Steve

for all the years @ DEC

Best

Mike Martin

July 2014

A Record of the United States Road Racing Championship 1963–1968

USRRC

By Mike Martin

Foreword by George Follmer, 1965 USRRC Champion

Library of Congress Control Number: **2012942227**

ISBN: **978-0-9857300-17**
Book design: **David Burngasser, DB Design, Seattle, WA**

Dustjacket photos—Top: *Don Devine at Laguna Seca 1963 by Allen Kuhn.*
Bottom: *Mark Donohue at Riverside 1968 by Ron Miller.*

Printed in China by Planet Ink, USA

Dead Pedal Press
6043 - 45th Ave SW
Seattle, WA 98136-1426
425-530-8021

This book is dedicated to the five D's that have been in my life:

Dot *Dorothy Aileen McDonald, aka Mom. RIP*

Doris *Doris Hilda (Hancock) McDonald, aka Aunt Doris. RIP*

Donna *Donna Jane (Martin) Onsager, aka Sis. RIP*

David *David Leroy Martin, aka The Dunk. Hang in there, man*

Diane *Diane(Carter) Martin, for years of love and support*

Also: Charles Eugene McDonald, aka Unk. RIP

Table of Contents

Foreword

For me, the USRRC series was my beginning, as it was for many of the sports car racers of the 60s and 70s. We owe, and should thank, the early leaders of the SCCA for having the vision to see ahead of the curve. Until that time, road racing was limited to production car and modified club racers, with the SCCA discouraging members from racing for money. Many SCCA racers went on to become the star drivers of the time, all because of the USRRC series.

From the USRRC we were given the Can-Am, Trans-Am, and Formula 5000 series to race in. My start in professional racing was at the 1965 Pensacola USRRC race. I used my wife's Pontiac station wagon with an open trailer to tow my Lotus 23-Porsche across the country in hopes of becoming a "Professional Race Driver". I didn't know much about running with the "Big Boys" like Jim Hall, Walt Hansgen, Ken Miles, and Hap Sharp. So winning my first Pro race of 1965 at the Pensacola USRRC was huge for me.

From that start I was able to move on and race in the Can-Am, Trans-Am, Formula 5000 series, at Indy, and in Formula 1, NASCAR, and the World Manufacturers races.

This book is a good documentation of the USRRC series and many of the American drivers that made Sports Car racing during the 60s.

It is a must read…

George Follmer

George Follmer
1965 USRRC Champion

7

Lothar Motschenbacher (left) won the pole at Mid-Ohio in 1968 but Mark Donohue in this blue Sunoco Special beat him to the finish line.

Author's Introduction

This is the story and record of the original USRRC series. I am surprised there has not been a book about it already. After all, the USRRC was the catalyst for the Trans-Am, Can-Am, and Formula 5000 series, and there are plenty of books about them.

There are two main reasons I wrote this book. First, I wanted a book about the USRRC, even if I had to write it myself. Second, the 1966 USRRC race at Pacific Raceways was the first major professional sports car race I attended. The month prior to that USRRC, I was at the SCCA regional races and was very bored because there was no action, just cars following each other at quite a distance. I told my buddy, Russ Taylor, "if this is what sports car racing is really like, I'll have to find another sport to follow". Russ told me to hold that thought until after we went to the USRRC race. I'm glad I took his advice. There were a number of elements to the race that kept my interest alive: Charlie Parsons debuted Randy Hilton's new McLaren M1B, there were lead and major place changes, and Mark Donohue won his first USRRC and pro race. My interest (some say, obsession) has just grown over the years.

This book is a chronological story of the whole series. There is a chapter for each year, with an appendix detailing the most and fastest. The index on page 335 has been keyed to easily find text about the race courses and drivers.

Hopefully you will find this book to be a good story and reference.

Mike Martin

Author's Note

A huge effort was made to have this book be a "complete" record of the USRRC. However, the passage of time and lack of foresight of the future importance of complete record-keeping has left some holes. That said, there are a number of missing qualifying times/ starting grids and fastest race laps I was not able to uncover. Also, there are a couple of races I could not find the number of laps all the finishers completed. If you have any of this data and are willing to share please contact me. I would love to use it, with due credit, in future editions of this book.

Finding good photographs from every race was a minor challenge. In most cases I did find good photos and got permission to use them. Still, good photos from a few races eluded me. In most cases, I did find photos, but could not locate the photographers to get their permission. So I have included some photos of a lesser quality, thinking they were better than nothing. My hope is they won't detract from the story of the series.

The results charts were constructed to give as much pertinent data about the race results as possible. There are, however, a few acronyms that could stand explanation:

DNF = Did Not Finish the race
DSQ = started the race, but was Disqualified
DNS = Did Not Start the race

Acknowledgements

Writing this book has taken longer than I care to admit. I do admit that I have enjoyed working with everyone who has contributed to this book. I am grateful for every minute I've spent with them, in person, on the phone, in letters and email. As with most b ooks like this, it would not have happened without their help and encouragement.

Bruce Perry is really the impetus for this book. Early on, he gave me a set of the SCCA "official" results for the whole series and said what he would really like is to have a book about the USRRC. Bruce has been a constant source of documents, information, contacts, proofreading and encouragement.

Jim Sitz has been a champion of this project from the beginning, sharing information, photo sources, contacts, proofreading and more.

Tom Brierley has given a lot of time, friendship and publishing advice. Plus "help" with the final push to get this to print. He also maintains www.motorbook-case.com.

Janos Wimpffen's expertise in all aspects of research is, obviously, second to none. His willingness to share has been invaluable and greatly appreciated. His friendship is beyond value.

Don Markle has been a terrific help finding race programs, information, and photo contacts. Thanks for all the program cover scans, Don.

A huge Thank You to George Follmer for the foreword. His racing exploits were always fun to watch and read about.

Aside from doing the design and layout for this book, David Burngasser has patiently helped guide me through the publishing process.

Randy Christensen led me into the world of auto racing literature shows and has traded numerous USRRC items to me. For a diehard Indy guy who dabbles in sports car racing stuff, Randy has steered me to a lot of useful information for this book.

For years, Martin Spetz has been a great help finding race programs, sources, and info.

My brother, Chad Martin, has been my computer support guy since forever and has always been supportive of this project. He's also a car guy and one of the proofreaders.

At times Diane Martin wanted this book done more than I did. Thanks for proofreading, prodding and years of support.

Mike Stinogel is my marketing idea guy. He's also my motorcycle riding buddy.

Jill Stinogel proofread the book from a non-racing fan's perspective and actually found it to be interesting.

Ike Smith was a wrench for Charlie Parsons during his championship winning year. Thanks for a weeklong tour of the Bay Area racing haunts and for making Gil Munz' photos available.

Gil Munz also wrenched for Charlie Parsons. Aside from wrenching, he took photos at most races.

Bill Green has shared info about the races at Watkins Glen and came through with a few starting grids and some nice photos. Thanks Bill, for the ride around the original Watkins Glen street course

Jerry Entin gave a nice interview and followed it up with emails, tips, hints, and good photo sources.

Pete Lovely always patiently answered my questions in great detail, whether at the races, or on the phone. RIP

Don Devine was kind enough to answer my questions about his and Harry Heuer's 1963 season.

Tom Schultz is one of the proofreaders and has supplied a lot of the Road America photos.

To Luc Ghys (aka Pedro917 on TNF) goes a big Thank You for the Mexican magazine "Record" which previewed the 1968 Mexico City race.

Ted Wilkinson of Wilkinson's Automobilia in Vancouver BC (www.eautomobilia.com) has been a great source of racing magazines and books.

Tam McPartland, who maintains Tam's Old Race Car site, gave me contact info for many photographers, whose work appears here.

Martin Krejci maintains the World's Sports Racing Prototype site and also gave me contact info for photographers, whose photos are in this book.

Alan Brown maintains the Old Racing Cars site and also supplied contact info for photographers.

At times, I wish I lived closer to the International Motor Racing Research Center at Watkins Glen. Everyone is so friendly and helpful. It is always a treat to spend time there.

Julie Sebranek and Erin at the Road America office allowed access to their files of race info, starting grids, timing reports, race programs, photos, and more.

Jim Orr was my go-to guy at the Henry Ford/Benson Ford Research Center for getting photos and made the whole process go smoothly.

Mark Patrick and Nadia Taliceo made getting photos from the REVS/Collier Museum a real pleasure.

Van Bagley at Planet Ink has been a delight to work with.

Karen Furlong at the Mansfield/Richland (OH) County Public Library, Patricia Golgart at the Augusta/Richmond County Public Library, Jody Habayeb at the Daytona Beach News-Journal and Sandra Hancock at the (Pensacola) West Florida Regional Library get my thanks for the info they sent.

Thanks also go to: Jack Brady, Ken Breslauer, Steve Calbaum, Rod Campbell, Dean Case, Art Conner, Tim Considine, Steve Fields, Joel Finn, Ross Fossbender, Joe Freeman, Dave Friedman, Jim Gessner, Logan Gray (Vintage Motorbooks), Rick Hayden, Paul House, Vince Howlett, Jan Hyde, Al Isselhard, Henry Jones, Robert Judy, Peter Klebinkov, Wolfgang Klopfer, Erin Kunz, Michael Ling, Dan Lipetz, Jim Martin, Dave Nicholas and the BARC Boys, James O'Keefe, Michael Oliver, Willem Oosthoeck, Steve Peterson (Longmont, CO), Bill Pohnan, David Pozzi, Jim Rice, David Seielstad, Michael Shoen, Tina Van Curren (www.autobooks-aerobooks.com), Craig Wheeldon, John Whitmore and Gillian Cowling.

My sincere apologies to anyone who helped, but is not mentioned. Please know your effort has been appreciated.

Photographer Acknowledgements

Without photos this book would be a rather dry tale of the USRRC. Many thanks to the Benson Ford Research Center at The Henry Ford museum. Also, thanks to Jim Orr, who was pleasantly professional and made the process easy. These are photos from the Dave Friedman collection. With all the books Dave supplied photos for, there were quite a few from Ford that have not been previously published.

The REVS Institute at the Collier Museum came through with some needed Bridgehampton shots. Mark Patrick and Nadia Taliceo were incredibly helpful, pleasant, and fast.

Many thanks to the following photographers who kept their photos for all these years and were willing to dig them out again and share them with us.

Dave Arnold is one of the first snappers I contacted for photos. His Mid-Ohio shots are quite evocative.

Robert Bohl took some nice shots at Bridgehampton and Watkins Glen.

Jack Brady travelled to many USRRC races and took hundreds of photos that appeared in many popular magazines of the day. I was lucky to get the Daytona shots.

Bob Brannon supplied photos his brother, Bill, took while working as a stringer for *Competition Press*.

Jim Caspary provided nice photos from gorgeous Road America.

I have to thank Dave Friedman for being there and capturing so many great USRRC moments, even if I was too slow to get them direct from him.

Bill Green, world famous historian at the International Motor Racing Research Center at Watkins Glen, supplied some nice shots from the races at the Glen.

Kirby Guyer is another person whose photos came via Jerry Entin.

Jim Hayes has some nice shots from Watkins Glen, Laguna Seca and Mid-Ohio.

Photos from the 1964 Augusta race came from Joe Cawley via Henry Jones.

Allen Kuhn's early Riverside and Laguna Seca photos really bring those races back to life. Check out his website at: www.vintage-sportscar-photos.com for great Southern California photos from the 50s and early 60s.

Tom Lebo's photos from Pacific Raceways appear courtesy his son, Bill.

Augusta photos from USRRC racer, Richard Macon, came via Jerry Entin.

John McCollister took photos of some of the more unusual USRRC cars at Road America. It's nice to be able to show cars that came out of the Midwest garages.

Jerry Melton has some nice shots from Mid Ohio and Watkins Glen.

I got in touch with Ron Miller just in time to get his shots from Pacific Raceways, Laguna Seca, and Riverside.

Gil Munz took a lot of photos while working for Charlie Parsons. His photos come courtesy his partner in crime, Ike Smith

Dave Nicholas provided shots from Bridgehampton. For East Coast race photos check out Dave's site: www.barcboys.com

Mike Odell not only supplied great photos from Meadowdale and Road America, but also proofread the whole book. Many thanks. Check out Mike's website of Forget-Me-Not-Pix at: www.sportsracingltd.com

Bob Raymond's Bridgehampton shots are a nice addition.

Tom Schultz generously supplied shots from Road America, Meadowdale, Bridgehampton, and Mid Ohio.

Ron Shaw took some nice shots at Continental Divide and Road America.

Bill Stowe gave some nice photos from Mid Ohio.

Larry Tomaras took the shot of Scuderia Tin Can in 1964. Thanks to his brother, for letting me use the photo.

Introduction: The USRRC Story

How sports car racing evolved into the United States Road Racing Championships

The USRRC did not just happen overnight. The Automobile Racing Club of America (ARCA) is recognized as the first club in America to regularly hold races for European type sports cars. It was organized by the Collier brothers, Barron Jr., Miles and Sam, and friends. ARCA held races and hill-climbs at various venues (public roads, fairground ovals and private estates) in the Northeastern states between 1934 and 1941. After the bombing of Pearl Harbor, ARCA disbanded and never restarted.

The Sports Car Club of America (SCCA) was the post-World War II successor to ARCA. Starting in 1944 as a gentleman's club, its main purpose was to preserve sports cars and provide a social atmosphere for its members. In fact, if a member chose to sell his sports car he was supposed to offer it to other club members first. SCCA members who sold their last sports car were supposed to lose their membership in the club.

Racing for amateurs only

Sports car racing was an organizational sideline of the SCCA that started in 1948, after fierce lobbying by a few key members. It grew beyond any idea the founding fathers had. Right from the start, the SCCA Board of Directors decided the races they sanctioned would be strictly amateur. For the most part, this was not a problem as American racers were just glad to be able to race. The opportunity to race sports cars professionally during this time was pretty much limited to Europe.

Most sports car races of the late forties and early fifties took place on public roads that were closed for the occasion. The Watkins Glen race of 1948 is generally acknowledged as being the first major post-war sports car race in the U.S. It was followed by races at Bridgehampton on Long Island, Elkhart Lake in Wisconsin, Palm Beach Shores in Florida and Pebble Beach on the Monterey Peninsula in California. In 1950 Alec Ulmann organized and promoted a six-hour handicap race at Hendricks Field in Sebring, Florida. This was the first endurance race sanctioned by the SCCA and one of the first races to run on airport runways.

In 1951 the SCCA instituted a National Championship for drivers and John Fitch

was the first champion. Basically it was just an East Coast championship as there were no races west of the Mississippi River. Professional sports car racing in America also began in 1951. The Sports Car Owners and Drivers Association (SCODA) was based in New York and affiliated with NASCAR. Most of the SCODA races were run on dirt oval tracks in the Northeastern U.S.

Alec Ulmann and Miles Collier had tried to get the SCCA to embrace professional racing as early as 1951. Unfortunately, the SCCA would not stand for it and caused a rift that would last for years. This led Ulmann to have the 1952 Sebring 12 Hours race sanctioned by the American Automobile Association (AAA), which sanctioned Indycar racing from 1909 through 1955. The SCCA retaliated by holding one, six and twelve hour races at Vero Beach two weeks prior to the Sebring race, in veiled hopes it would deplete the entries at Sebring. The 1952 SCCA National Championship included California races at Pebble Beach and Golden Gate Park, in addition to the East Coast races, and Sherwood Johnston was the champion.

Some car owners paid drivers under the table to drive their cars during this time. Since it was not obvious the SCCA turned a blind eye to it. However, the SCCA did publish articles in their newsletter discouraging members from competing in professional races. By 1954 the discouragement changed to the threat of suspension. The only way SCCA drivers could race professionally and maintain their SCCA membership was to race outside the U.S. Basically this meant racing in Europe, Nassau or Mexico. SCCA members who held AAA licenses were allowed to compete in "approved" races, like the Sebring 12 Hours, provided they did not accept any cash or trophies.

Racing on Air Force runways

During the early fifties, there were well-publicized fatal accidents during the public road races at Watkins Glen and Bridgehampton. It then became more difficult for the SCCA regions and civic groups to get insurance, or permission, for races on public roads. The answer to their problem came out of the blue, in the form of Air Force General Curtis LeMay. He was a racing fan and he was in charge of the U.S. Air Force Strategic

Air Command (SAC). The SCCA and SAC jointly promoted 14 sports car races on SAC airfields between 1952 and 1954.

In July of 1952 the SCCA announced the opening of a 1-1/2 mile enclosed road course at Thompson, Connecticut, with races to be held August 16 and 17. This planted the seed that sports cars racing could be done without using public roads. It took groups of people willing to find the finances to build the facility, get insurance, promote and hold the races. During the 1952 race at Watkins Glen an accident occurred which killed a seven year old boy and injured 12 others. The local race organizers realized they needed a closed road circuit on which to hold a race. Bonds were sold to raise the money to buy property on which the course was built and to lease the land around it for complete control. They built a 4.6 mile course that was Northwest of the town of Watkins Glen and the old road course. The first races were held on September 19, 1953.

Race courses for improved safety

1954 saw enclosed road courses open at Marlboro in Maryland, Wilmot Hills in Wisconsin and Willow Springs in California. The real eye-opener came in 1955 when Road America, in Wisconsin, opened for business. They had an inaugural race day crowd of 35,000 spectators. 1957 was the high-water mark for road course openings. On the West Coast, Riverside opened near Los Angeles and Laguna Seca replaced the roads of Pebble Beach in Northern California. New tracks opened on the East Coast at Lime Rock in Connecticut, Bridgehampton on Long Island and Virginia International Raceway. With these purpose-built race courses, the airfield courses and a few open-road courses, the SCCA was blessed with a wide geographical base of venues to hold races.

There was constant open debate in the pages of the SCCA's *Sports Car* magazine and *National Newsletter* and in the popular press magazines about the subject of professional sports car racing during the mid-fifties. The SCCA leadership held fast to the idea of amateurism, while some drivers chose to ignore it and risked their memberships. During this time, American drivers Phil

Hill, Masten Gregory, Carroll Shelby and a few others, found opportunities in Europe, Central America and South America to race and get paid for it.

USAC goes pro

In early 1958, the SCCA again reiterated their amateur-only policy. The United States Auto Club (USAC) sanctioned a professional National Championship that was based on points scored in thirteen races, run on dirt tracks, for sprint cars and oval tracks for Indianapolis 500 cars. USAC took notice of the SCCA's amateur-only policy and announced the creation of their Road Racing Division to oversee professional sports car races in May of 1958. The purpose was to develop a professional sports car racing series and to foster the growth of international race competition in the Americas.

USAC was quick to get their series started and the first race was held at Lime Rock in September, 1958. George Constantine drove Elisha Walker's Aston Martin to victory over Bruce Kessler and Allen Markelson in front of 7,000 spectators. George also won the next event at Marlboro. International racing star, Joakim Bonnier, won at Watkins Glen over Dan Gurney and Bruce Kessler. The final event of the year was held at Riverside. 70,000 spectators saw a thrilling duel between Phil Hill's Ferrari and Chuck Daigh's Scarab. While Hill retired, Daigh went on to win over Dan Gurney and Bill Krause. Dan Gurney was USAC's first road racing champion by virtue of USAC's scoring system. For a 100-mile race the winner got 200 points, second got 160, third 140 and 20 points less for each place down to eighth which got 50 points. The points dropped by ten for each place, down to 10 points for twelfth. A total of sixty-four drivers took part in the four races.

The USAC series expanded in 1959 to fourteen races. Races were run at Pomona, Daytona, Meadowdale, Lime Rock, Vacaville, Riverside and Watkins Glen. Augie Pabst won the championship driving the Meister Brauser Scarab. He scored three wins, a second and two third place finishes. Lloyd Ruby was second with one win, three seconds, a third and two fifth places. The

big money winner, though, was Ken Miles with $7,150. Ruby won $6,757 and Pabst $5,180. The series was a definite success. 137 drivers scored points and there were sixteen foreign drivers participating.

The 1960 USAC championship was scaled back to six races, at Riverside, Continental Divide Raceway, Road America and Laguna Seca. Carroll Shelby was the champion, with two wins, a fourth and two fifth place finishes. Jim Hall was second, with two seconds and one third place finish. Jim Jeffords was third and Bill Krause was fourth.

Ken Miles won the 1961 USAC Road Racing Championship, with one win, two second place and one fourth place finish. Jack Brabham, Bruce McLaren and Roger Penske were second, third and fourth. USAC proudly trumpeted their success of attracting foreign entries with Brabham and McLaren taking second and third in the championship. Stirling Moss was the only two-race winner and he placed seventh in the championship.

1962 was the swan song of USAC's Road Racing Championship. Roger Penske drove his controversial Zerex Special to the series championship, winning by sixty points over Dan Gurney. Roger had two wins, three second places and one third place finish. Gurney won five races and finished second in another. Such were the vagaries of the USAC scoring system.

Throughout the time of the USAC series, the SCCA kept their races as strictly amateur. To their credit, they allowed the discussion of professional racing to go on in the pages of *Sports Car* magazine. John Bishop, SCCA Executive Director, played a political poker game of trying to get the rest of the SCCA board of governors and SCCA general membership to adopt a professional series. In the Fall of 1962, there were rumblings that an SCCA professional road racing championship was on the horizon.

In the November 1962 issue of *Sports Car*, John Bishop stated the case that the races making up the SCCA's National Championship program were attractive only to competitors in the Northeast and Midwest parts of the U.S. and had less significance than the term "National" meant to have. He went on to say the SCCA needed to strengthen its position in United States road racing (i.e. beat

those USAC boys back to the circle tracks, where they belong) and make available to SCCA members the best road courses and premier racing events. The proposal for the USRRC was the middle topic of a five-point agenda for revamping the SCCA's racing program for 1963.

SCCA allows pro racing: USRRC

The United States Road Racing Championship (USRRC) was announced in the December 1962 issue of *Sports Car*. There would be two championship divisions, one for drivers and one for manufacturers. Each event was required to hold a race for the Drivers Championship and was encouraged to hold a separate race for the Manufacturers Championship, but not required to do so. The minimum duration for each race was 150 miles. Also, other competitions, like SCCA regional races, could be included in the same event program as the USRRC race. To score the championships, nine points would be awarded for winning, six points for second place, four points for third, three points for fourth, two for fifth place and one point for sixth place. And the drivers would finally win MONEY! That was the basic framework of the USRRC series.

The Drivers Championship races would have two classes, one for cars with engines over two liters and one for cars with engines under two liters. Cars expected to race in this series were Cooper Monaco and Lotus 19's with various V-8 engines, Lotus 23, Porsche RS models, various Ferraris, front-engine Chaparrals and Scarabs, Birdcage Maserati and homebuilt specials. Each driver's best six scores would count for the championship.

The Manufacturers Championship would be for Grand Touring cars with engines over two liters (122 cubic inches). This included cars like the Ferrari GTO, Chevrolet Corvette, Shelby Cobra and Jaguar XKE. Points were scored on the same basis as the drivers races. All points scored by each marque, in each race, would be counted for the championship.

So the scene is set for the first of the Sports Car Club of America professional race series. Sports car racing in America would never be the same.

1963

Daytona
Pensacola
Laguna Seca
Watkins Glen
Pacific Raceways
Continental Divide
Road America
Mid Ohio

Introduction 1963

Popular racing press of the day consisted of the twice-a-month newspapers, *Competition Press* and *Motoracing*; monthly magazines, *Sports Car Graphic*, *Road & Track*, *Car & Driver*, *Today's Motor Sports*, *US Auto Sports*, *Motor Sport Illustrated*, and of course the SCCA's *Sports Car*. These magazines and newspapers did a fine job of reporting on the upcoming series and the actual races. Unlike today's magazines, they did very little speculation about who would be competing in the series, or who would be driving for whom. They were quieter times when the fans mostly just wished for more information about the cars, drivers, and races. Those obsessed with the need for facts and details wrote letters to the teams, the drivers, the race organizers, and the circuits asking for specs of the cars, details about obscure championship and non-championship races, lap charts, race results, and race programs.

For 1963, the obvious driver choices came from those who competed in the 1962 USAC Road Racing series. The big money winner was Roger Penske in his controversial Zerex Special. Other drivers who had competed in the USAC races were Jim Hall, Jerry Grant, Chuck Daigh, Bill Krause, Augie Pabst, Harry Heuer, Ken Miles and Bob Holbert. These drivers were also active and successful in SCCA racing. Other SCCA racers who could give these guys a run for the money were Dr. Dick Thompson, the fast Washington, DC dentist; Doug Thiem, a 22-year-old college student; Tim Mayer; Bob Grossman; Don Yenko; Joe Buzzetta and Dave MacDonald, among others.

Coming out of 1962, the cutting edge of racecar technology was Roger Penske's infamous Zerex Special. At the time, this was basically a Formula One Cooper with sports car bodywork and a passenger seat just big enough for a hamburger-bun-sized butt. For 1963, Penske had the frame widened at the cockpit to include a more realistic passenger seat and altered the bodywork to fit. Jim Hall's new Chaparral II was also expected to be fiercely competitive. However, fans hoping to see it would be disappointed as

Jim decided to race Formula One in Europe during the 1963 season.

Grids were bolstered with Porsche RS models, Chaparral Mk I, the front-engine Scarab, Lotus 19's and 23's, Cooper Monaco's, and various Ferrari's. Grid-fillers were various older Elva, Lotus, Lister, Maserati, Corvette, and Jaguar models. Of course there were specials. On the East Coast there were Ferraris, Jaguars, Listers, and Maseratis with Chevrolet engines, plus specials like the Apache, Durant, Scrabeck, Edwards, Excalibur, and Fireball. From Canada came the Comstock, Sadler, and Kelly specials. On the West Coast there were the HWM-Chevrolet, Kurtis-Pontiac, Forsgrini, and Campbell specials.

The Shelby American Cobra team was the only real manufacturer to announce their support of the Manufacturers class. The Cobra was based on the A.C. Ace chassis that had a beefed up suspension to handle the torque from the Ford 260 engine. Racing fans were excited to see a new "American" sports car to compete with the Corvette and Ferraris. It was hoped that Ferrari, Chevrolet, or Jaguar would enter teams, or give good support to private entrants. Roger Penske and Mike Gammino would run privately entered Ferrari GTO's in various races. A fair number of private Corvettes and Jaguars also raced, but without factory support.

The series would race at some of the most exciting and challenging courses in the US. It started on the high banks at Daytona in February with a Drivers-only race. This was the only course to not host a Manufacturers race, or class. The second USRRC was held at the flat airfield of Corry Field Naval Air Station in Pensacola, Florida. A trip to the West Coast for a race at Laguna Seca in California was next. After that it went back east to Watkins Glen in New York, and then out west again to Pacific Raceways in Washington. The final swing took the racers to the high altitude of Colorado's Continental Divide Raceway, before finishing at Road America in Wisconsin and Mid-Ohio. This gave drivers from all parts of the U.S. a chance to participate at a race fairly close to home. Anticipation was high.

$1.00

200 MILE
US ROAD RACING DRIVER CHAMPIONSHIP RACE
February 3, 1963

SCCA REGIONAL RACES
February 2, 1963

DAYTONA INTERNATIONAL SPEEDWAY
DAYTONA BEACH, FLORIDA

The World's Finest and Fastest

OFFICIAL SOUVENIR PROGRAM   [1963 DAYTONA SPEEDWEEKS—PROGRAM 1]

200 KILOMETER
GRAND PRIX of UNITED STATES
February 10, 1963

OTHER USMC MOTORCYCLE RACES
February 9, 1963

1963 Daytona USRRC program cover. Scan courtesy Don Markle.

Getting ready to roll. Harry Heuer is on the pole, to the right, and Jim Hall #166 shares the front row. Tim Mayer #95 is on the second row, behind Heuer, and Don Devine in the #51 Meister Brauser Scarab is behind Hall. Photo by Jack Brady.

Bob Holbert led for the first fifteen laps, before pitting for a brake adjustment. Here he passes by Don Kirby's beached Ol Yaller. Photo by Jack Brady.

Daytona 1963

The USRRC series debuted February 3 at Daytona International Speedway with only a Drivers Championship race. The entry was a nice mix of pro, semi-pro and SCCA amateur racers. The pro drivers were Jim Hall, Bob Holbert, Harry Heuer, Herb Swan and Tom Terrell. All had participated in the previous USAC road racing series. The semi-pro drivers, or drivers who were using this series to cut their pro teeth, were Doug Thiem, Tim Mayer, Bill Eve and Don Devine.

One of the great attributes of the USRRC series was the opportunity it gave local drivers to compare their talent to that of the pro drivers. In this case, local meant east of the Mississippi River. Five racers from Florida were Bill Bencker, Bob Richardson, Charlie Kolb, Ed Cantrell and Bill Bowman. Jack Ryan from Georgia, Tommy Charles from Alabama and Harry Washburn from Louisiana were other southeast racers. A healthy contingent trekked down from the midwest included Charles Kurtz and Ray Heppenstall from Pennsylvania, Don Wolf and Bernie Keller from Ohio and Mike Rahal from Illinois. Also racing were Anson Johnson and Don Kirby from New York and Gordon Richardson from Maine.

This race also had a nice diversity of cars and drivers. Ten cars were in the over-two liter class: a Chaparral I for Harry Heuer, two Cooper Monacos (Jim Hall and Tim Mayer), two Corvettes (Bill Eve and Ed Cantrell), an Elva-Buick (Bernie Keller), two Ferraris, both with Corvette engines (Anson Johnson and Tommy Charles), an Ol' Yaller

(Don Kirby) and a Meister Brauser Scarab (Don Devine). The under-two liter class had fifteen cars: an Alfa Romeo Zagato (Bob Richardson), a Cooper Monaco with Maserati engine (Harry Washburn), Elvas (Don Wolf and Mike Rahal), Ferrari Dino (Doug Thiem), Lotus Monte Carlo (Tom Terrell), Lotus 23 (Gordon Richardson), OSCA (Ray Heppenstall) and seven Porsches (Bob Holbert, Charles Kurtz and Bill Bowman in RS-61's, Herb Swan and Charlie Kolb in Spyders, Bill Bencker in a Carrera and Jack Ryan in an RSK).

Daytona was typical of most USRRC weekends to come, with SCCA regional races and USRRC qualifying taking place on Saturday and the feature race happening on Sunday. Saturday was warm and sunny shirtsleeve weather. Harry Heuer in the Meister Brauser Chaparral won the pole position. Jim Hall was next to Heuer on the front row in Hap Sharp's Cooper Monaco. During the Friday practice session, a local entrant spun in front of Hall and the crash damaged the left side of the Cooper putting a hole in the gas tank. Hall's mechanic was able to get the Cooper repaired in time for the race. Third and fourth on the grid were Tim Mayer and Don Devine. Next were Bob Holbert and Doug Thiem.

Sunday morning dawned gray and angry, as torrential rain and wind swept across the racetrack. The start was postponed for half an hour. When the race was started, the rain had decreased to a steady drizzle. There were still several puddles around the infield part of the course. Seven drivers chose not to race

due to the weather, or weather-related problems. As the cars started the pace lap Chuck Cassel could not get his Porsche Abarth to fire. Only twenty-five cars completed the warm up lap. Harry Heuer dropped back with ignition problems and got hit in the face with a load of mud flung up by another car. He stopped at the pits while the other cars took the flag on the flying start. Heuer got back in the race but lasted just a few laps before a drowned magneto forced him out. His teammate, Don Devine, aquaplaned off the course on the second lap and got enough water in the fuel injection to drown the engine and put him out of the race.

In the meantime, Bob Holbert snatched the lead from Tim Mayer, Herb Swan and Jim Hall. Hall methodically worked his way past Herb Swan during the next few laps. Tim Mayer pitted for earplugs to muffle the loudness of broken exhaust pipes and Jim Hall took second place. Bob Holbert was building up a small lead, but on lap sixteen he pitted for a brake adjustment and that let Hall into the lead. Holbert got back on the track in second place and started to catch Hall. That came to a halt when Holbert pitted for another brake adjustment on lap twenty-four and dropped to fourth place.

Holbert set out again and spent the rest of the race working up to second place. He got within thirty seconds of Hall to take second place and first in the under two liter class. Herb Swan and Bill Bencker were third and fourth after smooth, steady drives. Fifth was Doug Thiem in his Ferrari Dino. Charlie Kolb should have been fifth after spend-

1963 DAYTONA • USRRC
February 3, 1963, Daytona International Raceway,   Daytona, Florida

Place	Driver	Car/Engine	Car #	Class	Laps	Points	Prize
1	Jim Hall	Cooper-Monaco T57-Climax	166	O2	53	9	$1,200
2	Bob Holbert	Porsche 718 RS61	14	U2	53	9	1,200
3	Herb Swan	Porsche 718 RS61	99	U2	53	6	900
4	Bill Bencker	Porsche- 356 B Carrera 2	44	U2	52	4	600
5	Doug Thiem	Ferrari Dino 196SP	8	U2	51	3	400
6	Tim Mayer	Cooper-Monaco T61-Climax	95	O2	49	6	900
7	Charles Kurtz	Porsche 718 RS61	157	U2	49	2	300
8	Bob Richardson	Alfa-Romeo Zagato	19	U2	48	1	200
9	Tom Terrell	Lotus 19-Climax	151	U2	48	-	100
10	Bill Eve	Chevrolet Corvette	25	O2	47	4	600
11	Don Wolf	Elva Mk 6-Climax	85	U2	46	-	50
12	Gordon Richardson	Lotus 23-Climax	5	U2	45	-	-
13	Bernie Keller	Elva Mk 3-Buick	89	O2	28	3	400
DNF	Charlie Kolb	Porsche 718 RS61	11	U2	52	-	-
DNF	Jack Ryan	Porsche 718 RSK	68	U2	-	-	-
DNF	Ray Heppenstall	OSCA	34	U2	-	-	-
DNF	Harry Heuer	Chaparral 1-Chevrolet	50	O2	4	-	-
DNF	Don Kirby	Ol' Yaller Mk 7	71	O2	21	-	-
DNF	Michael Rahal	Elva Mk 2-Climax	18	U2	-	-	-
DNF	Ed Cantrell	Chevrolet Corvette	1	O2	-	-	-
DNF	Anson Johnson	Ferrari 500-Chevrolet	61	O2	-	-	-
DNF	Bill Bowman	Porsche 718 RS61	144	U2	-	-	-
DNF	Tommy Charles	Ferrari-Chevrolet	88	O2	-	-	-
DNF	Harry Washburn	Cooper Monaco T61-Maserati	47	U2	-	-	-
DNF	Don Devine	Scarab Mk 2	51	O2	1	-	-
DNS	Chuck Cassel	Porsche-Abarth 356B Carrera GTL	16	U2	-	-	-
DNS	Buck Fulp	Ferrari Dino 196SP	26	U2	-	-	-
DNS	Bill Terrell	MG-A	90	U2	-	-	-
DNS	David Full	Chevrolet Corvette	60	O2	-	-	-
DNS	Hamilton Vose	Lister-Buick	33	O2	-	-	-
DNS	T.A. Rees	Lotus 23	48	U2	-	-	-
DNS	Dick Talbot	Elva Mk 5	86	U2	-	-	-
DNS	Jeff Stevens	Chevrolet Corvette	147	O2	-	-	-

Fastest Qualifier:	Harry Heuer	Chaparral 1-Chevrolet	2:05.01	108.852 mph
Race Distance:	200.64 miles	53 laps of 3.78 mile course		
Race Time:	2hr 13min 26sec			
Winner's Speed:	90.210 mph			
Victory Margin:	30 seconds			
Fastest Lap:	Bob Holbert	Porsche 718 RS61	2:29.14	92.241 mph

Don Kirby hit a puddle of water in his Ol Yaller, spun and took out a loudspeaker stand. Photo by Jack Brady.

Jim Hall splashing his way to victory in Hap Sharp's Cooper Monaco. Photo by Jack Brady.

ing most of the race there, but he pitted with two laps to go and very little gas left. He intended to wait and cross the finish line after Hall had passed but he mistook Terrell's Lotus Monte Carlo for Hall's Cooper Monaco and was committed to another lap. This was too far. He ran out of gas and battery power on the backstretch and DNF'd (did not finish). Tim Mayer was sixth after spending the early part of the race in third place. After pitting for earplugs he had to drive through some of the bigger puddles to put out an engine compartment fire. But sixth place netted him second in the over-two liter class.

With equal points awarded in both class-es, Hall and Holbert both left Daytona with 9 points, Swan and Mayer with 6 each, Bencker and Bill Eve with 4, Thiem and Bernie Keller with 3 each, Charles Kurtz with 2 and Bob Richardson with 1. There were no over-two liter cars running at the finish to take fifth and sixth place points.

1963 SOUVENIR PROGRAM —————————— 25¢

THE Fiesta OF Five Flags

Stamps Problem

SPORTS CAR RACES

U.S. ROAD RACING DRIVER CHAMPIONSHIP
·
USRRC MANUFACTURER'S CHAMPIONSHIP
·
GULF COAST REGIONALS

PENSACOLA, FLA.   MAY 25-26

1963 Pensacola USRRC program cover. Scan courtesy Don Markle.

The Mecom Ferrari 250 GTO in the pits. With this car, Roger Penske became the only driver to defeat the Cobras during the USRRC series. Photo by Bill Brannon, courtesy Bob Brannon.

1963 Pensacola Manufacturers Race

The Pensacola races took place on May 26, three months after the first race at Daytona. The wet chill of Daytona was replaced with ninety-degree temperatures shimmering off the pavement at the NAS Corry Field race course.

This was the first USRRC race meeting to include a Manufacturers race and the field was rather sparse. Five Cobras were entered for this race. The Shelby-American team of Ken Miles, Bob Holbert and Dave MacDonald were strong favorites. There were also the privately entered Cobras of Bob Johnson and Bob Hayes. Roger Penske, Mike Gammino and Ed Cantrell had Ferrari GTO's. Bill Cantrell (Ed's brother) entered a Corvette and George Demetropulos had an E-type Jaguar.

The Shelby team showed the way in qualifying with Dave MacDonald taking pole position from Holbert, Miles and Johnson. Next up were Penske, Gammino and Ed Cantrell in the Ferraris. Bill Cantrell, Bob Hayes and George Demetropulos completed the field.

At the start of the race, Dave MacDonald took the lead from Bob Holbert. Holbert re-took the lead before the end of the first lap, with Penske and Johnson in third and fourth. Ken Miles made a poor start and had an off course excursion trying to make up for it. After four laps Holbert had a five-second lead over MacDonald who had a similar margin over Penske and Johnson. They were followed by Mike Gammino, a hard charging Miles and Ed Cantrell. At six laps Miles was in his stride, passed Gammino and over the next three laps he got by Johnson and Penske to take third place.

By lap fourteen Holbert had stretched his lead to fifteen seconds. Miles caught and passed MacDonald to take second place. Holbert had lapped everyone except Miles and MacDonald. Penske was fourth, followed by Johnson, Gammino and Ed Cantrell. After six more laps, George Demetropulos retired his Jaguar. Dave MacDonald had also retired his Cobra with a broken distributor.

On lap twenty-two, Miles made a long pitstop to get fuel and new tires. This gave second place to Penske who had unlapped himself and was now about a minute behind Holbert. After two more laps Penske took the lead while Holbert made his pitstop for tires and fuel. Unfortunately for Holbert, one of his crew thought he'd cool him off by throwing a bucket of cold water on him. But Holbert got hit on the head with the bucket as he was getting out of the car. Holbert got back in the car and made it about half a lap before he got ill. He managed to get the Cobra back to the pits. MacDonald jumped into Holberts car and tore off in third place behind Miles. On the next lap, Miles began to dramatically close in on Penske. In the next five laps Miles closed the gap to fifteen seconds.

Miles pitted to have the differential checked on lap thirty-one because there was smoke coming out of the rear of the car on various corners. He was told nothing could be done and to just go back out for as long as the car would last. Miles returned to the race in fourth place, behind MacDonald and Johnson. MacDonald, in Holbert's car, retired on lap thirty-five with broken rear axle hangers. This moved Bob Johnson's Cobra up to third place behind Miles. Six laps later Johnson retired with a broken distributor. Penske was still leading and turning laps at a 2:25 pace with Miles about twenty seconds behind and turning 2:18 laps. It looked like it would be a very close finish. Then Miles' Cobra started smoking every time he let up on the gas. After forty-five laps he had closed the gap to fifteen seconds. On lap forty-six Miles was hanging his head out of the cockpit to get fresh air and to see, because the windshield was covered with oil. Miles retired on the next lap ending his great chase.

Penske cruised to victory, a lap ahead of Mike Gammino and two laps ahead of Ed Cantrell, all three in Ferrari GTO's and Bill Cantrell got fourth place in his Corvette. Four laps back in fifth place was Bob Hayes in his privately entered Cobra. This was not an auspicious start for the Shelby team, but it was certainly interesting to watch.

1963 PENSACOLA • USRRC MANUFACTURERS RACE

May 26, 1963, NAS Corry Field, Pensacola, Florida

Place	Driver	Car/Engine	Car #	Laps	Points	Prize
1	Roger Penske	Ferrari 250 GTO	17	50	9	$500
2	Mike Gammino	Ferrari 250 GTO	23	49	6	300
3	Ed Cantrell	Ferrari 250 GTO	29	48	4	200
4	Bill Cantrell	Chevrolet Corvette	29	46	3	-
5	Bob (R.E.L.) Hayes	Cobra	45	46	2	-
DNF	Ken Miles	Shelby Cobra	97	46	-	-
DNF	Bob Johnson	Cobra	33	40	-	-
DNF	Bob Holbert	Shelby Cobra	98	34	-	-
DNF	Dave MacDonald	Shelby Cobra	96	20	-	-
DNF	George Demetropulos	Jaguar E-Type	91	20	-	-

Fastest Qualifier:	Dave MacDonald	Shelby Cobra		
Race Distance:	150.0 miles	50 laps of 3.0 mile course		
Race Time:	1 hr 56 min 43.89 sec			
Winner's Speed:	77.10 mph			
Victory Margin:	1 lap			
Fastest Race Lap:	Bob Holbert	Shelby Cobra	2:14.0	80.7 mph

Ed Cantrell took his Ferrari 250 GTO to third place in the Manufacturers race. Photo by Bill Brannon, courtesy Bob Brannon.

Bob Johnson's private Cobra was running in third place when the distributor broke. Photo by Bill Brannon, courtesy Bob Brannon.

1963 Pensacola Drivers Race

Eleven drivers who had raced at Daytona showed up for the second round at Pensacola. New over two-liter racers included Roger Penske in the infamous Zerex Special, which was now owned by John Mecom Jr. Also entered were Hap Sharp in his Cooper-Monaco that Jim Hall used to win at Daytona, Enus Wilson in a Maserati T61, Ed Rahal in a D-type Jaguar, Chuck Nervine in a Ferrari-Corvette and Ralph Noseda in a Corvette. Additions to the under-two liter corps were Augie Pabst in a Lotus 19, Mason O'Kieff, Harry Braswell and Richard Macon in Lotus 23's, plus Mancil Smith in a Lotus 7.

Roger Penske won the pole in the Mecom Zerex Special. Bob Holbert had recovered from being hit by a bucket of water during the Manufacturers race. He lined up next to Penske in his Porsche RS-61. Third on the grid was Tim Mayer in a Cooper-Monaco.

When the race started Penske took off like a flash, followed at a distance by Sharp, Holbert, Washburn, Swan, Rahal, Mayer and Pabst. Mayer and Pabst tussled for a lap before Pabst started moving backward through the field when a fire broke out in his Lotus. Tim Mayer was moving up through the field and after four laps had taken second place. Pabst, Braswell and Noseda all retired within the first four laps. Hap Sharp retired his Cooper after eight laps with transmission problems. Charlie Kolb had worked his way through the field and was battling with Bob Holbert for third place.

As in so many previous races, Penske was making the Zerex fly. After twenty-three laps, he had lapped everyone, except Mayer. At thirty-six laps Penske had a seventy-five second lead and then Mayer had to pit with a broken shift linkage. It took his crew about four laps to get the car into third gear and give Mayer a push start to get back into the race. Meanwhile Holbert took second place, over a lap behind Penske.

Penske was driving the Zerex at a furious pace, increasing his lead with every lap. Surprisingly, Penske brought the Zerex into the pits on lap fifty and got out. He was visibly fatigued from over three hundred miles of racing in ninety-degree heat. A few moments later the Zerex was back on the racetrack with Hap Sharp at the wheel and still in the lead. Sharp brought the Zerex back to the pits on the next lap and jumped out. Penske added water to the car and Sharp jumped back in and rejoined the race. He made it one more lap before he stopped at the pits again, had a word with John Mecom and then raced off again. After another lap, Sharp was back at the pits again complaining about the water temperature. He was told the gauge was broken and sent back out. Holbert had taken the lead by now and was thirty seconds ahead of Sharp in the Zerex. The gap grew to over ninety seconds when Sharp spun. After the spin, Sharp settled into a fast pace and began eating into Holbert's lead.

The heat was getting to Holbert. He brought his Porsche into the pits on lap sixty-two and handed it over to Shelby teammate, Ken Miles. After two laps the gap between Miles and Sharp was thirty-seven seconds. It was twenty-one seconds after the next lap. By now Penske had taken up residence on a haybale and was signaling the gap to Sharp (and probably Miles). The gap was seventeen seconds on lap sixty six. Four laps later, Sharp had whittled Miles' lead down to five seconds. The difference was three seconds after four more laps and it appeared the Zerex would chalk up another win. However, on the next lap Sharp pitted the Zerex for good after over-revving the engine and losing oil pressure.

Miles was able to cruise the last thirteen laps to finish with a lead of two laps over Charlie Kolb, who had burned his car's clutch. Doug Thiem was third, just inches behind Kolb. Tim Mayer managed to bring his Cooper home in fourth place and first in the over two liter class. Jack Ryan was fifth with Bill and Ed Cantrell, sharing a Ferrari GTO, in sixth.

Most folks thought Holbert and Miles and the Cantrell brothers would share the points for their cars position. After a few days, the SCCA issued a bulletin stating shared drives in non-distance races (i.e. any race other than the Road America 500) would result in no points for either driver. Holbert filed a protest, but was turned down.

Tim Mayer led the Championship, after two races, with 15 points. Bob Holbert and Jim Hall were next with 9 points, followed by Doug Thiem and Bill Eve with 7 points each. Ferrari led the Manufacturers championship with 19 points over Corvette's 3 points and Cobra's 2 points.

1963 PENSACOLA · USRRC DRIVERS RACE

May 26, 1963, NAS Corry Field, Pensacola, Florida

Place	Driver	Car/Engine	Car #	Class	Laps	Points	Prize	Qualifying Place
1	Bob Holbert/Ken Miles	Porsche 718 RS61	14	U2	87	np *	$1,500	4
2	Charles Kolb	Porsche 718 RSK	21	U2	85	6	650	9
3	Doug Thiem	Ferrari Dino 196SP	9	U2	85	4	300	6
4	Tim Mayer	Cooper Monaco T57-Climax	4	O2	84	9	1,000	2
5	Jack Ryan	Porsche 718 RSK	69	U2	82	3	200	10
6	Ed Cantrell/Bill Cantrell	Ferrari 250 GTO	29	O2	82	np *	650	27
7	Ed Rahal	Jaguar D-type	39	O2	80	4	300	17
8	Bill Eve	Ferrari-Chevrolet	25	O2	78	3	200	19
9	Mancil Smith	Lotus Super 7	68	U2	76	2	100	20
10	Gordon Richardson	Lotus 23-Climax	15	U2	73	1	-	13
11	Bill Bowman	Porsche 718 RS61	11	U2	71	-	-	22
DNF	Roger Penske/Hap Sharp	Zerex Special-Climax	6	O2	74	-	-	1
DNF	Chuck Cassel	Porsche-Abarth 356B Carrera GTL	58	U2	74	-	-	16
DNF	Enus Wilson	Maserati Tipo 61	2	O2	72	-	-	11
DNF	Harry Washburn	Cooper T61-Maserati	47	U2	70	-	-	8
DNF	Herb Swan	Porsche 718 RS61	99	U2	57	-	-	7
DNF	Bill Fuller	Jaguar-Chevrolet	27	O2	51	-	-	12
DNF	Mason O'Keiff	Lotus 23	12	U2	36	-	-	18
DNF	Hap Sharp	Cooper T57-Climax	95	O2	8	-	-	3
DNF	Chuck Nervine	Ferrari-Chevrolet	18	O2	7	-	-	26
DNF	Richard Macon	Lotus 23-Alfa	8	U2	5	-	-	14
DNF	Ralph Noseda	Chevrolet Corvette	13	O2	3	-	-	21
DNF	Harry Braswell	Lotus 23-Climax	16	U2	2	-	-	15
DNF	Augie Pabst	Lotus 19-Climax	5	U2	2	-	-	5
DNS	Gordon Hadley	Elva Mk 7-Ford	55	U2	-	-	-	23
DNS	Edna Sherman	Lotus 23-Alfa Romeo	32	U2	-	-	-	24
DNS	Buck Fulp	Ferrari Dino 196SP	26	U2	-	-	-	25

* np = no points (race not long enough to have co-drivers)

Fastest Qualifier:	Roger Penske	Zerex Special-Climax	2:06.8	85.17 mph
Race Distance:	261.0 miles	87 laps of 3.0 mile course		
Race Time:	3 hr 41 min 16.8 sec			
Winner's Speed:	70.77 mph			
Victory Margin:	2 laps			
Fastest Race Lap:	Roger Penske	Zerex Special-Climax	2:03.0	87.8 mph

John Mecom bought the Zerex Special from Roger Penske and gave Roger a last drive at Pensacola. Penske made the most of it by getting pole position, setting the fastest race lap, and leading the race for the first fifty laps. Penske turned the car over to Hap Sharp who had a hard time with it and retired with thirteen laps left. Photo by Bill Brannon, courtesy Bob Brannon.

The now Mecom, Zerex Special in the paddock next to the transporter. Photo by Bill Brannon, courtesy Bob Brannon.

Hap Sharp brought his Cooper Monaco to Pensacola, but it lasted only eight laps. This is the car Jim Hall used to win at the Daytona USRRC race. Photo by Bill Brannon, courtesy Bob Brannon.

Bill Eve's Ferrari-Chevrolet finished in eighth place overall and fourth in the Over-Two-Liter class. Photo by Bill Brannon, courtesy Bob Brannon.

SCRAMP presents...

LAGUNA SECA
CHAMPIONSHIP
ROAD RACES

june 7-8-9

OFFICIAL PROGRAM

ONE DOLLAR

Cover from 1963 Laguna Seca race program. Scanned by Don Markle.

1963 Laguna Seca

After two races in the Southeast, the USRRC crossed the country to California for the Laguna Seca round. This would be one combined race for the Drivers and Manufacturers championships. Doug Thiem, Harry Heuer and Don Devine had raced at Daytona, Pensacola, or both in the Driver's races. The Shelby Cobra team of Dave MacDonald, Bob Holbert and Ken Miles, plus Ed Cantrell in his Ferrari GTO had all competed at Pensacola and followed the USRRC trail to Laguna Seca. Local drivers in the Manufacturers race were Ed Leslie in an XKE Jaguar and Stan Peterson in a Ferrari GTO. In the Drivers over two-liter section we had Skip Hudson, Jerry Grant, Dave Ridenour, Jerry Titus, Dan Parkinson, in the Campbell Special, Paul Reinhart, Bill Boldt and Bill Sherwood. Pedro Rodriguez in Kjell Qvale's new Genie added international flavor. Charlie Parsons, Don Wester, Walt Maas, Bill Molle, Dave Kyte, Dan Gillum, Frank Monise and Ken O'Niell were in the under two-liter class.

In qualifying, Jerry Grant took the pole position with a time of 1:16.6, or 89.3 mph. Sharing the front row with Grant were Charlie Parsons and Don Wester, both with a time of 1:17.0. Dave Ridenour in a Genie-Oldsmobile (1:17.2), Harry Heuer in a Chaparral 1-Chevy (1:17.7) and Don Devine in a Scarab (1:17.9) were on the next row. Pedro Rodriguez had a rough time in qualifying. He ran many laps in the 1:17's, but everytime he raised his hand to get a

qualifying time his car began to misfire. So his best timed lap was 1:20.8.

Jerry Grant took the lead at the start and began pulling away from everyone. Dave Ridenour was second, followed by Devine, Rodriguez, Wester, Heuer and Skip Hudson. On the fourth lap, Hudson spun his Chaparral 1 at turn six and had to wait for most of the field to go by before he could re-enter the track. On lap eight Rodriguez passed Devine for third place.

After ten laps, Grant had a six-second lead on Ridenour's Genie. Rodriguez was third in the new Genie with Devine's Scarab and Wester's Porsche right on his tail. Charlie Parsons had his little Lotus 23 in sixth place with Harry Heuer breathing up his tailpipe. Bob Holbert's Cobra was leading the Manufacturers class in ninth place with teammate Ken Miles second, in eleventh place.

On lap twelve, Rodriguez passed Ridenour for second place. But this lasted only five laps before Pedro retired the Genie with a broken water pump. Soon after this Don Devine eased his Scarab past Ridenour's Genie to take second place. Ridenour then had to battle with Don Wester's Porsche for third place. After a few laps, Wester began to fall back and Parsons took fourth place from him on lap twenty-six. Parsons then inherited third place on lap thirty-four when a water hose broke on Ridenour's Genie and he pitted for a long time.

At the halfway point, lap thirty-seven, Grant held a twelve-second lead over Don

Devine. Devine was busy with Parsons all over his rear-end and looking to get by. Don Wester was fourth and Harry Heuer fifth. Skip Hudson had worked his way back up to sixth place, one lap down from the leaders. Holbert still held the Manufacturers lead in seventh place with Miles in eighth. Heuer's Chaparral broke a rear axle after forty-three laps, elevating Hudson to fifth place.

Devine was unable to close the gap to Grant until lap fifty. That was when Grant retired his Lotus with a broken rod. Grant's crew could not pull the dipstick out because it had wrapped around the broken rod. This left Devine in the lead with a one-second lead over Parsons. Don Wester was third, twenty seconds back and Skip Hudson was fourth, still a lap down. Bob Holbert was still leading his class in fifth place. Ken Miles' Cobra lost a cotter pin in the shift linkage and he pitted to have it fixed. This moved Jerry Titus up to sixth place.

Devine was throwing the Scarab around the course with controlled abandon, but was unable to shake Parsons. They really gave the spectators their money's worth. After fifty-nine laps Ed Cantrell drove off the course to avoid another car, but in the process of coming back onto the track, he ran over something that ruptured an oil line. He managed to lay oil around the course for a lap and a half before being black flagged. Back in the pits, he said, "I was wondering who the son of a bitch was laying down all the oil."

Devine's lead lasted until lap sixty-two. When Devine retired the Scarab it had very little brakes left and a washer had broken loose and chewed the gears in the differential. This gave Parsons a twenty-second lead over Don Wester and two laps on Skip Hudson. On lap sixty-eight, Parsons hit some of Cantrell's oil in a corner and spun off the course. Parsons was able to recover and keep the lead, but it was down to six seconds. The race ran out with a jubilant Parsons taking the win with both hands raised as he crossed the finish line. Don Wester was second. Skip Hudson was third, but first in the over two-liter class. Bob Holbert took the Manufacturers win in fourth place with Jerry Titus fifth and Jim Parkinson sixth. Dave MacDonald was seventh and second in the Manufacturers section with Ed Leslie in eighth and Ken Miles in ninth.

After this race Tim Mayer still held the championship lead with 15 points. Second place was now a fourway tie between Bob Holbert, Jim Hall, Charlie Parsons and Skip Hudson, all with 9 points. Doug Thiem was sixth, with 8 points and Bill Eve was seventh, with 7 points. Eighth place was another four-way tie between Charlie Kolb, Herb Swan, Don Wester and Jerry Titus each with 6 points.

This was the second Manufacturers race and Ferrari still held the lead with 21 points to Cobra's 20. Jaguar had 4 points and Chevrolet (Corvette) had 3 points.

Don Wester's second place Porsche RS61 on the left and Charlie Parsons' winning Lotus 23 on the right, in the paddock at Laguna Seca. Photo by Allen R. Kuhn.

Skip Hudson in the #92 Team Meridian Chaparral Mk I, ahead of winner Charlie Parsons #10 Lotus 23 and Ed Leslie in Kjell Qvalle's #423 E-type Jaguar. Photo by Allen R. Kuhn.

Harry Heuer's Chaparral Mk I, next to the Meister Brauser transporter at Laguna Seca. Photo by Allen R. Kuhn.

Don Devine in the Meister Brauser Scarab gave Charlie Parsons a run for the money in the Meister Brauser Scarab. Unfortunately for Don the Scarab ran out of brakes and the differential packed up. Photo by Allen R. Kuhn.

Bob Holbert #196 leading Ken Miles #198, both in Shelby American Cobras and Don Devine #26 Meister Brauser Scarab. Photo by Allen R. Kuhn.

Don Devine #26 Meister Brauser Scarab leading winner Charlie Parsons #10 Lotus 23. Photo by Allen R. Kuhn.

1963 LAGUNA SECA • USRRC

June 9, 1963, Laguna Seca Raceways, Monterey, California

Place	Driver	Car/Engine	Car #	Class	Laps	Driver Points	Mfg Points	Prize	Qualifying Time
1	Charlie Parsons	Lotus 23-Ford	10	U2	78	9	-	$ 1,000	1:17.0
2	Don Wester	Porsche 718 RS61	60	U2	78	6	-	750	1:17.0
3	Skip Hudson	Chaparral 1-Chevrolet	92	O2	76	9	-	1,000	1:18.6
4	Bob Holbert	Shelby Cobra	196	MFR	76	-	9	-	-
5	Jerry Titus	Genie Mk 5-Corvair	16	O2	75	6	-	750	-
6	Jim Parkinson	Campbell Special	131	O2	75	4	-	500	1:19.4
7	Dave MacDonald	Shelby Cobra	197	MFR	75	-	6	-	-
8	Ed Leslie	Jaguar E-Type	423	MFR	74	-	4	-	-
9	Ken Miles	Shelby Cobra	198	MFR	73	-	3	-	-
10	Stan Peterson	Ferrari 250 GTO Berlinetta	7	MFR	71	-	2	-	-
11	Walt Maas	Cooper-Porsche	89	U2	70	4	-	500	1:22.8
12	Paul Reinhart	Chevrolet Corvette	6	O2	69	3	-	250	1:21.5
13	William Molle	Lotus 23-Climax	166	U2	69	*	-	250	1:25.0
14	Dave Kyte	Genie Mk 5-BMC	444	U2	66	3	-	-	1:28.7
15	Dan Gillum	Elva Mk 3	193	U2	64	2	-	-	1:28.6
16	Dave Ridenour	Genie Mk 8-Olds	146	O2	38	2	-	-	1:17.2
17	Doug Thiem	Ferrari Dino 196SP	1	U2	28	1	-	-	1:20.9
DNF	Don Devine	Scarab Mk 2-Chevrolet	26	O2	62	-	-	-	1:17.9
DNF	Ed Cantrell	Ferrari 250 GTO	9	MFR	60	-	-	-	1:24.1
DNF	Frank Monise	Lotus 23-Climax	44	U2	56	-	-	-	1:20.4
DNF	Jerry Grant	Lotus 19-Buick	18	O2	50	-	-	-	1:16.6
DNF	Harry Heuer	Chaparral 1-Chevrolet	24	O2	43	-	-	-	1:17.7
DNF	Bill Boldt	Kurtis 500X2-Pontiac	414	O2	36	-	-	-	1:20.0
DNF	Bill Sherwood	Chevrolet Corvette	183	O2	25	-	-	-	1:20.2
DNF	Pedro Rodriguez	Genie Mk 8-Chevrolet	448	O2	17	-	-	-	1:20.8
DNF	Ken O'Neill	Marlyn Mk HA	88	U2	9	-	-	-	1:26.3
DNS	Bill Sturgis	Cooper-Monaco	257	O2	-	-	-	-	1:17.6

* Disqualified for points due to tech violation

Fastest Qualifier:	Jerry Grant	Lotus 19-Buick	1:16.6	89.3 mph
Race Distance:	148.2 miles	78 laps of 1.9 mile course		
Race Time:	1hr 47min 20.3sec			
Winner's Speed:	86.2 mph			
Victory Margin:	6 seconds			
Fastest Race Lap:	Chuck Parsons	Lotus 23-Ford	1:17.8	87.92 mph

Don Devine #26 going around the outside of Bill Molle #166 Lotus 23. Photo by Allen R. Kuhn

WATKINS GLEN

SPORTS CAR GRAND PRIX WEEKEND

16th Annual

Where Road Racing Came of Age in America

**JUNE
28 - 29 - 30
1963**

50¢

Sunday

U. S. CHAMPIONSHIP

One for Manufacturers

One for Drivers

1963 Watkins Glen USRRC race program cover. Scan courtesy Don Markle.

1963 Watkins Glen Manufacturers Race

Three weeks after the Laguna Seca race, the USRRC went back across the US for the races at Watkins Glen, in upstate New York. At the time, the East Coast was having a heat-wave and it was sweltering at the Glen with ninety-degree weather.

The Manufacturers race entry comprised the Shelby Cobra team of Bob Holbert, Dave MacDonald and Ken Miles, and the privately entered Cobras of Bob Johnson, Bob Brown and Canadian Eppie Weitzes. Mike Gammino and Charlie Kolb were entered in Ferrari GTO's. Jack Moore, Alvin Forsyth and Millard Ripley raced their Corvettes.

Bob Johnson won the pole position with a time of 1:29.3 (92.72 mph) and blazed into the lead when the race started. Holbert was in second place and followed by MacDonald, Miles, Brown, Gammino, Weitzes, Kolb, Forsyth, Ripley and Moore. MacDonald passed Holbert on the next lap and

Weitzes retired with a blown clutch. Holbert pitted on the next lap, suffering a blown rear tire and a broken exhaust. Dave MacDonald took the lead from Johnson on the fifth lap. Mike Gammino dropped to seventh moving Kolb and Ripley up to fifth and sixth.

Johnson retook the lead from MacDonald on lap seven and Gammino passed Ripley for sixth place. Bob Holbert retired his Cobra on the next lap with a broken front suspension. After eight more laps, Charlie Kolb passed Bob Brown for fourth place.

MacDonald took the lead from Johnson on lap seventeen, with Miles third and Kolb fourth. Johnson ferociously dogged Mac-Donald and two laps later passed him to retake the lead. Although Johnson gradually extended his lead over the next few laps, it was more a matter of MacDonald falling back than Johnson pulling away. MacDonald kept slowing and fell back into the clutches of Miles, who took second place from him

on lap twenty-two. By now, Ripley had retired his Corvette and Charlie Kolb was in fourth place followed by Brown, Gammino, Moore and Forsyth. Gammino took fifth place from Brown on lap twenty-six.

Charlie Kolb pitted on lap thirty-six with fuel pump problems. This moved Gammino and Brown up to fourth and fifth places. Kolb retired his car after a few more laps, to get it fixed for the Drivers race. The race wound down with Miles dogging Johnson to the finish and MacDonald well behind in third place. Gammino spent the last fifteen laps inching closer to Brown's wheezing Cobra and eventually got by him to claim fourth place. Brown was fifth, Moore was sixth and Forsyth was a very distant seventh.

After this race Cobra assumed the lead in the championship with 41 points, to Ferrari's 24 points. Chevrolet (Corvette) now had 4 points and was tied with Jaguar for third place.

1963 WATKINS GLEN • USRRC MANUFACTURERS RACE
June 30, 1963, Watkins Glen Grand Prix Race Course, Watkins Glen, New York

Place	Driver	Car/Engine	Car #	Laps	Points	Prize
1	Bob Johnson	Cobra	33	66	9	$500
2	Ken Miles	Shelby Cobra	98	66	6	300
3	Dave MacDonald	Shelby Cobra	97	66	4	200
4	Mike Gammino	Ferrari 250 GTO	23	64	3	-
5	Bob Brown	Cobra	41	63	2	-
6	Jack Moore	Chevrolet Corvette	7	56	1	-
DNF	Alvin Forsyth	Chevrolet Corvette	81	51	-	-
DNF	Charles Kolb	Ferrari 250 GTO	21	40	-	-
DNF	Millard Ripley	Chevrolet Corvette	84	20	-	-
DNF	Bob Holbert	Shelby Cobra	99	7	-	-
DNF	Eppie Weitzes	Cobra	54	1	-	-

Fastest Qualifier:	Bob Johnson	Cobra	1:29.3	92.72 mph
Race Distance:	151.8 miles	66 laps of 2.3 mile course		
Race Time:	1 hr 38 min 38.4 sec			
Winner's Speed:	92.33 mph			
Victory Margin:	20.6 seconds			
Fastest Race Lap:	Dave MacDonald	Shelby Cobra	1:29.2	92.83 mph

Bob Johnson fought hard with the Shelby cars to win the Manufacturers race. Photo by Robert Bohl.

Doug Thiem placed ninth overall in his Ferrari 196SP. He would have scored a point for being sixth place in the under two-liter class, but driving help from Tom Peacock disqualified him from getting points. Photo by John McCollister.

Watkins Glen Drivers Race

The Glen had separate Drivers and Manufacturers races, so Bob Holbert entered his Penscacola-winning Porsche RS-61 in the Drivers race. To make things interesting and for more publicity, Carroll Shelby let Ken Miles enter the Drivers race in the Cobra he used in the Manufacturers race.

Harry Heuer, Skip Hudson, Don Wester, Ed Cantrell and Doug Thiem all made the trek from Laguna Seca. Herb Swan, Charlie Kolb and Charles Kurtz made another USRRC start at Watkins Glen. Twelve drivers were having their first USRRC race. Most notable were Joe Buzzetta, John Cannon, Ed Lowther and Peter Sachs.

Bob Holbert won the pole with a time of 1:28.1. Don Wester shared the front row with Holbert. Ken Miles started on the last row because his qualifying time was for only the Manufacturers race. Perrenial race starter, Tex Hopkins, had a style of his own for starting races. When the cars were lined up on the grid, revving their engines and all extraneous people were gone, Tex would strut ahead of the front row, on the outside of the track with a cigar clamped in his mouth. Somewhere between fifteen and thirty feet beyond the front row, Tex would suddenly turn ninety degrees, jump in the air with both lower legs bent up and furiously raise and wave the flag. When Tex did his trademark turn and jump to start this race Skip Hudson jumped from the second row into the lead. Behind were Holbert, Heuer, Swan, Lowther, Schall, Kelly (in a homemade Lotus 23 lookalike), John Cannon, Thiem, Kurtz and Miles was twenty-second and last.

Al Schall passed Lowther on the second lap, while Cannon passed Kelly, Sachs took Bucher, Kolb got by Buzzetta, Colombosian retired, Wester passed Cantrell and Miles passed Beimler and Clark. Lap three brought more excitement with Heuer taking second from Holbert, Cannon took sixth from Lowther, Kolb passed Snyder, Wester got by Buzzetta and Miles moved up to eighteenth. Peter Sachs got by Kurtz for tenth spot on lap four and Snyder retired.

Holbert took second place back from Heuer on lap five. Don Wester passed Kolb and Bucher for eleventh place and Charles Kurtz fell behind all three. On lap six, Peter Sachs and Don Wester passed Doug Thiem's Ferrari for ninth and tenth places and Joe Buzzetta passed Kurtz. Heuer passed Holbert again for second place. Sachs took eighth from Wayne Kelly, Wester fell back to fourteenth, Charlie Kolb retired and Ken Miles passed Cantrell for fifteenth place.

Peter Sachs was on a roll. On lap eight, he passed Ed Lowther to take seventh. Joe Buzzetta got by Bob Bucher for tenth when Doug Thiem fell behind both of them. Don Wester passed Charles Kurtz. On the next lap Buzzetta passed Kelly for ninth. A lap later, Heuer took the lead from Hudson, with Holbert in third and followed by Swan, Cannon, Schall, Sachs, Lowther, Buzzetta, Kelly, Bucher, Wester, Thiem, Kurtz and Miles. Holbert inherited second place on the eleventh lap when Hudson pitted. Wester passed Bucher, Kelly, Buzzetta and Lowther to take seventh. Bucher also passed Kelly for eighth.

Further back, Max Beimler retired.

The action continued on lap twelve as Buzzetta took eighth place from Lowther and Kelly repassed Bucher for ninth place. Schall pitted on the next lap and dropped to last. Peter Sachs had moved up to fifth place. Wayne Kelly took eighth place from Ed Lowther. Miles passed Kurtz for twelfth place on lap fourteen. On the next lap Sachs was passed by Wester and Buzzetta. Miles moved up to tenth by passing Thiem and Bucher. Thiem passed Bucher for eleventh spot. After one more lap, Miles passed Lowther for ninth place.

Along with the temperature, Ken Miles' driving was hot. He passed Kelly on lap eighteen for eighth place. Lowther and Bucher moved up to ninth and tenth as Kelly fell back. Wester pitted on lap twenty, moving Buzzetta up to fifth, followed by Sachs and Miles. Bucher passed Lowther for eighth place. Wester did one more lap and retired. Holbert took the lead from Heuer on lap twenty-two. Sachs passed Buzzetta on lap twenty-five for fifth place and then retired on the next lap. This left Buzzetta in fifth, with Miles closing in. Ken passed Buzzetta to take fifth place on lap thirty. Two laps later, Miles passed Cannon for fourth. On lap thirty-three Cannon pitted, giving fifth place to Buzzetta. That lasted for one lap and then Bucher passed Buzzetta.

On lap thirty-nine Harry Heuer retired leaving Herb Swan in second, Ken Miles in third, Bucher fourth, Buzzetta fifth and Kelly passed Lowther for sixth place. Kelly pitted on lap forty-one and dropped to eleventh. Skip Hudson passed Doug Thiem on lap forty-six to take eighth. Two laps later Thiem pitted and fell to tenth while John Cannon moved up to ninth place. But Cannon retired after three more laps leaving Thiem in eighth place. In the ensuing laps both Kelly and Schall pitted without losing places. On lap sixty-seven, Miles passed Swan to take second and Buzzetta got by Bucher for fourth. But on the next lap, Bucher pitted and lost only one place. Swan took second place back from Miles on lap seventy-three. There was no more passing and the race ended with Holbert winning over Swan and Miles, Buzzetta in fourth followed by Bucher, Lowther, Kurtz, Cannon, Thiem, Kelly, Lane and Schall.

Holbert and Miles both got 9 points for winning their classes. With the season at the halfway point, Bob Holbert was leading the championship with 18 points, followed by Tim Mayer with 15. Third was Herb Swan with twelve points and fourth was a four-way tie between Jim Hall, Charlie Parsons, Skip Hudson and Ken Miles all with 9 points. Doug Thiem was seventh with 8 points and Bill Eve was eighth with 7 points. Ninth place was another four-way tie between Charlie Kolb, Don Wester, Jerry Titus and Ed Lowther all with 6 points. Beyond this, there were seven drivers with 4 points, five with 3 points, three with 2 points and two with 1 point.

Bob Holbert and his trusty Porsche took pole position, stayed in the top three during the first quarter of the race, and then steadily drew away from the field to win by a lap. Photo by Bill Brannon, courtesy Bob Brannon.

Joe Buzzetta was fourth overall and third in the under two-liter class after an action-packed race. Photo by Don Rogerman.

1963 WATKINS GLEN SPORTS CAR GRAND PRIX • DRIVERS RACE
June 30, 1963, Watkins Glen Grand Prix Race Course, Watkins Glen, New York

Place	Driver	Car/Engine	Car #	Class	Laps	Points	Prize
1	Bob Holbert	Porsche 718 RS61	14	U2	82	9	$1,250
2	Herb Swan	Porsche 718 RS61	99	U2	81	6	500
3	Ken Miles	Shelby Cobra	98	O2	81	9	750
4	Joe Buzzetta	Porsche 718 RS61	7	U2	80	4	300
5	Bob Bucher	Porsche 718 RS60	29	U2	80	3	200
6	Ed Lowther	Lister-Chevrolet	72	O2	79	6	500
7	Charles Kurtz	Porsche 718 RS61	57	U2	78	2	150
8	John Cannon	Comstock-Ford	55	O2	78	4	300
9	Doug Thiem/Tom Peacock	Ferrari Dino 196SP	4	U2	78	-	100
10	Wayne Kelly	Kelly-Porsche	81	U2	77	-	-
11	Dick Lane	Ferrari 500 Mondial	48	U2	71	-	-
12	Al Schall	Lotus 23-Climax	40	U2	68	-	-
DNF	Skip Hudson	Chaparral 1-Chevrolet	92	O2	50	-	-
DNF	Harry Heuer	Chaparral 1-Chevrolet	1	O2	38	-	-
DNF	Peter Sachs	Lotus 23	37	U2	25	-	-
DNF	Ed Cantrell	Ferrari 250 GTO	21	O2	23	-	-
DNF	Don Wester	Porsche 718 RS61	60	U2	20	-	-
DNF	Max Beimler	Sadler-Stebro	63	O2	10	-	-
DNF	Charles Kolb	Porsche 718 RSK	3	U2	6	-	-
DNF	John Snyder III	Lister-Chevrolet	9	O2	3	-	-
DNF	Grant Clark	Lola Mk 1-Climax	65	U2	2	-	-
DNF	Robert Colombosian	Lotus 19-Buick	10	O2	1	-	-

Fastest Qualifier:	Bob Holbert	Porsche 718 RS61	1:28.1	93.98 mph
Race Distance:	188.6 miles	82 laps of 2.3 mile course		
Race Time:	2 hr 5 min 39.8 sec			
Winner's Speed:	90.63 mph			
Victory Margin:	1 lap			
Fastest Race Lap:	Harry Heuer	Chaparral 1-Chevrolet	1:27.7	94.31 mph

Ken Miles took third place overall and won the over two-liter class in the same car he used to take second place in the Manufacturers race. Photo by John McCollister.

U.S. ROAD RACING CHAMPIONSHIP

FOR SPORTS CARS AND GRAN TURISMO
PACIFIC RACEWAYS
JULY 20 AND 21, 1963

PROGRAM 50 CENTS

1963 Pacific Raceways race program cover. Scan courtesy Don Markle.

The Shelby American team. From the left, Dave MacDonald, Bob Holbert (open shirt) and Ken Miles plot their strategy. Photo by Ron Miller

Before they finished in race number order, the Shelby team traded places multiple times per lap. Here Ken Miles leads Bob Holbert and eventual winner, Dave MacDonald. Photo by Ron Miller

Frank Crane, #9 Ferrari 250 GTO, on his way to sixth place. Photo by Tom Lebo, courtesy Bill Lebo

1963 Pacific Raceways Manufacturers Race

For the fifth race of the series, teams and drivers had to go back across the country to Washington State and the Pacific Raceways course. The Shelby Cobra team of Holbert, MacDonald and Miles showed up and there was also the locally entered Cobra of John Razzelle. Mike Gammino made his second trip out West with his Ferrari GTO and Frank Crane brought his GTO up from the Bay area. Jerry Grant, Rick Stark, Pat McElreath and Jim Reese were all entered in Corvettes. Also, for the first time, there were the

Triumph TR4's of Bill Pendleton and Bob Rinde and the Sunbeam Alpine of L.C. Thomas.

Bob Holbert won the pole for the Manufacturers race with a time of 1:34.1 and he was joined on the front row of the grid by teammates Miles 1:34.5 and MacDonald 1:35.0. The next driver up was Mike Gammino with a time of 1:39.0 and Frank Crane at 1:39.6. Sixth on the grid was John Razzelle's Cobra with a time of 1:45.1.

When the race started, the first three Cobras flew off the grid and no one saw

them again until the Cobras came around to lap them. The one interesting feature of this race was watching Jerry Grant hustle Alan Green's Corvette around the track trying to get by Mike Gammino's Ferrari.

The race ran out with the Shelby Cobra of Dave MacDonald winning. Right on MacDonald's tail, Ken Miles was second and immediately following was Bob Holbert in third. Mike Gammino was fourth. Jerry Grant got close to Mike several times, but never quite made it and finished a worthy fifth.

1963 PACIFIC RACEWAYS • USRRC MANUFACTURERS RACE

July 21, 1963, Pacific Raceways, Kent, Washington

Place	Driver	Car/Engine	Car #	Laps	Points	Prize	Qualifying Place	Qualifying Time
1	Dave MacDonald	Shelby Cobra	97	67	9	$ 700	3	1:35.0
2	Ken Miles	Shelby Cobra	98	67	6	400	2	1:34.5
3	Bob Holbert	Shelby Cobra	99	67	4	375	1	1:34.1
4	Mike Gammino	Ferrari 250 GTO	23	66	3	350	4	1:39.0
5	Jerry Grant	Chevrolet Corvette	7	66	2	325	-	-
6	Frank Crane	Ferrari 250 GTO	9	65	1	250	5	1:39.6
7	Pat McElreath	Chevrolet Corvette	15	63	-	200	-	-
8	Jim Reese	Chevrolet Corvette	5	63	-	50	-	-
9	Bill Pendleton	Triumph TR4	56	60	-	50	-	-
10	Bob Rinde	Triumph TR4	21	60	-	50	-	-
11	John Razzelle	Cobra	59	60	-	-	6	1:45.1
12	L.C. (Leroy) Thomas	Sunbeam Alpine	42	55	-	-	7	1:54.4
DNF	Rick Stark	Chevrolet Corvette	11	15	-	-	-	-

Fastest Qualifier: Bob Holbert   Shelby Cobra   1:34.1   86.08 mph

Race Distance: 150.75 miles   67 laps of 2.25 mile course

Race Time: 1hr 48 min 20.4 sec

Winner's Speed: 83.49 mph

Victory Margin: 1 second

Fastest Race Lap: Unknown

Fifth place Jerry Grant, #7 Corvette, being lapped by third place, Bob Holbert. Photo by Tom Lebo, courtesy Bill Lebo.

Winner of the Driver's Race, Pedro Rodriguez is getting ready to do battle. Photo by Ron Miller.

After placing second and third in the Manufacturers race, Ken Miles #98 and Bob Holbert #99 raced their Cobras to fifth and fourth places, respectively, in the drivers race. Photo by Tom Lebo, courtesy Bill Lebo.

1963 Pacific Raceways Drivers Race

The Drivers race had Doug Thiem and Harry Heuer coming back out West. California drivers included Charlie Parsons, Skip Hudson, Jerry Titus, Dave Ridenour, Don Wester, Rod Carveth, Jack Nethercutt and Merle Brennan. Pedro Rodriguez was in Kjell Qvale's Genie. The local entries of Jerry Grant, Bob Clark, Lyle Forsgren, Blaise Lewark, George Miller, Paul Scott, Gene Lee and Jim Rattenbury enhanced the field.

Ken Miles started something at Watkins Glen: changing tires and refueling the Cobra after finishing the Manufacturers race, then running it again in the Drivers race (finishing third). At Pacific Raceways six drivers raced the same cars in both races. Mike Gammino, Pat McElreath and John Razzelle joined the three Shelby drivers. McElreath was the only one of these who didn't start from the rear of the grid. He'd made a point of qualifying his Corvette for both races. For the Driver's race, he started sixteenth. If Holbert had been able to use his Manufacturers race qualifying time, he would have started on the third row in eighth.

As it was, Jerry Grant got the pole for the Drivers race in Alan Green's Lotus 19-Buick with a time of 1:30.4. Pedro Rodriguez and Dave Ridenour filled out the front row of the grid, both with a time of 1:31.8. On the third row were Skip Hudson, Don Wester and Jerry Titus. Charlie Parsons and Harry Martin were on row four.

When the starter dropped the flag, it looked like a massive drag race. The front row all thundered off together, going three abreast through the turn one kink and

Rodriguez braked a smidge later than Grant to take the lead through turn two. Dave Ridenour was third, followed by Titus, Hudson, Wester, Nethercutt and Parsons. The Cobras of Holbert, Miles and MacDonald had worked up to ninth, tenth and eleventh on the second lap. On the third lap Grant passed Rodriguez between turns three and four and began to pull out a lead. Two laps later Jerry Titus pitted with fanbelt problems and Charlie Parsons pitted with low oil pressure, due to loose rings. This moved Bob Holbert up to seventh place. Grant had about a two-second lead over Rodriguez. Pedro's advantage over Ridenour stretched out when Ridenour heard strange noises coming from his engine and slowed down.

By the tenth lap Grant was three seconds ahead of Rodriguez, who had a fifteen-second lead on Ridenour. Skip Hudson was fourth with Holbert up to fifth. Don Wester, Ken Miles, Dave MacDonald and Jack Nethercutt followed them. Over the next few laps, the order stayed the same with Grant pulling out a couple more seconds over Rodriguez. In turn, Rodriguez also put more space between himself and Ridenour.

On lap twenty-two, Grant had just lapped Don Wester's sixth place Porsche when a rear hub carrier broke on his Lotus. Grant went for a wild ride through the grass on the outside of turn two. Rodriguez assumed the lead with thirty seconds over Ridenour. Skip Hudson's Chaparral 1 was third and gaining on Ridenour, but he also had Bob Holbert's Cobra rather close behind. Don Wester was fifth with Ken Miles sixth. Everyone maintained their places until lap thirty-

three when Hudson's engine blew. This put Holbert into third place.

On lap thirty-nine, Miles caught the fourth place Porsche of Don Wester and they began taking turns passing each other lap after lap and sometimes corner after corner. The big-engine Cobra would blow by the Porsche on the long straight and on the backside of the course. Then the Porsche would close up on, or pass, the Cobra on the tight turns. After about ten more laps, Miles was able to get the better of Wester and put a few seconds between them. After fifty laps rain, the great equalizer, entered the race. Wester began to reel in Miles' Cobra, which was a real handful on the wet track because of the wide stock car tires it was using.

After fifty-seven laps, Wester took fourth place from Miles and two laps later he took third place from Holbert. Back up front, Rodriguez had slowed his pace, but still won the race with a twenty-eight second lead over Ridenour. Wester took third place and first in the under two liter class. The Cobras of Holbert, Miles and Dave MacDonald were a lap back, in fourth, fifth and sixth. Rod Carveth and Jack Nethercutt were seventh and eighth with Doug Thiem ninth and second in the under two-liter class.

After this race Holbert extended his championship lead with 22 points, to the 15 points each, of Tim Mayer and Don Wester. Doug Thiem was fourth in the championship with 14 points, while Charlie Parsons was next with 13 points. Tied for sixth were Ken Miles and Herb Swan with 12 points. By now, thirty-five different drivers had scored points for the championship.

1963 PACIFIC RACEWAYS • USRRC DRIVERS RACE

July 21, 1963, Pacific Raceways, Kent, Washington

Place	Driver	Car/Engine	Car #	Class	Laps	Points	Prize	Qualifying Place	Qualifying Time
1	Pedro Rodriguez	Genie Mk 8-Chevrolet	448	O2	67	9	$ 1,500	2	1:31.8
2	Dave Ridenour	Genie Mk 8-Oldsmobile	146	O2	67	6	600	3	1:31.8
3	Don Wester	Porsche 718 RS61	60	U2	67	9	1,000	5	1:33.4
4	Bob Holbert	Shelby Cobra	99	O2	66	4	400	-	-
5	Ken Miles	Shelby Cobra	98	O2	66	3	300	-	-
6	Dave MacDonald	Shelby Cobra	97	O2	65	2	200	-	-
7	Rod Carveth	Lotus 19-Buick	54	O2	64	1	50	12	1:37.9
8	Jack Nethercutt	Lotus 19-Climax	102	O2	64	-	50	9	1:35.0
9	Doug Thiem	Lotus 19-Climax	4	U2	63	6	600	10	1:35.8
10	Charlie Parsons	Lotus 23-Ford	10	U2	63	4	400	7	1:33.6
11	Mike Gammino	Ferrari 250 GTO	23	O2	62	-	50	-	-
12	Merle Brennan	Jaguar E-Type	66	O2	62	-	50	-	-
13	Pat McElreath	Chevrolet Corvette	15	O2	61	-	50	16	1:40.0
14	Bob Clark	HWM-Chevrolet	45	O2	59	-	-	14	1:39.6
15	Lyle Forsgren	Forsgrini Veloce-Alfa Romeo	148	U2	55	3	300	-	-
16	Blaise Lewark	Lotus 23-Ford	67	U2	52	2	200	13	1:38.7
17	George Miller	Lotus 11	31	U2	50	1	50	-	-
18	Paul Scott	Lotus 15	123	U2	48	-	50	19	1:42.6
DNF	Skip Hudson	Chaparral 1-Chevrolet	92	O2	32	-	-	4	1:33.0
DNF	John Razzelle	Cobra	59	O2	29	-	-	-	-
DNF	Harry Martin	Lotus 23	3	U2	28	-	-	8	1:34.7
DNF	Bill Stephens	Lister-Corvette	62	O2	27	-	-	11	1:37.6
DNF	Jim Rattenbury	Porsche Special	51	U2	27	-	-	18	1:40.8
DNF	Gene Lee	Chev Special	35	O2	23	-	-	15	1:40.
DNF	Jerry Grant	Lotus 19-Buick	8	O2	21	-	-	1	1:30.4
DNF	Jerry Titus	Genie Mk 5-Corvair	16	U2	18	-	-	6	1:33.5

Fastest Qualifier:	Jerry Grant	Lotus 19-Buick	1:30.4	89.6 mph
Race Distance:	150.75 miles	67 laps of 2.25 mile course		
Race Time:	1hr 48 min 59.4 sec			
Winner's Speed:	82.99 mph			
Victory Margin:	28.5 seconds			
Fastest Race Lap:	Jerry Grant	Lotus 19-Buick	1:30.4	89.6 mph

Pedro Rodriguez on his way to victory at Pacific Raceways. Photo by Ron Miller.

FIRST CONTINENTAL DIVIDE NATIONAL OPEN
AUG. 17-18 1963

OFFICIAL PROGRAM

SCCA SANCTION No. DMC-6
SPONSORED BY:
ROAD RACING LTD.

ACCUS FIA INC.
SANCTION No. N-22

1963 Continental Divide program cover. Scan courtesy Don Markle.

Continental Divide

The series began its final leg east with a stop at Continental Divide Raceway in Colorado. This would be a combined race as there were only seven Manufacturers cars entered.

Shelby brought three Cobras, as usual. One of them had a Le Mans hardtop, to be raced by Dave MacDonald. This was not the Daytona coupe that was yet to come, but a roadster fitted with a permanent top. Bob Bondurant was having his first race for the Shelby team by filling in for the missing Ken Miles. Ken was not actually missing. He was in England to race a Cobra in the Tourist Trophy at Goodwood. Shelby let Bob Holbert run a Cobra roadster in the Driver's class, to help consolidate his championship lead. Other Manufacturer's entries were Bob Hayes in his own Cobra, Roy Kumnick in a Corvette, Bob Moore and Gordon Stalgren in Triumphs and John Barker in an MGA.

The Driver's race was blessed with a fine entry from East, West and in between. Entries included the Meister Brauser team of Harry Heuer in his Chaparral 1 and Augie Pabst in the front-engine Scarab, Jerry Grant with his potent Lotus 19-Buick and Chuck Daigh in a Cooper-Chevrolet. There were also Lotus 23's for Charlie Parsons, Blaise Lewark, Bob Markley and Dave Morgan, plus a Lotus 19 for Doug Thiem. Don Wester, Bob Wuesthoff, Herb Swan and Steve Baughman were entered in Porsches. Enus Wilson entered a Birdcage Maserati with a Buick engine.

The week before the race, the race promoters brought in Stirling Moss to work his PR magic at the local car dealerships and on local radio and TV shows. This turned out to be a smooth move because the track had a record crowd on race day.

Jerry Grant nailed down his third pole position of the year with a lap of 2:04.2. Harry Heuer moved his Chaparral around the course in 2:06.3 to line up next to Grant.

Taking the last front row position was Don Wester with a time of 2:06.9. Augie Pabst got the Scarab around in 2:07.9 and was joined on the second row by Hap Sharp, in a new Elva-Ford with a time of 2:08.1. The third row had Bob Holbert, 2:08.3, Charlie Parson, 2:08.6 and Bill Wuesthoff, 2:09.2.

Harry Heuer shot into the lead when the race started. Jerry Grant was well behind in second spot. Following in third place was Don Wester with Bob Holbert and Charlie Parsons right behind. Augie Pabst almost stalled the Scarab on the grid and was passed by almost everyone before he was able to get it moving. Hap Sharp made one lap before he stopped at the pits to have the sparkplugs changed.

The first ten laps saw Heuer drawing away from Grant, who in turn was putting distance between himself and Don Wester. Holbert was maintaining fourth spot in his Cobra. There were also six cars which had retired including Doug Thiem, Charlie Parsons, Hank Candler and Bud Morley. Hap Sharp was way down the order, but passing cars almost every other lap. After eighteen laps, Blaise Lewark retired his Lotus 23.

Heuer had a one-minute lead over Grant after twenty-four laps. On the next lap Grant retired his Lotus from second place with an engine that had been misfiring and a drivetrain that just gave up. Wester was now in second place. He had very little hope of catching Heuer as he was busy defending his place from Holbert's charging Cobra. Over the next seven laps, Holbert closed the gap to Wester who would put some distance between them on the tight section of the course only to have Holbert close it up on the main straight. On lap thirty-two, Holbert was able to stay close on Wester's tail through the last turn and sail past him on the front straight.

Also on the move was Augie Pabst who had recovered from his bum start and tenaciously worked his way up to fifth place

behind Bill Wuesthoff's Porsche. By lap thirty-four, Pabst had passed Wuesthoff for fourth place and had his sights set on Wester.

Harry Heuer's lead was big enough for him to pit on lap thirty-four for a drink of water and to have his tires inspected. He got back on the track, still with a healthy lead over Holbert's Cobra. Third was Wester, followed by Pabst and Wuesthoff. Further back was Bob Bondurant leading the Manufacturer's section.

Pabst caught and passed Wester on lap thirty-six. A couple of laps later Pabst caught up with Holbert's Cobra. Bob was able to keep Pabst behind him everywhere except the main straight. For two laps they roared down the straight side by side with the crowd roaring back. On lap forty, Pabst took the lead from Holbert, but immediately got repassed on the next lap and dropped back a few seconds.

Heuer had been sailing along in the lead until lap forty-two, when a tie rod broke sending him off course and into Enus Wilson's Maserati. Heuer got back to the pits and did one more lap before parking the Chaparral near the start/finish line. Bob Holbert now assumed the lead with Pabst eleven seconds back in second place. Don Wester was way back in third place and Bill Wuesthoff was even further back in fourth place. Bob Bondurant was still leading the Manufacturer's contingent a lap down in fifth place.

On lap forty-five, Herb Swan tried to lap Steve Baughman going into turn one, but they made heavy contact. The result was Baughman slewing down the escape road and Swan swerving madly but still on the course. With eight laps left Pabst was throwing the Scarab around the course and visibly catching Holbert. The crowd was on their feet pressing the fence and being very vocal. The gap was about seven seconds. After five more laps, there were three and a half

seconds between Holbert and Pabst and the crowd was yelling louder. On lap fifty-two, with two more laps left Pabst was one and a half seconds behind Holbert. On the backside of the course at turn five the crowd groaned. Holbert got the sun in his eyes, hit some oil in the middle of the turn and slid for about fifty yards as he help-lessly watched Pabst go by into the lead.

Pabst finished the race with a ten-second lead over Holbert. Don Wester and Bill Wuesthoff brought their Porsches home in third and fourth places taking first and second in the under two liter class. Wester's nine points moved him into second place in the championship with 24 points to Holbert's 28. Bob Bondurant was fifth overall, winning the Manufacturer's class. Hap Sharp recovered from his first lap pitstop and had methodically worked his way up to sixth place. Herb Swan was seventh and his fourth place points in the under two-liter class moved him into third place in the championship with 15 points. Dave MacDonald brought the Cobra hardtop home in eighth place ahead of Bob Hayes' private Cobra roadster.

Jerry Grant #8 and Harry Heuer #12 lead off the line, with Don Wester #60, Hap Sharp #95, Augie Pabst #14, and Bob Holbert #99 in pursuit. Photo from the collections of The Henry Ford.

Harry Heuer grabbed the lead at the start and kept pulling away from the field. He was able to make a pitstop and still retain the lead, setting the fastest race lap, until a tie rod broke after 42 laps. Photo from the collections of The Henry Ford.

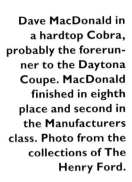

Dave MacDonald in a hardtop Cobra, probably the forerunner to the Daytona Coupe. MacDonald finished in eighth place and second in the Manufacturers class. Photo from the collections of The Henry Ford.

Don Wester #60 ran in third place, with Bob Holbert #99 in fourth place, for the first thirty-two laps. Holbert then got a run on Wester and passed him on the main straight. Photo from the collections of The Henry Ford.

Bob Bondurant #98 won the Manufacturers class and finished in fifth place overall. Behind Bondurant is Dave MacDonald in the Cobra hardtop #97. Photo from the collections of The Henry Ford.

1963 CONTINENTAL DIVIDE USRRC
August 18, 1963, Continental Divide Raceways, Castle Rock, Colorado

Place	Driver	Car/Engine	Car #	Class	Laps	Driver Points	Mfg Points	Prize
1	Augie Pabst	Scarab Mk 2-Chevrolet	14	O2	54	9	-	$1,00
2	Bob Holbert	Shelby Cobra	99	O2	54	6	-	500
3	Don Wester	Porsche 718 RS61	60	U2	54	9	-	1,000
4	Bill Wuesthoff	Porsche 718 RS61	77	U2	54	6	-	500
5	Bob Bondurant	Shelby Cobra	98	MFR	53	-	9	500
6	Hap Sharp	Elva Mk 7-Ford	95	U2	53	4	-	250
7	Herb Swan	Porsche 718 RS61	199	U2	52	3	-	150
8	Dave MacDonald	Shelby Cobra (hardtop)	97	MFR	52	-	6	250
9	Bob (R.E.L.) Hayes	Cobra	45	MFR	52	-	4	125
10	Roy Kumnick	Chevrolet Corvette	-	MFR	51	-	3	7
11	Harry Washburn	Cooper T61-Maserati	147	O2	51	4	-	2
12	Steve Baughman	Porsche 718 RSK	67	U2	51	2	-	100
13	Enus Wilson	Maserati-Buick	2	O2	50	3	-	150
14	Chuck Daigh	Cooper T61-Chevrolet	15	O2	49	2	-	100
15	Dave Morgan	Lotus 23-Climax	39	U2	47	1	-	
16	Chuck Frederick	Chevrolet Corvette	3	O2	47	1	-	-
17	Jim Kirbach	Lotus 11	19	U2	45	-	-	-
18	Harry Heuer	Chaparral 1-Chevrolet	12	O2	44	-	-	-
19	Stan Schooley	Elva Mk 5-Maserati	-	U2	44	-	-	-
20	Bob Moore	Triumph TR3	55	MFR	43	-	2	-
21	Bob Markley	Lotus 23	17	U2	37	-	-	-
DNF	John Barker	MG-A	89	MFR	35	-	-	-
DNF	Yale Thomas	Maserati	72	O2	31	-	-	-
DNF	Jim Eichorn	Devin-Corvair	114	O2	30	-	-	-
DNF	Jerry Grant	Lotus 19-Buick	8	O2	25	-	-	-
DNF	Chuck Trowbridge	Elva Mk 6	9	U2	25	-	-	-
DNF	Matt Raun	Chevrolet Corvette	99	MFR	25	-	-	-
DNF	Blaise Lewark	Lotus 23-Ford	24	U2	18	-	-	-
DNF	Doug Thiem	Lotus 19-Climax	4	U2	10	-	-	-
DNF	Gordon Stalgren	Triumph TR2	63	MFR	10	-	-	-
DNF	Hank Candler	Elva Mk 7-BMW	44	U2	10	-	-	-
DNF	Charlie Parsons	Lotus 23-Climax	10	U2	9	-	-	-
DNF	Bud Morley	Elva Mk 6	33	U2	6	-	-	-
DNF	Edna Sherman	Lotus 23-Alfa	23	U2	4	-	-	-

Fastest Qualifier:	Jerry Grant	Lotus 19-Buick	2:04.2	81.16 mph
Race Distance:	151.2 miles	54 laps of 2.8 mile course		
Race Time:	1 hr 57 min 31.8 sec			
Winner's Speed:	77.19 mph			
Victory Margin:	10 seconds			
Fastest Race Lap:	Harry Heuer	Chaparral 1-Chevrolet	2:06.9	79.43 mph

Augie Pabst was in second place, eleven seconds behind leader, Bob Holbert, with eight laps left to run. Augie was throwing the Scarab around the course to close in on Holbert. With two laps left Holbert spun when the sun got the better of his eyes and Pabst flew by into the lead and take the win. Photo from the collections of The Henry Ford.

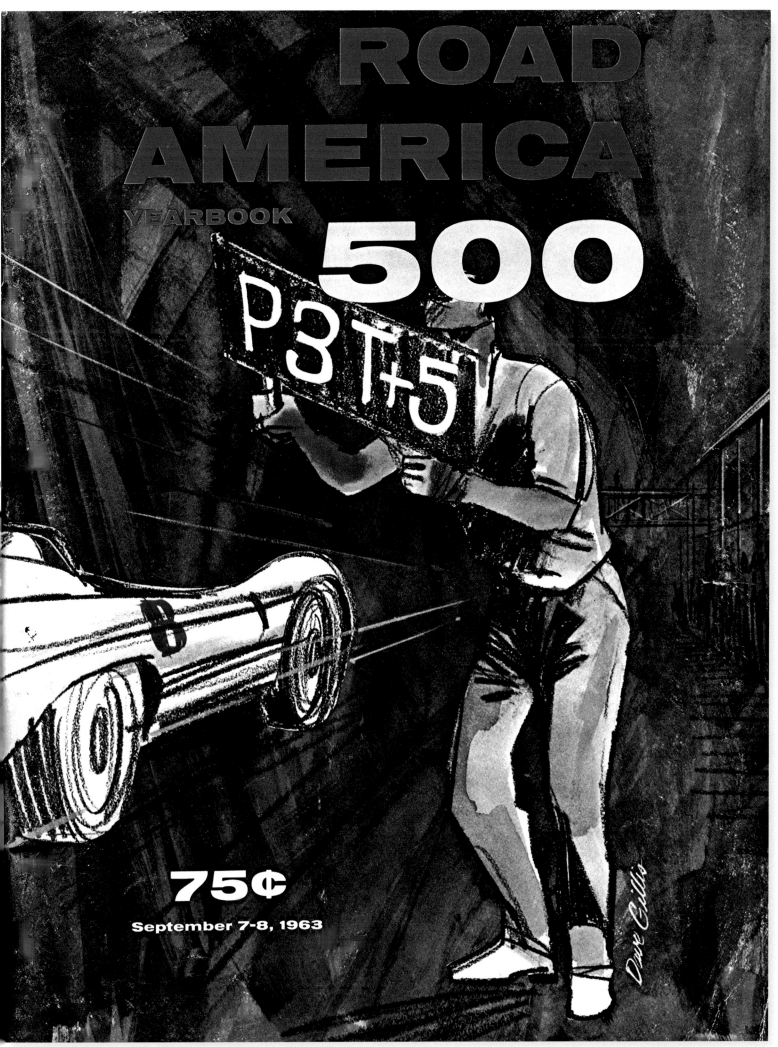

ROAD AMERICA YEARBOOK

500

P3T51

75¢

September 7-8, 1963

1963 Road America 500 race program cover. Scan courtesy Don Markle

1963 Road America

The series arrived at the beautiful Road America course in Elkhart Lake, Wisconsin for the seventh and penultimate race. In the past, the Road America 500 was an SCCA National race attracting a huge field of cars. This year was no different. There were seventy-eight cars entered and sixty-one cars ended up taking the starting flag.

The Manufacturers race was combined with the Drivers race and had only nine entries. The low entry was probably due in part to the Shelby team having already clinched the Manufacturers Championship and after the Pensacola race, having thoroughly stomped the competition at each race. Shelby entered two Cobras in the Manufacturer's class, for Bob Bondurant and Dave MacDonald, plus another for Bob Johnson and Lew Spencer. Tom Payne shared Dan Gerber's privately entered Cobra. Briggs Cunningham entered three E-type Jaguars for himself and John Fitch, Bob Grossman and Dick Thompson and for Walt Hansgen and Paul Richards. Dick Doane and Ralph Salyer had a Corvette Grand Sport while Americ Joslin shared his Sting Ray with Dick Lang. The final entry in the Manufacturer's class was the Ferrari 250 GT of John Baxter which he shared with Bill Tannhaeuser.

The entry for the Driver's section was stellar. Shelby entered a Cobra roadster that was "stock, but loose", so Bob Holbert could try to maintain his championship lead. Holbert had teammate Ken Miles co-driving. John Mecom entered a Ferrari GTO for Roger Penske and Augie Pabst. Harry Heuer's Meister Brauser team entered a Chaparral 1 for Harry and a Scarab for Don Devine and

Don Yenko. Doug Thiem shared his Ferrari Dino with Tom Terrell. Don Wester brought his Porsche RS-61out from California. Ollie Schmidt entered the brand new Elva Mark 7S with a 1.8 liter Porsche engine for Bill Wuesthoff, who intended to drive it solo. Chuck Dietrich was entered in the incredibly fast, little Bobsy. It now had a 1500cc twin cam Holbay Ford engine, instead of the previously used 1100cc unit. All told there were thirteen Elvas, eight Ferraris, five Porsches and five Lotuses among the Cobras, Chaparral, Scarab and other specials.

Holbert and Miles garnered the pole position with the new Elva-Porsche beside them on the front row. As the race started, Bill Wuesthoff pushed the little Elva-Porsche into the lead ahead of Miles' Cobra. Third was Don Sesslar in a Porsche RS-60, followed by Augie Pabst in Mecom's Ferrari, George Reed in a Ferrari 250 TR-59 powered by a 427 Ford and sixth was Curt Gonstead in a Lotus 23. During the pace lap, Harry Heuer found the gearshift was not attached to the linkage. At the end of the pace lap, Heuer brought his Chaparral into the pits to have it reattached. He got back in the race as everyone else completed the first lap.

Miles took the lead on the fourth lap with Wuesthoff and Sesslar close behind. Heuer was fourth on the track, one lap behind and charging like the devil. Don Yenko had the Scarab up to fifth behind Reed's Ferrari-Ford with Gonstead sixth and Pabst seventh. A few laps later, Bob Johnson in a Cobra, passed Pabst's Ferrari and started gaining on Yenko's Scarab. On lap nineteen Gonstead spun his Lotus and broke a water hose, resulting in immediate retirement.

Heuer thundered by Sesslar after twenty laps and was moving up on Wuesthoff. Heuer was still a lap down and trying to make up time and places. At the hundred-mile mark (twenty-five laps), Miles was leading Wuesthoff. Heuer was third on the road, but really in tenth place. Sesslar was in third place followed by Reed's Ferrari-Ford and the Scarab of Yenko. The Cobras of MacDonald and Johnson were sixth and seventh. Dick Doane in the Grand Sport, Pabst in Mecom's Ferrari and Dave Morgan in a Lotus 23 rounded out the top ten.

With nine more laps completed, Heuer's Chaparral blew its transmission and he was out. The next bit of excitement came when Bob Johnson brought his Cobra into the pits for gas, tires and to hand it over to Lew Spencer. As he raced off, Spencer heard a "ding" at the first corner. That "ding" was his left front knock-off falling off the car. Spencer ended up racing his left front tire to turn two before he eased the three-wheeled Cobra around the rest of the course and back to the pits. This time the knock-off was knocked on tightly and Lew set out racing again.

Back in the pack, Walt Hansgen was working his E-type Jag through the field. He got up to twelfth place behind Dietrich's little Bobsy. Don Sesslar had pitted for gas and gave his Porsche to Chuck Cassell. Cassell was working his way back up to third place when a tire blew and he limped back to the pits to have it changed. He returned to the track in tenth place, right in front of Dietrich's Bobsy. On lap thirty-five, Miles brought his Cobra into the pits for gas, tires and to handoff to Holbert. This dropped

Ken Miles in the Cobra he shared with Bob Holbert. They took second overall and first in the over two-liter Drivers class. Photo by John McCollister.

Harry Heuer retired the Meister Brauser Chaparral Mk I after 34 laps. Photo by Tom Schultz.

them to third place behind Wuesthoff's Elva-Porsche and Yenko's Scarab. Wuesthoff made his scheduled pitstop on lap forty-two, giving the lead to Yenko. When he returned to the track, Wuesthoff was still in second place and within sight of the Scarab. Yenko held the Scarab in the lead until lap fifty-nine when he made his scheduled pitstop and gave the car to Don Devine.

Holbert took the lead again with Wuesthoff second and Devine's Scarab in third. The Scarab lasted until lap seventy-four when the engine blew. Holbert pitted the Cobra on lap eighty-four to have the brake pads replaced and for Miles to take the final stint. This gave the lead back to Wuesthoff and put the Cobra more than a lap behind, still in second place. When Wuesthoff pitted two laps later he asked for relief. Augie Pabst had finished his last stint in the Ferrari GTO and agreed to finish the race for Wuesthoff. He had never sat in the Elva before and was given a very brief overview of the controls before he drove off, still

keeping the Elva in the lead.

During the last forty laps Miles was driving like a demon. He unlapped himself and whittled down the Elva's lead. As anything can happen in a long race, Miles wasn't about to let up. But the race wound down with Pabst taking the Elva around the course about ten seconds a lap slower than Miles, but still in the lead. On the last lap the Cobra started smoking under the hood from a ruptured oil line and Miles didn't let up. Right after the Cobra crossed the finish line, fifty-nine seconds behind Pabst, the engine blew up.

The Cassell/Sesslar Porsche finished in third place with the Bondurant/MacDonald Cobra in fourth place and first in the Manufacturers section. Chuck Dietrich brought the Bobsy home in fifth place with a solo drive. The Bob Johnson/Lew Spencer Cobra managed to keep all its wheels on for sixth place. The Ferrari Dino of Doug Thiem and Tom Terrell was seventh and the Ferrari GTO Roger Penske shared with Pabst

was eighth and second in the over two-liter Driver's section.

With this race completed, Bob Holbert clinched the Drivers title with the nine points he and Miles got for finishing in second place and first in over two-liters. Bob had a total of 37 points. Don Wester still held onto second place in the championship with 24 points. His was the hard luck story of this race. He brought his Porsche out from California only to have it expire on the first lap. Then the Elva-Porsche he shared with Ernie Erickson gave up after eighty-nine laps. Ken Miles moved up to third place in the championship with 21 points. Augie Pabst and Doug Thiem shared fourth place with 18 points each. The win moved Bill Wuesthoff into a tie for sixth place with Tim Mayer and Herb Swan at 15 points apiece. Charlie Parsons was ninth in the championship with 13 points and Skip Hudson rounded out the top ten with 10 points. There was still plenty of room for drivers to improve their championship standing with one race to go.

1963 ROAD AMERICA 500
September 8, 1963, Road America, Elkhart Lake, Wisconsin

Place	Driver	Car/Engine	Car #	Class	Laps	Driver Points	Mfg Points	Prize
1	Augie Pabst/Bill Wuesthoff	Elva Mk 7-Porsche	76	U2	125	9	-	$1,500
2	Bob Holbert/Ken Miles	Shelby Cobra	98	O2	125	9	-	1,000
3	Don Sesslar/Chuck Cassell	Porsche 718 RS60	73	U2	123	6	-	750
4	Bob Bondurant/Dave MacDonald	Shelby Cobra	97	MFR	123	-	9	500
5	Chuck Dietrich	Bobsy Mk 2-Ford	37	U2	122	4	-	500
6	Bob Johnson/Lew Spencer	Shelby Cobra	99	MFR	121	-	6	300
7	Doug Thiem/Tom Terrell	Ferrari Dino SP206	4	U2	121	3	-	300
8	Augie Pabst/Roger Penske	Ferrari 250 GTO	7	O2	120	6	-	750
9	Lee (E.L.) Hall/Glen Carroll	Porsche 718 RS60	66	U2	120	2	-	200
10	Doc (M.R.J.) Wyllie	Lola Mk 1-Cosworth	12	U2	117	1	-	150
11	Walt Hansgen/Paul Richards	Jaguar E-Type	61	MFR	116	-	4	200
12	Wayne Burnett/Luke Stear	Ferrari 250TR	94	O2	116	4	-	500
13	Mike Hall/Burdie Martin	Elva Mk 6-Ford	69	U2	114	-	-	125
14	Chuck Rickert/Sam Eller	Porsche Special	10	U2	114	-	-	100
15	Enus Wilson/Gary Wilson	Ferrari 250TR	19	O2	113	3	-	300
16	David Biggs/James Johnston	Ferrari 250TR	16	O2	112	2	-	200
17	Skip Hudson	Maserati Tipo 151	93	O2	112	1	-	150
18	Scott Beckett/Don Skogmo	Maserati T61-Ford	34	O2	112	-	-	125
19	Bob Kelce/Clint Lindberg	Elva Mk 7-BMW	5	U2	111	-	-	75
20	Briggs Cunningham/John Fitch	Jaguar E-Type	63	MFR	110	-	3	-
21	Howard Quick/Hal Ullrich	Lister-Jaguar	17	O2	110	-	-	100
22	Al Ross/Hank Candler	Elva Mk 7- BMW	25	U2	109	-	-	50
23	Jack Stone/Bill Stone	Elva Mk 5	38	U2	108	-	-	-
24	George Hadley/Roger Donovan	Elva Mk 7-Ford	55	U2	108	-	-	-
25	Alex Ratelle/Franklin Phillipps	Elva Mk 6	21	U2	107	-	-	-
26	Charles Edwards/Joseph Swanson	Elva Mk 6	58	U2	105	-	-	-
27	Homer Rader/Bob Markley	Lotus 23	43	U2	105	-	-	-
28	Mike Rahal/Stan Kozlowski	Elva Mk 6	42	U2	104	-	-	-
29	Herb Swan	Porsche 718 RS61	79	U2	102	-	-	-
30	Bob Dusinberre/Burrel Besancon	Elva Mk 6	6	U2	101	-	-	-
31	Dick Durant/A.R. Welch Jr.	Durant Special	46	O2	101	-	-	-
32	Bill Cooper/Dick Irish	Ferrari 500TR	22	U2	99	-	-	-
33	Bud Gates/Jack Ensley	Apache-Chevrolet	71	O2	98	-	-	-
34	Jerry Nelson/Charlie Cox	Stanguellini	88	U2	97	-	-	-
35	Keith Hardy/Chuck Frederick	Corvette Special	26	O2	96	-	-	-
36	Jerald Scrabeck/Dewey Brohaugh	Scrabeck Special	47	O2	92	-	-	-
37	Jack Moore	Chevrolet Corvette	81	O2	88	-	-	-
38	Tom Payne/Dan Gerber	Cobra	13	MFR	83	-	2	-
39	Bob Grossman/Dick Thompson	Jaguar E-Type	62	MFR	79	-	1	-

The Meister Brauser Scarab of Don Yenko and Don Devine. Photo by Tom Schultz.

DNF	Don Wolf/Dick Talbot	Elva Mk 6-Climax	86	U2	114	-	-	-
DNF	Dick Doane/Ralph Salyer	Corvette Grand Sport	29	MFR	93	-	-	-
DNF	John Baxter/William Tannhaeuser	Ferrari 250 GTO	78	O2	93	-	-	-
DNF	Ernie Erickson/Don Wester	Elva Mk 7-Porsche	27	U2	89	-	-	-
DNF	Dave Morgan/Hap Sharp	Lotus 23-Climax	39	U2	73	-	-	-
DNF	Don Yenko/Don Devine	Scarab Mk 2-Chev	2	O2	73	-	-	-
DNF	Americ Joslin/Dick Lang	Chevrolet Corvette	51	MFR	69	-	-	-
DNF	James Spencer/Richard Buedinger	Lotus 23-Ford	53	U2	40	-	-	-
DNF	Bill Niemeyer/Tom Cones	Bristol-Chevrolet	65	O2	39	-	-	-
DNF	Harry Heuer	Chaparral 1-Chev	1	O2	34	-	-	-
DNF	George Reed	Ferrari TR 59/60-Ford	95	O2	27	-	-	-
DNF	Jerry Dunbar/Walter Gray	Edwards Special	32	O2	22	-	-	-
DNF	Curt Gonstead	Lotus 23-Ford	3	U2	18	-	-	-
DNF	Roy Kumnick	Excalibur Hawk Mk4-Studebaker	44	O2	18	-	-	-
DNF	John Snyder	Lister-Corvette	11	O2	17	-	-	-
DNF	Pat Manning/Bob Liess	Ferrari-Chevrolet	45	O2	17	-	-	-
DNF	Ralph Trieschmann/Owen Coon	Elva Mk 7-Ford	56	U2	15	-	-	-
DNF	Dave Causey/Dean Causey	Lotus 19-Ford	24	O2	11	-	-	-
DNF	Charles Kolb	Maserati 200si-Chev	36	O2	8	-	-	-
DNF	Robert Spooner/Joe Scopelite	Bocar-Stilletto	83	O2	5	-	-	-
DNF	Richard Jordan/Dick Clicquennoi	Fireball Special	15	O2	3	-	-	-
DNF	Don Wester	Porsche 718 RS61	64	U2	0	-	-	-

Fastest Qualifier:	Ken Miles	Shelby Cobra	2:40.8	89.55 mph
Race Distance:	500 miles	125 laps of 4.0 mile course		
Race Time:	5 hr 0 min 55.2 sec			
Winner's Speed:	84.507 mph			
Victory Margin:	59 seconds			
Fastest Race Lap:	Ken Miles	Shelby Cobra	2:41.6	89.109 mph

Dave MacDonald in the Cobra he shared with Bob Bondurant. They took fourth overall and first in the Manufacturers class. Photo by John McCollister.

The #99 Cobra of Bob Johnson/Lew Spencer ended up sixth overall and second in the Manufacturers class. Photo by John McCollister.

The Mecom Racing Team Ferrari 250 GTO of Augie Pabst/Roger Penske getting a bit loose in front of the Ferrari-Chevrolet of Pat Manning/Bob Liess. Photo by John McCollister.

The Elva-Porsche of Bill Wuesthoff/Augie Pabst taking the checkered flag. Photo by Tom Schultz.

Skip Hudson in a Maserati 151 finished in fifteenth place and was sixth in the over two-liter class. Photo by John McCollister.

ABOVE–The Bobsy of Chuck Dietrich finished fifth overall and third in the under two-liter class. Photo by Tom Schultz.

LEFT–The Fireball Special of Richard Jordan/Dick Clicquennoi retired after three laps. Photo by John McCollister.

Roy Kumnick managed to complete eighteen laps in the Excalibur Hawk Mk 4 before retiring. Photo by John McCollister.

The Bocar Stiletto of Bob Spooner/Joe Scopelite completed five laps. Photo by John McCollister.

Ken Miles being chased by Don Sesslar and Bill Wuesthoff. Photo by Tom Schultz.

Jesse Wyllie in his Lola Mk 1-Climax finished tenth overall and sixth in the under two-liter class. Photo by John McCollister.

Doug Thiem and Tom Terrell took this Ferrari Dino to seventh place overall and fourth in the under two-liter class. Photo by John McCollister.

The Ferrari 250 TR of David Biggs and James Johnston placed sixteenth overall and fifth in the over two-liter class. Photo by John McCollister.

The Ferrari 250 GTO of John Baxter/Bill Tannhaeuser, ahead of the Ferrari-Corvette of Pat Manning/Bob Liess. Photo by John McCollister.

The Elva of Mike Hall/Burdie Martin spinning off. Photo by John McCollister.

Augie Pabst on the cool down lap after winning the race. Photo by John McCollister.

Rear-engined Excalibur ran in practice, but not in the race. Photo by John McCollister.

The Ferrari 250 TR of David Biggs and James Johnston placed sixteenth overall and fifth in the over two-liter class. Photo by John McCollister.

MID OHIO

SPORTS CAR COURSE

UNITED STATES
ROAD RACING CHAMPIONSHIP
SEPT 21-22 1963

FIFTY CENTS OFFICIAL PROGRAM • SANCTION NO. DMC-8-63

1963 Mid Ohio race program cover. Scan courtesy Don Markle.

1963 Mid-Ohio Manufacturers Race

The Mid-Ohio race course opened its gates for the first time in August of 1963, holding some SCCA regional races. One month later it hosted the final round of the 1963 USRRC series. Considering that both championships were already settled, the entry was very good and typical of the average USRRC event. The Manufacturer's race had nine entries with the Cobra team of Bob Holbert and Ken Miles, Bob Johnson's private Cobra, the Corvettes of Dick Lang, Tony Denman, Bob Bienerth and Jack Moore, Mike Gammino's Ferrari GTO and Al Rogers' Morgan SS.

Bob Holbert won the pole, while Miles and Johnson shared the front row with him. Mike Gammino and Dick Lang were on the second row.

Local driver, Bob Johnson, got the drop on everyone when the race started, to lead from Holbert, Miles, Gammino, Lang, Denman, Bienerth, Moore and Rogers. Johnson's lead lasted a lap and a half before the timing chain broke and his Cobra ground to a halt. Bob Holbert assumed the lead followed by Ken Miles with Dick Lang and Mike Gammino right behind. After a few laps, Miles overcooked it on a corner and slid off into the grass. This let Lang and Gammino into second and third spots.

It took a few laps for Miles to charge back and catch up with Gammino. Miles was passing Gammino and almost got by him when the Ferrari's left rear fender bashed the right front corner of the Cobra. The Ferrari came off the worse for the wear, having to pit for a few laps to have the bodywork pulled out and the wheel changed.

Miles quickly caught and passed Lang to reassume second place a few seconds behind Holbert. This lasted until lap twenty-four when an oil line broke on Miles' Cobra sending him to the pits for six minutes, or three laps. Miles was inspired, and during the next forty laps, he drove like a madman to reclaim second place and set the fastest race lap (1:48.4).

Dick Lang finished in third place, after having gearbox trouble and completing the race locked in third gear. Two laps behind Lang was Tony Denman. Bob Bienerth was fifth with Jack Moore sixth and Al Rogers seventh in his ailing Morgan. Mike Gammino got his Ferrari back in the race and finished in eighth place, twenty-four laps behind Holbert.

1963 MID-OHIO • USRRC MANUFACTURERS RACE

September 22, 1963, Mid-Ohio Sports Car Course, Lexington, Ohio

Place	Driver	Car/Engine	Car #	Laps	Points	Prize
1	Bob Holbert	Shelby Cobra	99	70	9	$1,000
2	Ken Miles	Shelby Cobra	98	67	6	500
3	Dick Lang	Chevrolet Corvette	85	67	4	300
4	Tony Denman	Chevrolet Corvette	19	65	3	200
5	Bob Bienerth	Chevrolet Corvette	5	62	2	150
6	Jack Moore	Chevrolet Corvette	14	57	1	100
7	Al Rogers	Morgan SS	1	47	-	-
8	Mike Gammino	Ferrari 250 GTO	23	46	-	-
DNF	Bob Johnson	Cobra	33	2	-	-

Fastest Qualifier:	Bob Holbert	Shelby Cobra		
Race Distance:	168 miles	70 laps of 2.4 mile course		
Race Time:	1 hr 19 min 7.86 sec			
Winner's Speed:	75.67 mph			
Victory Margin:	3 laps			
Fastest Race Lap:	Ken Miles	Shelby Cobra	1:48.4	79.71 mph

Shelby mechanics on the right with signs asking Miles if he wants coffee or tea and Bob Holbert if he wants milk. Bob Johnson's mechanic, Tom Greatorex, on the left, holding a paper cup of...? Photo by John McCollister

1963 Mid-Ohio Drivers Race

The final Drivers race had twenty-five entries, headed by Shelby's Cobras. Other significant over two-liter entries were Skip Hudson in a Cooper-Chev and Ed Lowther in a Lister, plus Bud Gates (Genie-Chev), Ed Hamill (Cooper-Ford), Dave Causey (Lotus 19) and Jack Ensley (Apache). The under two-liter class had Herb Swan, Chuck Stoddard, Jack Ryan and Joe Buzzetta in Porsches, Hap Sharp, Roger Donovan and Bill Malion in Elvas, Chuck Dietrich in a Bobsy, Doc Wyllie in a Lola, Wayne Kelly in the Kelly Special, plus Skip Barber and Dave Sheff in Lotus 23's.

Skip Hudson earned the pole with a time of 1:48.6. Unfortunately, the clutch blew shortly after Skip set this time and he was not able to get it repaired in time for the race. Next up was Bob Holbert at 1:48.9. Hap Sharp in a 1600cc Elva with a time of 1:49.0 had the third fastest time. Chuck Dietrich got the Bobsy around the course in 1:49.9 followed by Ken Miles with the same time. Joe Buzzetta and Wayne Kelly were both timed at 1:51.0. Dave Causey and Herb Swan also set identical times at 1:51.6.

The cars lined up on the starting grid with Holbert and Sharp on the front row. Dietrich and Miles were on the second row while Buzzetta and Kelly were on the third row. Trouble brewed right away when the starter in Sharp's Elva wouldn't catch and Hap was pushed off the grid. Holbert left the line in the lead and Miles muscled his Cobra alongside Holbert and took command before the end of the first lap. Keeping up with the Cobras was Chuck Dietrich in the little Bobsy. There was a gap between Dietrich and Wayne Kelly who was leading Dave Causey, Joe Buzzetta, Ed Lowther, Chuck Stoddard, Bud Gates and Herb Swan.

Hap Sharp had the starter catch just as three quarters of the field had gone by. Since Hap was on the grass when he dropped the clutch, dirt and grass flew everywhere as he got under way. His car slithered back onto the course in last place and he began to rip through the field. Ed Hamill also got a slow start off the line and followed that with a pit stop on the second lap to fix a water leak.

Holbert was the first to retire on lap twelve with a wheel bearing failure. Miles

held a ten second lead over Dietrich and he began to stretch that to thirty seconds over the next ten laps. Wayne Kelly was third until lap twenty when Hap Sharp blasted by. Next, Hap stalked Dietrich for ten laps before taking second place from him.

On lap thirty-two, Kelly retired from fourth place with a broken piston. That moved Dave Causey into fourth place for one lap before he retired with a broken gearbox. Chuck Dietrich kept his Bobsy in third place until lap forty, when the radiator cap worked loose. Dietrich pitted a few times before finally tying it down with wire so he could finish the race.

Miles kept a thirty-second lead over Sharp and, by the end of the race, they were a lap ahead of Herb Swan and Chuck Stoddard's pair of Porsches. Ed Lowther finished in fifth place overall and second in over two-liters. Bud Gates was sixth, while Ed Hamill worked his way up to seventh place and set the fastest race lap. Chuck Dietrich was able to get the Bobsy to the finish line in eighth place. Miles' win gave him enough points to take second place in the championship.

Bob Holbert, about to DNF, leading Chuck Dietrich in a Bobsy, and in the background, Wayne Kelly in the Kelly Special. Photo by John McCollister

Wayne Kelly in the Kelly Special held third, then fourth, place before retiring with a blown engine. Photo by John McCollister

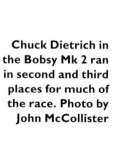

Chuck Dietrich in the Bobsy Mk 2 ran in second and third places for much of the race. Photo by John McCollister

Ed Hamill, #69 Cooper-Ford, finished seventh overall and fourth in the over two-liter class. Photo by John McCollister

Ed Hamill, getting a little frisky and high-siding off a corner. Photo by John McCollister

1963 MID-OHIO • USRRC DRIVERS RACE
September 22, 1963, Mid-Ohio Sports Car Course, Lexington, Ohio

Place	Driver	Car/Engine	Car #	Class	Laps	Points	Prize	Qualifying Place	Qualifying Time
1	Ken Miles	Shelby Cobra	98	O2	70	9	$1,500	2	1:49.9
2	Hap Sharp	Elva Mk 7-Ford	95	U2	70	9	1,000	12	1:53.6
3	Herb Swan	Porsche 718 RS61	89	U2	69	6	500	10	1:52.2
4	Chuck Stoddard	Porsche 718 RS61	4	U2	69	4	300	13	1:53.8
5	Ed Lowther	Lister-Chevrolet	7	O2	67	6	500	-	-
6	Bud Gates	Genie Mk 8-Chevrolet	6	O2	67	4	300	16	1:56.0
7	Ed Hamill	Cooper T61-Ford	69	O2	67	3	200	3	1:50.8
8	Chuck Dietrich	Bobsy 2-Ford	37	U2	66	3	200	9	1:52.0
9	Jack Moore	Chevrolet Corvette	14	O2	64	2	150	19	2:00.6
10	Doc (M.R.J.) Wyllie	Lola Mk 1-Cosworth	2	U2	64	2	150	14	1:54.8
11	Roger Donovan	Elva Mk 7	55	U2	64	1	100	18	2:00.6
12	Harry Washburn	Cooper T61-Maserati	15	O2	64	1	100	15	1:55.9
13	Jack Ensley	Apache-Chevrolet	28	O2	64	-	-	22	2:01.8
14	Bob Bienerth	Chevrolet Corvette	5	O2	61	-	-	23	2:02.4
15	Jack Ryan	Porsche 718 RSK	68	U2	59	-	-	6	1:51.2
16	Joe Buzzetta	Porsche 718 RS61	74	U2	55	-	-	5	1:51.0
DNF	Anson Johnson	Ferrari-Chevrolet	61	O2	46	-	-	24	2:05.4
DNF	Owen Russell	Lishin Special	18		38	-	-	21	2:01.4
DNF	Dave Scheff	Lotus 23	25	U2	35	-	-	-	-
DNF	Dave Causey	Lotus 19-Ford	24	O2	32	-	-	8	1:51.6
DNF	Wayne Kelly	Kelly Special-Porsche	87	U2	32	-	-	11	1:53.6
DNF	Skip Barber	Lotus 23-Porsche	13	U2	29	-	-	17	2:00.2
DNF	Bill Malion	Elva Mk 6	3	U2	24	-	-	-	-
DNF	Bob Holbert	Shelby Cobra	99	O2	12	-	-	7	1:51.6
DNS	Skip Hudson	Cooper T61-Chevrolet	9	O2	-	-	-	1	1:48.6

Fastest Qualifier:	Skip Hudson	Cooper T61-Chevrolet	1:48.6	79.56 mph
Race Distance:	168.0 miles	70 laps of 2.4 mile course		
Race Time:	1 hr 59 min 30.42 sec			
Winner's Speed:	77.41 mph			
Victory Margin:	30 seconds			
Fastest Race Lap:	Ed Hamill	Cooper T61-Ford	1:44.24	82.89 mph

**Ed Hamill getting back on the course behind hard-charging
Hap Sharp. Photo by John McCollister**

Winner, Ken Miles, taking the race queen on the
victory lap. Photo by John McCollister

Ken Miles giving the race queen a ride. Photo by John McCollister

1963 Driver's Points

Place	Driver	Daytona	Pensacola	LagSeca	WatGlen	PacRace	ContDiv	RoadAm	Mid-Ohio	Total Points
1	Bob Holbert	9	np*	-	9	4	6	9	-	37
2	Ken Miles	-	np*	-	9	3	-	9	9	30
3	Don Wester	-	-	6	-	9	9	-	-	24
4	Herb Swan	6	-	-	6	-	3	-	6	21
5	Doug Thiem	6	4	-	-	6	-	3	-	19
6	Augie Pabst	-	-	-	-	-	9	9	-	18
7	Tim Mayer	6	9	-	-	-	-	-	-	15
8	Bill Wuesthoff	-	-	-	-	-	6	9	-	15
9	Hap Sharp	-	-	-	-	-	4	-	9	13
10	Charlie Parsons	-	-	9	-	4	-	-	-	13
11	Ed Lowther	-	-	-	6	-	-	-	6	12
12	Skip Hudson	-	-	9	-	-	-	1	-	10
13	Jim Hall	9	-	-	-	-	-	-	-	9
14	Pedro Rodriguez	-	-	-	-	9	-	-	-	9
15	Dave Ridenour	-	-	2	-	6	-	-	-	8
16	Chuck Dietrich	-	-	-	-	-	-	4	3	7
17	Bill Eve	4	3	-	-	-	-	-	-	7
18	Enus Wilson	-	-	-	-	-	3	3	-	6
19	Roger Penske	-	-	-	-	-	-	6	-	6
20	Don Sesslar	-	-	-	-	-	-	6	-	6
21	Chuck Cassel	-	-	-	-	-	-	6	-	6
22	Charlie Kolb	-	6	-	-	-	-	-	-	6
23	Jerry Titus	-	-	6	-	-	-	-	-	6
24	Harry Washburn	-	-	-	-	-	4	-	1	5
25	Wayne Burnett	-	-	-	-	-	-	4	-	4
26	Luke Stear	-	-	-	-	-	-	4	-	4
27	Charles Kurtz	2	-	-	2	-	-	-	-	4
28	John Cannon	-	-	-	4	-	-	-	-	4
29	Joe Buzzetta	-	-	-	4	-	-	-	-	4
30	Bill Bencker	4	-	-	-	-	-	-	-	4
31	Ed Rahal	-	4	-	-	-	-	-	-	4
32	Jim Parkinson	-	-	4	-	-	-	-	-	4

1963 Season Summary

The first year of the USRRC was a definite success. The cars and drivers were an interesting assortment. There was a good spectator turnout at all races, except Daytona. Even the weather cooperated at all races, except Daytona.

The racing was good, intense and varied in the Drivers races. At Daytona there was the drama of a full-on rain race. At Pensacola, Laguna Seca, Pacific Raceways and Road America, the early leader retired or dropped back. The lead was fought for at Watkins Glen and Continental Divide. The closest victory margin was eight seconds at Laguna Seca. The greatest victory margin was two laps, or six miles, at Pensacola.

Overall car wins were shared, at four each, for over two-liter and under two-liter cars. Jim Hall took Hap Sharp's 2.7 liter Cooper Monaco to victory at Daytona. At Pacific Raceways, Pedro Rodriguez won in Joe Huffaker's new Genie Mk 8-Chevrolet. Augie Pabst won at Continental Divide, in the last major pro victory for the Scarab Mk 1. At Mid-Ohio, Ken Miles won the Drivers race in a "stock, but loose" Cobra that he used earlier the same day to take second place in the Manufacturers race. The under two-liter wins were Bob Holbert and Ken Miles at Pensacola, in Bob's Porsche RS-61. Bob also used his Porsche to win again at Watkins Glen. Charlie Parsons took his Lotus 23 to victory at Laguna Seca. Bill Wuesthoff and Augie Pabst shared the brand new Elva-Porsche to win its first major race at Road America.

No driver entered all eight races and Bob Holbert was the only driver to enter seven races. He actually entered and ran eight, but at the combined Laguna Seca race he ran in the Manufacturers class. When the series got to Continental Divide, the Cobra team had clinched the Manufacturers class and Shelby let Holbert run in the Drivers class to chase the title. Herb Swan and Doug Thiem both entered six races while Ken Miles, Don Wester and Harry Heuer all entered five Drivers races. Five drivers entered four races while six drivers entered three races. There were thirty-one drivers who entered two races and 127 drivers who entered only one race. In all, 175 individual drivers entered races and sixty-three drivers scored points.

The Manufacturers series was not as competitive as the Drivers series. This was undoubtedly due to Shelby American being the only manufacturer to enter a factory team in the series. The grids were small with an average starting field of nine cars. The grid of six cars at Laguna Seca was the smallest of the series. The largest grid was thirteen cars starting at Pacific Raceways.

The Ferraris and Corvettes put up a good fight, but without manufacturer/factory support, they were basically also-rans. After Roger Penske won the first race at Pensacola in a Ferrari, the Cobras waxed the competition in the rest of the races. The Shelby American team took at least first and second in five of the seven races and Bob Johnson won the Watkins Glen race in his private Cobra.

The SCCA Board was pleased with the results of the first season of the USRRC series. Attendance was pretty good everywhere, except at Daytona. The severe rain at Daytona kept the reported paid admissions down to 1,200. On the low end, there were 10,000 spectators at Pensacola and 12,000 at Continental Divide. The high end had 23,000 at Laguna Seca and 38,000 at Road America. The total paid admissions for all eight races was 142,000, which was an average of 17,750 per race. Seven race promoters were happy and looking forward to 1964.

Place	Driver	Daytona	Pensacola	LagSeca	WatGlen	PacRace	ContDiv	RoadAm	Mid-Ohio	Total Points
33	Charles Stoddard	-	-	-	-	-	-	-	4	4
34	Bud Gates	-	-	-	-	-	-	-	4	4
35	Walt Maas	-	-	4	-	-	-	-	-	4
36	Lyle Forsgren	-	-	-	-	3	-	-	-	3
37	Bob Bucher	-	-	-	3	-	-	-	-	3
38	Jack Ryan	-	3	-	-	-	-	-	-	3
39	Bernie Keller	-	-	-	-	-	-	-	-	3
40	Paul Reinhart	-	-	3	-	-	-	-	-	3
41	Dave Kyte	-	-	3	-	-	-	-	-	3
42	Tom Terrell	-	-	-	-	-	-	3	-	3
43	MRJ (Doc) Wyllie	-	-	-	-	-	-	1	2	3
44	Gary Wilson	-	-	-	-	-	-	3	-	3
45	Ed Hamill	-	-	-	-	-	-	-	3	3
46	Dan Gillum	-	-	2	-	-	-	-	-	2
47	Steve Baughman	-	-	-	-	-	2	-	-	2
48	Chuck Daigh	-	-	-	-	-	2	-	-	2
49	Blaise Lewark	-	-	-	-	2	-	-	-	2
50	Dave MacDonald	-	-	-	-	2	-	-	-	2
51	Mancil Smith	-	2	-	-	-	-	-	-	2
52	E.L. (Lee) Hall	-	-	-	-	-	-	2	-	2
53	Glen Carroll	-	-	-	-	-	-	2	-	2
54	Dave Briggs	-	-	-	-	-	-	2	-	2
55	Jim Johnston	-	-	-	-	-	-	2	-	2
56	Jack Moore	-	-	-	-	-	-	-	2	2
57	Bob Richardson	1	-	-	-	-	-	-	-	1
58	Gordon Richardson	-	1	-	-	-	-	-	-	1
59	Rod Carveth	-	-	-	-	1	-	-	-	1
60	George Miller	-	-	-	-	1	-	-	-	1
61	Dave Morgan	-	-	-	-	-	1	-	-	1
62	Chuck Frederich	-	-	-	-	-	1	-	-	1
63	Roger Donovan	-	-	-	-	-	-	-	1	1

np = no points for sharing the drive in a short race

1963 Manufacturers Championship Points

Place	Manufacturer	Daytona*	Pensacola	Laguna Seca	WatGlen	PacRace	ContDivide	RoadAm	Mid-Ohio	Total Points
1	Shelby-American (Cobra)	-	2	18	21	19	19	17	15	111
2	Ferrari	-	19	2	3	4	-	-	-	28
3	Chevrolet (Corvette)	-	3	-	1	2	3	-	10	19
4	Jaguar	-	-	4	-	-	-	8	-	12
5	Triumph	-	-	-	-	-	2	-	-	2

* No Manufacturers race at Daytona

1964

START POWER/NG **FIN**

Augusta
Pensacola
Riverside
Laguna Seca
Pacific Raceways
Watkins Glen
Greenwood
Meadowdale
Mid Ohio
Road America

1964 Introduction

The 1964 USRRC series had all the makings of being great before it even started. USRRC racers dominated USAC's 1963 "Fall Pro Series" of sports car races, taking three wins out of five races and thirty top ten places. The only races they did not win were the first two at Pacific Raceways. USAC racer Lloyd Ruby won both races at Pacific Raceways from Rodger Ward. Of the USRRC drivers, Dave Ridenour managed third place in the second race, while Don Wester, Stan Burnett, Paul Scott and Lyle Forsgren finished in the top ten in both races. Jerry Grant and John Razzelle each finished one race in the top ten.

The Canadian Grand Prix for sports cars at Mosport was won by Pedro Rodriguez. Don Devine was third and Bill Wuesthoff fourth. Ken Miles had trouble with his Cobra and was beaten into seventh place by local Cobra driver, Eppie Weitzes. Herb Swan was ninth in his Porsche.

The Riverside Times Grand Prix was next. This was the Big Daddy of the fall pro races. It was sponsored by the Los Angeles Times newspaper and featured international Formula One stars Jim Clark, Graham Hill, John Surtees, Dan Gurney and Richie Ginther. Dave MacDonald ran away with the race in one of Carroll Shelby's King Cobras. This was actually a modified and strengthened Cooper-Monaco T61M chassis with a Ford V8 in the rear. Roger Penske was second in the Mecom-owned Zerex Special and Pedro Rodriguez took third place. Bill Krause, Bob Bondurant and Don Wester were all in the top ten.

At Laguna Seca Dave MacDonald won again. USAC driver, A.J. Foyt was second. Jim Hall, Dave Ridenour, Harry Heuer and Tim Mayer were third through sixth. Don Wester, Ed Leslie and Don Devine were eighth, ninth and tenth.

The Bahamas Speedweek was an end-of-season series of parties that were interrupted with sports car races. The races were held at the Oakes Field course, which was a bumpy 4.5 mile airfield race course. USRRC drivers made their presence known there. Chuck Cassel, Augie Pabst, Charlie Kolb and Roger Penske all won at least one of the various 5 lap races. Augie Pabst won the twenty-two lap Tourist Trophy for "GT" cars, driving John Mecom's Lola Coupe. Mike Gammino was second, Chuck Cassel was third and Art Riley was ninth. Although USAC racer A.J. Foyt won the Governor's Trophy, the next eight places were captured by USRRC drivers: Pedro Rodriguez, Roger Penske, Augie Pabst, Buck Fulp, Dick Thompson, Bob Grossman, Ed

Hugus and Chuck Cassel. Charlie Kolb won the twenty-five lap Formula Vee race from Bill Bencker. USRRC drivers took eight of the top ten places in the big Nassau Trophy race. Foyt won in Mecom's Scarab with Pedro Rodriguez second. Next were Tim Mayer, Dick Thompson, Skip Hudson and Mike Gammino. John Cannon was eighth, Ray Heppenstall and Bob Holbert shared the ninth place Cooper Monaco and Chuck Cassel was tenth. Try as they might, the Shelby Cobras couldn't even buy a win during these races. The best a Cobra managed was fifth place in the five-lap over two-liter GT race.

The Chaparral team of Jim Hall and Hap Sharp committed to run the 1964 USRRC series. They had spent 1963 building and testing the Chaparral 2, with a pole position at Riverside and a third place at Laguna Seca to show for it. The Chaparrals were constantly being developed, so Hall and Sharp were ready to race for the USRRC Championship. Challenging the Chaparrals were Carroll Shelby's King Cobras driven by Dave MacDonald and Bob Holbert. Ollie Schmidt's Scuderia Tin Can was set to contest the under two-liter class with Elva-Porsches for Charlie Hayes, Chuck Dietrich, Bob Markley and Bill Wuesthoff. During 1964, Ken Miles planned to use his Manufacturers class Cobra roadster in most of the Drivers races.

For 1964 the Manufacturers Championship would have separate classes for over two-liters and under two-liters and each class would have their own points. Another change was that only the highest place finisher for a marque would score points. Like the Drivers Championship, the Manufacturer with the most points would be the champion, regardless of class. The spectators would enjoy two races on Sundays as the Manufacturers classes would have a separate race before the Drivers race at all circuits, except Greenwood and Road America where they ran combined with the Drivers' cars. The Shelby Cobra team was again the only team to sign up for the whole series. That is, until the second race at Pensacola where Team Lotus showed up with two Lotus Cortinas for the under two-liter class. Otto Zipper, the Los Angeles Porsche distributor, entered three of the new 904's at the Riverside race.

The number of races in the series increased from eight to ten. The race at Daytona was gone. It was replaced with races at Riverside, California; Meadowdale, Illinois; and new courses at Augusta, Georgia, and Greenwood, Iowa.

UNITED STATES ROAD RACING CHAMPIONSHIP FOR DRIVERS AND MANUFACTURERS CHAMPIONSHIPS

FEBRUARY 29 – MARCH 1, 1964

ACCUS, FIA, and NATIONAL OPEN, SCCA Sanction Number N6

Augusta International Speedway
Augusta, Georgia

Conducted by The ATLANTA REGION SPORTS CAR CLUB OF AMERICA

Sponsored by The AUGUSTA INTERNATIONAL SPEEDWAY, INC., AUGUSTA, GEORGIA

Augusta, Georgia

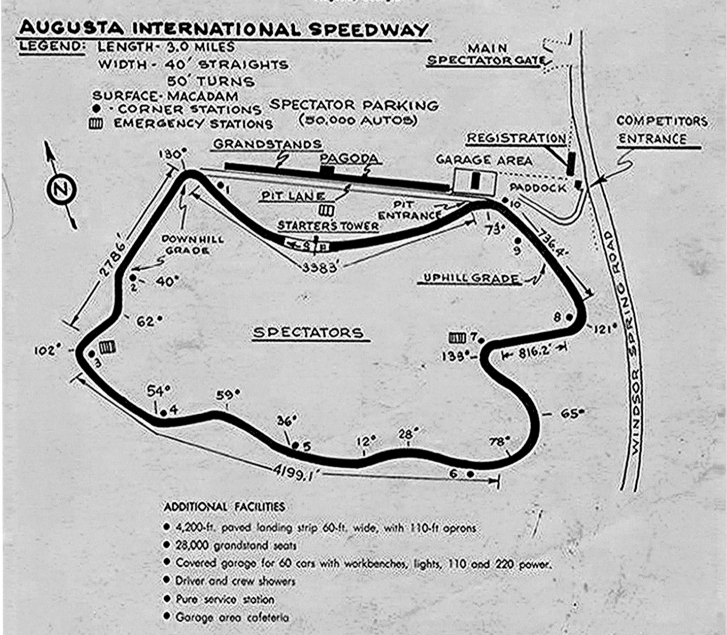

AUGUSTA INTERNATIONAL SPEEDWAY
LEGEND: LENGTH - 3.0 MILES
WIDTH - 40' STRAIGHTS
50' TURNS
SURFACE - MACADAM
● - CORNER STATIONS
▥ EMERGENCY STATIONS

SPECTATOR PARKING
(50,000 AUTOS)

ADDITIONAL FACILITIES
● 4,200-ft. paved landing strip 60-ft. wide, with 110-ft. aprons
● 28,000 grandstand seats
● Covered garage for 60 cars with workbenches, lights, 110 and 220 power.
● Driver and crew showers
● Pure service station
● Garage area cafeteria

1964 Augusta USRRC info sheet. Scan courtesy Don Markle.

Dave MacDonald #16 and Ken Miles, to the right, get a jump on the field at the start. Behind the parked Austin Healey is Graham Shaw's Cobra. Bruce Jennings in the #79 Porsche, on the second row, won the under two-liter class. Photo from the collections of the Henry Ford.

Augusta Manufacturers Race

When the players assembled for the first race of the 1964 season at Augusta Raceway, Shelby American was the only real team entered in the Manufacturers race. Their drivers were Ken Miles and Dave MacDonald. Privately entered Cobras were in the hands of Graham Shaw and Ralph Noseda. Bruce Jennings, Chuck Cassel, Jack Ryan and Ted Tidwell all had Porsches. Peter Gregg was entered in a Corvette and Art Riley in a Volvo P1800.

In practice, the Shelby cars were much faster than the private Cobras. Miles won the pole with a time of 1:54.0 and MacDonald turned in a 1:55.0 to claim the front row. Next up was Graham Shaw, whose time was 2:03.0. He was followed by Ralph Noseda at 2:05.0. Next were the Porsches of Bruce Jennings (2:09.0), Chuck Cassel (2:13.0) and Jack Ryan (2:14.0). Peter Gregg and Ted Tidwell both turned in a 2:14.0. Art Riley got

his Volvo P1800 around in 2:15.0.

Graham Shaw got the jump on Miles and MacDonald at the start and took the lead for the first nine laps. On the tenth lap a wheel came off Shaw's Cobra putting him out of the race. Miles took over the lead with MacDonald right on his heels. Ralph Noseda was third and already out of touch with the leaders. Bruce Jennings was leading the under two-liter class in fourth place and Chuck Cassel was running in fifth place. Racing hard for sixth place were Jack Ryan in a Porsche Super 90 and Art Riley in a Volvo P1800. They traded places back and forth, lap after lap, until lap twenty-seven. Riley went on the outside at turn three trying to get by Ryan, but slid off the course, up the sandbank, crested the dune sideways and somehow steered the Volvo down the dune and back onto the course. Riley was now nineteen seconds behind Ryan.

Miles and MacDonald were up front trading the lead until lap thirty-four. MacDonald spun on a corner and lost over a minute to Miles, who drove the last eighteen laps with MacDonald almost a minute and a half behind, in second place. Noseda shared his Cobra with Jef Stevens and they brought it home in third place, two laps behind the leading duo. Bruce Jennings and Chuck Cassel both drove lonely races in fourth and fifth places. Peter Gregg worked his Corvette past Riley's Volvo and Ryan's Porsche to claim sixth place.

This year only the leading car from each Manufacturer would score points in the races. So, Cobra and Porsche each scored nine points for their class wins. Chevrolet (Corvette) and Volvo each got three points for fourth place finishes. Morgan scored one point, from TJ Kelly's eleventh place and sixth in class finish.

Miles #15 and MacDonald #16 just ran away with the race, finishing two laps ahead of the third place private Cobra of Ralph Noseda and Jef Stevens. Photo from the collections of the Henry Ford.

Dave MacDonald #16 lapping the under two-liter winner, Bruce Jennings #79. Photo from the collections of the Henry Ford.

The Shelby Cobras of Dave MacDonald #16 and Ken Miles #15 in the Augusta garage with a spare engine. Photo by Joe Cawley, courtesy Henry Jones.

Dave MacDonald's Shelby Cobra #16 on pit lane. Photo by Richard Macon.

Art Riley #11, going over the banking, after a failed attempt to wrestle sixth place from Jack Ryan. Photo from the collections of the Henry Ford.

The Cobra #3 of Ralph Noseda and Jef Stevens. Photo by Joe Cawley, courtesy Henry Jones.

1964 AUGUSTA • USRRC MANUFACTURERS RACE
March 1, 1964, w, Augusta, Georgia

Place	Driver	Car & Engine	Car #	Class	Laps	Points	Prize	Qualifying Place	Qualifying Time
1	Ken Miles	Shelby Cobra	15	GTO	52	9	$ 1,500	1	1:54
2	Dave MacDonald	Shelby Cobra	16	GTO	52	-	500	2	1:55
3	Ralph Noseda-Jef Stevens	Cobra	3	GTO	50	-	300	4	2:05
4	Bruce Jennings	Porsche Carrera 356B	79	GTU	49	9	1,000	5	2:09
5	Chuck Cassel	Porsche 356B-Abarth	50	GTU	48	-	500	6	2:13
6	Peter Gregg	Chevrolet Corvette	41	GTO	47	3	200	8	2:14
7	Jack Ryan	Porsche 356 S-90	72	GTU	47	-	300	7	2:14
8	Art Riley	Volvo P1800	11	GTU	47	3	200	10	2:15
9	Ted Tidwell	Porsche 356 S-90	51	GTU	46	-	150	9	2:14
10	Bill Floyd-Jack Rogers	Chevrolet Corvette	88	GTO	45	-	150	-	-
11	T.J. Kelly	Morgan Plus 4	84	GTU	36	1	100	-	-
12	George Parsons	Austin Healey Sprite	-	GTU	29	-	-	-	-
DNF	Graham Shaw	Cobra	24	GTO	9	-	-	3	2:03

Fastest Qualifier:	Ken Miles	Shelby Cobra	1:54.0	94.74 mph	
Race Distance:	156.0 miles	52 laps of 3.0 mile course			
Race Time:	1 hr 46 min 29.0 sec				
Victory Margin:	1 minute 25 seconds				
Winner's Speed:	87.9 mph				
Fastest Race Lap:	Unknown				

Chuck Cassel's Porsche on its trailer. Photo by Joe Cawley, courtesy Henry Jones.

Graham Shaw's Cobra #24 on pit lane. Photo by Joe Cawley, courtesy Henry Jones.

Augusta Drivers Race

Qualifying for the Drivers race saw a lot of activity with Jim Hall taking the pole with a time of 1:47.2 in his Chaparral II with a new, revised nose section. Dave MacDonald was second on the grid (1:48.2) in a Shelby King Cobra. Bob Holbert, in another Shelby King Cobra, filled the outside of the front row with a time of 1:49.0. Charlie Hayes set the fourth fastest time of 1:51.0 in an under two-liter Elva-Porsche. Beside Hayes was Buck Fulp in a brand new Ferrari 250LM at 1:52.0. Filling out the top ten were Harry Heuer in a Chaparral I (1:54.0), Chuck Dietrich in an Elva-Porsche (1:56.0), George Koehne in a Genie-Ford (1:56.0), Bud Gates in a Genie-Chevrolet (1:57.0) and Don Yenko in a Corvette (1:57.0).

The cars lined up on the grid, which had a slight bank to it. The slight bank caused gasoline in Hall's Chaparral to exit from the overflow tube and puddle under his rear wheels. When the flag dropped Hall went nowhere. His wheels spun in the puddle and he watched eight cars go by before his tires gripped and he got underway. MacDonald grabbed the lead with Holbert in second

place. George Koehne was third in his Genie-Ford and Ken Miles fifth, in the Cobra roadster he used to win the earlier Manufacturers race. By the end of the first lap Hall had passed four cars to take fifth place.

By the end of the second lap, Hall had passed Miles and Koehne for third place. Harry Heuer was sixth and followed by Charlie Hayes, who was first in the under two-liter class, and Chuck Dietrich. Unfortunately, on lap thirteen, Dietrich went up and over the banking at the Alligator Hole turn, dropped twenty feet and landed flat on all four wheels. Dietrich was out of the race and came away with a minor cut on his arm.

As the race closed in on the halfway point, Hall's Chaparral had consumed enough gas that he was able to pick up his pace and close in on Bob Holbert, who was in second place, about fifteen seconds behind MacDonald. After six more laps, Hall got by Holbert and set out after MacDonald.

George Koehne had his Genie in fourth place since early in the race. Partway through the race the mirror on his Genie had worked loose. To use it, Koehne had to reach up and steady it. This race was, by

far, the longest race Koehne had driven in competition and the cockpit of the Genie was hot. Behind Koehne was Ken Miles, who had Harry Heuer right behind him. On lap forty-five, Heuer was able to get past Ken and then started reeling in Koehne.

Up front, Hall was rapidly closing in on MacDonald at a rate of about a second a lap. At the start of the last lap the gap between them was three seconds and Hall was still gaining. Halfway around on the last lap, Hall slid off course on the banked S-turn. He gathered it together and got back on the track in time to keep second place, ahead of Holbert.

Behind Holbert, George Koehne had become too tired to reach out and hold up the mirror to see if anyone was behind him. Harry Heuer had moved up to striking distance and blew past into fourth place before Koehne even knew he was there. Ken Miles held his Cobra roadster in sixth place and Charlie Hayes was seventh overall and the first under two liter finisher. Buck Fulp brought his new Ferrari home in eighth place. Ninth and tenth places went to Hap Sharp and George Wintersteen, both driving Elva-Porsches.

Jim Hall fell back to fifth place at the start and worked his way up to within striking distance of MacDonald by the end of the race. Photo from the collections of the Henry Ford.

Bob Holbert ran a smooth and steady race about fifteen seconds behind Dave MacDonald. He lost second place to Jim Hall at half-distance, but still finished in third place. Photo from the collections of the Henry Ford.

Charlie Hayes qualified his under two-liter Elva-Porsche fourth fastest, got away in seventh place and held for the entire race. He did win the under two-liter class. Photo from the collections of the Henry Ford.

Budd Clusserath's Cheetah in the garage. Clusserath was out of the race after 28 laps. Photo by Richard Macon.

The Scuderia Tin Can Elvas in the garage. Chuck Dietrich drove #76 and Charlie Hayes won the under two-liter class in #77. In the foreground is the rear cover of Jim Hall's Chaparral. Photo by Richard Macon.

1964 AUGUSTA · USRRC DRIVERS RACE

March 1, 1964, Augusta International Raceway, Augusta, Georgia

Place	Driver	Car/Engine	Car #	Class	Laps	Points	Prize	Qualifying Place	Qualifying Time
1	Dave MacDonald	Shelby Cooper T61M-Ford	97	O2	52	9	$1,500	2	1:48.2
2	Jim Hall	Chaparral 2A-Chevrolet	66	O2	52	6	500	1	1:47.3
3	Bob Holbert	Shelby Cooper T61M-Ford	98	O2	52	4	300	3	1:49.0
4	Harry Heuer	Chaparral 1-Chevrolet	2	O2	50	3	200	6	1:54.0
5	George Koehne	Genie Mk 8-Ford	95	O2	50	2	150	8	1:56.0
6	Ken Miles	Shelby Cobra	16	O2	50	1	100	-	-
7	Charlie Hayes	Elva Mk 7S-Porsche	77	U2	49	9	1,000	4	1:51.0
8	Buck Fulp	Ferrari 250LM	26	O2	49	-	-	5	1:52.0
9	Hap Sharp	Elva Mk 7S-Porsche	65	U2	49	6	500	13	1:59.0
10	George Wintersteen	Elva Mk 7S-Porsche	12	U2	49	4	300	14	1:59.0
11	Don Yenko	Corvette Grand Sport	14	O2	49	-	-	10	1:57.0
12	Millard Ripley	Porsche 718 RS-61	78	U2	48	3	200	11	1:58.0
13	Richard Young	Elva Mk 7-Ford	8	U2	47	2	150	15	2:00.0
14	Augie Pabst	Maserati T64-Ford	6	O2	46	-	-	17	2:00.0
15	Roger Heftler	Elva Mk 7-BMW	93	U2	46	1	100	12	1:58.0
DNF	Budd Clusserath	Chevie GT (Cheetah)	46	O2	28	-	-	-	-
DNF	Charlie Kolb	Lotus 30-Ford	11	O2	45	-	-	-	-
DNF	Anson Johnson	RWB Special (Ferrari 500 TRC)	13	O2	40	-	-	-	-
DNF	Richard Macon	Cooper Monaco T61-Climax	4	U2	31	-	-	-	-
DNF	Bob Ward	Ferrari 500 Mondial-Chev	91	O2	26	-	-	-	-
DNF	Bob Bondurant	Lotus 23-Climax	69	U2	26	-	-	19	2:00.0
DNF	Bud Gates	Genie Mk 8-Chevrolet	38	O2	21	-	-	9	1:57.0
DNF	Chuck Dietrich	Elva Mk 7S-Porsche	76	U2	12	-	-	7	1:56.0
DNF	Ralph Salyer	Cheetah	25	O2	11	-	-	16	2:00.0
DNF	Bill Floyd	Chevrolet Corvette	88	O2	9	-	-	-	-
DNF	Dick Doane	McKee Mk 1 (Chevette)-Chev	29	O2	7	-	-	20	2:04.0
DNF	Wilbur Morgan	Devin-Chevrolet	9	O2	4	-	-	-	-
DNS	Jack Ensley	Apache-Chevrolet	17	O2	-	-	-	18	2:00.0

Fastest Qualifier: Jim Hall   Chaparral 2A-Chevrolet   1:47.2   100.8 mph
52 laps of 3.0 mile course

Race Distance: 156.0 miles
Race Time: 1 hr 35 min 50.98 sec
Winner's Speed: 97.65 mph
Victory Margin: 28 seconds
Fastest Race Lap: Unknown

Buck Fulp finished in eighth place with his brand new Ferrari 250LM.
Photo by Richard Macon.

Augie Pabst's Maserati about to be unloaded.
Photo by Joe Cawley, courtesy Henry Jones.

The Shelby Cooper-Fords of Bob Holbert #98 and Dave MacDonald #97 took third and first places, respectively. Photo by Richard Macon.

George Koehne drove his Genie Mk 8 to fifth place. Photo by Joe Cawley, courtesy Henry Jones.

Richard Young finished thirteenth overall and scored two points for fifth place in the under two-liter class. Photo by Joe Cawley, courtesy Henry Jones.

Dick Doane drove the Chevette (McKee Mk I) but lasted only seven laps. Photo by Joe Cawley, courtesy Henry Jones.

Bob Ward entered his Ferrari 500 Mondial, with Chevrolet engine, as the "Birmingham Special". It lasted twenty-six laps before retiring. Photo by Joe Cawley, courtesy Henry Jones.

Roger Heftler's Elva. The fifteenth and last finisher. Roger got one point for being sixth in the under two-liter class. Photo by Richard Macon.

U.S.R.R.C.

SPORTS CAR RACES

APRIL 4 & 5

PENSACOLA, FLA.

1964 Pensacola **USRRC** program cover. Scan courtesy Don Markle.

Start of the Manufacturers race with Graham Shaw in the lead followed by Ken Miles, Ralph Noseda and the rest of the field. Photo by Larry Tomaras, courtesy John Tomaras.

This was the first USRRC appearance of the Team Lotus Cortinas. Mike Spence #54 is leading John Whitmore #55. Spence dnf'd while Whitmore won the under two-liter class with a fourth overall finish. Photo by Larry Tomaras, courtesy John Tomaras.

Pensacola Manufacturers Race

The entry for the Manufacturers race was similar to that of the Augusta race. The Shelby Cobra team was present with Ken Miles and Graham Shaw was drafted into the team to take Dave Mac-Donald's place. Ralph Noseda and George Wills had their private entry Cobras. The only other over two-liter entry was Wayne Benton in a Corvette. The under two-liter class had the Lotus Cortina team, from England, making its USRRC debut with John Whitmore and Mike Spence. To add a little more continental sounding flavor, Count d'Herbois was entered in an Austin Healey Speedwell Sprite.

Ken Miles won the pole position for the Manufacturers race. Graham Shaw and Ralph Noseda also had their Cobras on the front row with Miles.

When the race started, Noseda grabbed the lead for the first two laps with Miles and Shaw right behind. The Cortinas of Spence and Whitmore were leading the under two-liter class. Miles passed Shaw and Noseda on the third lap to assume the lead. Miles stopped at the pits on lap fifteen, for a drink of water and a few words with his crew. He roared back onto the track in second place and began to chase down Shaw. Jim Manley's Porsche expired after thirteen laps.

Bill Bencker and Mike Spence both retired after eighteen laps and Count d'Herbois' Sprite lasted for twenty-four laps. Miles pitted again on lap twenty-two and fell thirty seconds behind Shaw. This time, it took Miles only three laps to re-take the lead. George Wills took his Cobra to the pits on lap twenty-five with a fuel leak. He pulled into the pits only to have

his car surrounded by a bunch of gawkers. As flames began to erupt from the car, one of the gawkers suggested the car might explode. That sent everyone, except the crew, running. The crew calmly dealt with the fire and gas leak. Unfortunately, the car was not repairable on the spot.

Miles was now leading Shaw and Noseda. Whitmore was fourth and Michael Needham, in a Triumph, was fifth. By lap thirty Miles was basically on cruise control, half a lap ahead of Shaw. To keep himself alert, Miles really stood on the gas for the last twenty laps. He lapped third place Noseda and finished thirty-five seconds ahead of second place Shaw. Whitmore brought his Lotus-Cortina home in fourth place, three laps down. Michael Needham was the final finisher, in fifth place and ten laps behind Miles.

1964 PENSACOLA • USRRC MANUFACTURERS RACE

April 5, 1964, NAS Corry Field, Pensacola, Florida

Place	Driver	Car/Engine	Car #	Class	Laps	Points	Prize
1	Ken Miles	Shelby Cobra	14	GTO	50	9	$400
2	Graham Shaw	Cobra	15	GTO	50	-	200
3	Ralph Noseda	Cobra	3	GTO	49	-	150
4	John Whitmore	Lotus-Cortina	55	GTU	47	9	400
5	Michael Needham	Triumph	8	GTU	40	6	200
DNF	George Wills	Cobra	41	GTO	25	-	-
DNF	Count d'Herbois	Austin Healey Sprite	57	GTU	24	-	-
DNF	Mike Spence	Lotus Cortina	54	GTU	18	-	-
DNF	Bill Bencker	Porsche 904GTS	-	GTU	18	-	-
DNF	Wayne Benton	Chevrolet Corvette	36	GTO	-	-	-
DNF	Jim Manley	Porsche	5	GTU	13	-	-

Fastest Qualifier:	Ken Miles	Shelby Cobra	2:12.6	81.45 mph	
Race Distance:	150.0 miles	50 laps of 3.0 mile course			
Race Time:	1 hr 59 min 15.54 sec				
Winner's Speed:	75.47 mph				
Victory Margin:	35 seconds				
Fastest Race Lap:	Ken Miles	Shelby Cobra	2:12.6	81.45 mph	

Start of the Drivers race with Hap Sharp #65 leading off the line, closely followed by Roger Penske #67, Ken Miles #98 and Bob Holbert #97. To the right, Charlie Hayes, in an under two-liter Elva-Porsche, is keeping up with the big boys. Photo by Larry Tomaras, courtesy John Tomaras.

Pensacola Drivers Race

The entry for the Drivers race was impressive. The Chaparral Team entered a Chevrolet powered 2A for Jim Hall, an Oldsmobile powered 2A for Hap Sharp and a Cooper Monaco-Chevrolet for Roger Penske. The Mecom team was present with the rear-engine Scarab for Augie Pabst and the old Penske Zerex Special, with an under two-liter Climax engine, for John Cannon. The Shelby team had two King Cobras for Bob Holbert and Ken Miles. Other over two-liter entries included Jef Stevens in a Cobra, Bill Fuller in a homemade Rebel Special and Bob Bienerth in a Corvette. The rest of the under two-liter contingent included seven Elva-Porsches, four Lotus 23's, an Elva-Ford, a Porsche RS and a Lotus 11.

In qualifying, Roger Penske took six seconds off last year's pole time with a lap of 2:00.8 (89.4 mph). Hap Sharp had the next fastest time (2:02.3) and Jim Hall completed the front row with (2:02.7). Bob Holbert (2:06.2) and John Cannon (2:06.5) shared the second row. Augie Pabst was sixth, in the Mecom Scarab with a 2:06.8.

When the race started, Hap Sharp jumped into the lead with Roger Penske right behind. They were followed by Ken Miles, Bob Holbert and Augie Pabst. Jim Hall messed up his start and fell back to ninth place. Before the end of the first lap Hall got up to sixth place.

After three laps, Sharp was still leading Penske and Jim Hall was now in third place.

The Shelby cars were fourth and fifth, while the Mecom cars of Pabst and Cannon were sixth and seventh. During the next twenty-five laps, Sharp, Penske and Hall put on a show trading places several times a lap.

John Cannon led the under two-liter class until he retired on lap eleven with a broken oil line. Bill Wuesthoff then assumed the under two-liter lead with Skip Scott, in another Elva-Porsche, right behind.

Holbert had brake problems and pitted from fourth place on lap twenty. He visited the pits a number of times before retiring after thirty-six laps. Hap Sharp retook the lead from Penske on lap twenty-seven, but it lasted only one lap. Jim Hall passed both Penske and Sharp to take the lead on lap

1964 PENSACOLA • USRRCDRIVERS RACE
April 5, 1964, NAS Corry Field, Pensacola, Florida

Place	Driver	Car/Engine	Car #	Class	Laps	Pts	Prize	Qualifying Place	Qualifying Time
1	Jim Hall	Chaparral 2A-Chevrolet	66	O2	74	9	$1,000	3	2:02.7
2	Roger Penske	Cooper T61-Chevrolet	67	O2	74	6	700	1	2:00.8
3	Ed Hugus	Lotus 23-Ford	23	U2	70	9	1,000	-	-
4	George Wintersteen	Elva Mk 7S-Porsche	12	U2	69	6	500	-	-
5	Bud Gates	Genie Mk 8-Ford	38	O2	68	4	300	-	-
6	Mike Hall	Elva Mk 7S-Ford	68	U2	68	4	300	-	-
7	Bill Wuesthoff	Elva Mk 7S-Porsche	7	U2	68	3	200	8	2:10.7
8	Jef Stevens	Cobra	3	O2	67	3	200	-	-
9	Bill Fuller	Rebel Special	17	O2	65	2	150	-	-
10	Wick Williams	Lotus 23-Ford	22	U2	61	2	150	-	-
11	Bob Bienerth	Chevrolet Corvette	4	O2	60	1	100	-	-
DNF	Hap Sharp	Chaparral 2A-Oldsmobile	65	O2	68	-	-	2	2:02.3
DNF	Chuck Dietrich	Elva Mk 7S-Porsche	76	U2	67	-	-	-	-
DNF	Augie Pabst	Scarab Mk 2-Chevrolet	30	O2	63	-	-	6	2:06.8
DNF	Ken Miles	Shelby Cooper T61M-Ford	14	O2	61	-	-	-	-
DNF	Skip Scott	Elva Mk 7S-Porsche	11	U2	56	-	-	-	-
DNF	Chuck Cassel	Porsche 718 RS	51	U2	50	-	-	-	-
DNF	Bob Holbert	Shelby Cooper T61M-Ford	97	O2	36	-	-	4	2:06.2
DNF	Nat Adams	Lotus 23-Climax	16	U2	32	-	-	-	-
DNF	Bob Markley	Elva Mk 7S-Porsche	75	U2	22	-	-	-	-
DNF	Charlie Hayes	Elva Mk 7S-Porsche	77	U2	22	-	-	7	2:08.3
DNF	Roy Kumnick	Cooper T61-Ford	44	O2	19	-	-	-	-
DNF	Harry Shaw	Lotus 11	73	U2	17	-	-	-	-
DNF	John Cannon	Zerex Special-Climax	31	U2	11	-	-	5	2:06.5
DNF	Richard Macon	Lotus 23-Alfa Romeo	2	U2	10	-	-	-	-
DNF	George Koehne	Genie Mk 8-Ford	93	O2	9	-	-	-	-
DNF	Joe Buzzetta	Elva Mk 7S-Porsche	71	U2	8	-	-	-	-
DNF	John Snyder	Lister-Ford	1	O2	8	-	-	-	-

Fastest Qualifier:	Roger Penske	Cooper T61-Chevrolet	2:00.8	89.4 mph
Race Distance:	222.0 miles	74 laps of 3.0 mile course		
Race Time:	2 hr 38min 9.433 sec			
Winner's Speed:	84.22 mph			
Victory Margin:	2 seconds			
Fastest Race Lap:	Roger Penske	Cooper T61-Chevrolet	2:03.8	87.24 mph

twenty-eight. Penske and Sharp traded second and third places lap after lap.

Ken Miles inherited fourth place when Holbert retired. Pabst was driving the wheels off the Scarab, in fifth place, trying to catch Miles. Miles' King Cobra lasted until just past the halfway point. He then started a series of pitstops for new tires, an ailing clutch and a broken suspension. There were too many problems and Miles retired after sixty-one laps. Augie Pabst pitted for new tires and fell back to tenth place. He worked his way back up to fifth place, only to run out of gas after sixty-three laps.

Bill Wuesthoff held the under two-liter lead from lap eleven until around lap sixty when he had to pit to have his Elva's frame re-welded. Ed Hugus moved into the under two-liter lead when Wuesthoff pitted. Hugus had a suspenseful drive to the finish, as his Lotus had a gas leak. To avoid further

suspense, Hugus made a quick pitstop to have it taken care of.

For a while it looked like George Wintersteen might have taken the under two-liter lead during Hugus' pitstop, but he spun off the course. Wintersteen recovered and got back into the race, a further lap down, but still in fourth place.

The race finished with Hall winning over Penske by two seconds. Ed Hugus was third, winning the under two-liter class. George Wintersteen was fourth, Bud Gates fifth and Mike Hall sixth. Bill Wuesthoff recovered from his pitstop and finished in seventh place.

After two races, Hall led the championship with fifteen points. Dave MacDonald, Charlie Hayes and Ed Hugus were tied for second place with nine points each. Next were Sharp, Wintersteen and Penske, each with six points.

Ed Hugus took the lead in the under two-liter class after Wuesthoff pitted. He finished in third place overall and won the class. Photo by Larry Tomaras, courtesy John Tomaras.

Roger Penske and Hap Sharp followed and passed each other, and Jim Hall, for the whole race. Penske finished second to Hall and Sharp dropped out of the race with six laps left. Photo by Larry Tomaras, courtesy John Tomaras.

Bill Wuesthoff led the under two-liter class for most of the race, but had to pit to have the car's frame welded. He returned to the race to finish seventh overall and fourth in the under two-liter class. Photo by Larry Tomaras, courtesy John Tomaras.

Hall's Chaparral is on jackstands, while the nose of Penske's Cooper is laying on the pavement to right of Hall's exhaust pipes. Photo by Larry Tomaras, courtesy John Tomaras.

Hap Sharp's Chaparral looks like it's almost ready to go, while Hall's car is being serviced. Photo by Larry Tomaras, courtesy John Tomaras.

OFFICIAL 50¢ PROGRAM

US ROAD RACING CHAMPIONSHIP

RIVERSIDE INTERNATIONAL RACEWAY

RIVERSIDE, CALIFORNIA

april 25/26 1964

CONDUCTED BY—California Sports Car Club Region of SCCA

1964 Riverside USRRC program cover. Scanned by Don Markle.

Front row of the grid. On the left is Scooter Patrick in a Porsche 904 who qualified third. Next is Ed Leslie in a Cobra and Ken Miles is on the far right, on the pole. Photo by Allen R. Kuhn

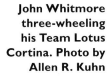

John Whitmore three-wheeling his Team Lotus Cortina. Photo by Allen R. Kuhn

1964 Riverside Manufacturers Race

There were twenty-two entries for the Riverside Manufacturers race. Ken Miles and Ed Leslie piloted two Shelby Cobras. Four Corvettes, a Jaguar XKE and a Ford Falcon in the over two-liter class challenged them. The under two-liter class had three brand new Porsche 904's, entered by Otto Zipper, for Scooter Patrick, Don Wester and Kurt Neumann. Also there were three older Porsches, two Lotus Cortinas for John Whitmore and Peter Arundell (1963 European Formula Junior champion and current #2 to Jimmy Clark on the GP team), an AC Bristol, two MG-B's, a Sunbeam Alpine, an Alfa Romeo and a Lotus Elite.

Ken Miles won the pole position with a time of 1:38.4. Ed Leslie in the other Cobra was next to Ken with a time of 1:40.0. Scooter Patrick, in a Porsche 904, was third and also on the front row with a time of 1:40.4. Next up were Don Wester and Dick Guldstrand (Corvette) with times of 1:40.4 and 1:41.8. Kurt Neumann headed up the third row with a 1:42.2. Next to him were Bill Krause (Corvette) 1:43.9 and Dennis Harrison (Porsche 1600) 1:44.4. The Lotus Cortinas were back on the sixth row. Arundell had a time of 1:49.5 and Whitmore turned in a lap at 1:50.8.

When the flag dropped to start the race, Ken Miles tore off with Ed Leslie right behind him. Already losing ground were Scooter Patrick and Don Wester in the Porsche 904's. Next up were the Corvettes of Dick Guldstrand, Doug Hooper and Joe Freitas. They all finished in this order. The only real crowd-pleasing excitement was watching the Lotus Cortinas. Arundell and Whitmore were back in eleventh and twelfth places and they swapped positions a couple of times a lap and two-wheeled through the corners.

The Shelby Cobras now led the Manufacturer's Series with 27 points to Porsche's 18. Lotus and Chevrolet (Corvette) both had 10 points. Following them were Volvo (3 points), Triumph (2) and Morgan (1).

The Lotus Cortinas of Peter Arundell and John Whitmore finished in eleventh and twelfth places respectively. They were totally outpaced by the Porsche 904's. Photo by Allen R. Kuhn

Second place, Ed Leslie, lapping the Falcon Sprint of Pete Cordts. Photo by Allen R. Kuhn

Ken Miles crossing the finish line in first place. Photo by Allen R. Kuhn

1964 RIVERSIDE • USRRC MANUFACTURERS RACE

April 26, 1964, Riverside International Raceway. Riverside, California

Place	Driver	Car/Engine	Car #	Class	Laps	Pts	Prize	Qualifying Place	Qualifying Time
1	Ken Miles	Shelby Cobra	50	GTO	48	9	$ 1,200	1	1:38.4
2	Ed Leslie	Shelby Cobra	198	GTO	48	-	400	2	1:40.0
3	Scooter Patrick	Porsche 904GTS	33	GTU	48	9	700	3	1:40.4
4	Don Wester	Porsche 904GTS	60	GTU	47	-	400	4	1:40.4
5	Dick Guldstrand	Chevrolet Corvette	56	GTO	47	4	250	5	1:41.8
6	Doug Hooper	Chevrolet Corvette	4	GTO	46	-	125	10	1:44.8
7	Joe Freitas	Chevrolet Corvette	77	GTO	46	-	100	9	1:44.6
8	Kurt Neumann	Porsche 904GTS	32	GTU	45	-	250	6	1:42.2
9	Alan Johnson	Porsche 1600	21	GTU	45	-	125	11	1:47.5
10	Dennis Harrison	Porsche 1600	701	GTU	44	-	100	8	1:44.4
11	Peter Arundell	Lotus-Cortina	2	GTU	44	1	50	14	1:49.5
12	John Whitmore	Lotus-Cortina	1	GTU	44	-	-	15	1:50.8
13	Gil Ranney	AC Bristol	113	GTU	43	-	-	16	1:51.8
14	Richard Smith	Porsche Carrera 356B	171	GTU	43	-	-	20	1:55.0
15	John Lumpkin	MG-B	62	GTU	43	-	-	17	1:52.1
16	Pete Cordts	Ford Falcon Sprint	17	GTO	40	-	50	19	1:54.8
17	Jim Adams	MG-B	55	GTU	21	-	-	13	1:49.1
DNF	Serge May	Sunbeam Alpine	54	GTU	45	-	-	21	1:55.8
DNF	Bob Challman	Lotus Elite	22	GTU	33	-	-	18	1:53.4
DNF	Dino Seraguso	Alfa-Romeo	61	GTU	18	-	-	22	1:45.3
DNF	Max Norris	Jaguar E-Type	63	GTO	12	-	-	12	1:48.3
DNF	Billy Krause	Chevrolet Corvette	3	GTO	2	-	-	7	1:43.9

Fastest Qualifier:	Ken Miles	Shelby Cobra	1:38.4	95.12 mph
Race Distance:	124.8 miles	48 laps of 2.6 mile course		
Race Time:	1 hr 20 min 54.48 sec			
Winner's Speed:	92.55 mph			
Victory Margin:	35 seconds			
Fastest Race Lap:	Ken Miles	Shelby Cobra	1:40.0	93.6 mph

Ken Miles being congratulated on winning, while Marilyn Fox (soon to be Marilyn Motschenbacher) is walking around the back of the Cobra to give Ken a kiss and a flag. Photo by Allen R. Kuhn.

The grid all lined up. Dave MacDonald #97 on the pole, with Skip Hudson #9 to the left and Jerry Titus' #58 Cheetah on the outside. Jim Hall's Chaparral is on the left of the second row and next to him is Bob Holbert #114. Photo by Allen R. Kuhn.

1964 Riverside Drivers Race

A week before the Riverside USRRC races, there was an SCCA FIA Open race at Phoenix International Raceway. It was like a USRRC race, being open to two-seater sports racing and grand touring race cars, although it was not part of the USRRC series. Twenty of the twenty-nine Phoenix starters would race in the Riverside and Laguna Seca USRRC races. Dave Mac-Donald won the race by just over a minute. Rick Muther, driving a Lotus 23, was third and first in the under two liter class. Ken Miles finished in eighth place and first in the GT class in Carroll Shelby's Cobra roadster.

The Riverside Drivers race entry featured USRRC regulars Jim Hall, in the sole Chaparral, Dave MacDonald and Bob Holbert in the Shelby Cooper-Cobras and Ken Miles in the GT winning Cobra roadster. The rest of the over two-liter field was made up of West Coast locals; Skip Hudson in the Nickey Cooper-Chevrolet, Chuck Daigh (Lotus 19), Jerry Titus and Don Jensen (Cheetah), Bart Martin (Cooper-Chevrolet), Don Hulette (Townsend Special), Dave Ridenour (Genie), Bill Krause (Old Yaller), Jim Parkinson (Cooper-Buick) and Stan Peterson (Lotus 19-Buick).

The major under two-liter entries were the Scuderia Tin Can Elva-Porsches for Charlie Hayes, Chuck Dietrich and record producer Bob Markley. West Coast under two-liter entries with Lotus 23 variants were Bobby Unser (of Indy car fame), Rick Muther, Chuck Kessinger, Ed Leslie, Bob Winkelmann, Frank Monise, Charlie Parsons,

George Follmer (using a destroked Corvair engine) and Tony Settember. Don Wester, Jim Kennedy, Dave Jordan and Al Cadrobbi all had various Porsches. Miles Gupton had a Merlyn-Porsche and Lothar Motschenbacher had an Elva-Cosworth.

Dave MacDonald got the pole position with a lap time of 1:32.6. Next to Dave was Skip Hudson with a time of 1:34.3 and Jerry Titus wheeled the Cheetah around in 1:35.3. Jim Hall had oil pressure problems in the Chaparral so he headed up the second row with a 1:35.6. Bob Holbert was next to Hall with the same lap time. The third row had Dave Ridenour (1:35.7), Don Jensen (1:35.9) and Bobby Unser (1:36.8), who was the fastest under two-liter contender.

When the race started MacDonald led the way with Titus and Hall not very far behind. Back in the pack at turn four, Chuck Dietrich hit the tires lining the corner and spun across the track. Bob Markley, Bob Winkelmann and Al Cadrobbi tried to take evasive action. Markley went up the bank, came back down, hit Winkelmann's Lotus and was severely rear-ended by Cadrobbi. Miraculously, there were no injuries and the race was red-flagged. Everyone except Winkelmann and Cadrobbi made the re-start.

MacDonald led the restart ahead of Hall, Titus and Hudson. By lap five, Chuck Daigh had moved his Arciero Lotus from the back of the grid up to fifth place. MacDonald kept increasing his lead, lap after lap, until lap twelve when he pitted with the clutch gone. His crew jacked the car up, locked the gear-

box in gear and gave him a pushstart back into the race. Jim Hall had taken over the lead when MacDonald pitted and Hudson stayed right with Hall's Chaparral.

Bob Holbert retired his Shelby Cooper with engine problems right after his teammate, Dave MacDonald, returned to the race. Don Jensen, in a Cheetah, dropped back through the field right from the start. Don found the Cheetah was hot and uncomfortable and he retired after twenty laps. On lap twenty-one, Chuck Daigh moved his Lotus past Titus' Cheetah into third place. Charlie Hayes had his Elva-Porsche in eighth place overall and first in the under two-liter class, but this ended in retirement after twenty-one laps.

Up front, Jim Hall was just barely keeping Skip Hudson at bay. Hudson was pushing hard and on lap thirty four he took the lead from Hall. Four laps later, Hall retook the lead but Hudson kept his Cooper very close. Hudson passed Hall for the lead again on lap forty-one. Three laps later, Hall was one second behind Hudson when the Chaparral's brakes locked up in turn seven. The Chaparral went off the race course into the hay bales and Hall was out of the race.

At this point Chuch Daigh was second, more than a minute behind Hudson. Jerry Titus was third and Bobby Unser was in fourth place, leading the under two-liter class. Ken Miles was fifth, in the Cobra he used to win the earlier Manufacturer's race. Charlie Parsons was sixth and the last racer on the lead lap. Following Parsons were Jim Kennedy, Rick Muther and Don Wester.

As the race progressed, Titus was feeling the heat in the poorly ventilated Cheetah cockpit. He pitted to have a bucket of cold water thrown on him. Jerry continued racing but the oilpan drain plug fell out with only five laps left. Titus coasted to a stop on the back straight when he saw the oil pressure suddenly drop. This moved Bobby Unser into third place and Ken Miles into fourth place. Charlie Parsons was in fifth place for three laps before he spun out of the race on the oil Titus dropped.

Skip Hudson had eased up and brought his Cooper to the finish line, the winner by eighty-five seconds over Chuch Daigh. Bobby Unser held onto third place with Miles in fourth place ahead of Kennedy, Wester, Muther and Bob Markley. Oddly enough, this was the only overall pro win of Hudson's career.

Jim Hall continued to lead the series with 15 points to George Wintersteen's 10 points. Hudson and Unser moved into a five-way tie for third place with Dave Mac-Donald, Charlie Hayes and Ed Hugus, each with 9 points. Chuch Daigh and Jim Kennedy were tied with Hap Sharp and Roger Penske for eighth place with 6 points.

1964 RIVERSIDE • USRRC DRIVERS RACE

April 26, 1964, Riverside International Raceway, Riverside, California

Place	Driver	Car/Engine	Car #	Class	Laps	Pts	Prize	Qualifying Place	Qualifying Time
1	Skip Hudson	Cooper T61-Chevrolet	9	O2	70	9	$ 1,225	3	1:34.3
2	Chuck Daigh	Lotus 19-Chevrolet	5	O2	70	6	400	-	-
3	Bobby Unser	Lotus 23B-Climax	95	U2	69	9	700	8	1:36.8
4	Ken Miles	Shelby Cobra	50	O2	68	4	250	-	-
5	Jim Kennedy	Porsche 718 RS	132	U2	66	6	400	24	1:42.9
6	Rick Muther	Lotus 23B-Ford	11	U2	66	4	250	11	1:37.7
7	Don Wester	Porsche 904GTS	60	U2	66	3	125	-	-
8	Bob Markley	Elva Mk 7-Porsche	175	U2	65	2	50	25	1:43.5
9	Bart Martin	Cooper T49-Chevrolet	78	O2	65	3	125	17	1:38.8
10	Lothar Motchenbacher	Elva Mk 7S-Porsche	20	U2	61	1	50	21	1:41.0
11	Don Hulette	Townsend Mk 3-Pontiac	204	O2	56	2	100	14	1:38.6
12	Chuck Kessinger	Lotus 23-Climax	101	U2	53	-	-	30	1:52.3
DNF	Charlie Parsons	Lotus 23B-Ford	10	U2	68	-	-	12	1:37.9
DNF	Chuck Dietrich	Elva Mk 7S-Porsche	176	U2	66	-	-	22	1:41.4
DNF	Jerry Titus	Cheetah	58	O2	65	-	-	3	1:35.3
DNF	Jim Hall	Chaparral 2A-Chevrolet	166	O2	44	-	-	4	1:35.6
DNF	Jim Parkinson	Cooper-Buick	187	O2	31	-	-	9	1:37.6
DNF	Frank Monise	Lotus 23B-Ford	44	U2	30	-	-	10	1:37.7
DNF	Dave Ridenour	Genie Mk 5-Mercury	146	O2	27	-	-	6	1:35.7
DNF	Dave MacDonald	Shelby Cooper T61M-Ford	97	O2	25	-	-	1	1:32.6
DNF	Miles Gupton	Merlyn Mk 4-Porsche	75	U2	25	-	-	16	1:38.8
DNF	Billy Krause	Ol' Yaller 9-Ford	53	O2	23	-	-	13	1:38.4
DNF	Don Jensen	Cheetah	8	O2	23	-	-	7	1:35.9
DNF	Charlie Hayes	Elva Mk 7S-Porsche	177	U2	21	-	-	15	1:38.6
DNF	Bob Holbert	Shelby Cooper T61M-Ford	114	O2	17	-	-	5	1:35.6
DNF	George Follmer	Lotus 23-Corvair	16	U2	7	-	-	29	1:51.4
DNF	Stan Peterson	Lotus 19-Buick	37	O2	5	-	-	19	1:40.3
DNS	Al Cadrobbi	Porsche 718 RS60	111	U2	-	-	-	26	1:43.6
DNS	Bob Winkelmann	Lotus 23B-Climax	110	U2	-	-	-	27	1:43.7
DNS	Dave Jordan	Porsche Spyder	14	U2	-	-	-	18	1:40.0
DNS	Paul Reinhart	Genie Mk 8-Chevrolet	6	O2	-	-	-	23	1:41.9
DNS	Jerry Entin	Ol' Yaller 2-Buick	71	O2	-	-	-	28	1:44.6
DNS	Ed Leslie	Lotus 23B-Climax	98	U2	-	-	-	20	1:40.9

Fastest Qualifier:	Dave MacDonald	Shelby Cooper T61M-Ford	1:32.6 mph	101.08 mph
Race Distance:	182.0 miles	70 laps of 2.6 mile course		
Race Time:	1hr 53min 53.82sec			
Winner's Speed:	95.8 mph			
Victory Margin:	1 minute, 25 seconds			
Fastest Race Lap:	Dave MacDonald	Shelby Cooper T61M-Ford	1:34.0	99.58 mph

The start is a drag race between MacDonald, in the Lang Cooper, and Titus in the Cheetah. Photo by Allen R. Kuhn.

Jim Hall leading Jerry Titus. Both ran strong, but neither finished the race. Photo by Allen R. Kuhn.

Sideview of Titus' Cheetah in action. Photo by Allen R. Kuhn.

Jim Hall drifting the Chaparral. Photo by Allen R. Kuhn.

Skip Hudson on his way to victory, after battling with Jim Hall. Photo by Allen R. Kuhn.

Ken Miles, #50 Cobra, passing Don Hulette, in the Townsend Special #204. Photo by Allen R. Kuhn.

Dave MacDonald in the Lang Cooper about to pass Titus in the Cheetah. Photo by Allen R. Kuhn.

Skip Hudson drifting out of a corner and on to victory. Photo by Allen R. Kuhn.

Ken Miles finished the Driver's race in fourth place. Again, this was after winning the Manufacturers race in the same car. Photo by Allen R. Kuhn.

Stan Peterson in a Lotus 19 leads Don Jensen in a Cheetah and Don Wester in a Porsche 904. Wester placed seventh overall and fourth in the under two-liter class. Peterson and Jensen both DNF'd. Photo by Allen R. Kuhn.

Jerry Titus in the Bill Thomas Cheetah. Titus ran with the leaders in the early laps, then held third or fourth place until he DNF'd after 65 laps. Photo by Allen R. Kuhn.

Early in the race Titus #58 leads eventual winner Hudson #9. Photo by Allen R. Kuhn.

Don Jensen brought his new Cheetah to Riverside and ran in mid-pack until retiring after 23 laps. Photo by Allen R. Kuhn.

U.S. ROAD RACING CHAMPIONSHIP

/ MAY: 1964

LITHOGRAPHED BY COPY/CO S.F.

JULIAN VEOVICH PHOTO COURTESY ROAD AND TRACK

LAGUNA SECA / OFFICIAL PROGRAM / ONE DOLLAR

1964 Laguna Seca USRRC program cover. Scan courtesy Don Markle

The first lap with Ken Miles (#50) and Ed Leslie (#98) already pulling away from the field. Photo from the collections of The Henry Ford.

Laguna Seca Manufacturers Race

The entry for the Laguna Seca Manufacturers race was much the same as at Riverside. There were Shelby's Cobras for Ken Miles and Ed Leslie. Bob Johnson entered his very quick private Cobra. Otto Zipper entered three Porsche 904's, for Don Wester, Scooter Patrick and Kurt Neumann. Dick Guldstrand and Joe Freitas were racing their Corvettes. John Whitmore was teamed with Mike Spence in the Lotus Cortinas. Other entries included Merle Brennan in an E-Type Jaguar, Red Faris, Ron Craven, John Coyle and Rick Sullivan in Corvettes, Jack Dalton and Jim Adams in MG-B's, Foster Alexander and Dick Carter in Triumph TR4's, Dick Stephens and Walt Maas in Elva Couriers and Stan Peterson in a Lotus Elite.

Qualifying was held while it was raining and the wet conditions affected the timing equipment. The officials knew they were in trouble when a MG-B "broke" the course record by four seconds. They nullified all the times for both the Manufacturers and the Drivers races and asked each team to turn in the best time for their cars. The overwhelming majority of teams and drivers felt the times turned in were a fair representation of what the grid should look like. Ed Leslie was on the pole and Ken Miles was second on the grid.

The weather for Sunday's races was nice and dry. As the race started, Leslie and Miles tore off the line, side by side, in a thundering drag race. Leslie got the lead by virtue of having the inside line through turn two. Miles stayed right with Ed and pulled up beside him a few times, but could not get by. On the fourth lap, Ken tried too hard and went off the course at turn three, doing about 100 mph. He got back on the course in eighth place, about forty seconds behind Leslie. This gave second place to Bob Johnson, who was leading the Porsches of Don Wester, Scooter Patrick and Kurt Neumann. Dick Guldstrand kept his Corvette in sight of the Porsches, but could not pass them.

Miles spent the race working his way past Guldstrand's Corvette and the three Porsches. On lap forty-five, Miles caught and passed Johnson's Cobra for second place. Johnson knew Miles was gaining on him all the time and tried to build up a cushion. He used a few too many revs and overextended his engine. Right before the last corner on the last lap Johnson's engine blew up. He didn't know it was the last lap and headed for the pits, only to find his crew waving like crazy for him to get back on the course to finish. Johnson steered back onto the course at the last moment and let his Cobra roll to the finish line. His front wheels crossed the finish line, but his rear wheels did not. That was good enough for third place.

Don Wester finished in fourth place with teammate Scooter Patrick right on his tail in fifth place. They spent the whole race driving nose to tail. Patrick tried everything he knew to get by Wester. Laguna was Wester's home track and after following Patrick at Riverside he was not about to do the same here. Dick Guldstrand finished in sixth place with Kurt Neumann behind him in seventh. Merle Brennan brought his Jaguar home in eighth, followed by the Corvettes of Joe Freitas and Red Faris. Jack Dalton took eleventh place and fourth in under two-liters, after a race long battle with John Whitmore's Lotus Cortina.

After four races Cobra led Porsche 36 points to 27 points. Lotus Cortina was third with 12 points and Chevrolet (Corvette) was fourth with 10 points. Triumph was fifth with 6 points, followed by MG and Volvo with 3 points each, Jaguar with 2 points, while Morgan and Ford (Falcon) had 1 point each.

Bob Johnson #33 leading Don Wester #60. Johnson finished in third place and Wester in fourth place. Photo from the collections of The Henry Ford.

Ken Miles goes off course on lap 4 as Kurt Neumann whistles by. Miles eventually worked his way back up to second place, while Neumann finished in seventh place. Photo from the collections of The Henry Ford.

1964 LAGUNA SECA • USRRC MANUFACTURERS RACE

May 3, 1964, Laguna Seca Raceway, Monterey, California

Place	Driver	Car/Engine	Car #	Class	Laps	Points	Prize
1	Ed Leslie	Shelby Cobra	98	GTO	53	9	$800
2	Ken Miles	Shelby Cobra	50	GTO	53	-	600
3	Bob Johnson	Cobra	33	GTO	53	-	500
4	Don Wester	Porsche 904GTS	60	GTU	52	9	300
5	Scooter Patrick	Porsche 904GTS	33	GTU	52	-	200
6	Dick Guldstrand	Chevrolet Corvette	56	GTO	52	3	100
7	Kurt Neumann	Porsche 904GTS	32	GTU	52	-	-
8	Merle Brennan	Jaguar E-Type	66	GTO	50	2	-
9	Joe Freitas	Chevrolet Corvette	177	GTO	49	-	-
10	Red Faris	Chevrolet Corvette	11	GTO	49	-	-
11	Jack Dalton	MGB	40	GTU	48	3	-
12	John Whitmore	Lotus Cortina	1	GTU	48	2	-
13	Richard Smith	Porsche Carrera	171	GTU	48	-	-
14	Ron Craven	Chevrolet Corvette	67	GTO	46	-	-
15	John Coyle	Chevrolet Corvette	-	GTO	46	-	-
16	Mike Spence	Lotus Cortina	2	GTU	46	-	-
17	Foster Alexander	Triumph TR4	-	GTO	45	-	-
18	Stan Peterson	Lotus Elite Climax	-	GTU	43	-	-
DNF	Milt Minter	Porsche Carrera	-	GTU	37	-	-
DSQ	Jim Adams	MGB	55	GTU	32	-	-
DSQ	Dick Stephens	Elva Courier	69	GTU	19	-	-
DSQ	Dick Carter	Triumph TR4	-	GTO	18	-	-
DSQ	Rick Sullivan	Chevrolet Corvette	266	GTO	18	-	-
DSQ	Walt Maas	Elva Courier	36	GTU	-	-	-

Fastest Qualifier:	Ken Miles	Shelby Cobra	time unknown	
Race Distance:	100.7 miles	53 laps of 1.9 mile course		
Race Time:	1hr 9min 7.82sec			
Winner's Speed:	87.4 mph			
Victory Margin:	17 seconds			
Fastest Race Lap:	Ed Leslie	Shelby Cobra	1:17.58	88.17 mph

Ed Leslie takes the checkered flag and wins the race.
Photo from the collections of The Henry Ford.

During qualifying bemused officials knew something was wrong when an MG clocked the fastest time. Photo from the collections of the Henry Ford.

Laguna Seca Drivers Race

The Drivers race had twenty-one entries that had raced at Riverside. Roger Penske joined Jim Hall and drove the second Chaparral. John Cannon was racing John Mecom's rear-engine Scarab. George Koehne, Paul Reinhart and Jack Flaherty all had Genies. Bat Masterson was in a Porsche-Buick and Frank Crane entered a Ferrari Testa Rossa. The under two-liter troops were bolstered by Tony Settember, Bob Keyes and Bill Molle in Lotus 23's, plus Steve Froines and Eldon Beagle in Porsche RS61's.

Qualifying for the Drivers race was held in the same wet conditions as the Manufacturers race qualifying and also suffered from the wet, malfunctioning, timing equipment. The race officials had the teams turn in qualifying times for their drivers they had timed themselves. From those times, Bob Holbert ended up on the pole with Jim Hall next to him. Roger Penske and Skip Hudson were on the second row. John Cannon and Chuck Daigh started from the third row. Race officials received no complaints about the grid. Consensus among the competitors was that everyone was pretty much where they belonged on the grid.

Holbert jumped into the lead when the race started. Jim Hall was about a car length behind and followed by Skip Hudson, Roger Penske, Chuck Daigh, Dave Ridenour, John Cannon, Ed Leslie, Dave MacDonald and George Koehne. By the end of the first lap, MacDonald and Dave Ridenour had worked up to third and fourth places. Hudson passed Ridenour on the second lap. This did not last long as Ridenour charged back, hit the rear of Hudson's Cooper and sent it spinning off course. Ridenour was blackflagged into the pits to have the front-end bodywork repaired before he was allowed back into the race. When he returned to the race, he was about ten laps behind the leaders.

Jim Hall had Holbert sized up by the fourth lap and blew by him to take the lead. It took six more laps for Holbert to retake the lead from Hall. On lap eighteen MacDonald took second place from Hall.

Charlie Hayes, in an Elva-Porsche, and Jerry Titus, in a Cheetah, passed each other many times as they worked their way through the field. By lap thirty they were fifth and sixth overall, behind Holbert, MacDonald, Hall and Penske. On lap thirty-six the suspension on Titus's Cheetah broke, putting him out of the race.

Hall moved past MacDonald into second place on lap fifty-nine. On the next lap, the suspension broke on Holbert's Cooper-Ford and Hall assumed the lead with MacDonald in second place. Holbert was able to get his car back to the pits, but his crew sent him back out to rejoin the race. Bob managed just one more lap before retiring.

Hall was able to put a lot of distance between himself and MacDonald during the last twenty laps and won by twelve seconds. Roger Penske brought the second Chaparral home in third place, one lap behind Mac-Donald. Charlie Hayes was fourth overall and first in the under two-liter class. Ed Leslie, in the Cobra roadster he used to win the Manufacturers race, was fifth. John Cannon had a heck of a time keeping the Scarab pointed in the right direction because it was too heavy and too powerful. Cannon teetered on the brink of a spin going into corners and laid rubber when he exited, but was still able to bring it home in sixth place. Frank Monise was seventh overall and second in under two-liters. Jim Kennedy, Chuck Dietrich and Bob Markley, all in under two-liter cars, rounded out the top ten.

Jim Hall left Laguna Seca with 24 points to lead the series championship. Charlie Hayes was second with 18 points and Dave MacDonald had 15 points for third place. Roger Penske, George Wintersteen and Jim Kennedy were tied for fourth place with 10 points each.

Bob Holbert #114 taking off like a scalded cat, with Jim Hall #366, Roger Penske #367, and Skip Hudson #9 a car length behind. Photo from the collections of The Henry Ford.

Holbert #114 led all but six of the first sixty laps. Jim Hall #366 led laps five through ten. Photo from the collections of The Henry Ford.

Dave Ridenour #146 is about to be passed by hard-charging Dave MacDonald #97. The nose of Ridenour's car was re-arranged when he hit the back of Skip Hudson's car, early in the race. Photo from the collections of The Henry Ford.

Charlie Hayes #77 placed fourth overall and won the under two-liter class. Here he is leading Jerry Titus' Genie-Corvair (#58) and Jack Flaherty #4 in a Genie-Climax. Both Titus and Flaherty dropped out of the race around the halfway mark. Photo from the collections of The Henry Ford.

1964 LAGUNA SECA • USRRC DRIVERS RACE
May 3, 1964, Laguna Seca Raceway, Monterey, California

Place	Driver	Car/Engine	Car #	Class	Laps	Points	Prize
1	Jim Hall	Chaparral 2A-Chevrolet	366	O2	80	9	$800
2	Dave MacDonald	Shelby Cooper T61M-Ford	97	O2	80	6	600
3	Roger Penske	Chaparral 2A-Chevrolet	367	O2	78	4	500
4	Charlie Hayes	Elva Mk 7S-Porsche	77	U2	77	9	800
5	Ed Leslie	Shelby Cobra	98	O2	77	3	300
6	John Cannon	Scarab-Chevrolet	8	O2	77	2	200
7	Frank Monise	Lotus 23B-Climax	-	U2	76	6	600
8	Jim Kennedy	Porsche 718 RS	-	U2	76	4	500
9	Chuck Dietrich	Elva Mk 7S-Porsche	76	U2	75	3	300
10	Bob Markley	Elva Mk 7S-Porsche	75	U2	75	2	200
11	Frank Crane	Ferrari 250 TRI/61	9	O2	75	1	100
12	George Koehne	Genie Mk 8-Ford	93	O2	75	-	-
13	Tony Settember	Lotus 23B-Climax	198	U2	74	1	100
14	Steve Froines	Porsche 718 RS-61	48	U2	71	-	-
15	Dave Ridenour	Genie Mk 8-Mercury	46	O2	69	-	-
16	Bob Keyes	Lotus 23B-Climax	136	U2	69	-	-
17	Bob Winkelmann	Lotus 23B-Climax	110	U2	69	-	-
18	Ken Miles	Lotus 23B-Climax	96	U2	69	-	-
19	Eldon Beagle	Porsche 718 RS-61	12	U2	68	-	-
DNF	Chuck Daigh	Lotus 19-Climax	5	O2	75	-	-
DNF	Bob Holbert	Shelby Cooper T61M-Ford	114	O2	60	-	-
DNF	Rick Muther	Lotus 23B-Ford	111	U2	47	-	-
DNF	Jack Flaherty	Genie Mk 5-Climax	4	U2	43	-	-
DNF	Paul Reinhart	Genie Mk 8-Chevrolet	6	O2	42	-	-
DNF	Jerry Titus	Genie-Corvair	58	O2	35	-	-
DNF	Jim Parkinson	Cooper-Buick	21	O2	33	-	-
DNF	Bat Masterson	Porsche-Buick	222	O2	25	-	-
DNF	Skip Hudson	Cooper T61-Chevrolet	91	O2	21	-	-
DNF	Charlie Parsons	Lotus 23-Ford	10	U2	17	-	-
DNF	Miles Gupton	Merlyn Mk 4-Porsche	175	U2	16	-	-
DNF	Bill Molle	Lotus 23-Climax	166	U2	13	-	-
DNF	Bart Martin	Cooper T49-Chevrolet	78	O2	6	-	-

Fastest Qualifier: Bob Holbert — Shelby Cooper T61M-Ford
Race Distance: 152.0 miles — 80 laps of 1.9 mile course
Race Time: 1 hr 23 min 38.16 sec
Winner's Speed: 88.0 mph
Victory Margin: 12 seconds
Fastest Race Lap: Unknown

John Cannon #8 drove John Mecom's rear-engined Scarab to sixth place. Behind Cannon, Roger Penske #367 has just passed Jerry Titus #58. Penske finished in third place. Photo from the collections of The Henry Ford.

Jim Hall #366 has just passed Dave MacDonald #97 for second place on lap fifty-nine, which turned into the lead on the next lap, when Bob Holbert dropped out. Photo from the collections of The Henry Ford.

1964 Pacific Raceways USRRC program cover. Scan courtesy Don Markle.

The front row of the grid blasting off at the start. From the right are Ken Miles #50 on the pole and slightly ahead of Ed Leslie in his black "Dragonsnake" Cobra. Don Wester in the #60 Porsche 904 was third on the grid and fourth in the race. Lurking on the second row is Bob Johnson in #133 Cobra who took third place in the race. Photo from the collections of the Henry Ford.

Bob Johnson #133 has the drop on Dick Guldstrand #56. Guldstrand was the only retirement of the race. Merle Brennan #66 Jaguar XKE is edging ahead of John Razzelle's Cobra #59 and Mike Eyerly's Porsche 904 #64. Photo from the collections of the Henry Ford.

Pacific Raceways Manufacturers Race

Eleven cars showed up for the Manufacturers race at Pacific Raceways. The Shelby Cobra team of Ken Miles, Ed Leslie and Bob Johnson were joined by local racer John Razzelle. Dick Guldstrand and Joe Freitas brought their Corvettes, while Merle Brennan entered his E-type Jaguar. In the under two-liter class Don Wester was entered in Otto Zipper's Porsche 904. Mike Eyerly was also entered in a 904 that he had received during the week before this race. Team Lotus entered Cortinas and they were driven by mechanic, Ray Parsons and local driver, Pete Lovely.

When the race started, Miles grabbed the lead. Don Wester unexpectedly pushed his Porsche into second place ahead of the Cobras of Ed Leslie and Bob Johnson. Wester was right with Miles for the first lap. On the second lap Miles began to draw away. Ed Leslie blew by Wester's Porsche and into second place on the fourth lap. After eight more laps, Wester fell back into the clutches of Johnson. Miles was in first place, seven seconds ahead of Leslie after twenty laps. There was a seven-second gap back to Bob Johnson, who was eleven seconds ahead of Wester.

Further back in the field, Pete Lovely and Ray Parsons were putting on the best show of the race. They were trading places lap after lap while two and three-wheeling around the corners.

The spaces between Miles and Leslie and Leslie and Johnson began to decrease over the next fifteen laps. Johnson was able to sneak by Leslie and Miles to take the lead on lap thirty-five. This lasted just one lap because Leslie took the lead after passing both Miles and Johnson on the backside of the course. It appeared that Miles had been toying with Leslie and Johnson because a few laps later he passed both of them and began to draw away.

Miles won by ten seconds with Leslie second and Johnson third. Don Wester was in fourth place and first in the under two-liter class. He was also the last competitor on the lead lap. Mike Eyerly brought his new Porsche home in fifth place, ahead of Merle Brennan's Jaguar. Pete Lovely was seventh in the Lotus Cortina, just a few feet ahead of teammate, Ray Parsons.

1964 PACIFIC RACEWAYS • USRRC MANUFACTURERS RACE

May 10, 1964, Pacific Raceways, Kent, Washington

Place	Driver	Car/Engine	Car #	Class	Laps	Pts	Prize	Qualifying Place
1	Ken Miles	Shelby Cobra	50	GTO	46	9	$800	1
2	Ed Leslie	Shelby Cobra	98	GTO	46	-	600	2
3	Bob Johnson	Cobra	133	GTO	46	-	500	4
4	Don Wester	Porsche 904GTS	60	GTU	46	9	300	3
5	Mike Eyerly	Porsche 904GTS	64	GTU	45	-	200	10
6	Merle Brennan	Jaguar E-Type	66	GTO	44	3	100	6
7	Pete Lovely	Lotus Cortina	2	GTU	42	4	-	8
8	Ray Parsons	Lotus Cortina	1	GTU	42	-	-	9
9	John Razzelle	Cobra	59	GTO	41	-	-	7
10	Joe Freitas	Chevrolet Corvette	177	GTO	30	-	-	11
DNF	Dick Guldstrand	Chevrolet Corvette	56	GTO		-	-	5

Fastest Qualifier: Ken Miles — Shelby Cobra
Race Distance: 103.5 miles — 46 laps of 2.25 mile course
Race Time: 1 hr 12 min 17.58 sec
Winner's Speed: 85.9 mph
Victory Margin: 2 seconds
Fastest Race Lap: Unknown

LEFT–Don Wester had his #60 Porsche 904 wound up and flying. He grabbed second place away from Leslie and Johnson right after the start. However Leslie got by after four laps and Johnson demoted him to fourth place after twelve laps. At least he won the under two-liter class. Photo from the collections of the Henry Ford.

BELOW–Flying along, Miles #50 is lapping Merle Brennan's XKE. Right behind are Ed Leslie #98 and Bob Johnson #133 who took second and third places, respectively. Photo from the collections of the Henry Ford.

Local driver, Pete Lovely, got a ride in the second Team Lotus Cortina. He finished in seventh place and third in the under two-liter class. Photo from the collections of the Henry Ford.

Ken Miles on a victory lap with the race queen. Photo by Tom Lebo, courtesy Bill Lebo.

Ed Leslie's Cobra and Joe Freitas' Corvette were transported to and from the race by the Shelby team. Photo Tom Lebo, courtesy Bill Lebo.

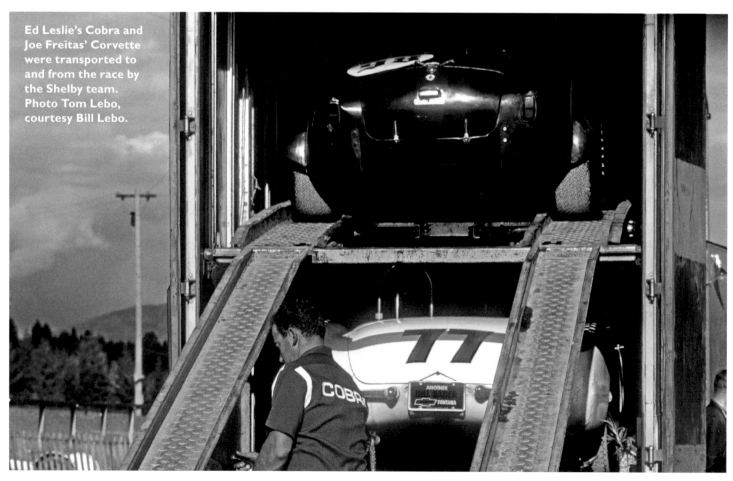

The remains of Dave MacDonald's Lang Cooper, after Bob Holbert lost control during practice. From the collections of the Henry Ford.

Stan Burnett's Mk 2 Special was a one of the victims of Holberts crash. Burnett was sitting in the car without a helmet when it was hit. Burnett's head hit the rollbar, giving him a concussion. From the collections of the Henry Ford.

Pacific Raceways Drivers Race

This round of the series fell just one week after the Laguna Seca race. Eighteen drivers made the trek to Washington State. Jim Hall and Hap Sharp had their Chaparrals. Bob Holbert and Dave MacDonald drove the Shelby Cooper-Cobras. Ken Miles and Ed Leslie decided, between races, to enter the Cobras they used in the earlier Manufacturers race. Other over two-liter entries were Jerry Titus in a Cheetah, Skip Hudson, Dave Ridenour, Bart Martin and Dick Guldstrand. Local over two-liter entries included Allan Grant in a Cheetah, Dave Tatum in a Lotus 19, Stan Burnett, Ken Beckman and Stan Bennett.

In the under two-liter class Charlie Hayes and Chuck Dietrich were racing Ollie Schmidt's Elva-Porsches. There were six Lotus 23's entered by Charlie Parsons, Gerry Bruihl, Tony Settember, Frank Monise, Bob Winkelmann and Canadian Bob McLean. Don Wester and Mike Eyerly both raced Porsche 904's. Other under two-liter entries were Lyle Forsgren in his Forsgrini, Jim Kennedy in a Porsche RS and Stan Schooley in an Elva-Maserati.

In the days leading up to the race, the Seattle area was having its usual May showers. The weather cleared up for Friday's practice and Jim Hall moved his Chaparral around the course in 1:25.0, breaking Bob Holbert's old record of 1:26.5. However, Friday was just practice. The rain returned for qualifying on Saturday and Hall won pole position with a time of 1:38.7.

Bob Holbert set the third fastest qualifying time in his Shelby Cooper-Cobra on Saturday. Because Dave MacDonald was at Indianapolis and due to arrive raceday morning, Holbert took MacDonald's Lang Cooper out to qualify it for him. Holbert came flying out of the last turn and lost control. The car went down the straight backward and spun into the pits. It slammed into Skip Hudson's Cooper, throwing mechanic, Ron Kaplan, into the air. Then it hit Stan Burnett's new Mark 2 Special. Stan was sitting in his car without a helmet and was knocked unconscious when his head hit the rollbar. The Lang Cooper spun back into the middle of the track with a ruptured fuel tank and burst into flames. Holbert was hospitalized with burns. Ron Kaplan suffered a broken leg and many bruises. Burnett was hospitalized with a concussion. Trevor Harris, Burnett's partner and Larry Webb, mechanic for Alan Grant, were also injured in the melee. Only half of the field posted qualifying times on Saturday. They were hoping for a dry track during the final qualifying session Sunday morning.

Sunday was dry, but clouds loomed overhead. MacDonald arrived at the track Sunday morning and found out he would be driving Holbert's King Cobra instead of the Lang Cooper. The Lang Cooper was damaged well beyond immediate repair and Holbert thought it was only right for Mac-Donald to use his car.

When the race started, Hall and Mac-Donald blasted off the grid and put some distance between themselves and Hap Sharp in third place. Dave Ridenour, Ken Miles, Jerry Titus and Charlie Hayes closely followed Sharp. Hayes passed Miles and Titus to take fifth place on the third lap. The next time around, MacDonald had relieved Hall of the lead. Hall kept the Chaparral right on MacDonald's tail and they lapped the rest of the field by the twenty-sixth lap.

MacDonald spun the King Cobra at the esses on lap thirty-one, while lapping backmarkers and Hall pounced into the lead. MacDonald got going immediately, but had trouble keeping the car in gear. He got the hang of it over the next few laps and then started to move back up.

Meanwhile Charlie Hayes was leading the under two-liter class, far ahead of Charlie Parsons, but gearbox trouble set in and Hayes retired after forty-five laps. Parsons kept the under two-liter lead until near the end of the race when he too had gearbox problems. Tony Settember now took over the under two-liter lead with Chuck Dietrich second in class.

MacDonald was ten seconds behind Hall after forty-six laps. By lap sixty-six, MacDonald was six seconds behind Hall. Suddenly, Hall's Chaparral slowed to a stop on the backside of the course. It was the victim of a failed fuel pump. MacDonald whizzed by and won by a margin of two laps over Hap Sharp's Chaparral. Dave Ridenour was third. Ken Miles was three laps back in fifth place. Tony Settember won the under two-liter class with a sixth place overall finish. Next up were Chuck Dietrich and Mike Eyerly. Dave Tatum, Don Wester and Bob McLean rounded out the top ten.

On the cooling down lap MacDonald stopped to give Hall a lift back to the pits. They came away from this race tied for first place in the championship with 24 points each. Unfortunately, this would be Mac-Donald's last race before losing his life in a huge first lap crash at the Indy 500. This was also Bob Holbert's last race. After crashing in practice and having his teammate die at Indy, Bob retired from racing.

Skip Hudson's Cooper was the other car involved. Mechanic, Ronnie Kaplan was tossed in the air, broke an arm and received a bunch of bruises. From the collections of the Henry Ford.

Dave MacDonald leads the field in the car Bob Holbert was going to race. He is followed by the Chaparrals of Jim Hall #66 and Hap Sharp #67. In fourth place is Dave Ridenour in his Genie. Photo by Tom Lebo, courtesy Bill Lebo.

Halfway through the race MacDonald spun at the esses as he was about to put a lap on Dick Guldstrand #56. Jim Hall is waiting to see which way MacDonald goes. Photo by Tom Lebo, courtesy Bill Lebo.

MacDonald spins into the infield and Hall assumes the race lead. Photo by Tom Lebo, courtesy Bill Lebo.

A few laps later and MacDonald is right on Hall's tail, ready to pounce. Photo by Tom Lebo, courtesy Bill Lebo.

Dave Ridenour #146 spent the race in fourth place and moved up to third when Hall retired. Here he has Ken Miles #50 on his tails. From the collections of the Henry Ford.

Charlie Hayes spent two-thirds of the race holding down sixth place and first in the under two-liter class, before he retired. Ken Miles is about to put Hayes a lap down. From the collections of the Henry Ford.

1964 PACIFIC RACEWAYS • USRRC DRIVERS RACE

May 10, 1964, Pacific Raceways, Kent, Washington

Place	Driver	Car & Engine	Car #	Class	Laps	Points	Prize
1	Dave MacDonald	Shelby Cooper T61M-Ford	14	O2	68	9	$800
2	Hap Sharp	Chaparral 2A-Chevrolet	67	O2	66	6	600
3	Dave Ridenour	Genie Mk 8-Mercury	146	O2	66	4	500
4	Ken Miles	Shelby Cobra	50	O2	65	3	300
5	Tony Settember	Lotus 23-Climax	3	U2	63	9	800
6	Chuck Dietrich	Elva Mk 7S-Porsche	76	U2	63	6	600
7	Mike Eyerly	Porsche 904GTS	64	U2	62	4	500
8	Dave Tatum	Lotus 19-Climax	78	O2	62	2	200
9	Don Wester	Porsche 904GTS	60	U2	61	3	300
10	Bob McLean	Lotus 23-Climax	101	U2	61	2	200
11	Dick Guldstrand	Chevrolet Corvette	56	O2	61	1	100
12	Gerry Bruihl	Lotus 23-Climax	41	U2	58	1	100
13	Charlie Parsons	Lotus 23-Ford	110	U2	58	-	-
14	Allen Grant	Cheetah	8	O2	57	-	-
15	Lyle Forsgren	Forsgrini Veloce-Alfa	148	U2	57	-	-
16	Stan Bennett	Lister	82	O2	55	-	-
17	John Antons	Lotus 6-Buick	24	U2	52	-	-
18	Bart Martin	Cooper T49-Chevrolet	178	O2	51	-	-
19	Jerry Titus	Cheetah	16	O2	48	-	-
20	Frank Monise	Lotus 23-Climax	-	U2	19	-	-
DNF	Jim Hall	Chaparral 2A-Chevrolet	66	O2	66	-	-
DNF	Charlie Hayes	Elva Mk 7S-Porsche	77	U2	45	-	-
DNF	Bob Winkelmann	Lotus 23-Climax	-	U2	43	-	-
DNF	Ken Deckman	Chevrolet Corvette	88	O2	18	-	-
DNF	John Razzelle	Cobra-Ford	59	O2	8	-	-
DNF	Ed Leslie	Cobra-Ford	98	O2	8	-	-
DNF	Jim Kennedy	Porsche 718 RS	32	U2	3	-	-
DNF	Stan Schooley	Elva Mk 6-Maserati	-	U2	2	-	-
DNS	Bob Holbert	Shelby Cooper T61M-Ford	97	O2	-	-	-
DNS	Skip Hudson	Cooper T61-Chevrolet	9	O2	-	-	-
DNS	Stan Burnett	Burnett Mk 1-Chevrolet	36	O2	-	-	-

Fastest Qualifier:	Jim Hall	Chaparral 2A-Chevrolet	1:38.7	82.07 mph	
Race Distance:	153.0 miles	68 laps of 2.25 mile course			
Race Time:	1 hr 40 min 19.68 sec				
Winner's Speed:	91.5 mph				
Victory Margin:	2 laps				
Fastest Race Lap:	Jim Hall	Chaparral 2A-Chevrolet	1:26.8	93.318 mph	

Hap Sharp #67 spent most of the race in third place. He took second place, two laps behind MacDonald, when teammate Hall retired. From the collections of the Henry Ford.

Tony Settember on his way to winning the under two-liter class, after Hayes and Parsons had problems. From the collections of the Henry Ford.

1948
FRANK GRISWOLD
with close second
BRIGGS CUNNINGHAM

1949
MILES COLLIER

1950
**ERWIN
GOLDSCHMIDT
AND WIFE**

1953 ★ 1957
1959 ★ 1962
WALTER HANSGEN

1954
PHIL WALTERS

1955
**SHERWOOD
JOHNSTON**

1956 ★ 1961
**GEORGE
CONSTANTINE**

1958
ED CRAWFORD

1960
AUGIE PABST

1963
BOB HOLBERT

17th ANNUAL

GRAND PRIX SPORTS CAR WEEKEND

Watkins Glen, N. Y.

JUNE 26-27
SCCA
Regional Races

JUNE 28
USRRC
1964

OFFICIAL PROGRAM 50 CENTS

1964 Watkins Glen Sports Car Grand Prix race program cover. Scan courtesy Don Markle.

On the pace lap, Ken Miles #98, on the left, is on the pole with teammate, Ed Leslie #99, beside him. Bob Johnson #33 and Mike Gammino #23 are on the second row with Hal Keck #88 and Graham Shaw # 44 behind on row three. They almost finished in this order. Gammino retired after thirty-six laps while Shaw finished fourth ahead of Keck. Photo by William Green.

Watkins Glen Manufacturers Race

After a six-week break the USRRC series moved across the country to Watkins Glen. This year the whole course had been repaved and lap times were expected to drop considerably.

The Shelby team, with Cobras for Ken Miles and Ed Leslie, were present, as were, four privately entered Cobras driven by Bob Johnson, Graham Shaw, Hal Keck and John Everly. Challenging the Cobras were Al Forsyth's Corvette and Mike Gammino's Ferrari Berlinetta. John Whitmore and Mike Spence were driving the Team Lotus Cortinas. Taking on the Cortinas were four Porsches, two Abarth-Simcas, an Alfa Romeo TZ, a Morgan +4, a Volvo P1800 and a TVR.

Ken Miles (1:24.3) and Ed Leslie (1:24.5) were on the front row of the grid. Miles' time beat last year's pole time by five seconds. Bob Johnson (1:26.2) and Mike Gammino (1:28.0) were on the second row. Next up were Hal Keck (1:29.1) and Graham Shaw (1:29.4). Rounding out the top ten were John Everly (1:31.8), Bud Patterson (1:36.3), Chuck Stoddard (1:36.7) and John Whitmore (1:37.0).

Although Miles had the pole position, he was third at the end of the first lap. Bob Johnson had shot off the grid to take the lead from Ed Leslie. Hal Keck (Cobra) was fourth with Mike Gammino (Ferrari), Graham Shaw(Cobra), Bud Patterson (Abarth-Simca),

John Whitmore (Lotus Cortina), Chuck Stoddard (Alfa Romeo TZ) and Al Forsyth (Corvette) following. On the next lap Whitmore and Stoddard passed Patterson's Abarth. Forsyth fell back a few places and Mike Spence moved into tenth place. Shaw's Cobra demoted Gammino's Ferrari to sixth place on the third lap.

Up front, the Cobras of Johnson, Leslie and Miles were drawing away from Keck's Cobra at a quick rate. On the fourth lap, Miles got by Leslie for second place and then took the lead from Johnson on the next lap. Ed Leslie pushed Johnson down to third place on lap seven. After two more laps, Leslie came around in the lead with Miles and Johnson right on his tail. Back in the next pack, Shaw had moved up to fourth place with Keck fifth and Gammino sixth. Following them were Stoddard's Alfa and the Cortinas of Whitmore and Spence.

On lap eleven Shaw spun in front of the pits, hitting Keck who was right behind. Keck pitted and Gammino flew by Shaw for fourth place. Miles took the lead on lap fifteen and Johnson passed Leslie for second place. On the next lap, Johnson took the lead for two laps, with Miles in second place. Miles took the lead the following lap, with Leslie second and Johnson third. On lap nineteen Ed Leslie passed Miles to take the lead. This lasted until lap twenty-two when both Miles and

Johnson got by Leslie. Behind the leaders Gammino was running in fourth place ahead of Shaw, Stoddard, Whitmore, Spence, Jennings and Keck.

Johnson passed Miles and then Leslie to take the lead on lap thirty-one. Miles followed Johnson and took second place from Leslie. Hal Keck was getting back into his stride and had passed Jennings, Spence and Whitmore, to take seventh place. On lap thirty-four, Miles took the lead from Johnson and Keck passed Gammino for sixth place. Leslie pushed Johnson down to third place on the next lap while Keck took fifth place from Stoddard. Johnson regained second place from Leslie on lap thirty-seven, while Gammino retired.

Leslie squeezed passed Johnson on lap forty-two to reassume second place, just behind Miles. These three stayed two seconds apart through the end of the race, all of them a lap ahead of Graham Shaw. Keck and Stoddard were fifth and sixth, three laps behind the leaders. Mike Spence was seventh with Bruce Jenning eighth.

This win gave Cobra a total of 54 points. Porsche was still in second place with 40 points. The Lotus Cortinas were third with 22 points. Chevrolet (Corvette) increased their total to 12 points to stay in fourth place. Chuck Stoddard's win put Alfa Romeo in fifth place with 9 points.

1964 WATKINS GLEN • USRRC MANUFACTURERS RACE

June 28, 1964, Watkins Glen Grand Prix Course, Watkins Glen, New York

Place	Driver	Car/Engine	Car #	Class	Laps	Pts	Prize	Qualifying Place	Qualifying Time
1	Ken Miles	Shelby Cobra	98	GTO	44	9	$750	1	1:24.3
2	Ed Leslie	Shelby Cobra	99	GTO	44	-	300	2	1:24.5
3	Bob Johnson	Cobra	33	GTO	44	-	150	3	1:26.2
4	Graham Shaw	Cobra	44	GTO	43	-	125	6	1:29.4
5	Hal Keck	Cobra	88	GTO	41	-	100	5	1:29.1
6	Chuck Stoddard	Alfa Romeo TZ	22	GTU	41	9	500	9	1:36.7
7	Mike Spence	Lotus Cortina	12	GTU	40	6	300	13	1:37.8
8	Bruce Jennings	Porsche 356B Carrera	77	GTU	40	4	150	12	1:37.3
9	John Kelly	Porsche 356B Carrera	34	GTU	39	-	125	15	1:39.5
10	Alvin Forsyth	Chevrolet Corvette	81	GTO	39	1	75	11	1:37.1
11	Dick Holquist	Abarth Simca	96	GTU	39	2	100	14	1:38.5
12	Bud Patterson	Abarth Simca	18	GTU	39	-	75	8	1:36.3
13	Arch McNeill	Morgan Plus 4	17	GTU	37	-	-	16	1:45.8
14	Jacques Duval	Porsche	58	GTU	37	-	-	17	1:47.8
15	Art Riley	Volvo P1800	24	GTU	36	-	-	19	no time
16	McLane Tilton Jr	TVR Mk 3	16	GTU	36	-	-	20	no time
DNF	Mike Gammino	Ferrari 250 GTO	23	GTO	36	-	-	4	1:28.0
DNF	John Whitmore	Lotus Cortina	11	GTU	32	-	-	10	1:37.0
DNF	Ron Grable	Porsche	28	GTU	21	-	-	18	1:48.4
DNF	John Everly	Cobra	21	GTO	0	-	-	7	1:31.8

Fastest Qualifier:	Ken Miles	Shelby Cobra	1:24.3	98.23 mph
Race Distance:	101.2 miles	44 laps of 2.3 mile course		
Race Time:	1 hr 4 min 57.3.sec			
Winner's Speed:	93.48 mph			
Victory Margin:	1 second			
Fastest Race Lap:	Ken Miles	Shelby Cobra	1:24.8	97.67 mph

Jim Hall won the race going away. He went from a one second lead on lap one, to over a lap by the end of the race. Photo by William Green.

Roger Penske finished in second place in the second Chaparral. This was after stalling at the start and working his way up from twenty-first place. Photo by William Green.

Watkins Glen Drivers Race

The over two-liter Drivers race entry was rather thin. There were eight over two-liter racers, plus the two Cobras Ken Miles and Bob Johnson had raced in the earlier Manufacturers race. The Chaparral team of Jim Hall and Roger Penske headed up the entry. The Shelby team had Skip Scott driving their Cooper-Cobra. Ludwig Heimrath had his Cooper-Ford and George Wintersteen fielded his Chevrolet-powered Cooper. Bud Gates entered his Genie-Chevrolet and James Flynn had a Ferrari.

There were sixteen under-two liter entries; Elva was the most prevalent chassis. Charlie Hayes, Don Wester, Bill Wuesthoff and Joe Buzzetta had Porsche powered Elvas. George Alderman, Alan Friedland, Peter Goetz and Don Wolf were entered in Elva-Fords. Lotus 23 entries consisted of Bob Bucher, Mike Goth, John Morton and Wick Williams. Also Ray Parsons, the Lotus Cortina mechanic/driver, was racing the Kelly-Porsche.

Jim Hall won pole position with a time of 1:20.0, which took 8.1 seconds off last year's pole time. Roger Penske was second with a 1:20.4. Skip Scott completed the first row with a time of 1:24.1, just over four seconds

behind Hall. Sharing the second row of the grid were Ken Miles, using the 1:24.3 he won the manufacturers pole with and Ludwig Heimrath (1:24.9). Ed Lowther (1:25.1), Charlie Hayes (1:25.6) and Bob Johnson (1:26.2) were on the third row. Peter Sachs (1:26.3) and George Wintersteen (1:26.4) completed the top ten qualifiers.

After a parade lap the race started and Jim Hall jumped into the lead with Skip Scott already falling back. Roger Penske had stalled at the start and saw most of the field pass by while he restarted his Chaparral. At the end of the first lap, Hall was leading Skip Scott by ten seconds. Ed Lowther was third, with Ludwig Heimrath, Ken Miles, Charlie Hayes and Bill Wuesthoff following him. Penske completed the first lap in twenty-second position. Charlie Hayes took fourth place away from Ken Miles on the second lap. The next lap Don Wester took eighth place from George Wintersteen and Penske moved up four places. The first eight places stayed the same until lap twelve when Don Wester passed Bill Wuesthoff and Roger Penske moved up to ninth place. On lap fourteen Skip Scott fell from second to sixth

place. Charlie Hayes and Ken Miles moved up to third and fourth places which demoted Ludwig Heimrath to fifth place.

Roger Penske took seventh place from Wuesthoff and Wester on lap seventeen. After two more laps Skip Scott retired and Penske passed Heimrath for fifth place. The running order was now Jim Hall, with a huge lead over Ed Lowther, then Hayes, Miles, Penske, Heimrath, Wuesthoff, Wester, Johnson and Bob Bucher. After three more laps, Ken Miles got his Cobra close enough to Charlie Hayes to pass him for third place and make it stick. This lasted until Penske blew by both of them to claim third place on lap twenty-eight.

Hall had lapped everyone by now. Lowther maintained second place with Penske third, but moving closer. Miles was fourth while Charlie Hayes was fifth overall and first in the under two-liter class. Ludwig Heimrath was running in sixth place and Wuesthoff, Wester, Johnson and John Morton followed him. On lap forty-six Bob Johnson pitted for a new tire and some gas and fell back to fourteenth. Penske sailed past Lowther on the next lap to take over second place.

Ludwig Heimrath #55 is leading Skip Scott #96 and Charlie Hayes #71, early in the race. Scott retired after eighteen laps, while Hayes finished in third place and first in the under two-liter class. Heimrath finished in fourth place. Photo by William Green.

Lowther started drifting back on lap fifty-two and Ken Miles pounced on him to take third place. After three more laps Don Wester pitted for fuel and dropped to eleventh. This elevated Bob Bucher to eighth place. Bud Gates was ninth with John Morton tenth.

Places remained static until lap sixty-six when Charlie Hayes passed Ed Lowther for fourth place and Bill Wuesthoff retired with a dropped valve in his engine. This moved Bud Gates up to seventh place and he was followed by John Morton, Don Wester and Bob Johnson. Don Wester was into his stride and recovering from his earlier pit-

stop. He blew by Morton and Gates on lap seventy-one to take seventh place.

On lap seventy-four Ed Lowther retired with a broken suspension, moving Heimrath up to fifth place. Wester, Gates, Morton and Johnson also moved up behind Heimrath. After three more laps, Gates retired and that moved John Morton up to seventh place. On lap eighty-two, Miles brought his Cobra into the pits so his mechanics could check the transmission. They found the casing was cracked and sent Miles back to finish the race. He dumped it in gear, re-entered the race in fourth place and tried to nurse it to the end. One lap

later Heimrath caught and passed Miles.

The race ended with the Chaparrals of Hall and Penske in first and second places. Charlie Hayes was third and first in the under two-liter class. Ludwig Heimrath was fourth and Miles was fifth. Don Wester, John Morton, Bob Johnson, Tibor Imrey and Charles Kurtz followed them.

Hall, with 33 points, maintained his championship lead over Charlie Hayes (27). Penske moved up to fourth place with 16 points (behind Dave MacDonald). Don Wester and Hap Sharp were next with 12 points and Miles moved up to seventh place with 11 points.

1964 WATKINS GLEN • USRRC DRIVERS RACE

June 28, 1964, Watkins Glen Grand Prix Course, Watkins Glen, New York

Place	Driver	Car/Engine	Car #	Class	Laps	Pts	Prize	Qualifying Place	Qualifying Time
1	Jim Hall	Chaparral 2A-Chevrolet	66	O2	87	9	$1,500	1	1:20.0
2	Roger Penske	Chaparral 2A-Chevrolet	67	O2	86	6	500	2	1:20.4
3	Charlie Hayes	Elva Mk 7S-Porsche	71	U2	85	9	750	7	1:25.6
4	Ludwig Heimrath	Cooper T61-Ford	55	O2	85	4	300	5	1:24.9
5	Ken Miles	Shelby Cobra	98	O2	85	3	200	4	1:24.3
6	Don Wester	Elva Mk 7S-Porsche	76	U2	83	6	500	13	1:26.9
7	John Morton	Lotus 23-Climax	97	U2	83	4	300	14	1:27.1
8	Bob Johnson	Cobra	33	O2	82	2	150	8	1:26.2
9	Tibor Szaba Imrey	Ferrari Dino	22	U2	80	3	200	25	1:31.7
10	Charles Kurtz	Porsche 718 RS-61	57	U2	78	2	150	24	1:30.8
11	Mike Goth	Lotus 23-Alfa Romeo	18	U2	77	1	100	29	1:33.2
12	Robert Mouat	Cooper Monaco T61-Climax	79	U2	76	-	-	27	1:32.2
13	Peter Sachs	Brabham BT8-Climax	37	U2	69	-	-	9	1:26.3
14	Ray Parsons	Kelly Special-Porsche	81	U2	67	-	-	23	1:30.5
15	James Flynn	Ferrari 290MM	85	O2	64	1	100	32	1:48.8
16	Uwe Buehl	Porsche 718 RS	11	U2	42	-	-	28	1:32.4
DNF	Bud Gates	Genie Mk 8-Chevrolet	16	O2	77	-	-	19	1:28.5
DNF	Ed Lowther	Genie Mk 8-Ford	17	O2	73	-	-	6	1:25.1
DNF	Don Wolf	Elva Mk 7S-Ford	25	U2	73	-	-	18	1:28.2
DNF	Bill Wuesthoff	Elva Mk 7S-Porsche	77	U2	65	-	-	11	1:26.7
DNF	Bob Bucher	Lotus 23B-Ford	29	U2	62	-	-	15	1:27.6
DNF	John Dennis	Denmacher-Porsche	19	U2	58	-	-	21	1:29.5
DNF	Alan Friedland	Elva Mk 7-Ford	24	U2	36	-	-	22	1:30.4
DNF	Peter Goetz	Elva Mk 7S-Ford	9	U2	33	-	-	30	1:37.0
DNF	George Alderman	Elva Mk 7-Ford	23	U2	29	-	-	17	1:28.1
DNF	Doc (M.R.J.)Wyllie	Lola Mk 1-Cosworth	2	U2	27	-	-	20	1:29.0
DNF	Skip Scott	Shelby Cooper T61M-Ford	96	O2	18	-	-	3	1:24.1
DNF	Wick Williams	Lotus 23B-Ford	82	U2	16	-	-	31	1:48.7
DNF	Joe Buzzetta	Elva Mk 7S-Porsche	7	U2	9	-	-	12	1:26.9
DNF	George Wintersteen	Cooper T61-Chevrolet	12	O2	7	-	-	10	1:26.4

Fastest Qualifier:	Jim Hall	Chaparral 2A-Chevrolet	1:20.0	103.53 mph
Race Distance:	100.7 miles	87 laps of 2.3 mile course		
Race Time:	1 hr 2 min 24.66 sec			
Winner's Speed:	96.81 mph			
Victory Margin:	1 lap, 26 seconds			
Fastest Race Lap:	Jim Hall	Chaparral 2A-Chevrolet	1:22.2	100.72 mph

Don Wester in a Scuderia Tin Can Elva-Porsche. Don finished in sixth place overall and second in the under two-liter class. Photo by William Green.

GREENWOOD ROADWAY, INC.
U.S.R.R.C. RACES/JULY 18th, 19th, 1964

SOUVENIR PROGRAM
SEVENTY-FIVE CENTS

1964 Greenwood USRRC race program. Scan courtesy Don Markle.

His win at Greenwood was Ed Leslie's first race in the Shelby Cooper. Photo by John McCollister.

Greenwood USRRC Race

The next round of the series was held at the new Greenwood course at Indianola, Iowa, south of Des Moines. This was a combined race with the Drivers and Manufacturers entries racing together. Throughout the race weekend the temperature was in the high nineties.

Heading up the over two-liter drivers entries were Jim Hall and Hap Sharp in the Chaparrals. Ed Leslie was having his first ride in Shelby's Cooper-Ford. Charles Cox was driving his Cooper-Ford. Ralph Salyer was entered in a Cheetah-Chevrolet. Gary Wilson, Dick Durant and Floyd Aaskov completed the over two-liter entries.

Bill Wuesthoff, Charlie Hayes, Bob Markley, Don Wester, Joe Buzzetta and Lee Hall were all entered in Elva-Porsches in the under two-liter class. Mike Hall, Mak Kronn, Don Wolf and Ernie Harris had Elvas, with other engines. John Morton, Hank Candler, Bob Shaw and Tom Terrell all had Lotus 23's.

Cobra was the only marque in the Manufacturers over two-liter class, with Ken Miles, Hal Keck, Bob Johnson, Charlie Parsons, Dan Gerber and Tom Payne driving. The Shelby Cobra team mechanics provided the excitement of the day. They could not get the wheel alignment right on the Cobras and decided to drive them into Des Moines, to use the Ford dealer's alignment rack. They had a police escort up to the Des Moines city limits. As soon as they got inside the Des Moines city limits, they were pulled over by the Des Moines police. Somehow they talked the police into letting them deliver the cars to the Ford dealer, before getting hauled off to jail. Shelby did not think it was funny to have to go into town to bail them out. The Lotus Cortinas of Sir John Whitmore and Henry Taylor headed up the under two-liter class. They were joined by Chuck Stoddard in his Alfa Romeo TZ and John Ryan in a Porsche 904.

Jim Hall stormed to the pole position with a time of 1:57.0. Hap Sharp was next fastest, 2.4 seconds slower with a 1:59.40. Amazingly, Charlie Hayes was third fastest in his Elva-Porsche (2:01.59). Ed Leslie had the fourth fastest time (2:01.8) and shared the second row of the grid with Hayes. Bill Wuesthoff (2:02.4) and Ken Miles (2:03.0) were on the third row. Joe Buzzetta (2:03.3), Bob Markley (2:05.4), Ralph Salyer (2:06.0) and Bob Johnson (2:06.0) completed the top ten qualifiers.

During the warm-up on Sunday, Jim Hall had a wheel break that sent his Chaparral spinning into the barriers. His car was too badly damaged to race. Hap Sharp, ever the gracious teammate, stepped down and let Hall race his Chaparral that had a manual transaxle. When the starter dropped the flag Hall immediately grabbed the lead. Ed Leslie was right on Hall's tail and they were closely followed by Charlie Hayes, Ken Miles and Bob Johnson. For the first ten laps they were neck and neck. Then Hall stepped on the gas and began pulling away. Leslie ran in second place and had Charlie Hayes within worrying distance. Bill Wuesthoff worked his way up to fourth place, ahead of Miles and Johnson. John Ryan had his Porsche 904 wound up and was leading the under two-liter manufacturers class over Chuck Stoddard's Alfa GTZ and the Lotus Cortinas of Whitmore and Taylor.

Hall had a lead of fifty seconds after twenty-two laps. His engine suddenly lost oil pressure and he pulled into the pits for more oil. Leslie took the lead with Hall eleven seconds back in second place. Three laps later, Charlie Hayes ground to a halt along the turn eight guardrail. His Elva had a broken halfshaft. This put Bill Wuesthoff into third place, for a moment or two. Miles pounced on Wuesthoff and took third place.

For a few laps it looked like Hall was going to reel Leslie in. The Chaparral's engine then lost a cylinder and considerable power. Hall fell back twenty seconds in one lap. Leslie sweated through fifteen laps with a slipping clutch that somehow cured itself. Miles dropped to fifth place as his brakes disappeared. Wuesthoff retook third place and Bob Johnson was running in fourth place.

Hall stopped at the pits again for more oil and this allowed Wuesthoff into second place. Hall came out of the pits in third place with Johnson very close behind. On lap forty-seven, Johnson lost control of his Cobra and went off course doing too much damage to continue. This elevated Miles to fourth place and the Manufacturers over two-liter lead.

The race finished with Ed Leslie picking up his first overall win with 47.4 seconds in hand over Bill Wuesthoff, the under two-liter winner. Jim Hall's Chaparral limped home in third place, ahead of Miles' Cobra. Charlie Cox drove an inspired race to take fifth place. This was after having a push-start, then making a mandatory pitstop to stop and restart his engine. Right at the end of the race Mike Hall took sixth place and second in under two-liters, from Bob Markley. Gary Wilson, in a Chaparral 1 was eighth, with Tom Terrell ninth in a Lotus 23. Sir John Whitmore was tenth and first in the Manufacturers under two-liter class in his Lotus Cortina. For most of the race Whitmore ran third in class behind Jack Ryan's Porsche 904 and Chuck Stoddard's Alfa TZ. Sir John picked up the win after these two both had engine problems.

Hall increased his championship lead to twelve pointws over Charlie Hayes (39 points to 27). Dave MacDonald's 24 points kept him, posthumously, in third place. Roger Penske was fourth with 17 points.

Bill Wuesthoff was second overall and first in the under two-liter class. Photo by Larry Tomaras, courtesy John Tomaras.

Jim Hall salvaged a third place and second in the over two-liter class. Photo by Ron Miller.

Ken Miles raced to fourth place overall and first in the over two-liter GT class. Photo by Tom Schultz.

John Whitmore was first in the under two-liter GT class. Photo by John McCollister.

1964 GREENWOOD • USRRC

July 19, 1964, Greenwood Raceway, Indianola, Iowa

Place	Driver	Car/Engine	Car #	Class	Laps	Points	Prize	Qualifying Place	Qualifying Time
1	Ed Leslie	Shelby Cooper T61M-Ford	96	O2	55	9	$2,000	4	2:01.8
2	Bill Wuesthoff	Elva Mk 7S-Porsche	71	U2	55	9	1,200	5	2:02.4
3	Jim Hall	Chaparral 2A-Chevrolet	65	O2	54	6	900	1	1:57.0
4	Ken Miles	Shelby Cobra	98	GTO	53	9	1,200	6	2:03.0
5	Charlie Cox	Cooper T61M-Ford	39	O2	53	4	500	27	2:15.6
6	Mike Hall	Elva Mk 7S-Ford	69	U2	52	6	600	15	2:09.0
7	Bob Markley	Elva Mk 7S-Porsche	75	U2	52	4	450	8	2:05.4
8	Gary Wilson	Chaparral 1-Chevrolet	9	O2	51	3	200	29	2:17.0
9	Tom Terrell	Lotus 23B-Climax	55	U2	51	3	150	18	2:10.2
10	Sir John Whitmore	Lotus Cortina	15	GTU	50	9	600	22	2:14.2
11	Hal Keck	Cobra	88	GTO	50	-	350	17	2:10.2
12	Henry Taylor	Lotus Cortina	16	GTU	49	-	350	26	2:15.4
13	Lee (E. L.) Hall	Elva Mk 7S-Porsche	66	U2	49	2	50	28	2:16.8
14	Bob Shaw	Lotus 23B-Climax	84	U2	48	1	50	20	2:11.4
15	Chuck Stoddard	Alfa Romeo TZ	5	GTU	48	4	250	25	2:15.0
16	Bill Allen-Mak Kronn	Elva Mk 7S-BMW	13	U2	47	-	50	30	2:21.0
17	Joe Buzzetta	Elva Mk 7-Porsche	7	U2	45	-	50	7	2:03.3
18	John Ryan	Porsche 904GTS	68	GTU	43	3	50	31	2:22.8
19	Hank Candler	Lotus 23-Climax	41	U2	31	-	50	14	2:08.4
20	Dick Durant	Durant Special-Chevrolet	46	O2	30	2	50	23	2:14.3
DNF	Bob Johnson	Cobra	33	GTO	46	-	-	10	2:06.0
DNF	Don Wolf	Elva Mk 7S-Ford	85	U2	27	-	-	12	2:07.2
DNF	Ernie Harris	Elva Mk 7S-Ford	17	U2	26	-	-	19	2:11.2
DNF	Charlie Hayes	Elva Mk 7S-Porsche	77	U2	25	-	-	3	2:01.6
DNF	Charlie Parsons	Cobra	10	GTO	22	-	-	13	2:07.2
DNF	Dan Gerber	Cobra	19	GTO	17	-	-	24	2:14.4
DNF	Ralph Salyer	Cheetah	25	O2	8	-	-	9	2:06.0
DNF	Don Wester	Elva Mk 7S-Porsche	76	U2	2	-	-	33	2:30.8
DNF	Tom Payne	Cobra	14	GTO	2	-	-	11	2:06.6
DNF	Floyd Aaskov	Genie Mk 8-Chevrolet	3	O2	1	-	-	-	-
DNS	Hap Sharp	Chaparral 2A-Chevrolet	67	O2	-	-	-	2	1:59.4
DNS	Jerry Hansen	McKee Mk 2 (Chevette)-Chev	44	O2	-	-	-	-	-
DNS	John Morton	Lotus 23-Climax	97	U2	-	-	-	-	-

Fastest Qualifier:	Jim Hall	Chaparral 2A-Chevrolet	1:57.0	92.31 mph	
Race Distance:	165.0 miles	55 laps of 3.0 mile course			
Race Time:	1 hr 43 min 28.8 sec				
Winner's Speed:	87.24 mph				
Victory Margin:	47.4 seconds				
Fastest Race Lap:	Charlie Cox	Cooper T61M-Ford	1:56.4	92.78mph	

Chuck Stoddard took his Alfa TZ to third place in the under two-liter GT class. Photo by John McCollister.

UNITED STATES
ROAD RACING
CHAMPIONSHIPS

BENEFIT
ILLINOIS EPILEPSY LEAGUE

AUGUST 8-9, 1964

Management By
MID-AMERICA
AUTO RACING
INC.
'Meadowdale International Raceway'

MEADOWDALE

50¢

1964 Meadowdale race program cover. Scan courtesy Don Markle.

LEFT–Ken Miles leads Bob Johnson and gave the Shelby team another 1-2. Photo by Tom Schultz.

BELOW–Jerry Hansen and Tom Payne in their private Cobras finished fourth and third, respectively. Photo by Tom Schultz.

Meadowdale Manufacturers Race

There were ten entries for this race and seven of them were Cobras. Ken Miles and Bob Johnson were the Shelby team entries. Private entries consisted of Jerry Hansen, Tom Payne, John Everly, Ray Cuomo and Pat Manning. The under two-liter class included Chuck Stoddard in an Alfa Romeo TZ, plus Trevor Taylor and Dave Clark, in Team Lotus Cortinas.

Ken Miles was fastest in qualifying with a time of 2:05.2. When the race started, Miles took the lead with Johnson in second, Payne third and Hansen fourth. Miles and Johnson looked like they were racing by taking turns with the lead during the first five laps. Payne passed them both to lead the sixth lap. Jerry

Hansen then passed all three of them to lead the next five laps. After that, Miles re-took the lead and held it. Even though Johnson would pull even with Miles, he could not pull off a pass. For a while, Jerry Hansen also kept the pressure on Johnson. Near the end of the race Hansen fell back to fourth place, behind Payne. John Everly was the only retirement of the race, lasting just seventeen laps.

Trevor Taylor and Dave Clark in the Cortinas kept the crowd excited by making attempt after attempt trying to get by Stoddard. They would draw up beside him in the corners, but Stoddard was always able to power away from them coming out of the corners.

The race finished with Miles winning by a car length from Johnson. Tom Payne was third, Jerry Hansen was fourth and Ray Cuomo was fifth. Chuck Stoddard won the under two-liter class with a sixth place finish just ahead of Dave Clark. Trevor Taylor was eighth, a lap behind Stoddard and Clark. Pat Manning finished in ninth place eight laps behind the winner.

With the win at this race, the Shelby Cobra team clinched the Manufacturers championship with a maximum of 72 points. Porsche was in second place with 43 points. The Team Lotus Cortinas were third with 36 points and Alfa Romeo had 22 points, for fourth place in the championship.

1964 MEADOWDALE • USRRC MANUFACTURERS RACE

August 9, 1964, Meadowdale Raceway, Carpenterville, Illinois

Place	Driver	Car/Engine	Car #	Class	Laps	Points	Prize	Qualifying Place	Qualifying Time
1	Ken Miles	Shelby Cobra	98	GTO	37	9	$700	1	2:05.2
2	Bob Johnson	Shelby Cobra	99	GTO	37	-	400	2	2:07.8
3	Tom Payne	Cobra	13	GTO	37	-	200	3	2:10.0
4	Jerry Hansen	Cobra	44	GTO	36	-	150	-	-
5	Ray Cuomo	Cobra	14	GTO	35	-	100	-	-
6	Chuck Stoddard	Alfa Romeo TZ	5	GTU	35	9	500	-	-
7	Dave Clark	Lotus Cortina	15	GTU	35	6	400	-	-
8	Trevor Taylor	Lotus Cortina	16	GTU	34	-	300	-	-
9	Pat Manning	Cobra	45	GTO	28	-	50	-	-
DNF	John Everly	Cobra	21	GTO	17	-	-	-	-

Fastest Qualifier:	Ken Miles	Shelby Cobra	2:05.2	94.03 mph
Race Distance:	120.99 miles	37 laps of 3.27 mile course		
Race Time:	1 hr 19 min 20.76 sec			
Winner's Speed:	91.49 mph			
Victory Margin:	0.2 second			
Fastest Race Lap:	Ken Miles	Shelby Cobra	2:04.6	94.48 mph

Trevor Taylor in a Lotus Cortina leads class winner, Chuck Stoddard, in his Alfa TZ. Photo by Tom Schultz.

Ken Miles in the winning Shelby Cobra. Photo by John McCollister.

Bob Johnson finished second to Miles by a car length. Photo by John McCollister.

Chuck Stoddard in the under two-liter class winning Alfa Romeo TZ. Photo by John McCollister.

The Lotus Cortina of Dave Clark placed second in the under two-liter class. Photo by John McCollister.

Trevor Taylor in the second Team Lotus Cortina. Photo by John McCollister.

Meadowdale winner Jim Hall at speed in his Chaparral. Photo by Tom Schultz.

Meadowdale Drivers Race

The entry for the Meadowdale Drivers race had twice as many over two-liter cars as the Greenwood race. Jim Hall and Roger Penske were on hand with the Chaparrals. Ed Leslie was driving the Shelby Cooper-Ford and Gary Wilson brought his Chaparral 1. Dr. Dick Thompson was debuting Bob McKee's new Chevette (McKee Mk 1). George Wintersteen and Skip Hudson each had Cooper-Chevrolets and Roy Kumnick entered his Ford powered Cooper. Bobby Unser was entered in the Arciero Lotus 19, Don Skogmo in a Genie and a couple of Ford powered Maseratis. There were six Elva-Porsches in the under two-liter class, driven by Bill Wuesthoff, Charlie Hayes, Joe Buzzetta, Mike Hall, Bob Markley

and Ralph Treischmann. Peter Goetz was entered in an Elva-Ford. Tom Terrell, Al Unser and Mike Goth were racing in Lotus 23's. Herb Swan was entered in a Porsche RS-61 and Doc Wyllie had his Lola Mk 1.

The highlight of qualifying was the duel between Jim Hall's Chaparral and Ed Leslie in the Shelby Cooper-Ford. Augie Pabst in a Scarab had set the previous lap record at 2:04.8. Hall and Leslie swapped the lap record many times before Leslie sealed the pole position with a time of 1:58.4. Hall's time of 1:59.6 put him on the front row of the grid next to Leslie. Roger Penske started from the last row of the grid because he did not arrive until Sunday morning. Jim Hall had qualified Penske's car with the third

quickest qualifying time at 2:00.8, but it was not an allowed time for Penske. Also starting from the rear of the grid were Dick Thompson in the McKee Chevette, Skip Hudson in the Nickey Cooper-Chevrolet that had been rebuilt after the Pacific Raceways debacle and Ken Miles in the Cobra roadster he had used to win the earlier Manufacturers race.

Ed Leslie grabbed the lead when the race started while Bobby Unser got second place, Jim Hall third and George Wintersteen was fourth in his Cooper. In the under two-liter class Joe Buzzetta took the lead when Charlie Hayes had his Elva-Porsche expire on the parade lap. From the back two rows, Penske, Hudson, Thompson and Miles all

Pace lap with Ed Leslie, in a Shelby Cooper-Ford, on pole with Jim Hall sharing the front row. On the second row are Bobby Unser #69 in an Arciero Lotus 19 and George Wintersteen #12 in a Cooper-Chevrolet. Al Unser #97 in an Arciero Lotus 23 and Charlie Hayes #77 Elva-Porsche are on the third row. Bob Markley #75 Elva-Porsche and Bud Gates #28 Genie-Chevrolet are on row four. Photo by Tom Schultz.

Bobby Unser leading Jim Hall, Ed Leslie and George Wintersteen, during the early laps. Photo by Tom Schultz.

On the third lap Roger Penske had worked his way from the back of the grid to take the lead. Following are Bobby Unser, Jim Hall, Ed Leslie and George Wintersteen. Photo by John McCollister.

used the long main straight to pass at least ten cars before the first turn. Penske was in seventh place at the end of the first lap. After two laps, Penske was fourth, behind Leslie, Unser and Hall. Penske took the lead on the third lap. It took eight laps for Ed Leslie to retake the lead and for Hall to regain second place. One lap later the suspension broke on Leslie's Shelby Cooper.

Joe Buzzetta was leading the under two-liter class ahead of Bob Markley. Markley held second place until lap forty-two. His car suffered a broken suspension, went up an embankment and into retirement. Tom Terrell inherited second place upon Markley's demise, but this lasted just a few laps before his engine expired. Ralph Treischmann

was next to hold second place in the under two-liter class ahead of Herb Swan. Bill Wuesthoff qualified close to Buzzetta, but suffered a bent wheel and had to pit early to have it changed. With the wheel fixed, Bill set out to tear through the field.

After Ed Leslie had retired, Jim Hall was leading the race from Penske, Unser, Wintersteen and Dick Thompson. On lap twenty-five Bobby Unser hit the guardrail on the Monza wall and almost collected George Wintersteen on his way down the banking. George was able to avoid Unser and continued in third place. In the meantime, Thompson was edging up on Wintersteen.

The rest of the race was led by Hall, who

won by forty-three seconds from teammate, Roger Penske. Dick Thompson brought the McKee Chevette home in third place, ahead of Wintersteen and Ken Miles. Joe Buzzetta won the under two-liter class with a sixth place finish. Bill Wuesthoff passed Ralph Treischmann a couple of laps before the finish to take seventh place.

With this win, Jim Hall clinched the Drivers Championship. He had a total of 48 points. So the race was on for second place in the championship. Charlie Hayes was currently in second place with 27 points. Dave MacDonald's 24 points kept him in third place. Roger Penske moved up to fourth place with 22 points and Bill Wuesthoff was fifth with 18 points.

Ed Leslie has got past Jim Hall and is about to put a move on Bobby Unser. George Wintersteen follows in fifth place. Photo by John McCollister.

Bob Markley leading the under two-liter class, ahead of eventual winner, Joe Buzzetta. Photo by Tom Schultz.

Dick Thompson took third place in the debut race for Bob McKee's Chevette. Photo by Tom Schultz.

Ed Leslie lasted 11 laps before the suspension of his Shelby Cooper gave out. Photo by John McCollister.

George Wintersteen, in his Cooper with eyeballs, finished in fourth place. Photo by John McCollister.

1964 MEADOWDALE • USRRC DRIVERS RACE

August 9, 1964. Meadowdale Raceway, Carpenterville, Illinois

Place	Driver	Car/Engine	Car #	Class	Laps	Points	Prize
1	Jim Hall	Chaparral 2A-Chevrolet	66	O2	52	9	$1,000
2	Roger Penske	Chaparral 2A-Chevrolet	67	O2	52	6	600
3	Dick Thompson	McKee Mk 1 (Chevette)-Chev	29	O2	52	4	400
4	George Wintersteen	Cooper T61-Chevrolet	12	O2	52	3	300
5	Ken Miles	Shelby Cobra	98	O2	51	2	200
6	Joe Buzzetta	Elva Mk 7S-Porsche	7	U2	51	9	800
7	Bill Wuesthoff	Elva Mk 7S-Porsche	71	U2	49	6	600
8	Ralph Trieschmann	Elva Mk 7S-Porsche	74	U2	49	4	400
9	Herb Swan	Porsche 718 RS61	99	U2	49	3	300
10	Gary Wilson	Chaparral 1-Chevrolet	19	O2	48	1	100
11	Don Skogmo	Genie Mk 8-Ford	31	O2	47	-	-
12	Peter Goetz	Elva Mk 7S-Ford	9	U2	47	2	200
13	Tom Terrell	Lotus 23B-Climax	55	U2	46	1	100
14	Bud Gates	Apache-Chevrolet	28	O2	46	-	-
15	Tossie Alex	Jaguar XK-SS	5	O2	39	-	-
16	Doc (M.R.J.)Wyllie	Lola Mk 1-Cosworth	2	U2	37	-	-
DNF	Bob Markley	Elva Mk 7S-Porsche	75	U2	42	-	-
DNF	Lee (E.L.) Hall	Elva Mk 7S-Porsche	68	U2	26	-	-
DNF	Skip Hudson	Cooper T61-Chevrolet	8	O2	25	-	-
DNF	Hamilton Vose	Maserati T-64-Ford	4	O2	25	-	-
DNF	Bobby Unser	Lotus 19-Chevrolet	69	O2	24	-	-
DNF	Roy Kumnick	Cooper T61-Ford	41	O2	21	-	-
DNF	Scott Beckett	Maserati T-61-Ford	34	O2	14	-	-
DNF	Ed Leslie	Shelby Cooper T61M-Ford	96	O2	11	-	-
DNF	Mike Goth	Lotus 23-Alfa Romeo	1	U2	5	-	-
DNF	Al Unser	Lotus 23-Climax	97	U2	1	-	-
DNF	Bud Gates	Genie Mk 8-Chevrolet	28	O2	0	-	-
DNF	Charlie Hayes	Elva Mk 7S-Porsche	77	U2	0	-	-
DSQ	Jerry Dunbar	Jaguar D-Chevrolet	32	O2	-	-	-
DSQ	Owen Rutherford	Cooper T-49-Maserati	11	O2	-	-	-

Fastest Qualifier:	Ed Leslie	Shelby Cooper T61M-Ford	1:58.4	99.43 mph
Race Distance:	170.04 miles	52 laps of 3.27 mile course		
Race Time:	1 hr 46 min 56.68 sec			
Winner's Speed:	95.4 mph			
Victory Margin:	43.8 seconds			
Fastest Race Lap:	Ed Leslie	Shelby Cooper T61M-Ford	1:59.4	98.59 mph

Gary Wilson, in his Chaparral 1, finished tenth overall and sixth in the over two-liter class. Photo by Tom Schultz.

Roger Penske did not arrive to qualify his Chaparral. Consequently, he started from the back of the grid. Photo by Tom Schultz.

Jim and Sandy Hall coming in from a victory lap. Photo by Tom Schultz.

The pace lap with Ed Leslie, in #96 Shelby Cooper-Ford, on pole with Jim Hall sharing the front row. On the second row are Bobby Unser #69 in an Arciero Lotus 19 and George Wintersteen #12 in a Cooper-Chevrolet. Al Unser #97 in an Arciero Lotus 23 and Charlie Hayes #77 Elva-Porsche are on the third row. Bob Markley #75 Elva-Porsche and Bud Gates #28 Genie-Chevrolet are on row four. Photo by John McCollister.

Early laps with Bobby Unser ahead of Ed Leslie and Jim Hall. Photo by John McCollister.

Bobby Unser leading Jim Hall and Ed Leslie. Photo by John McCollister.

Bobby Unser, in the Arciero Lotus 19 lapping Jerry Dunbar's D-type Jaguar. Photo by John McCollister.

Roger Penske drifting #67 Chaparral through a turn, on his way to second place. Photo by John McCollister.

Ed Leslie at speed in the Shelby Cooper-Ford. Photo by Tom Schultz.

Jim Hall won the race by 43 seconds, from teammate Roger Penske. Photo by John McCollister.

Jim Hall coming into the pits after winning the race. Photo by Tom Schultz.

Meadowdale was the race debut for Bob McKee's new Chevette. Dick Thompson drove it to third place. Photo by John McCollister.

ABOVE–The Shelby mechanics working on Ed Leslie's Cooper, with Ken Miles looking on. Photo by John McCollister.

LEFT–Bent rod was found after the engine was pulled from Leslie's Cooper. Photo by John McCollister.

UNITED STATES
ROAD RACING
CHAMPIONSHIP
•
AUGUST 29 - 30, 1964
•
OFFICIAL PROGRAM
THIRTY-FIVE CENTS

88 FP

MID·OHIO SPORTS CAR COURSE LEXINGTON, O.

ACCUS · FIA · SCCA
SANCTION NO. N-14

Program cover for 1964 Mid Ohio USRRC race. Scan courtesy Don Markle.

The start of the Manufacturers race. It's all Cobras at the front. From the right: Miles #98 is on the pole, Tom Payne #13 finished in third place, Pete Harrison #87 was fourth, and Bob Johnson #99 won the race. Photo by Dave Arnold.

Miles #98 led Johnson #99 for most of the race. Photo by Dave Arnold.

Mid-Ohio Manufacturers Race

There were eleven entries for the Mid-Ohio Manufacturers race. Once again, the Cobras were the only over two-liter contenders. Ken Miles and Bob Johnson drove the Shelby cars. Tom Payne, Lew Draper, John Everly and Pete Harrison all had privately entered Cobras. The under two-liter class saw Pete Lovely and Jim Spencer in the Team Lotus Cortinas, Bill Wuesthoff in a Porsche 904, Bruce Jennings in a Porsche Carrera and Chuck Stoddard in his Alfa Romeo TZ.

Ken Miles roared away at the start. He built up a fifteen second lead over Tom Payne and Bob Johnson during the first five laps. Johnson desperately wanted to get by Payne and finally succeeded after a few laps. Miles had a lead of twenty seconds and Johnson could keep pace with him but could not reduce the gap. Payne and Dick Lang diced with each other until Lang's Corvette expired on lap thirty-five.

Miles gradually slowed down after twenty-one laps, allowing Johnson to reel him in. Johnson was able to pass Miles after thirty-three laps. Ken took the lead back on the next lap. Although they swapped places for a few laps, it appeared that Miles was just letting Johnson lead.

In the under two-liter class Bill Wuesthoff led the way right from the start. Chuck Stoddard's Alfa was following, with Bruce Jennings in a Porsche right on his tail. After thirty-three laps of running nose to tail, Jennings pulled off a pass that stuck and he kept second place in class. Behind Stoddard were the Lotus Cortinas of Pete Lovely and Jim Spencer, running fourth and fifth in class and ninth and tenth overall.

Johnson took the win with Miles second, Tom Payne third. These three all shared the fastest lap of the race at 1:51.0. Pete Harrison was fourth, also in a Cobra. Bill Wuesthoff took fifth place overall and first in the under two-liter class. Lew Draper was sixth, in a Cobra. The top ten was filled out with Bruce Jennings in a Porsche Carrera, Chuck Stoddard in an Alfa Romeo TZ, Pete Lovely and Jim Spencer, both in Lotus Cortinas.

The Cobra team had already clinched the championship with the maximum amount of points (72). Porsche enhanced their second place with a total of 52 points while Lotus was a secure third with 39 points. Alfa Romeo was fourth with 26 points and Chevrolet was fifth with 12 points.

Early in the race Pete Harrison #87 is in second place and leading Tom Payne #13, Bob Johnson #99, Dick Lang #85 Corvette,
and Lew Draper #33. Miles is off in the distance, leading the
race. Photo by John McCollister.

In the paddock,
the Porsche 904
Bill Wuesthoff
used to win the
under two-liter
class. Photo by
Dave Arnold.

1964 MID-OHIO • USRRC MANUFACTURERS RACE

August 30, 1964, Mid-Ohio Sports Car Course, Lexington, Ohio

Place	Driver	Car/Engine	Car #	Class	Laps	Points	Prize
1	Bob Johnson	Shelby Cobra	99	GTO	42	9	$600
2	Ken Miles	Shelby Cobra	98	GTO	42	-	200
3	Tom Payne	Cobra	13	GTO	42	-	100
4	Pete Harrison	Cobra	87	GTO	-	-	75
5	Bill Wuesthoff	Porsche 904GTS	17	GTU	-	9	500
6	Lew Draper	Cobra	33	GTO	-	-	50
7	Bruce Jennings	Porsche Carrera	79	GTU	-	-	200
8	Chuck Stoddard	Alfa Romeo TZ	5	GTU	-	4	100
9	Pete Lovely	Lotus Cortina	15	GTU	-	3	75
10	Jim Spencer	Lotus Cortina	16	GTU	-	-	50
11	Larry Wehr	Jaguar E-Type	-	GTO	-	1	25
12	Max Nerriere	Lotus Elite-Climax	42	GTU	-	1	25
13	Red Crim	Austin Healey 3000	11	GTO	-	-	-
DNF	Dick Lang	Chevrolet Corvette	85	GTO	-	-	-
DNF	John Everly	Cobra	21	GTO	-	-	-
DNF	John Cannon	Simca Abarth 2000	18	GTU	-	-	-

Fastest Qualifier:	Unknown		
Race Distance:	100.8 miles	42 laps of 2.4 mile course	
Race Time:	1 hr 19 min 7.86 sec		
Winner's Speed:	76.43 mph		
Victory Margin:	1 second		
Fastest Race Lap:	Bob Johnson, Ken Miles, & Tom Payne	Shelby Cobra	1:51.0	85.55 mph

Tom Payne #13 leading Pete Harrison #87, Bob Johnson #99 and Dick Lang #85. Photo by John McCollister.

The start of the race with Jerry Grant leading. Jim Hall is second and behind Grant's Lotus. Ken Miles #98 is third, Hap Sharp #67 and Charlie Hayes #77 to his left. Photo by Dave Arnold.

Jim Hall #66 leading teammate and eventual winner, Hap Sharp #67, Owen Russell in the #81 Lishin Special, and Charlie Hayes #77. Photo by Dave Arnold.

Mid-Ohio Drivers Race

Twenty-six cars started the Mid-Ohio Drivers race with ten in the over two-liter class and sixteen in under two-liters. The strong over two-liter contenders were the Chaparrals of Jim Hall and Hap Sharp, along with Jerry Grant in a Lotus 19, George Wintersteen in a Cooper-Chevrolet, Bud Gates in Genie-Chevrolet and Gary Wilson in a Chaparral 1. Again, Ken Miles raced the Cobra he used in the Manufacturers race. The under two-liter contingent was headed by the Elva-Porsches of Joe Buzzetta, Mike Hall, Charlie Hayes, Jim Johnston, Bob Markley and Bill Wuesthoff. Elva's, with other engines, were entered by Peter Goetz, Ernie Harris, Phil Seitz and Don Wolf. Doc Wyllie in his Lola and Chuck Dietrich in a Bobsy were the other main contenders.

Qualifying was a shootout between Jim Hall and Jerry Grant. Hall set the early fastest lap at 1:43.4. Jerry Grant went out near the end of the last qualifying sesssion and turned in a 1:42.8. While Grant was on the track, Jim Hall slipped into his Chaparral, fired it up and went back onto the track. He turned in a 1:42.6 to take the pole position. Grant had time for one last qualifying lap, but it wasn't as fast as his previous time. Hap Sharp had the third fastest time. He joined Hall and Grant on the first row of the grid. Next up were Charlie Hayes and Ken Miles on the second row. Chuck Dietrich, George Wintersteen and Bud Gates were on the third row.

Jerry Grant grabbed the lead when the race started. Hall and Sharp were close behind. Charlie Hayes and Chuck Dietrich had an early battle for the under two-liter lead. On lap twenty they tried to occupy the same piece of the track. That did not work. Hayes dropped to twenty-fifth position and Dietrich retired after a pitstop. Jerry Grant brought his Lotus into the pits on lap twenty-one with a lack of brakes. This gave the lead to Jim Hall, who immediately poured on the coal and began to pull away from Sharp and George Wintersteen. Ken Miles was in fourth place while Bill Wuesthoff and Joe Buzzetta battled for fifth place and the under two-liter lead.

Jim Hall built up a one-minute lead during the middle of a race, while Charlie Hayes turned in a dynamic drive and carved through the field. Hall eventually backed off his pace and let Sharp pass him, to win by a car length. George Wintersteen was the only other driver on the lead lap, in third place. Ken Miles brought his Cobra home in fourth place, ahead of under two-liter class winner, Bill Wuesthoff. Joe Buzzetta was a lap behind Wuesthoff in sixth place. Charlie Hayes was seventh overall and third in under two-liters. Bud Gates had Bob Johnson co-drive his Genie, so they got prize money, but no championship points.

1964 MID-OHIO • USRRC DRIVERS RACE

August 30, 1964, Mid-Ohio Sports Car Course, Lexington, Ohio

Place	Driver	Car/Engine	Car #	Class	Laps	Points	Prize
1	Hap Sharp	Chaparral 2A-Chevrolet	67	O2	70	9	$1,250
2	Jim Hall	Chaparral 2A-Chevrolet	66	O2	70	6	500
3	George Wintersteen	Cooper T61-Chevrolet	12	O2	70	4	200
4	Ken Miles	Shelby Cobra	98	O2	69	3	150
5	Bill Wuesthoff	Elva Mk 7S-Porsche	71	U2	69	9	1,000
6	Joe Buzzetta	Elva Mk 7S-Porsche	7	U2	68	6	500
7	Charlie Hayes	Elva Mk 7S-Porsche	77	U2	68	4	200
8	Bud Gates-Bob Johnson	Genie Mk 8-Chevrolet	28	O2	67	-	150
9	Don Wolf	Elva Mk 7S-Ford	86	U2	67	3	150
10	Doc (M.R.J.) Wyllie	Lola Mk 1-Cosworth	2	U2	67	2	150
11	Mike Hall	Elva Mk 7S-Ford	69	U2	66	1	100
12	Bob Markley	Elva Mk 7S-Porsche	75	U2	66	-	100
13	Gary Wilson	Chaparral 1-Chevrolet	39	O2	64	1	100
14	Jack Ensley	Apache-Chevrolet	29	O2	64	-	100
15	John Dennis	Denmacher-Porsche	41	U2	62	-	75
16	Jim Johnston-Slim Helson	Elva Mk 7S-Porsche	25	U2	62	-	50
17	Tom Yeager	Merlyn-Ford	44	U2	61	-	50
18	Jim Flynn	Ferrari 290MM	58	O2	56	-	75
19	Art Seyler	Jaguar C-Type	-	O2	56	-	50
20	Don Nissen	Cooper-Maserati	59	U2	51	-	-
21	Phil Seitz	Elva Mk 6-Climax	22	U2	45	-	-
DNF	Jerry Grant	Lotus 19-Chevrolet	8	O2	31	-	-
DNF	Owen Russell	Lishin Special	81	-	28	-	-
DNF	Chuck Dietrich	Bobsy Mk 2-Ford	88	U2	24	-	-
DNF	Ernie Harris	Elva Mk 7S-Ford	37	U2	6	-	-
DSQ	Peter Goetz	Elva Mk 7S-Ford	19	U2	-	-	-

Fastest Qualifier:	Jim Hall	Chaparral 2A-Chevrolet	1:42.8	84.21 mph
Race Distance:	168.0 miles	70 laps of 2.4 mile course		
Race Time:	1 hr 59 min 30.42 sec			
Winner's Speed:	80.33 mph			
Victory Margin:	1 second			
Fastest Race Lap:	Jim Hall	Chaparral 2A-Chevrolet	1:44.0	83.01 mph

Charlie Hayes #77 Elva-Porsche passing Jim Flynn #58 Ferrari 290MM. Photo by Bill Stowe.

George Wintersteen finished in third place in his Cooper-Chevrolet. Photo by Dave Arnold.

Hap Sharp taking the win, after Jim Hall had built up a one minute lead and then backed off. Photo by Dave Arnold.

Road
America 500

SEPTEMBER 12 - 13 / 1964

75¢

1964 Road America 500 USRRC program cover. Scan courtesy Don Markle.

The pace lap with Jim Hall #68 Chaparral on the pole with Bud Gates #28 Genie sharing the front row. On the second row are the #59 McKee Chevette of Dick Thompson-Dick Doane and the #26 Cheetah of Ralph Salyer and Nate Karras. The #98 Cobra of Ken Miles and Ron Bucknum and the #92 Cooper of George Wintersteen and Ed Lowther are on the third row. Photo by Mike Odell.

Road America 500

When the teams and drivers arrived at Road America, the only championship battles left were for second through tenth places. Charlie Hayes was in second place with 31 points, coming into this race and Bill Wuesthoff was third with 27 points. Roger Penske had 22 points and Hap Sharp had 21 points. Both were trying to take third place from Wuesthoff. George Wintersteen with 17 points, Ken Miles with 16 points and Joe Buzzetta with 15 all had a slim chance to take fourth place from Penske.

Even though Jim Hall had secured the USRRC title at Meadowdale, there was a very strong turnout for the Road America 500. The Chaparral team of Jim Hall, Hap Sharp and Roger Penske were down for driving a Chaparral II and a Corvette Grand Sport. The Mecom team entered the Lola Mk 6 coupe and a Ferrari 250LM, both shared by Augie Pabst and Walt Hansgen. Dick Thompson was sharing the McKee Chevette (Mk 1) with Dick Doane and Jerry Hansen was entered in a McKee Mk 2 Chevette. Bud Gates and Ed Lowther entered their Genies. Charlie Cox entered his Cooper-Ford and George Wintersteen brought his Chevrolet powered Cooper. The Causey brothers had their Lotus 19, the Wilson brothers brought their Chaparral Mk 1 and Ralph Salyer entered his Cheetah. The under two-liter contingent was strong with Elva's. There were seven Porsche powered examples entered for Bill Wuesthoff and Joe Buzzetta, Lee and Mike Hall, Johnston and Seaverns and Charlie Hayes shared cars with John Cannon, Ralph Treischmann and Bob Markley. There were also ten Elva's with Ford

or BMW engines, three Lotus 23's and two Porsches. In the Manufacturers classes the Shelby team had three Cobras for Ken Miles and Ron Bucknum, John Morton and Skip Scott and Bob Johnson and Ed Leslie. There were also three private Cobras and a Ferrari 250GT. Only four cars were entered in the Manufacturers under two-liter class. Chuck Stoddard had his Alfa Romeo TZ. The Lotus team brought Cortinas for Dave Clark, to drive solo, and for David Hobbs (making his US racing debut) and Chris Craft. Art Riley entered his Volvo P1800.

Jim Hall qualified the Chaparral on the pole with a time of 2:32.0. Bud Gates was second fastest and shared the front row with Hall. Dick Doane in the Chevette and Ralph Salyer in the Cro-Sal Cheetah were on the second row. Ken Miles, George Wintersteen, Roger Penske, Walt Hansgen, Bob Johnson and Bill Wuesthoff completed the top ten.

Jim Hall, in the Chaparral, grabbed the lead right at the start. George Wintersteen, Bud Gates and Ralph Salyer were second, third and fourth at the end of the first lap. Roger Penske, in the Corvette Grand Sport was fifth, followed by Dick Doane, Ken Miles (first in Manufacturers over two-liter class), Bob Johnson and Bill Wuesthoff (first in the under two-liter Drivers class). Augie Pabst started in twenty-fifth place, in the Mecom Lola-Chevrolet coupe and had it up to tenth place by the end of the first lap. Dave Clark led the Manufacturers under two-liter class, in his Lotus Cortina, in fortieth place.

Penske passed Salyer and Gates on the second lap, to take third place. Then Pabst got by Salyer to take fifth. Walt Hansgen brought the Mecom Ferrari into the top ten. Pabst

moved up two more places, to third, on lap three. Miles moved his Cobra up to fifth place, behind Penske and in front of Salyer and Doane. Gates fell out of the top ten and Hansgen passed Johnson to take eighth place. Doug Revson worked his Elva up to tenth place and into the under two-liter drivers lead. Ralph Salyer fell to eighth place on lap four, after getting passed by Doane, Miles and Hansgen. Augie Pabst took second place from Wintersteen on the sixth lap. The Wuesthoff/Buzzetta Elva-Porsche moved up to tenth place taking the under two-liter class lead.

Dick Doane had the Chevette up to third place, ahead of Wintersteen and Penske, on the seventh lap. On the next lap Wintersteen pitted and fell out of contention. Penske was now up to fourth place. On the ninth lap he passed Doane for third place. After ten laps Hall was still leading in the Chaparral, followed by Pabst in the Lola coupe and Penske was third in the Corvette leading Doane, Miles, Hansgen, Salyer, Johnson, Skogmo and Wuesthoff. Dave Clark was still leading the Manufacturers under two-liter class, now in thirty-first place.

Doane took third place from Penske on lap eleven. Charlie Hayes moved his Elva-Porsche ahead of Wuesthoff's similar car to take tenth place and the under two-liter Drivers lead. Bob Johnson and Ralph Salyer gave the spectators a good show by trading sixth and seventh places many times during the next ten laps. Augie Pabst had the Lola coupe back in the top ten after twenty-two laps. On the next lap he was ninth and on lap twenty-four he took eighth place from Dave Causey.

The race winning Mecom Ferrari 250LM, piloted by Walt Hansgen and Augie Pabst. This was the third Road America 500 win for both Hansgen and Pabst. Photo by Mike Odell.

The Mecom Lola coupe was a very popular entry admired by many. Augie Pabst started in 25th position and got up to eighth place before retiring with a punctured oil cooler. Photo by Mike Odell.

Pabst in the winning Mecom Lola coupe passesBill Wuesthoff, his co-winner from 1963. Photo by Tom Schultz.

Hall's Chaparral was leading Doane's Chevette, Penske's Corvette, Miles' Cobra and Hansgen's Ferrari on lap thirty. Further back were Salyer, Johnson, Pabst, Causey and Charlie Hayes. Pabst retired the Lola on the next lap, with a punctured oil cooler. This elevated Miles to third place and Hansgen to fourth. The motor in Johnson's Cobra started running rough after thirty-five laps and it lasted seven more laps before he retired it. Miles took second place from Doane on lap thirty-six and Penske had the Corvette in fifth place, followed by the Causey brother's Lotus and the class leading Elva of Wuesthoff/Buzzetta. The Cobra of Skip Scott, John Morton and Ed Leslie had finished the first lap in twenty-first place and steadily worked up to eighth after thirty-six laps. On the next lap, they passed the Elva-Porsche of Wuesthoff/Buzzetta for seventh place.

The Chaparral had a two-minute lead over Dick Doane's Chevette after forty-two laps.

In third place was Hansgen's Ferrari, followed by Penske, Miles, Causey, Skip Scott, Wuesthoff, Roy Kumnick and Ralph Salyer. Dave Clark's Lotus Cortina was leading the Manufacturers under two-liter class, now in twenty-fourth place. The Chaparral pitted on the next lap, handing the lead to Doane's Chevette, with Hansgen in third place. On lap forty-four, Hansgen brought the Ferrari into the pits and handed it over to Augie Pabst. They dropped to third place behind the Chaparral and Chevette. The Cobra of Miles and Ron Bucknum took fourth place from Penske's Corvette. The Chaparral dropped to sixth place on lap forty-nine. The Hansgen/Pabst Ferrari moved into second place with the Miles/Bucknum Cobra in third, Penske's Corvette fourth and the Causey brother's Lotus in fifth place.

Doane gave up the lead on lap fifty-one when a bolt fell out of the transaxle. This put the Hansgen/Pabst Ferrari into the lead with the Miles/Bucknum Cobra in second.

The Penske Corvette was third with the Causey's in fourth, the Chaparral in fifth and Ralph Salyer in sixth. They were chased by the Wuesthoff/Buzzetta Elva, Scott/Morton Cobra, Roy Kumnick and Ralph Spooner's Cooper and Doug Revson. Chuck Stoddard took his Alfa Romeo TZ past Clark's Cortina into twenty-first place and the Manufacturers under two-liter lead.

During the next ten laps, the Miles/Bucknum Cobra traded the lead, back and forth, with the Hansgen/Pabst Ferrari while the Scott/Morton Cobra traded places with the Wuesthoff/Buzzetta Elva. Ralph Salyer then dropped from sixth to tenth place. The Causey brothers took third place from the Chaparral and Corvette. On lap sixty-two the Chaparral and Corvette overtook the Causey Lotus. The Chaparral got by the Miles/Bucknum Cobra for second place after three more laps.

After seventy laps, the Hansgen/Pabst Ferrari was leading the Chaparral, the Miles/

Jim Hall at speed in the #68 Chaparral. Hall led the first forty-two laps before falling back with problems. Photo by John McAllister.

The McKee Chevette of Dick Thompson and Dick Doane passes the Genie of Don Skogmo. Photo by John McCollister.

Chuck Stoddard in the #5 Alfa Romeo TZ won the Manufacturers under two-liter class. Here he leads the #36 Lotus Cortina of David Hobbs and Chris Craft and the #37 Lotus Cortina of Dave Clark. Photo by Tom Schultz.

Bucknum Cobra, the Penske/Hall/Sharp Corvette, the Scott/Morton Cobra and the Elva of Wuesthoff/Buzzetta. The excitement on lap seventy-one was the Chaparral having a lengthy pitstop and returning to the track in eighth place. After eight more laps the Chaparral moved up to sixth place. Bucknum then retired the Cobra he and Miles had driven so hard. This put the Penske/Hall/Sharp Corvette into second place and the Scott/Morton Cobra in third place. The Chaparral retired to the pits after four more laps and came out again, only to complete a final, slow lap at the end of the race. The Wuesthoff/Buzzetta Elva was now in fifth place on lap eighty-three. The Scott/Morton Cobra came into the pits for Ken Miles to take over the driving on lap eigthty-four.

The Hansgen/Pabst Ferrari was leading the Penske/Hall/Sharp Corvette after ninety laps and the Causey's Lotus was in third place. The Scott/Morton/Miles Cobra

was leading the Manufacturer over two-liter class in fourth place followed by the Cooper of Kumnick/Spooner and the Elva-Porsche of Wuesthoff/Buzzetta. Dick Doane and Dick Thompson had the Chevette in seventh place, with the Elva of Mike and Lee Hall in eighth and Doug Revson's Elva-BMW in ninth. Tenth was Chuck Stoddard, leading the Manufacturers under two-liter class. On the next lap the Cooper of Kumnick/Spooner dropped to seventh place, behind Wuesthoff/Buzzetta and Doane/Thompson. On lap ninety-two Dick Doane took fifth place from Wuesthoff and Charlie Hayes took tenth place from Chuck Stoddard.

The Causey Lotus got by Penske's Corvette for second place on lap 102, but this lasted for only eight laps before the engine in the Lotus expired. Hansgen and Pabst still led the race, with fifteen laps to go. The Penske Corvette was in second place and the Scott/Morton/Miles Cobra in third. Dick Doane was in fourth place and followed by Kum-

nick/Spooner, Wuesthoff/Buzzetta, the Hall's Elva, Doug Revson, Charlie Hayes and Chuck Stoddard. On the next laps Revson retired. Miles moved the Cobra into second place, as he passed the Penske Corvette with ten laps to go to. Dick Thompson retired the Chevette, handing fourth place to Wuesthoff/Buzzetta.

The race wound down with Hansgen and Pabst bringing the Mecom Ferrari home in first place, over the Cobra that Miles drove for the last fifty-three laps. Penske/Hall/Sharp brought the Corvette Grand Sport to the finish in third place, ahead of the Wuesthoff/Buzzetta class winning Elva-Porsche. The points Bill Wuesthoff gained from this win allowed him to take second place in the championship from Charlie Hayes. Father and son, Lee and Mike Hall finished in fifth place ahead of the Kumnick/Spooner Cooper, the Elva-Porsche of Charlie Hayes and John Cannon and Chuck Stoddard's class winning Alfa Romeo TZ.

1964 ROAD AMERICA
Road America 500, September 13, 1964, Road America, Elkhart Lake, Wisconsin

Place	Driver	Car/Engine	Car #	Class	Laps	Pts	Prize	Qualifying Place
1	Augie Pabst/Walt Hansgen	Ferrari 250LM	2	O2	125	9	$ 1,500	8
2	John Morton/Skip Scott-Ken Miles	Shelby Cobra	97	GTO	124	9	1,750	13
3	Roger Penske/Hap Sharp-Jim Hall	Corvette Grand Sport	67	O2	123	6	1,000	7
4	Bill Wuesthoff/Joe Buzzetta	Elva Mk 7S-Porsche	79	U2	121	9	1,350	10
5	Lee (E.L.) Hall/Mike Hall	Elva Mk 7S-Porsche	66	U2	119	6	950	20
6	Roy Kumnick/Bob Spooner	Cooper T49-Ford	61	O2	116	4	450	11
7	John Cannon/Charlie Hayes	Elva Mk 7-Porsche	76	U2	114	4	375	12
8	Chuck Stoddard	Alfa Romeo TZ	5	GTU	111	9	450	59
9	Peter Goetz/Frank Widman	Elva Mk 7S-Ford	49	U2	111	3	150	42
10	Jerry Dunbar/Chuck Cantwell Jr.	Elva Mk 7S-BMW	16	U2	110	2	-100	33
11	Dave Clark	Lotus Cortina	37	GTU	109	6	225	47
12	Roger Donovan	Elva Mk 7	35	U2	106	1	75	54
13	George Dickinson/Sheldon Brown	Porsche 718 RS	3	U2	105	-	75	55
14	David Hobbs/Chris Craft	Lotus Cortina	36	GTU	106	-	150	53
15	Stanley Kozlowski/Don Kirby	Ol' Yaller Mk7-Chevrolet	63	O2	104	3	75	61
16	Jack Stone/Ted Rand	Elva Mk 5	38	U2	103	-	65	57
17	Bud Gates	Genie Mk 8-Chevrolet	28	O2	102	2	65	2
18	Art Riley	Volvo P1800	4	GTU	100	3	65	56
19	Robert Stelloh/Bob Lyon	Ferrari 250GT	11	GTO	99	6	65	60
20	Robert Shaw/Homer Rader	Lotus 23B-Climax	84	U2	96	-	65	29
21	Doc (M.R.J.) Wyllie	Lola Mk 1-Cosworth	22	U2	95	-	50	37
22	Ralph Trieschmann/Charlie Hayes	Elva Mk 7S-Porsche	4	U2	93	-	50	23
23	Otto Klein Jr./Don Johnson	Maserati 250S-Chevrolet	77	O2	90	1	50	46
24	Horst Kwech/Pete Helferich	Ausca Mk 2-Alfa Romeo	25	U2	90	-	50	35
25	Dick Durant/John Martin	Durant Special-Chevrolet	46	O2	89	-	50	41
26	Pete Harrison/Art Huttinger	Cobra	89	GTO	87	-	50	24
27	Jim Hall-Roger Penske/Hap Sharp	Chaparral 2A-Chevrolet	68	O2	83	-	50	1
28	Ken Miles/Ron Bucknum	Shelby Cobra	98	GTO	82	-	50	5
29	Don Wolf/Dick Talbot	Elva Mk 7S-Ford	86	U2	81	-	50	27
30	Jerry Nelson/Robert Fox	Porsche 718 RS-60	18	U2	79	-	50	39
31	O.M. MacLeran/Bob Anderson	Elva Mk 7	71	U2	79	-	-	52
32	Pat Manning/Robert Liess	Cobra	65	GTO	78	-	-	43

continued

Dick Doane in his McKee Chevette which he shared with Dick Thompson. Doane led this race for 9 laps after the Chaparral pitted. Photo by John McCollister.

The #67 Chaparral-entered Corvette Grand Sport driven by Jim Hall, Hap Sharp, and Roger Penske finished in third place. Photo by Tom Schultz.

1964 Road America, continued

DNF	Dick Doane/Dick Thompson	McKee Mk 1 (Chevette)	59	O2	118	-		-	3
DNF	Doug Revson/Lake Underwood	Elva Mk 7S-BMW	64	U2	110	-		-	14
DNF	Dave Causey-Dean Causey	Lotus 19-Ford	24	O2	109	-		-	1
DNF	John Everly	Cobra	32	GTO	96	-		-	40
DNF	James Scott-Curt Gonstead	Elva Mk 7-BMW	7	U2	81	-		-	21
DNF	Charlie Cox-Dan Fowler	Cooper T61M-Ford	39	O2	75	-		-	17
DNF	Wayne Burnett-Dudley Davis	Ferrari TR250	94	O2	70	-		-	44
DNF	Ralph Salyer-Nate Karras	Cro-Sal Special (Cheetah)	26	O2	69	-		-	4
DNF	Bob Markley-Charlie Hayes	Elva Mk 7S-Porsche	75	U2	68	-		-	26
DNF	Gary Wilson-Enus Wilson	Chaparral 1-Chevrolet	9	O2	67	-		-	18
DNF	Jack Ensley	Apache-Chevrolet	17	O2	59	-		-	16
DNF	Bob Johnson-Ed Leslie	Shelby Cobra	99	GTO	42	-		-	9
DNF	James Johnston-Bud Seaverns	Elva Mk 7S-Porsche	15	U2	40	-		-	38
DNF	Alex Ratelle-Frank Phillips	Elva Mk 6-Climax	6	U2	39	-		-	50
DNF	Augie Pabst	Lola Mk 6-Chevrolet (coupe)	1	O2	30	-		-	25
DNF	George Wintersteen-Ed Lowther	Cooper T61-Chevrolet	92	O2	30	-		-	6
DNF	Don Skogmo-Scott Becker	Genie Mk 8-Ford	31	O2	30	-		-	15
DNF	David Evans	Lotus 11	41	U2	29	-		-	51
DNF	Tom Terrell-Mak Kronn	Lotus 23B-Climax	55	U2	27	-		-	30
DNF	Robert Shufelt-Jack Brady	Lotus 11	42	U2	26	-		-	58
DNF	Owen Rutherford-Hamilton Vose	Cooper T49-Maserati	12	O2	24	-		-	34
DNF	Jack Baker	Black Jack Special (Jag-Ford)	91	O2	20	-		-	49
DNF	Edmond Cicotte	Lotus 23B	29	U2	9	-		-	31
DNF	Richard Young/Warren Shamalian	Elva Mk 7-Ford	82	U2	6	-		-	36
DNF	Jerry Hansen	McKee Mk 2 (Chevette)	44	O2	5	-		-	22
DNF	Ed Fuchs/Ray Cuomo	Bobsy Mk 2	14	U2	4	-		-	48
DNF	Walter Gray/Jerry Dunbar	Allard Gray Special	51	O2	1	-		-	62
DNS	Dan Gerber	Cobra	19	GTO	-	-		-	32
DNS	Frank Phillips-Zane Mann	Porsche 718 RS	85	U2	-	-		-	45
DNS	Ernie Erickson-Don Sesslar	Elva Mk 7-Porsche	27	U2	-	-		-	63
DNS	Sam Eller-Lloyd Barton	Porsche 718 RSK	69	U2	-	-		-	64
DNS	George Reed	Ferrari 250 TR59/60-Ford	95	O2	-	-		-	-

Fastest Qualifier:	Jim Hall	Chaparral 2A-Chevrolet	2:32.0	94.7 mph
Race Distance:	500.0 miles	125 laps of 4.0 mile course		
Race Time:	5 hr 42 min 13.86 sec			
Winner's Speed:	87.66			
Victory Margin:	1 lap, 1 min, 17.4 seconds			
Fastest Race Lap:	Jim Hall	Chaparral 2A-Chevrolet	2:32.2	94.55 mph

Augie Pabst at speed in the Mecom Lola coupe.
Photo by John McCollister.

The winning Mecom Ferrari with Walt Hansgen at the wheel. Photo by John McCollister.

The Elva-BMW of Jerry Dunbar and Chuck Cantwell was tenth overall and fifth in the under two-liter class. Photo by John McCollister.

Robert Stelloh and Bob Lyon shared this Ferrari 250 GTO. They finished nineteenth overall and second in the Manufacturers over two-liter class. Photo by John McCollister.

Ralph Salyer's Cro-Sal Special with Nate Karras driving. This was a Cheetah with top chopped. Edmund Cicotte's Lotus 23 is in the weeds. Photo by John McCollister.

The Causey brothers got their Lotus 19 up to second place late in the race, only for the engine to expire with sixteen laps left to run. Photo by Tom Schultz.

Ralph Salyer at speed in his Cro-Sal Special. Photo by Mike Odell.

Jim Hall leading George Wintersteen and Bud Gates. Photo by Tom Schultz.

1964 USRRC Drivers Championship Points

Aug=Augusta, Pens=Pensacola, River=Riverside, LagSec=LagunaSeca, PacRace=Pacific Raceways, WatGlen=Watkins Glen, Green=Greenwood, M'dale=Meadowdale, MidOh=Mid Ohio, Road Am=Road America

Place	Driver	Aug	Pens	River	LagSec	PacRace	WatGlen	Green	M'dale	MidOh	RoadAm	Total Points
1	Jim Hall	6	9	DNF	9	DNF	9	6	9	6	6	60
2	Bill Wuesthoff	-	3	-	-	-	DNF	9	6	9	9	36
3	Charlie Hayes	9	DNF	DNF	9	DNF	9	DNF	DNF	4	4	35
4	Roger Penske	-	6	-	4	-	6	-	6	-	6	28
5	Hap Sharp	6	DNF	-	-	6	-	-	-	9	6	27
6	Dave MacDonald	9	-	-	6	9	-	-	-	-	-	24
7	Joe Buzzetta	-	DNF	-	-	-	DNF	-	9	6	9	24
8	Mike Hall	-	4	-	-	-	-	6	-	1	6	17
9	George Wintersteen	4	6	-	-	-	DNF	-	3	4	DNF	17
10	Ken Miles	1	DNF	4	-	3	3	-	2	3	-	16
11	Ed Leslie	-	-	DNF	3	DNF	-	9	DNF	-	-	12
12	Don Wester	-	-	3	-	3	6	DNF	-	-	-	12
13	Jim Kennedy	-	-	6	4	-	DNF	-	-	-	-	10
14	Tony Settember	-	-	-	1	9	-	-	-	-	-	10
15	Skip Hudson	-	-	9	-	-	-	-	-	-	-	9
16	Bobby Unser	-	-	9	-	-	-	-	-	-	-	9
17	Ed Hugus	-	9	-	-	-	-	-	-	-	-	9
18	Chuck Dietrich	-	-	-	3	6	-	-	-	-	-	9
19	Augie Pabst	-	-	-	-	-	-	-	-	-	9	9
20	Walt Hansgen	-	-	-	-	-	-	-	-	-	9	9
21	Bob Markley	-	-	2	2	-	-	4	-	-	-	8
22	Lee Hall	-	-	-	-	-	-	2	-	-	6	8
23	John Cannon	-	-	-	2	-	-	-	-	-	4	6
24	Bud Gates	-	4	-	-	-	-	-	-	-	2	6
25	Frank Monise	-	-	-	6	-	-	-	-	-	-	6
26	Chuck Daigh	-	-	6	-	-	-	-	-	-	-	6
27	Peter Goetz	-	-	-	-	-	-	-	2	-	3	5
28	Gary Wilson	-	-	-	-	-	-	3	1	1	-	5
29	Tom Terrell	-	-	-	-	-	-	3	1	-	-	4
30	Rick Muther	-	-	4	-	-	-	-	-	-	-	4
31	Charles Cox	-	-	-	-	-	-	4	-	-	-	4
32	Bob Holbert	4	-	-	-	-	-	-	-	-	-	4
33	Ludwig Heimrath	-	-	-	-	-	4	-	-	-	-	4
34	John Morton	-	-	-	-	-	4	-	-	-	-	4
35	Dave Ridenour	-	-	-	-	4	-	-	-	-	-	4
36	Mike Eyerly	-	-	-	-	4	-	-	-	-	-	4
37	Roy Kumnick	-	-	-	-	-	-	-	-	-	4	4
38	Bob Spooner	-	-	-	-	-	-	-	-	-	4	4
39	Dick Thompson	-	-	-	-	-	-	-	4	-	-	4
40	Ralph Treischman	-	-	-	-	-	-	-	4	-	-	4
41	Frank Wildman	-	-	-	-	-	-	-	-	-	3	3
42	Stan Kozlowski	-	-	-	-	-	-	-	-	-	3	3
43	Don Kirby	-	-	-	-	-	-	-	-	-	3	3
44	Don Wolf	-	-	-	-	-	-	-	-	3	-	3
45	Herb Swan	-	-	-	-	-	-	-	3	-	-	3
46	Bart Martin	-	-	3	-	-	-	-	-	-	-	3
47	Jef Stevens	-	3	-	-	-	-	-	-	-	-	3
48	Harry Heuer	3	-	-	-	-	-	-	-	-	-	3
49	Millard Ripley	3	-	-	-	-	-	-	-	-	-	3
50	Tibor Imrey	-	-	-	-	-	3	-	-	-	-	3
51	Dave Dunbar	-	-	-	-	-	-	-	-	-	2	2
52	Chuck Cantwell	-	-	-	-	-	-	-	-	-	2	2
53	Doc (M.R.J.) Wyllie	-	-	-	-	-	-	-	-	2	-	2
54	Dick Durant	-	-	-	-	-	-	2	-	-	-	2
55	Dave Tatum	-	-	-	-	2	-	-	-	-	-	2
56	Bob McLean	-	-	-	-	2	-	-	-	-	-	2
57	Bill Fuller	-	2	-	-	-	-	-	-	-	-	2
58	Wick Williams	-	2	-	-	-	-	-	-	-	-	2
59	Richard Young	2	-	-	-	-	-	-	-	-	-	2
60	George Koehne	2	-	-	-	-	-	-	-	-	-	2
61	Don Hulette	-	-	2	-	-	-	-	-	-	-	2

	Driver	Aug	Pens	River	LagSec	PacRace	WatGlen	Green	M'dale	Mid-O	RdAm	Total
62	Charles Kurtz	-	-	-	-	-	2	-	-	-	-	2
63	Bob Johnson	-	-	-	-	-	2	-	-	-	-	2
64	Bob Shaw	-	-	-	-	-	-	1	-	-	-	1
65	Mike Goth	-	-	-	-	-	1	-	-	-	-	1
66	Roger Heftler	1	-	-	-	-	-	-	-	-	-	1
67	Bob Biernerth	-	1	-	-	-	-	-	-	-	-	1
68	Lothar Motschenbacher	-	-	1	-	-	-	-	-	-	-	1
69	Frank Cane	-	-	-	1	-	-	-	-	-	-	1
70	Dick Guldstrand	-	-	-	-	1	-	-	-	-	-	1
71	Jerry Bruihl	-	-	-	-	1	-	-	-	-	-	1
72	James Flynn	-	-	-	-	-	1	-	-	-	-	1
73	Otto Klein	-	-	-	-	-	-	-	-	-	1	1
74	Don Johnson	-	-	-	-	-	-	-	-	-	1	1
75	Roger Donovan	-	-	-	-	-	-	-	-	-	1	1

1964 USRRC Manufacturers Championship Points

Aug Augusta, Pens Pensacola, River Riverside, LagSec LagunaSeca, PacRace Pacific Raceways, WatGlen Watkins Glen, Green Greenwood, M'dale Meadowdale, MidOh Mid Ohio, Road Am Road America

Place	Driver	Aug	Pensa	River	LagSec	PacRace	WatGlen	Green	M'dale	Mid-O	RdAm	Best 8 Points	Total Points
1	Shelby-American (Cobra)	9	9	9	9	9	9	9	9	9	9	72	90
2	Porsche	9	-	9	9	9	4	3	-	9	-	52	52
3	Ford of England (Cortina)	-	9	1	2	4	6	9	6	3	6	45	46
4	Alfa-Romeo	-	-	-	-	-	9	4	9	4	9	35	35
5	Chevrolet (Corvette)	3	-	4	3	1	1	-	-	-	-	12	12
6	Ferrari	-	-	-	-	-	-	-	-	-	6	6	6
7	Triumph	-	6	-	-	-	-	-	-	-	-	6	6
8	Jaguar	-	-	-	2	3	-	-	-	1	-	6	6
9	Volvo	3	-	-	-	-	-	-	-	-	3	6	6
10	BMC	-	-	-	3	-	-	-	-	-	-	3	3
11	Abarth	-	-	-	-	-	2	-	-	-	-	2	2
12	Morgan	1	-	-	-	-	-	-	-	-	-	1	1
13	Ford	-	-	1	-	-	-	-	-	-	-	1	1
14	Lotus (Elite)	-	-	-	-	-	-	-	-	1	-	1	1

1964 Summary

The 1964 USRRC championships were bigger and better than the previous year. There were more races, bigger grids, more paid admissions and more prize money paid. There were ten Drivers races and eight separate Manufacturers races. The Manufacturers races at Greenwood and Road America were combined with the Drivers races.

There were 298 starters in all of the Drivers races, with 72 drivers earning championship points. Jim Hall was the only driver to compete in all ten races. Charlie Hayes started nine races and Ken Miles started eight races. Bill Wuesthoff, Bob Markley and Bud Gates each had seven race starts. Four drivers started in six races and two drivers started five races. There were ten drivers starting in four races, twelve in three races and twenty-six drivers started two races.

The series enjoyed great racing drama during the first five races with Jim Hall and Dave MacDonald dueling to tie for the championship lead with twenty-four points each. Tragically, MacDonald died in a fiery crash at the Indy 500 and Hall clinched the championship with two races left to run. Charlie Hayes was in the championship hunt until he didn't finish at Greenwood. Then Bill Wuesthoff came on strong, taking three under two-liter wins and a second in the final four races to steal second place away from Hayes.

The closest finish was Hap Sharp's one-second win, over teammate Jim Hall, at Mid-Ohio. Hall won by two seconds over Penske and Sharp at Pensacola and by twelve seconds from MacDonald at Laguna Seca. Other than those, three races were won by less than a minute and three races were won by more than a lap. The largest victory margin was two laps, or 4.5 miles, at Pacific Raceways.

The ranks of the Manufacturers championship swelled to 147 starters, compared to 68 starters in 1963. Fourteen marques scored points in 1964, which was ten more than in 1963. There were three races that had ten entries, two had eleven, while Riverside and Laguna Seca had twenty-two and twenty-four entries, respectively.

The Shelby Cobras dominated the series by winning every single race. Ken Miles stamped his authority on the over two-liter class by winning six of the eight Manufacturers races and winning his class in the two combined events. Most often the excitement in the Manufacturers races was provided by the under two-liter cars. Colin Chapman wanted more exposure for Lotus cars and thought the USRRC would be a good publicity vehicle for his Lotus Cortinas. With drivers like Jackie Stewart, Mike Spence, Sir John Whitmore and Peter Arundell, plus their spectacular wheel-lifting on corners, the Cortinas spiced up the under two-liter class. However, Porsche won the under-two liter class with a greater number of privately entered cars which took five class wins and fifty-two points to the Lotus team's two victories and forty-five points.

The victory margins of the Manufacturers races were a lot closer this year. The Meadowdale race was won by .2 seconds, while three other races were won by two seconds, or less. Three races were won by less than a minute. The race at Augusta had the largest victory margin of eighty-five seconds.

1965

Pensacola
Riverside
Laguna Seca
Bridgehampton
Watkins Glen
Pacific Raceways
Continental Divide
Mid Ohio
Road America

1965 Introduction

Nineteen sixty-five promised to be a good year for the USRRC. The Chaparrals showed their continuous development and reliability during the 1964 Fall Pro races. Jim Hall broke his arm during the Canadian GP at Mosport when his car hit a puddle and slid off the road. After that, Roger Penske subbed for Hall and took second place at Riverside, behind Parnelli Jones, but in front of Jim Clark, Ed Leslie and Bob Bondurant. Penske again used the Chaparral to win both heats at Laguna Seca over Dan Gurney, Bondurant, Ron Bucknum and Don Wester. The Chaparrals won all three races they entered at the Nassau Speedweek. To kick off 1965, before the first USRRC race at Pensacola, the Chaparral team won the 12 hours of Sebring, in dry-wet-dry conditions.

The London Racing Car Show, in January, was the debut of new sports racers from Lola, Lotus and McLaren. The new Lola was the striking T70 model, which was built to hold either a Chevrolet or Ford V8. Lotus displayed a rolling chassis of the new type 40, which was basically a strengthened type 30, or as some folks later said, "it's a Lotus 30 with ten more mistakes". The McLaren was an Elva customer version of the M1A that Bruce raced in the 1964 Fall Pro races. It was built to hold Chevrolet, Ford, or Oldsmobile engines.

The pre-season speculation centered on the Chaparral team making another bid for the championship, with cars for Jim Hall and Hap Sharp. Their main competition

was expected to come from the Mecom and Shelby teams. Guys like Joe Buzzetta, Mike Hall, Charlie Hayes, Ed Leslie, Don Wester, George Wintersteen and Bill Wuesthoff were expected to give them all a run for their money. Before the season started, the Robert Bosch Corp. (maker of spark plugs) announced they would be entering Augie Pabst in a Chaparral I, with a Chevy engine.

For 1965 the SCCA scaled the series back to 9 events. Gone were the races at Meadowdale, Augusta and Greenwood. Meadowdale would hold one more professional road race, in 1968, before closing. Augusta and Greenwood did not have enough investment or profit to continue operations. This year, the USRRC returned to Continental Divide and added a race at Bridgehampton.

The series would start in April, at Pensacola, Florida. Then it would go west to California for races at Riverside and Laguna Seca. The next two rounds would be back on the East Coast at Bridgehampton and Watkins Glen, in New York. The racers had another cross country trip to Pacific Raceways, in Washington, before the final swing east to Continental Divide Raceway, in Colorado, then on to Mid-Ohio and finishing at Road America, in Wisconsin.

This year the SCCA was combining all but two of the Manufacturers races with the Drivers races. Riverside and Laguna Seca would both hold separate races for the Manufacturers. The minimum purse for a race in 1965 was increased to $10,000, with the hope it would result in more entries.

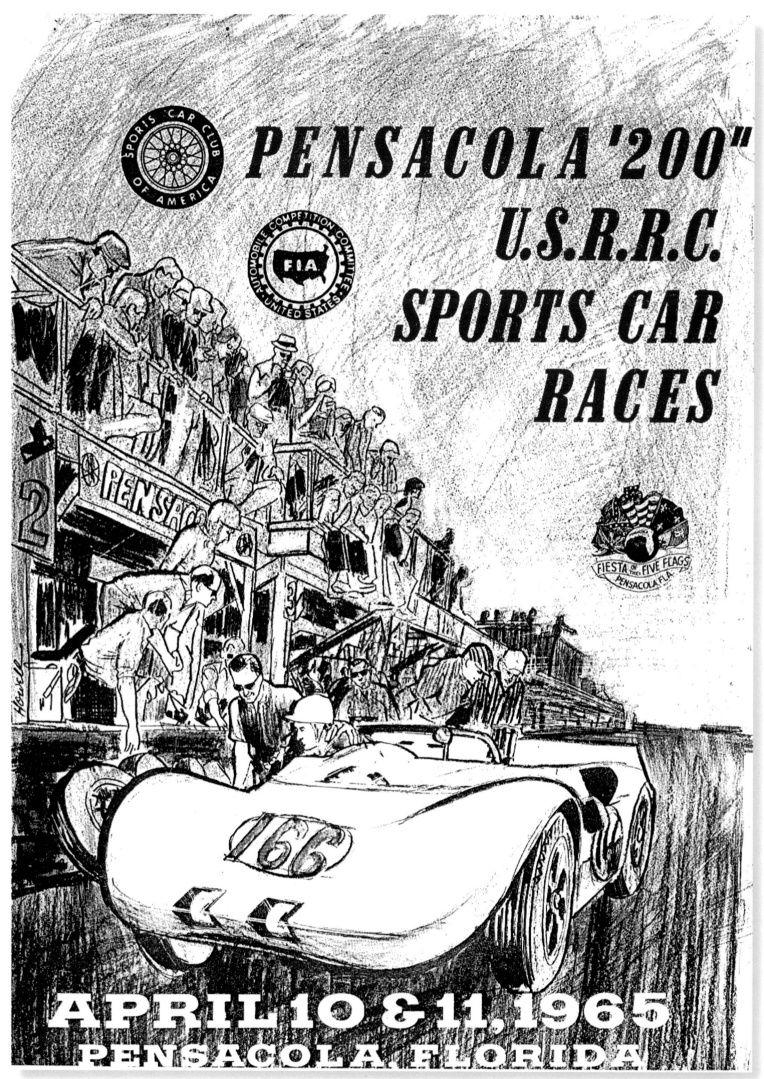

SPORTS CAR CLUB OF AMERICA

AUTOMOBILE COMPETITION COMMITTEE FOR THE UNITED STATES • FIA

PENSACOLA '200"
U.S.R.R.C.
SPORTS CAR
RACES

FIESTA OF THE FIVE FLAGS
PENSACOLA FLA.

APRIL 10 & 11, 1965
PENSACOLA FLORIDA

George Follmer was the surprise victor of the first race of the 1965 season. It was the last overall victory for an under two-liter car. Photo by Jack Brady.

Mike Hall was the second place finisher and first in the over two-liter class. Photo by Tom Schultz.

Pensacola Combined Race

The 1965 series opened at NAS Corry Field, in Pensacola, Florida with a large field of forty-plus entries. The Chaparrals of Jim Hall and Hap Sharp and the Mecom team's brand new Lola T70 for Walt Hansgen looked to be the strongest entries. Mike Hall was entered in a new McKee Mk 4 that had a 427 Ford stuffed in the engine bay. Charlie Hayes was entered in the Lang Cooper. This was basically a Cooper Monaco chassis with a Chevrolet engine and a body designed by Pete Brock (designer of the Cobra Daytona Coupe). Skip Scott ran a 427 Cobra roadster which had to compete with the sports racers as it was not homologated to run in the Manufacturers championship. Other notable over two-liter entries were Dan Gerber, in the Gerber-Payne Special (a McKee Mk 3), Charles Cox in his Cooper-Ford, Dick Doane in the McKee Mk 1 Chevette and Bud Gates in a Genie-Chevrolet.

The under two-liter drivers had a fit when they arrived. Without letting the racers know beforehand, the race promoters decided to pay only on overall results, rather than class results. The under two-liter drivers felt it was unfair that they were not told before they arrived at the course. There was a lot of talk during the driver's meeting about under two-liter cars costing almost as much to run as an over two-liter car. This prompted Jim Hall to ask, "Is there any money for over two-liters?" Only half of the crowd laughed. The under two-liter entries

had the usual East Coast contingent of variously powered Elvas driven by Bill Bowman, Joe Buzzetta, Chuck Dietrich, Roger Heftler, Mak Kronn and Herb Swan. From the West Coast, George Follmer brought his Lotus 23 with a Porsche engine. It was a reward for all the winter work his crew put in. He thought if he picked up some points and money that would be so much the better. Gerry Bruihl, from Portland, Oregon, brought his Enduro Special, a highly modified Lotus 23.

The Manufacturers over two-liter class had just four entries with two Cobras for Tom Payne and Bob Johnson, Bob Bienerth in a Corvette and Richard Macon in a Ford Mustang. The under two-liter class had eleven entries with Porsche 904's entered for George Drolsom, Peter Gregg, Charlie Kolb and Ted Tidwell. The rest was a mixture of Lotus Elans, Alfa Romeo TI's and Porsche Speedsters.

Qualifying was a straight-up fight between Jim Hall and Walt Hansgen. Walt won the pole with a time 1:45.2. Hall was second at 1:45.6 and Hap Sharp was third with a 1:46.0. The next fastest qualifier was Mike Hall, a full eight seconds slower than Sharp with a time of 1:54.0. Joe Buzzetta was fifth on the grid and the fastest under two-liter qualifier at 1:54.4. Augie Pabst hurled the front-engine Chaparral I around in 1:54.6 for the sixth fastest qualifying time and George Follmer was next up with a 1:56.0.

Charlie Hayes was qualifying the Lang Cooper when he had a suspension failure

that sent him spinning though the pits, almost mowing down two officials. Later, Don Skogmo also had a suspension failure, slid past the pits and did knock down a race official, giving him minor injuries. Skogmo was out of the race and it was thought that Hayes would also be out. However, Hayes' crew worked through the night to rebuild the car and had it ready to take the start.

The Chaparrals had been consistently out-dragged at the start of races the previous year. So it was a real surprise when Hall got off the line before Hansgen and assumed the lead right from the start. Hansgen was second with Hap Sharp right up his tailpipes. They were followed by Joe Buzzetta, Bob Johnson and George Follmer. Hansgen was close to Hall for the first six laps. Then Hansgen had gearbox problems and pitted. His crew gave him third and fourth gears to use and sent him back into the race.

Charlie Hayes had started from the back of the grid, due to not having a qualifying time. On the first lap he motored up to twelfth place and then he started having handling problems because the rear tires rubbed on the bodywork. Hayes pitted and had the wheelwells cut away to give the tires room to bounce. However, anytime the car hit a bump it would get sideways. Hayes retired after thirteen laps, rather than risk further damage to his car. At the same time, Hansgen had to retire the new Lola from second place with no clutch. Bob Johnson dropped from fourth place when he had to

Walt Hansgen won the pole position in John Mecom's brand new Lola T70. However, his car was plagued with transmission problems and he retired early. Photo from the collections of The Henry Ford.

Jim Hall looked to be running away with the race when electrical problems bit his Chaparral. Hall did repair work on the course and brought his car home in fifteenth place and sixth in the over two-liter class. Photo by Ron Miller.

pit to have an ignition wire replaced.

After fourteen laps, Hall had lapped everyone except his teammate, who was thirty-three seconds behind.

By lap thirty Follmer got his Lotus close enough to hassle Buzzetta for third place. For the next five laps they had a real ding-dong tussle that left Follmer with a dented fender, but possession of third place. Buzzetta retired on the next lap with a broken clutch. At about the same time, Hap Sharp retired his Chaparral with suspected transmission problems. This left Jim Hall with a two-lap lead over George Follmer, who had about thirty seconds on Mike Hall's 427-powered McKee.

Hall's lead lasted four more laps when the Chaparral suffered an electrical failure and died out on the circuit. Hall set about diagnosing the problem. It took him ten minutes to run to the pits for parts, fix the ignition and get back into the race. Follmer was now leading the race with Mike Hall about thirty seconds behind. Skip Scott was third in the 427 Cobra, Chuck Dietrich was fourth and Augie Pabst was fifth. Bob John-

son had been leading the Manufacturers over two-liter class since the start, but now his Cobra was making funny noises and he started slowing down. Tom Payne, in another Cobra, took the lead. Charlie Kolb, in a Porsche 904, was leading the Manufacturers under two-liter section by over a minute from Ted Tidwell, in another 904.

George Follmer finished the race in first place. Mike Hall tried to catch Follmer, but figured he would break his car trying. So he backed off, finished a safe second place and collected 9 points for the over two-liter class win. Chuck Dietrich took third place from Skip Scott when the 427 Cobra started sputtering. Augie Pabst was fifth. Tom Payne was sixth, and first in the Manufacturers over two-liter class. Charlie Kolb was in eighth place overall and won the Manufacturers under two-liter class. Jim Hall did get the Chaparral repaired and back in the race. He spent the last twenty laps going faster than in qualifying and set a new course record at 1:45.0. He finished in fifteenth place overall and got 1 point for being sixth in class.

1965 P ensacola • Combined Race • Pensacola 200

April 11, 1965, NAS Corry Field, Pensacola, Florida

Place	Driver	Car/Engine	Car #	Class	Laps	Driver Points	Mfr Points	Prize
1	George Follmer	Lotus 23-Porsche	16	U2	67	9	-	$ 2,500
2	Mike Hall	LMD McKee Mk 4-Ford	4	O2	67	9	-	1,700
3	Chuck Dietrich	Elva Mk 7-BMW	57	U2	66	6	-	1,200
4	Skip Scott	Cobra 427	91	O2	66	6	-	1,000
5	Augie Pabst	Chaparral 1-Chevrolet	7	O2	66	4	-	600
6	Tom Payne	Cobra	96	GTO	65	-	9	800
7	Dan Gerber	Gerber-Payne Special (McKee Mk 3)	19	O2	65	3	-	
8	Charlie Kolb	Porsche 904GTS	1	GTU	64	-	9	500
9	Ted Tidwell	Porsche 904GTS	51	GTU	64	-	-	250
10	Gerry Bruihl	Lotus 23-Climax	41	U2	63	4	-	200
11	Bill Bowman	Elva Mk 7S-Porsche	78	U2	63	3	-	50
12	Jerry Crawford	Lotus 30	73	O2	62	2	-	50
13	Bob Johnson	Cobra	98	GTO	62	-	-	50
14	George Drolsom	Porsche 904GTS	34	GTU	61	-	-	50
15	Jim Hall	Chaparral 2A-Chev	66	O2	61	1	-	50
16	Norm Evenden	Cooper T61-Chev	55	O2	60	-	-	50
17	Gene Parsons	Lotus Elan	47	GTU	59	-	3	50
18	Lance Pruyn	Lotus Elan	15	GTU	58	-	-	50
19	Monty Winkler	Alfa-Romeo TI	27	GTU	58	-	1	50
20	Roger West	MG-B	48	GTU	57	-	-	50
21	Richard Macon	Ford Mustang	14	GTO	54	-	4	50
22	Marty Gifford	Porsche 356 S90	45	GTU	53	-	-	50
23	Horst Kwech	Alfa-Romeo TI	26	GTU	52	-	-	50
24	Spurgeon May	Porsche 356 Speedster	5	GTU	50	-	-	50
25	Charles Cox	Cooper T61M-Ford	39	O2	39	-	-	50
DNF	Dick Doane	McKee Mk 1 (Chevette)-Chevrolet	29	O2	58	-	-	-
DNF	Ken Leith	Lotus 23B-Ford	77	U2	52	-	-	-
DNF	Dave Reilly	Lotus 23B-Ford	43	U2	49	-	-	-
DNF	Bob Bienerth	Chevrolet Corvette	10	GTO	33	-	-	-
DNF	Bud Gates	Genie Mk 8-Chevrolet	28	O2	36	-	-	-
DNF	Joe Buzzetta	Elva Mk 7S-Porsche	17	U2	36	-	-	-
DNF	Hap Sharp	Chaparral 2A-Chevrolet	65	O2	35	-	-	-
DNF	Mak Kronn	Elva Mk 7S-BMW	71	U2	17	-	-	-
DNF	Roger Heftler	Elva Mk 7S-BMW	93	U2	14	-	-	-
DNF	Charlie Hayes	Lang Cooper T61M-Chevrolet	97	O2	12	-	-	-
DNF	Walt Hansgen	Lola T70-Chevrolet	11	O2	12	-	-	-
DNF	Peter Gregg	Porsche 904GTS	-	GTU	12	-	-	-
DNF	John Norris	Lotus 23B	72	U2	7	-	-	-
DNF	Charles Slade	Porsche 718 RS60	44	U2	2	-	-	-
DNF	Herb Swan	Elva Mk 7-BMW	89	U2	1	-	-	-

Fastest Qualifier:	Walt Hansgen	Lola T70-Chevrolet	1:45.2	102.66 mph
Race Distance:	201 miles	67 laps of 3.0 mile course		
Race Time:	2 hr 10 min	58.98 sec		
Winner's Speed:	92.073 mph			
Victory Margin:	35 Seconds			
Fastest Race Lap:	Jim Hall	Chaparral 2A-Chevrolet	1:45.0	102.85 mph

Chuck Dietrich was third overall one lap behind Follmer and Mike Hall. Photo by Dave Arnold.

MAY 1&2 1965

UNITED STATES
ROAD RACING
CHAMPIONSHIP
RIVERSIDE INTERNATIONAL RACEWAY
CONDUCTED BY—California Sports Car Club Region of SCCA

1965 Riverside USRRC race program. Scan courtesy Don Markle.

Riverside Manufacturers Race

Riverside had a field of twenty-one cars that took the starters flag for the Manufacturers race. Of the seven over two-liter cars, three were Cobras driven by Ken Miles, Bob Johnson and Ed Leslie. Dick Guldstrand and Neben Evol challenged them in Corvettes. The other over two-liter starters were Pete Cordts in a Ford Falcon and Carl Cardey in an Austin Healey. Porsche 904's dominated the under two-liter class with six cars entered for Scooter Patrick, Dave Jordan, Jim Adams, Briggs Cunningham, Kurt Neumann and Bill Neal. Joe Ward and Terry Hall entered their Lotus Elans while Tony Hegbourne and Jackie Stewart piloted the Team Lotus Cortinas. There were also the two Alfa Romeos of Lloyd Berghagen and Frank Smith.

In qualifying, Ed Leslie took his privately entered Cobra around in 1:36.5—a surprising 1.5 seconds quicker than Ken Miles managed. Scooter Patrick equaled Miles' time of 1:38.0, in the Precision Motors Porsche 904.

Dave Jordan headed up row two in Otto Zipper's 904 at 1:39.2. Next to Jordan was Dick Guldstrand's Corvette (1:40.0). Bob Johnson (1:40.3), Kurt Neumann (1:40.8) and Jim Adams (1:41.1) occupied the third row of the grid. The Lotus Cortinas of Jackie Stewart (1:50.3) and Tony Hegbourne (1:50.5) started from the seventh row.

Ed Leslie shot off the grid with Miles and Patrick right on his tail. Miles passed Leslie for the lead on the backstretch. Charlie Gates hit some oil on the fourth lap at turn nine and spun his Triumph. When the leaders came through on the next lap, Miles hit the oil, spun and dropped to third place. This handed the lead to Ed Leslie's Cobra, but Scooter Patrick quickly passed him. Miles recovered from his spin and it took a couple of laps for him to re-take the lead. Miles spun again at a different corner and worked his way back into the lead again, which he then kept to the finish.

Bob Johnson worked his way up to fourth place and began to challenge Ed Leslie for third. Johnson got third place when Leslie retired his Cobra with a shredded a tire. Dave Jordan ran a steady race to take fourth place. Dick Guldstrand spent the first fifteen laps in fifth place, then he spun and dropped down to tenth place. By the end of the race, Guldstrand had worked his way back into fifth place. Jim Adams was sixth in another Porsche 904. The Lotus Elan drivers, Joe Ward and Terry Hall, spent most of the race passing each other, often multiple times per lap. At the end of the race, Ward had pulled out eight seconds, for seventh place, ahead of Hall. The Lotus Cortinas put on a great show for the crowd. Stewart and Hegbourne were lifting wheels and trading places until Stewart stopped at the pits, which put him one lap behind Hegbourne at the finish.

Cobra and Porsche came away from Riverside tied for first place with 18 points each. Ford was third with 7 points and Lotus had 6 points for fourth place.

1965 Riverside • Manufacturers Race • USRRC

May 2, 1965, Riverside International Raceway, Riverside, California

Place	Driver	Car/Engine	Car #	Class	Laps	Points	Prize	Qualifying Place	Qualifying Time
1	Ken Miles	Shelby Cobra	98	GTO	48	9	$ 700	2	1:38.0
2	Scooter Patrick	Porsche 904GTS	33	GTU	48	9	500	3	1:38.0
3	Bob Johnson	Shelby Cobra	97	GTO	48	-	300	6	1:40.3
4	Dave Jordan	Porsche 904GTS	34	GTU	48	-	300	4	1:39.2
5	Dick Guldstrand	Chevrolet Corvette	56	GTO	47	4	150	5	1:40.0
6	Jim Adams	Porsche 904GTS	55	GTU	47	-	150	8	1:41.1
7	Joe Ward	Lotus Elan	14	GTU	45	3	100	10	1:44.3
8	Terry Hall	Lotus Elan	1	GTU	45	-	50	11	1:45.1
9	Briggs Cunningham	Porsche 904GTS	31	GTU	45	-	-	12	1:45.2
10	Pete Cordts	Ford Falcon	17	GTO	44	3	100	16	1:47.9
11	Neben Evol	Chevrolet Corvette	-	GTO	44	-	50	14	1:46.3
12	Tony Hegbourne	Lotus Cortina	6	GTU	42	-	-	18	1:50.5
13	Lloyd Berghagen	Alfa Romeo TI	8	GTU	42	-	-	20	1:53.9
14	Frank Smith	Alfa Romeo TI	-	GTU	42	-	-	-	-
15	Jackie Stewart	Lotus Cortina	7	GTU	41	-	-	17	1:50.5
16	Carl Cardey	Austin Healey 3000	-	GTO	41	1	-	19	1:52.7
DNF	Phil Halbert	AC Bristol	71	GTU	42	-	-	21	2:10.1
DNF	Kurt Neumann	Porsche 904GTS	32	GTU	20	-	-	7	1:40.8
DNF	Ed Leslie	Shelby Cobra	2	GTO	18	-	-	1	1:36.5
DNF	Bill Neal	Porsche 904GTS	35	GTU	10	-	-	9	1:43.6
DNF	Charlie Gates	Triumph TR4	4	GTU	3	-	-	15	1:47.7
DNS	Doug Hooper	Chevrolet Corvette	3	GTO	-	-	-	13	1:45.5

Fastest Qualifier:	Ed Leslie	Shelby Cobra		1:36.5	96.995 mph
Race Distance:	124.8 miles	48 laps of 2.6 mile course			
Race Time:	1 hr 20 min 0.0 sec				
Winner's Speed:	93.60 mph				
Victory Margin:	28 seconds				
Fastest Race Lap:	Unknown				

Ken Miles #98 leading Scooter Patrick #33. Miles won, after spinning twice. Patrick put the Porsche into the lead, for a few laps, after Miles spun and he passed Ed Leslie. Photo from the collection of The Henry Ford.

Dick Guldstrand #56 about to be passed by Dave Jordan #34. Jordan finished in fourth place and Guldstrand, a lap down, in fifth. Photo from the collection of The Henry Ford.

The Lotus Elans of Terry Hall #1 and Joe Ward #14 put on a good show, passing and repassing each other for the whole race. Ward finished in seventh place and Hall in eighth. Photo from the collection of The Henry Ford.

Jim Hall #66 leading Walt Hansgen #12, in the Mecom Scarab, and Hap Sharp #65, early in the race. Hall and Sharp finished first and second, respectively, and Hansgen retired with a broken suspension after twenty-seven laps. Photo from the collection of The Henry Ford

Riverside Drivers Race

There were twenty-seven starters for the Drivers Race. Making their second USRRC starts for 1965 were Jim Hall and Hap Sharp with their Chaparrals, Walt Hansgen in the Mecom Lola, Charlie Hayes in the Lang Cooper, plus George Follmer and Gerry Bruihl in the under two-liter class. Other drivers in the over two-liter class were Ken Miles and Lothar Motschenbacher in 427 Cobras, Jack Weimer and Robs Lamplough in Coopers, Paul Reinhart and Don Wester driving Genies, Bob Challman and Charlie Parsons in Lotus 30's, Bob Montana in his McKee-Plymouth and Andre Gessner in his Front Runner Special.

Contesting the under two-liter section with Bruihl and Follmer were Bud Morley and Ralph Wood in Elvas, plus Tony Settember, Jim Paul, Frank Monise and Bill Molle in Lotus 23's. Jerry Titus in the Webster Special, Miles Gupton in his Platypus, Joe Ward and Terry Hall in Lotus Elans and Rudy Bartling in a Porsche RS61 were the other entries.

Hap Sharp led the way in qualifying with a pole-winning time of 1:28.0. This broke Dan Gurney's track record of 1:29.3. Jim Hall was second on the grid with a 1:28.2 and Walt Hansgen had the third quickest time of 1:29.3. Fourth and fifth fastest quali-

fiers were Don Wester (1:29.8) and Charlie Hayes (1:31.6). John Cannon had the sixth fastest time (1:34.7) in the Mecom rear-engine Scarab. George Follmer was seventh and the fastest under two-liter qualifier, with a time of 1:36.0. Ken Miles (1:36.3), Jerry Titus (1:36.7) and Paul Reinhart (1:37.2) completed the top ten qualifiers.

During the Sunday morning warm-up session, the Mecom mechanics discovered that Hansgen's Lola had developed a crack in the engine. The Lola would not race, so Hansgen took the Scarab that his teammate, John Cannon, had qualified. Walt started from sixth spot, which moved Don Wester onto the front row of the grid. When the race started, Don Wester surprisingly got the drop on the Chaparrals. However, by the end of the first lap, Charlie Hayes was leading Walt Hansgen, Jim Hall, Don Wester and Hap Sharp. Wester passed both Hall and Hansgen on the next lap to take second place. Hall passed Hansgen for third place on the third lap. After three more laps, Hall took second place from Wester and on the next lap he took the lead from Hayes.

Charlie Hayes, Don Wester and Hap Sharp were dueling for second place while Walt Hansgen was in fifth and falling further behind. Charlie Hayes suffered a broken

suspension on the fourteenth lap that sent his Cooper flying off the track at the second turn. Hayes just missed taking Don Wester off course with him. The order now was Jim Hall in first place, Hap Sharp in second, Don Wester third, Walt Hansgen fourth and Jerry Titus was in fifth place and leading the under two-liter class.

Titus maintained the under two-liter lead until lap twenty when his engine went sour. This moved George Follmer into fifth place and into the under two-liter class lead. Fifth place turned into fourth place for Follmer when Hansgen's Scarab broke its suspension after twenty-seven laps.

Hall led the last forty laps to win by sixteen seconds over Hap Sharp. Don Wester finished in third place, thirty-five seconds behind Sharp. George Follmer was fourth and first in the under two-liter class, four laps behind the first three finishers. Bud Morley and Gerry Bruihl were fifth and sixth.

With two races completed, George Follmer led the championship with 18 points to Jim Hall's 10. Mike Hall was third with 9 points and Gerry Bruihl was fourth with 8 points. Hap Sharp, Skip Scott and Chuck Dietrich were tied for fifth place with 6 points each.

1965 Riverside • Drivers Race

May 2, 1965, Riverside International Raceway, Riverside, California

Place	Driver	Car/Engine	Car #	Class	Laps	Points	Prize	Qualifying Place	Qualifying Time
1	Jim Hall	Chaparral 2A-Chevrolet	66	O2	70	9	$2,000	2	1:28.2
2	Hap Sharp	Chaparral 2A-Chevrolet	65	O2	70	6	1,200	1	1:28.0
3	Don Wester	Genie Mk 10-Ford	0	O2	70	4	900	4	1:29.8
4	George Follmer	Lotus 23-Porsche	16	U2	66	9	1,050	7	1:36.0
5	Bud Morley	Elva Mk 7S-BMW	61	U2	66	6	600	12	1:38.3
6	Gerry Bruihl	Lotus 23-Climax	41	U2	64	4	350	11	1:37.5
7	Miles Gupton	Platypus-Porsche	75	U2	62	3	250	15	1:39.5
8	Bob Challman	Lotus 30-Ford	2	O2	62	3	200	16	1:39.8
9	Paul Reinhart	Genie Mk 8-Chevrolet	6	O2	59	2	150	10	1:37.2
10	Tony Settember	Lotus 23-Climax	36	U2	59	2	100	13	1:39.0
11	Jim Paul	Lotus 23-Climax	-	U2	58	1	100	29	1:46.6
12	Terry Hall	Lotus Elan	19	U2	58	-	100	-	-
13	Joe Ward	Lotus Elan	14	U2	58	-	100	-	-
14	Bob Montana	McKee Mk 5-Plymouth	15	O2	57	1	100	19	1:40.6
15	Frank Monise	Lotus 23-Climax	44	U2	57	-	100	14	1:39.2
16	Andre Gessner	Front Runner Special	-	O2	57	-	100	30	1:47.2
17	Jack Weimer	Cooper T61	51	O2	57	-	100	27	1:45.7
18	Bill Molle	Lotus 23-Climax	6	U2	46	-	50	-	-
DNF	Robs Lamplough	Cooper-Chevrolet	3	O2	55	-	-	23	1:42.6
DNF	Walt Hansgen	Scarab-Chevrolet	12	O2	27	-	-	3	1:29.0
DNF	Rudy Bartling	Porsche 718 RS-61	-	U2	19	-	-	28	1:45.9
DNF	Ken Miles	Shelby Cobra	98	O2	25	-	-	8	1:36.3
DNF	Jerry Titus	Webster-Climax	7	U2	20	-	-	9	1:36.7
DNF	Lothar Motchenbacher	Cobra 427	1	O2	21	-	-	20	1:41.0
DNF	Charlie Hayes	Lang Cooper T61M-Chev	97	O2	13	-	-	5	1:31.6
DNF	Ralph Wood	Elva Mk 7S-Porsche	87	U2	9	-	-	22	1:42.3
DNF	Charlie Parsons	Lotus 30	17	O2	8	-	-	25	1:45.1

Fastest Qualifier:	Hap Sharp	Chaparral 2A-Chevrolet	1:28.0	106.363 mph
Race Distance:	182.0 miles	70 laps of 2.6 mile course		
Race Time:	1 hr 48 min 49.8 sec			
Winner's Speed:	100.34 mph			
Victory Margin:	16 seconds			
Fastest Race Lap:	Unknown			

Charlie Hayes in the Lang Cooper #97 led the first seven laps from Jim Hall #66, Don Wester #60, and Hap Sharp #65. Hayes retired after thirteen laps with a broken suspension. Photo from the collection of The Henry Ford.

Lothar Motschenbacher #1 in 427 Cobra leading Bob Challman #2 Lotus 30, Bob Montana #15 McKee-Plymouth, and Charlie Parsons #17 Lotus 40. Challman finished in eighth place and Montana in fourteenth. Parsons and Motschenbacher both retired. Photo from the collection of The Henry Ford.

One of the more interesting cars was the Front Runner Special of Andre Gessner. Photo from the collection of The Henry Ford.

1965 Laguna Seca USRRC program cover. Scan courtesy Don Markle.

Ken Miles #98 and Ed Leslie #96 lead from the start. Close behind are the Cobras of Ernie Kesling #1 and Bob Johnson #97 with the Porsche 904's of Dave Jordan #31, Kurt Neumann #34, and Scooter Patrick #32 in hot pursuit. Photo from the collections of the Henry Ford.

Laguna Seca Manufacturers Race

This was the last separate race for Manufacturers cars and there were twenty-seven starters. In the over two-liter class, there were five Cobras driven by Ken Miles, Ed Leslie, Bob Johnson, Foster Alexander and Ernie Kesling. Driving Corvettes were Dick Guldstrand, Bill Neal and Herb Caplan. Merle Brennan raced his Jaguar E-Type and Dick Carter ran a Ford Mustang. There were also a couple of Triumph TR4's, a Plymouth Valiant and an Austin Healey in the over two-liter class. The under two-liter class was dominated by Porsche with four 904's for Scooter Patrick, Dave Jordan, Kurt Neumann and Briggs Cunningham, and two Carreras. Joe Ward drove a Lotus Elan while Jackie Stewart and Tony Hegbourne handled the Team Lotus Cortinas. Gene Smith had an Alfa Romeo

TZ while Lloyd Berghagen and Frank Smith raced TI's. Bob Keyes was in an Elva Courier.

Ken Miles won the pole position with a time of 1:14.79. Ed Leslie (1:15.02), Ernie Kesling (1:15.34) and Bob Johnson (1:16.27) filled the next three places. Scooter Patrick (1:16.36) and Dave Jordan (1:18.03) were next on the grid.

When the race started, Miles scooted into the lead from Leslie. Kesling and Johnson were third and fourth, a little ways behind Leslie. Scooter Patrick led the under two-liter class in fifth place. Patrick had his Porsche right up Johnson's tailpipes for six laps, when Johnson pitted for more oil. Patrick moved up and started challenging Kesling. Patrick took third place from Kesling on the next lap. Dave Jordan moved his 904 up to hassle Kesling until lap twenty,

when Kesling spun into the haybales.

Since there was a lack of passing at the front of the race, the excitement for the spectators was the dice between Dick Guldstrand and Merle Brennan for sixth place. Guldstrand eventually got by Brennan and started pulling away. Jackie Stewart and Tony Hegbourne tried very hard to get by the Alfa TZ of Gene Smith, but just could not pull it off. This race was one week before Stewart would win his first Formula One race, at Silverstone in England.

The race ran out with Miles winning over Ed Leslie. Scooter Patrick was third and first in the under two-liter class. Dave Jordan and Kurt Neumann finished fourth and fifth. Dick Guldstrand brought his Corvette home in sixth place, a lap ahead of Merle Brennan's Jaguar.

1965 Laguna Seca • Manufacturer's Race

May 9, 1965, Laguna Seca Raceway, Monterey, California

Place	Driver	Car/Engine	Car #	Class	Laps	Points	Prize
1	Ken Miles	Shelby Cobra	98	GTO	53	9	$ 600
2	Ed Leslie	Shelby Cobra	96	GTO	53	-	400
3	Scooter Patrick	Porsche 904GTS	32	GTU	52	9	400
4	Dave Jordan	Porsche 904GTS	31	GTU	52	-	300
5	Kurt Neumann	Porsche 904GTS	34	GTU	52	-	200
6	Dick Guldstrand	Chevrolet Corvette	56	GTO	51	4	250
7	Merle Brennan	Jaguar E-Type	61	GTO	50	3	150
8	Herb Kaplan	Chevrolet Corvette 396	8	GTO	50	-	100
9	Dick Carter	Ford Mustang	27	GTO	48	2	-
10	Briggs Cunningham	Porsche 904GTS	3	GTU	48	-	100
11	Joe Ward	Lotus Elan	41	GTU	48	2	-
12	Gene Smith	Alfa Romeo TZ	71	GTU	47	1	-
13	Jackie Stewart	Lotus Cortina	33	GTU	47	-	-
14	Tony Hegbourne	Lotus-Cortina	22	GTU	47	-	-
15	Foster Alexander	Cobra	47	GTO	47	-	-
16	Bob Johnson	Shelby Cobra	97	GTO	46	-	-
17	Frank Smith	Alfa Romeo Spider	9	GTU	46	-	-
18	Lloyd Berghagen	Alfa Romeo TI	25	GTU	46	-	-
19	Bob Keyes	Elva Courier	24	GTU	45	-	-
20	Bill Martin	Triumph TR4	83	GTO	45	-	-
21	Wayne Schmad	Plymouth Valiant	73	GTO	44	-	-
22	Rolf Soltau	Porsche 356 Carrera	7	GTU	44	-	-
23	Dick Smith	Porsche 356 Carrera	72	GTU	33	-	-
DNF	Charlie Gates	Triumph TR4A	-	GTO	32	-	-
DNF	Bill Neal	Chevrolet Corvette	35	GTO	30	-	-
DNF	Carl Cardey	Austin Healey 3000	17	GTO	21	-	-
DNF	Ernie Kesling	Cobra	1	GTO	20	-	-

Fastest Qualifier:	Ken Miles	Shelby Cobra	1:14.79	91.46 mph
Race Distance:	101.76 miles	53 laps of 1.9 mile course		
Race Time:	1hr 8min 59.7sec			
Winner's Speed:	88.494 mph			
Victory Margin:	2 seconds			
Fastest Race Lap:	Ken Miles	Shelby Cobra	1:16.24	89.72 mph

ABOVE–Corvette stalwart Dick Guldstrand #56 had an early dice with Merle Brennan's Jaguar XKE before pulling away to finish in sixth place and fourth in the over two-liter class. Photo from the collections of the Henry Ford.

RIGHT– Ken Miles #98 and Ed Leslie #96 just drove away from the rest of the field to take first and second places, respectively. Photo from the collections of the Henry Ford.

Scooter Patrick #32 brought his Otto Zipper Porsche 904 home in third place overall and first in the under two-liter class. Photo from the collections of the Henry Ford.

Jackie Stewart three-wheels his Lotus Cortina around a corner. Laguna Seca was not a Cortina-friendly circuit. Stewart finished the race in thirteenth place and seventh in the under two-liter class. Photo from the collections of the Henry Ford.

Jim Hall #66 leads away from Don Wester #60, Walt Hansgen #11, Dave Ridenour #14 and Charlie Hayes #97. Following are Jerry Titus in the Webster Special #76 leading Miles Gupton's Platypus #75, and a line of Lotus 23's: Gerry Bruihl #41, George Follmer #16, and Tony Settember #86. Photo from the collections of the Henry Ford.

Laguna Seca Drivers Race

The field for the Laguna Seca Drivers race was split, almost evenly, with twelve over two-liter cars and thirteen under two-liter runners. Jim Hall in the solo Chaparral and Walt Hansgen in the Mecom Lola were the leading over two-liter contenders. Charlie Hayes had the Lang Cooper and Robs Lamplough ran his Cooper. Paul Reinhart, Dave Ridenour and Don Wester all had Genies, but each with a different engine (Chevrolet, Mercury and Ford, respectively). Other runners were Lothar Motschenbacher in a 427 Cobra, Stan Peterson in a Lotus, Jim Williams in a Huffaker, Jerry Entin in a Cheetah and Bob Erickson in a Lister-Chevrolet. George Follmer and Gerry Bruihl were the under two-liter leading racers. They were challenged by Jerry Titus, in the Webster Special, Ed Marshall and Tony Settember in Lotus 23's and Mike Watson, Bud Morley, Ralph Wood and Ready Davis in Elvas. Other under two-liter runners included Miles Gupton, Harry Banta, Tom Tobin and Nade Bourgeault.

Jim Hall got the pole position with a qualifying lap time of 1:09.81. Don Wester qualified second fastest and Walt Hansgen got third place on the grid with a 1:10.52.

Jim Hall led away from the start with Don Wester and Walt Hansgen close behind. On lap five, Hansgen passed Wester and closed up on Hall. Walt tried every move in the book to get by Hall during the next ten laps, but the Chaparral was just too fast. Hansgen's engine lost the fan belt and he retired after fifteen laps. Don Wester regained second place and Charlie Hayes had the ill-handling Lang Cooper in third place.

Jerry Titus initially lead the under two-liter class, but his car had problems. He pitted at the end of the second lap and retired after six. George Follmer took over the under two-liter lead for a few laps and then Gerry Bruihl sailed by Follmer into the class lead. Bud Morley in his Elva-BMW moved up to worry Follmer. Their battle moved them closer to Bruihl, but he put in some hot laps to maintain a nice cushion over them.

After twenty-seven laps, Jim Hall had lapped third place, Charlie Hayes. Wester was still in second place. Dave Ridenour and Paul Reinhart were having quite a battle for fourth place. Ridenour maintained the upperhand with Reinhart looking for any opportunity to get by.

On lap thirty-seven Morley got by Follmer, but almost immediately had to pit with problems that dropped him way back. Even Follmer had to pit late in the race and finished second in class to Bruihl, but still four laps ahead of third in class, Ed Marshall.

Hayes took his Cooper to the pits after fifty laps, to have the steering fixed. He got back into the race, but was well down. Hall lapped Wester on lap sixty. Wester was two laps ahead of the Reinhart/Ridenour battle. Gerry Bruihl was fifth and still leading the under two-liter class. George Follmer was sixth and Lothar Motschenbacher had his 427 Cobra in seventh place.

During the last few laps, Reinhart was able to get by Ridenour for third place. A slower car balked Reinhart on the last corner of the last lap and Ridenour was able to retake third place. The race ran out with Hall winning by a lap over Wester, who in turn, was a lap ahead of Ridenour and Reinhart. Gerry Bruihl won the under two-liter class with a fifth place finish, a lap ahead of George Follmer.

With three races completed, George Follmer was still leading the championship with 24 points to second place Jim Hall's 19 points. Gerry Bruihl moved into third place with 17 points, while Don Wester was fourth with 10 points and Mike Hall was fifth with nine points. Sixth place was a four-way tie between Hap Sharp, Skip Scott, Chuck Dietrich and Bud Morley, who each had 6 points.

Jim Hall, wheeling his Chaparral through a corner, had competition for just the first nine laps, then drove on to win. Photo from the collections of the Henry Ford.

George Follmer #16 is on his way to finishing in sixth place overall and second in the under two-liter class. Following Follmer is Jim Williams in the front-engine Huffaker Special. Photo from the collections of the Henry Ford.

Don Wester #60 was second, a lap behind Hall. Behind Wester, and still waving to him, is Ready Davis in an Elva Mk 5. Photo from the collections of the Henry Ford.

1965 Laguna Seca • Drivers Race

May 9, 1965, Laguna Seca Raceway, Monterey, California

Place	Driver	Car/Engine	Car #	Class	Laps	Points	Prize
1	Jim Hall	Chaparral 2A-Chevrolet	66	O2	79	9	$ 1,500
2	Don Wester	Genie Mk 10-Ford	60	O2	78	6	1,200
3	Dave Ridenour	Genie Mk 8-Mercury	14	O2	75	4	1,000
4	Paul Reinhart	Genie Mk 8-Chevrolet	6	O2	75	3	800
5	Gerry Bruihl	Lotus 23-Climax	41	U2	74	9	700
6	George Follmer	Lotus 23-Porsche	26	U2	73	6	600
7	Lothar Motchenbacher	Cobra-Ford 427	1	O2	71	2	500
8	Charlie Hayes	Lang Cooper T61M-Chev	97	O2	70	1	400
9	Ed Marshall	Lotus 23B-Climax	99	U2	69	4	300
10	Tony Settember	Lotus 23B-Climax	36	U2	68	3	200
11	Tom Tobin	Genie Mk 5-Alfa	69	U2	67	2	100
12	Nade Bourgeault	Borgeault Special	88	U2	64	1	100
13	Bob Erickson	Lister-Chevrolet	68	O2	62	-	-
14	Mike Watson	Elva-Climax	104	U2	62	-	-
15	Bud Morley	Elva Mk 7S-BMW	16	U2	55	-	-
DNF	Jim Williams	Huffaker	5	O2	47	-	-
DNF	Robs Lamplough	Cooper-Chevrolet	4	O2	34	-	-
DNF	Ralph Wood	Elva Mk 7S-Porsche	87	U2	25	-	-
DNF	Stan Peterson	Lotus 19-Buick	37	O2	22	-	-
DNF	Miles Gupton	Platypus-Porsche	75	U2	18	-	-
DNF	Ready Davis	Elva Mk 5	34	U2	17	-	-
DNF	Walt Hansgen	Lola T70-Chevrolet	11	O2	16	-	-
DNF	Harry Banta	Genie Mk 5-Climax	7	U2	8	-	-
DNF	Jerry Entin	Cheetah	77	O2	7	-	-
DNF	Jerry Titus	Webster-Climax	76	U2	6	-	-

Fastest Qualifier:	Jim Hall	Chaparral 2A-Chevrolet	1:09.19	98.386 mph
Race Distance:	101.76 miles	53 laps of 1.9 mile course		
Race Time:	1 hr 8 min 59.7 sec			
Winner's Speed:	94.622 mph			
Victory Margin:	1 lap, 15 seconds			
Fastest Race Lap:	Jim Hall	Chaparral 2A-Chevrolet	1:10.05	97.65 mph

Walt Hansgen in the Mecom Lola T70 ran right on Jim Hall's tail for the first nine laps, before a fan belt broke and toasted the engine. Photo from the collections of the Henry Ford.

Charlie Hayes qualified well in the Lang Cooper #97, but a revised front suspension was not to his liking. Hayes finished the race in eighth place and sixth in the over two-liter class. Tom Tobin in a Genie Mk 5 #69 is behind Hayes. Tobin finished in eleventh place and fifth in the under two-liter class. Photo from the collections of the Henry Ford.

THE BRIDGEHAMPTON RACE CIRCUIT

Presents

The Vanderbilt

1904   *1965*

Cup Race

OFFICIAL SOUVENIR PROGRAM

Jim Hall easily won the Bridgehampton race. All weekend long Hall was shadowed by a reporter and photographer for "Newsweek" magazine. Photo by Tom Schultz.

Joe Buzzetta #3 overtaking George Follmer early in the race. Buzzetta retired after forty-one laps and left Follmer to win the under two-liter class. Photo by Tom Schultz.

Bridgehampton

After the Riverside and Laguna Seca races, the series moved back across the country to the Brideghampton circuit on Long Island. The Chaparral team of Jim Hall and Hap Sharp was present. Joining the fun were Mike Hall in the LMD McKee-Ford, George Wintersteen and Charlie Cox in Coopers, Skip Scott in a 427 Cobra roadster, Dan Gerber in the Gerber-Payne Special (McKee Mk 3), Bob Grossman in a Ferrari 330P, Bill Wonder and Bob Brown in Genies, Gerry Georgi in a Lotus 30 and Augie Pabst in an old Chaparral I. George Follmer made the cross-country trip for championship points and was challenged by Elva drivers Joe Buzzetta, Chuck Dietrich, Bruce Jennings, Mak Kronn, and Doc Wyllie, plus Mike Goth in a Lotus 23, Lew Kerr in a Brabham and Walt Mann in a Porsche.

Naturally, Cobra was the car of choice for the Manufacturers over two-liter class, with Bob Johnson, Tom Payne and Ray Cuomo doing the driving. Bob Bienerth in a Corvette and Walt Luftman in a Ferrari GTO, added a bit of flavor to the over two-liter class. Peter Gregg and George Drolsom in a couple of Porsche 904's were the under two-liter favorites. Pete Pulver, Fred Ashplant and Russ McGrotty were driving Lotus Elans. Harry Theodorocopolus in an Alfa Romeo TZ, Art Riley in a Volvo P1800 and Horst Kwech in an Alfa Romeo TI were the other under two-liter Manufacturers competitors.

Qualifying was dominated by the Chaparrals. Hap Sharp broke the lap record by three seconds with a time of 1:40.3. Jim Hall was second at 1:40.4. George Wintersteen was third on the grid, almost six seconds back,

with a time 1:46.1. Charlie Hayes had the fourth fastest time, at 1:46.5, while Augie Pabst pedaled the old Chaparral around in 1:46.8. Bob Johnson was sixth on the grid and the first Manufacturer qualifier at 1:47.0.

The drivers voted to have a flying start. Hap Sharp stalled his Chaparral on the parade lap, but caught up with the pace car before the end of the lap and was able to take the starters flag. The cars came around with their engines roaring and flew across the starting line. Jim Hall wasted no time and immediately took the lead, while George Wintersteen moved ahead of Sharp. Hall pulled out a five-second lead over Wintersteen by the end of the first lap. Bob Johnson was fourth; Augie Pabst, fifth; Mike Hall sixth and George Follmer, seventh.

Over the next few laps there was a general shuffling of the order. Sharp passed Wintersteen for second place. Augie Pabst wound up the engine in the old Chaparral 1, threw the car around the course and took fifth place from Johnson. Skip Scott moved his 427 Cobra roadster up to sixth place and Gerry Georgi had his Lotus 30 in seventh place. Bob Johnson was leading the Manufacturer over two-liter class in eighth place and he had George Follmer and Joe Buzzetta right on his tail.

Positions at the front of the field stayed the same for the next twenty laps. Buzzetta got by Follmer and Johnson to take over sixth place. Jim Hall was leading Sharp by twenty-six seconds. In turn, Sharp had a twenty-second lead over Wintersteen, who

had Mike Hall and Augie Pabst snapping at his heels. Skip Scott and Gerry Georgi were driving lonely races in sixth and seventh places, with no other competitors in sight of them. Augie Pabst retired after thirty-three laps with transmission trouble. After forty-one laps, the engine in Joe Buzzetta's Elva blew up and Bob Johnson stopped at the pits for more fuel. Gerry Georgi retired his Lotus 30 by stuffing it in a sandbank, elevating George Follmer to sixth place and the under two-liter class lead. Bob Johnson came out of the pits in tenth place behind Tom Payne and Dan Gerber and made quick work of passing both of them.

The race ran out without any more changes in the top ten. Jim Hall won by seventy-six seconds from Hap Sharp. Mike Hall was two laps down in third place. George Wintersteen was another lap back in fourth place and Skip Scott took fifth place, a lap behind Wintersteen. George Follmer was sixth overall and won the under two-liter class from seventh place, Chuck Dietrich. Bob Johnson won the Manufacturers over two-liter class with an eighth place finish. George Drolsom, in a Porsche 904, won the Manufacturers under two-liter class in thirteenth place.

With Jim Hall and George Follmer both winning their classes, the championship battle continued in Follmer's favor 33 points to 29 points. Gerry Bruihl's 17 points kept him in third place. Mike Hall moved up to fourth place with 17 points. Hap Sharp and Chuck Dietrich both moved into a tie for fifth place with 12 points each. Then came Don Wester with 10 points, Skip Scott with 8 and Bud Morley with 6 points.

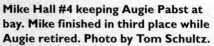

Mike Hall #4 keeping Augie Pabst at bay. Mike finished in third place while Augie retired. Photo by Tom Schultz.

Second place Hap Sharp in his Chaparral. Photo by Tom Schultz.

George Wintersteen took his Cooper to fourth place. Photo by Tom Schultz.

Skip Scott #91 passing Doc Wyllie #21. Scott's ride was a 427 Cobra that he drove to fifth place. Wyllie was driving an Elva Mk 8-BMW and retired after sixty laps. Photo by Tom Schultz.

Bob Johnson #33 Cobra won the Manufacturers class with an eighth overall finish. Here he is leading Augie Pabst. Photo by Tom Schultz.

1965 Bridgehampton • Combined Race • Vanderbilt Cup Race
May 23, 1965, Bridgehampton Race Circuit, Long Island, New York

Place	Driver	Car/Engine	Car #	Class	Laps	Driver Points	Mfg Points	Prize
1	Jim Hall	Chaparral 2A-Chevrolet	66	O2	75	9	-	$2,000
2	Hap Sharp	Chaparral 2A-Chevrolet	65	O2	75	6	-	1,600
3	Mike Hall	LMD McKee Mk 4-Ford	4	O2	73	4	-	900
4	George Wintersteen	Cooper Monaco T61-Chev	2	O2	72	3	-	700
5	Skip Scott	Cobra-Ford 427	91	O2	71	2	-	500
6	George Follmer	Lotus 23-Porsche	16	U2	71	9	-	800
7	Chuck Dietrich	Elva Mk 8-BMW	57	U2	70	6	-	500
8	Bob Johnson	Cobra	33	GTO	70	-	9	600
9	Dan Gerber	McKee Mk 3-Ford	19	O2	68	1	-	50
10	Tom Payne	Cobra	13	GTO	68	-	-	350
11	Ray Cuomo	Cobra	50	GTO	67	-	-	250
12	Walter Mann	Porsche 718 RS-61	81	U2	67	4	-	250
13	George Drolsom	Porsche 904GTS	34	GTU	66	-	9	55
14	Mak Kronn	Elva Mk 7S-BMW	79	U2	66	3	-	50
15	Pete Pulver	Lotus Elan	59	GTU	65	-	6	350
16	Mike Goth	Lotus 23-Climax	1	U2	65	2	-	50
17	Fred Ashplant	Lotus Elan	61	GTU	65	-	-	250
18	Bob Bienerth	Chevrolet Corvette	10	GTO	60	-	3	50
19	Art Riley	Volvo P1800	49	GTU	58	-	3	50
DNF	Bruce Jennings	Elva Mk 7S-Porsche	15	U2	63	-	-	-
DNF	Doc (M.R.J.) Wyllie	Elva Mk 8-BMW	21	U2	60	-	-	-
DNF	Horst Kwech	Alfa Romeo TI	26	GTU	44	-	-	-
DNF	Garry Georgi	Lotus 30-Ford	38	O2	42	-	-	-
DNF	Lew Kerr	Brabham BT8-Climax	48	U2	42	-	-	-
DNF	Joe Buzzetta	Elva Mk 7S-Porsche	3	U2	41	-	-	-
DNF	George Ralph	Lola Mk 1-Climax	20	U2	38	-	-	-
DNF	Augie Pabst	Chaparral 1-Chevrolet	7	O2	33	-	-	-
DNF	Bob Brown	Genie Mk 10-Chevrolet	41	O2	29	-	-	-
DNF	Bill Wonder	Genie Mk 8-Ford	77	O2	25	-	-	-
DNF	Peter Gregg	Porsche 904GTS	44	GTU	25	-	-	-
DNF	Charles Cox	Cooper Monaco T61M-Ford	39	O2	19	-	-	-
DNF	Walt Luftman	Ferrari 250 GTO	47	GTO	16	-	-	-
DNF	Bob Grossman	Ferrari 330P	96	O2	11	-	-	-
DNF	Harry Theodoracopulos	Alfa Romeo TZ	45	GTU	10	-	-	-
DNF	Jody Porter	Simca-Abarth 2000 GT	17	GTU	4	-	-	-
DNF	Russ McGrotty	Lotus Elan	31	GTU	3	-	-	-
DNS	Charlie Hayes	Lang Cooper T61M-Chevrolet	97	O2	-	-	-	-
DNS	Dick Holquist	Ferrari 275LM	69	O2	-	-	-	-
DNS	Walt Hansgen	Lola T70-Chevrolet	11	O2	-	-	-	-

Fastest Qualifier:	Hap Sharp	Chaparral 2A-Chevrolet	1:40.3	101.29 mph
Race Distance:	213.75 miles	75 laps of 2.85 mile course		
Race Time:	2hr 11min 35.58sec			
Winner Speed:	97.46 mph			
Victory Margin:	1 minute, 16.8 seconds			
Fastest Lap:	Jim Hall	Chaparral 2A-Chevrolet	1:38.8	103.8 mph

Walt Mann in the #81 Porsche RS-61 is leading George Drolsom in the #34 Porsche 904 and Harry Theodorocopolous in the #45 Alfa Romeo TZ. Mann finished twelfth place overall, third in the under two-liter class. Drolsom won the under two-liter Manufacturers class, and Theodorocopolous retired after ten laps. Photo by Tom Schultz.

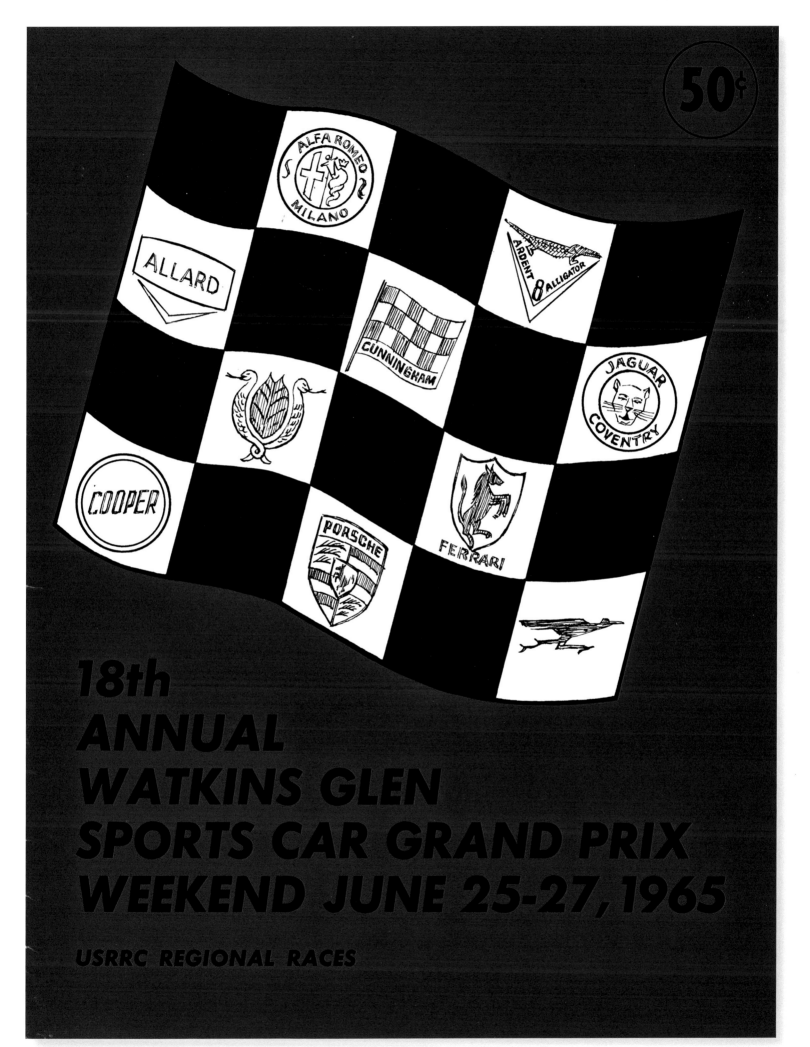

50¢

18th ANNUAL WATKINS GLEN SPORTS CAR GRAND PRIX WEEKEND JUNE 25-27, 1965

USRRC REGIONAL RACES

1965 Watkins Glen USRRC program cover. Scan courtesy Don Markle.

Watkins Glen

Fifty-five cars were entered for the Watkins Glen race. The organizers decided that all thirty grid places would be open to only the thirty fastest qualifiers. No places were held open to fill the smaller classes. The Chaparral team of Jim Hall and Hap Sharp were the favored over two-liter contenders. Challenging them were Buck Fulp and Rick Muther in Lola T70's, Don Wester and Don Skogmo in Genies, Skip Scott and Hal Keck in 427 Cobra roadsters. Other entries were George Wintersteen and Charlie Hayes in Coopers, Mike Hall in the LMD McKee, Ludwig Heimrath in a McLaren, Newton Davis in a Lotus 30, Dick Holquist in a Ferrari 275LM and Al Schall in the Carliss Special.

The leading under two-liter contenders were George Follmer, Gerry Bruihl, Mike Goth and Doug Revson in Lotus 23's, George Ralph, Mak Kronn, Joe Buzzetta, Chuck Dietrich, Bruce Jennings and Dick Brown in Elva's and Lew Kerr in a Brabham BT8.

The Chaparrals qualified on the front row of the grid. Hall set a new track record with a time of 1:16.5 while Sharp turned in a 1:17.2. Don Wester and Rick Muther occupied the second row, both with a time of 1:19.2. Next up were Buck Fulp (1:21.0), Mike Hall

(1:21.1), George Wintersteen (1:21.2) and Ludwig Heimrath (1:22.7). George Follmer was the first under two-liter qualifier in ninth spot with a 1:23.3. Skip Scott filled out the top ten at 1:23.5. Bob Johnson and Tom Payne, both in Cobras, were the only over two-liter Manufacturers entries to qualify for the race. Herb Wetanson did not qualify for the race in his under two-liter Porsche 904. His time of 1:29.3 put him on the pole for the consolation race. He moved up to the USRRC race when Charlie Hayes withdrew his entry.

During the morning warm-up, the fuel tank in Hall's Chaparral developed a leak. It was patched, but with the championship so close, they decided that Jim would race Hap's car, just in case the patch didn't hold.

Tex Hopkins did his turn-around jump and waved the green flag to start the race. The Chaparrals leapt ahead with Hall in the lead. When they came around on the first lap, Don Wester was behind them in third place, followed by Rick Muther. Buck Fulp, Mike Hall, George Wintersteen, George Follmer, Skip Scott and Ludwig Heimrath completed the top ten. On the next lap, Wester fell way back and Muther took third place.

Heimrath passed Skip Scott for eighth place on the third lap. Then Wintersteen passed Mike Hall and George Follmer fell to tenth, behind Skip Scott. Wintersteen retired after five laps with an oil leak, moving Mike Hall up to fifth place. On the next lap Mike Hall retired the LMD McKee with a broken transaxle. This moved Ludwig Heimrath up to fifth place with Skip Scott in sixth and Follmer in seventh place. Bob Johnson was in eighth with Chuck Dietrich ninth and Tom Payne tenth. Dietrich passed Johnson on the tenth lap for eighth place. Payne took ninth place from Johnson on the next lap.

Heimrath took fourth place from Buck Fulp on the fourteenth lap. They both moved up a spot when Rick Muther retired with an oil leak on the next lap. The Chaparrals were way out in front with Hall leading Sharp. Heimrath held down third place with Fulp in fourth place, Scott was fifth, Follmer sixth and Dietrich, Payne, Johnson and Joe Buzzetta completed the top ten. Tom Payne got around Dietrich on the next lap, only to pit to have the fanbelt checked. Heimrath retired with a broken suspension after nineteen laps. This moved Buck Fulp up to third place, with Scott fourth, Follmer fifth and Dietrich sixth. Behind them were Bob Johnson, Joe Buzzetta,

Augie Pabst and Don Skogmo.

Spectators had to look below sixth place for any good racing during the next twenty laps. Johnson took sixth from Dietrich. Augie Pabst first took eighth place from Buzzetta, then seventh from Dietrich and finally sixth from Johnson. Buck Fulp retired on lap forty and this moved Skip Scott's 427 Cobra into third place, already a lap behind the Chaparrals. George Follmer was now in fourth place, followed by Pabst, Johnson, Don Skogmo, Dietrich, Buzzetta and Gerry Bruihl. Dietrich whizzed by Skogmo on lap forty-five, but then retired when his engine blew a head gasket.

Hall and Sharp looked like they were running in formation with fifty laps run. They were two laps ahead of Skip Scott. George Follmer was fourth, Augie Pabst fifth

and Bob Johnson sixth. They were followed by Skogmo, Buzzetta, Bruihl and George Ralph. Johnson took fifth from Pabst on lap fifty-five, only to be re-passed three laps later. The final laps wound down with Skip Scott pitting for more fuel and getting back on the track in third place. The engine in Joe Buzzetta's Elva-Porsche went off-song and Gerry Bruihl took eighth place as Joe began falling back. Gerry also got by Don Skogmo for a few laps, before giving seventh place back to him. Augie Pabst and Bob Johnson traded places a few more times before Augie took and kept fifth place.

Jim Hall won the race by one car length in front of Hap Sharp. Skip Scott was third, three laps behind the Chaparrals. George Follmer brought his Lotus-Porsche home in fourth place, a lap ahead of Augie Pabst. Bob

Johnson finished in sixth place, snapping at Augie's heels. Don Skogmo was two laps back, in seventh place. Following Don were Gerry Bruihl, Al Schall and George Ralph. Herb Wetanson finished the race in thirteenth place, winning the Manufacturers under two-liter class.

The championship battle between Follmer and Hall was still a five point difference with Follmer's 42 points to Hall's 37. Gerry Bruihl and Hap Sharp were also five points apart in third and fourth place with 23 and 18 points. Mike Hall was fifth with 13 points. Chuck Dietrich and Skip Scott were tied for sixth place with 12 points each.

In the Manufacturers championship Cobra and Porsche were still tied with 45 points each. The next closest challenger was Lotus with 14 points.

1965 Watkins Glen • Combined Race • Sports Car Grand Prix
June 27, 1965, Watkins Glen Grand Prix Course, Watkins Glen, New York

Place	Driver	Car/Engine	Car #	Class	Laps	Points	Prize	Qual Place	Qual Time
1	Jim Hall	Chaparral 2A-Chevrolet	65	O2	87	9	$2,900	1	1:16.5
2	Hap Sharp	Chaparral 2A-Chevrolet	66	O2	87	6	1,500	2	1:17.2
3	Skip Scott	Cobra-Ford 427	91	O2	84	4	1,200	10	1:23.
4	George Follmer	Lotus 23-Porsche	16	U2	84	9	1,600	9	1:23.3
5	Augie Pabst	Chaparral 1-Chevrolet	7	O2	83	3	700	20	1:25.7
6	Bob Johnson	Cobra	33	GTO	83	9	1,000	11	1:23.5
7	Don Skogmo	Genie Mk 10-Ford	35	O2	81	2	400	16	1:25.0
8	Gerry Bruihl	Lotus 23-Climax	28	U2	81	6	700	24	1:27.0
9	Al Schall	Carliss-Schall Special	71	O2	79	1	200	26	1:27.3
10	George Ralph	Elva Mk 7S-BMW	20	U2	78	4	300	28	:27.6
11	Dick Holquist	Ferrari 275LM	69	O2	78	-	100	23	1:26.7
12	Mak Kronn	Elva Mk 7S-BMW	77	U2	77	3	100	18	1:25.3
13	Herb Wetanson	Porsche 904GTS	14	GTU	76	9	500	30	1:29.3
14	Newton Davis	Lotus 30	38	O2	74	-	100	19	1:25.5
15	Mike Goth	Lotus 23-Alfa Romeo	1	U2	71	2	100	29	1:28.2
16	Joe Buzzetta	Elva Mk 7S-Porsche	3	U2	69	1	100	12	1:24.1
17	Hal Keck	Cobra-Ford 427	88	O2	66	-	100	21	1:26.0
DNF	Roger Heftler	Elva Mk 7S-BMW	83	U2	38	-	50	25	1:27.2
DNF	Doug Revson	Lotus 23-Climax	93	U2	5	-	50	13	1:24.4
DNF	Don Wester	Genie Mk 10-Ford	60	O2	9	-	50	3	1:19.2
DNF	Chuck Dietrich	Elva Mk 7S-BMW	57	U2	46	-	100	15	1:24.9
DNF	Buck Fulp	Lola T70-Chevrolet	52	O2	40	-	100	5	1:21.0
DNF	Lew Kerr	Brabham BT8-Climax	48	U2	11	-	50	14	1:24.8
DNF	Rich Brown	Elva Mk 7S-BMW	36	U2	11	-	50	22	1:26.1
DNF	Rick Muther	Lola T70-Chevrolet	24	O2	14	-	50	4	1:19.2
DNF	Ludwig Heimrath	McLaren M1A-Chevrolet	18	O2	18	-	50	8	1:22.7
DNF	Tom Payne	Cobra	13	GTO	51	-	300	17	1:25.1
DNF	George Wintersteen	Cooper T61-Chevrolet	12	O2	5	-	50	7	1:21.2
DNF	Bruce Jennings	Elva Mk 7S-Porsche	6	U2	15	-	50	27	1:27.4
DNF	Mike Hall	LMD McKee Mk 4-Ford	4	O2	6	-	50	6	1:21.1
DNS	Charlie Hayes	Lang Cooper T61M-Chevrolet	97	O2	-	-	-	5	1:19.3

Fastest Qualifier:	Jim Hall	Chaparral 2A-Chevrolet	1:16.5	108.09 mph
Race Distance:	200.1 miles	87 laps of 2.3 mile course		
Race Time:	2hr 1min 8.28sec			
Winner's Speed:	99.11 mph			
Victory Margin:	0.2 second			
Fastest Race Lap:	Hap Sharp	Chaparral 2A-Chevrolet	1:19.9	103.6 mph

Hap Sharp taking his place on the grid. Photo by William Green.

Don Skogmo #35 qualified sixteenth, steadily worked his way into the top ten, and finished in seventh place. Here he is about to be lapped by Hap Sharp. Photo by William Green.

1965 Pacific Raceways race program cover. Scan courtesy Don Markle.

UNITED STATES
ROAD RACING
CHAMPIONSHIP

JULY 31st - AUG. 1st, 1965

SOUVENIR
PROGRAM
ONE DOLLAR

Pacific Raceways

A month after the Watkins Glen race, the series reconvened on the West Coast at Pacific Raceways. The Pacific Northwest was in the midst of a heat-wave, with the temperature hovering around one hundred degrees.

There was a strong entry for this race with fourteen over two-liter sports racers and nine under two-liter starters. The Manufacturers classes had a total of seven entries (four over two-liters and three under two-liters). The top contenders were the Chaparrals of Jim Hall and Hap Sharp, plus local driver, Jerry Grant, in a Lotus 19. Also, there were five Genies driven by Pete Harrison, Charlie Parsons, Paul Reinhart, Dave Ridenour and Don Wester. This was Parsons' first drive in Randy Hilton's Genie Mk 10. Also in the over two-liter field were Rick Muther, who had the mumps, in a brand new Lola T70, Richard Macon in a McLaren-Olds, Stan Burnett in his Burnett Special, Gary Gove in a Cheetah, Bob Erickson in a Costin Lister and Wayne Schmad in a Plymouth Valiant.

George Follmer and Gerry Bruihl were the top contenders of the under two-liter brigade. Pierre Phillips and Paul Scott ran their Lotus 23's. Jerry Titus and Bud Morley in Elva's, and Ed Leslie in the Webster Special, also looked to be strong contenders.

The Manufacturers Championship was beginning to bleed entries. There were four Cobras and one Corvette in the over two-liter class and three Porsche 904's in under two-liters.

During qualifying, Hap Sharp set a new track record at 1:22.0 to take the pole position. Grant's car had a sticking throttle, but he still managed to set the second fastest time at 1:22.3. Jim Hall completed the front row of the grid with a time of 1:22.4. Don Wester (1:26.1) and Charlie Parsons (1:26.4) were on the second row and more than four seconds slower than the front row. The third row had Dave Ridenour (1:28.2), Paul Reinhart (1:29.3) and George Follmer (1:29.4). Follmer's main competition, Ed Leslie (1:30.1) and Jerry Titus (1:30.2), were on the next row. The under two-liter qualifying action was intense as Leslie and Titus traded fastest times. Right at the end of the session, Follmer went out and put in his hot lap. Surprisingly enough, a Cobra did not set the fastest Manufacturers qualifying time. Dick Guldstrand qualified his Corvette in fourteenth place, with a time of 1:30.8. Bob Johnson qualified his Cobra at 1:31.9.

Hap Sharp messed up his start and almost stalled the Chaparral's engine, dropping back to mid-field. This left Jim Hall and Jerry Grant hurtling toward turn one together. Grant nosed out Hall for the lead. Rick Muther was third and Don Wester was fourth at the end of the first lap. Charlie Parsons, Dave Ridenour and Hap Sharp filled the next three spots. George Follmer was leading Ed Leslie in the under two-liter class, while Monte Shelton lead the Manufacturers entries in a Cobra.

The Chaparral plan had been for Sharp to lead at the start and try to wear out Grant, or his car, with a fast pace. When that didn't work, Hall ran fast and close to Grant, figuring the pace was harder on Jerry's car than his. Hall took the lead from Grant after four laps. Grant's problem was still a sticking throttle. He had to stomp on the brakes to slow the car down.

Sharp moved up to third place after eight laps. Monte Shelton retired his Cobra after twelve laps, giving the Manufacturers lead to Bob Johnson. Ed Leslie took the under two-liter lead from Follmer on lap seventeen. Gerry Bruihl was third and having a bit of cockpit drama trying to put out a dashboard fire that was under a pressurized fuel line. Fortunately, Bruihl got the fire out. The front suspension on Grant's car broke, putting him out of the race after nineteen laps. That moved Hap Sharp into second place, with Don Wester in third and Rick Muther in fourth. Behind were the Genies of Dave Ridenour, Charlie Parsons and Paul Reinhart.

In the under two-liter class, Ed Leslie's Webster Special lost power. The battery was not able to supply enough power to run the electric fuel pump. Follmer retook the class lead. Then he had shift linkage problems and spun at turn six, two laps in a row. This, along with some inspired driving, allowed Jerry Titus to close up and take the class lead from Follmer.

Tom Payne took the Manufacturers over two-liter lead when Bob Johnson retired his Cobra on lap thirty-eight. Payne had local driver, Lew Florence, in another Cobra, right on his tail. The Porsche 904's of Scooter Patrick and Dave Jordan were humming along leading the Manufacturers under two-liter class. Stan Burnett had the brakes lock on his Special after forty-one laps and he hit a dirt bank and retired. Paul Reinhart dropped out with a broken wheel spindle a few laps later.

The race ran out with Jim Hall taking the win, ten seconds in front of Hap Sharp. Don Wester brought his Genie home in third place, a lap ahead of Rick Muther and Dave Ridenour. Charlie Parsons was sixth, a lap behind Ridenour. Jerry Titus was seventh place overall and first in the under two-liter class, a lap ahead of George Follmer. Tom Payne just barely beat Lew Florence for the Manufacturers over two-liter class win. Scooter Patrick won the Manufacturers under two-liter class from Dave Jordan.

With this win, Jim Hall reduced Follmer's championship lead to two points. Follmer's second in class gave him a total of 48 points to Hall's 46. Gerry Bruihl's third place in class gave him a total of 27 points. Hap Sharp had 24 points to keep him in fourth place, but closer to Bruihl. Don Wester moved up to fifth place with 14 points. The 9 points he got for winning the under two-liter class put Jerry Titus in ninth place in the championship. Jim Hall was so pleased Titus beat Follmer, he gave him a bottle of champagne.

Gary Gove #81 and George Follmer #16 spent the last part of the race dicing for eighth place. Eventually Follmer got passed Gove, who finished in ninth spot. Photo by Ron Miller.

Heading downhill toward turn 3, Monte Shelton #57 leads Bob Johnson #33, Tom Payne #13, Richard Macon #6, and Ed Leslie #76. Photo by Tom Lebo, courtesy Bill Lebo.

Ed Leslie in the Webster Special makes room for Gary Gove #81 and Richard Macon #6. Photo by Ron Miller.

Jim Hall thunders along the back-stretch. He won the race by ten seconds, from teammate Hap Sharp. Photo by Tom Lebo, courtesy Bill Lebo.

Jerry Grant #8 has passed George Follmer #16 and is lining up Gary Gove #81. Photo by Ron Miller.

Hap Sharp motors down the front straight, to take second place. Photo by Tom Lebo, courtesy Bill Lebo.

1965 Pacific Raceways • Combined Race

United States Road Racing Championship • August 1, 1965, Pacific Raceways, Kent, Washington

Place	Driver	Car/Engine	Car #	Class	Laps	Driver Points	Mfg Points	Prize	Place	Time
1	Jim Hall	Chaparral 2A-Chevrolet	66	O2	68	9	-	$2,000	3	1:22.4
2	Hap Sharp	Chaparral 2A-Chevrolet	65	O2	68	6	-	1,400	1	1:22.0
3	Don Wester	Genie Mk 10-Ford	60	O2	67	4	-	900	5	1:26.4
4	Rick Muther	Lola T70-Chevrolet	11	O2	66	3	-	700	4	1:26.1
5	Dave Ridenour	Genie Mk 8-Mercury	7	O2	66	2	-	500	7	1:28.2
6	Chuck Parsons	Genie 10-Chevrolet	70	O2	65	1	-	300	6	1:27.5
7	Jerry Titus	Elva Mk 7S-Porsche	11	U2	64	9	-	700	11	1:30.2
8	George Follmer	Lotus 23-Porsche	16	U2	63	6	-	450	9	1:29.4
9	Gary Gove	Cheetah	81	O2	63	-	-	100	15	1:31.1
10	Gerry Bruihl	Lotus 23-Climax	17	U2	62	4	-	250	17	1:32.0
11	Tom Payne	Cobra	13	GTO	62	-	9	550	22	1:33.6
12	Lew Florence	Cobra	20	GTO	62	-	-	350	20	1:33.2
13	Pierre Phillips	Lotus 23B-Ford	18	U2	62	3	-	50	18	1:32.2
14	Scooter Patrick	Porsche 904GTS	38	GTU	61	-	9	550	21	1:33.2
15	Dave Jordan	Porsche 904GTS	37	GTS	61	-	-	350	23	1:34.
16	Wade Carter	Porsche 904GTS	22	GTU	60	-	-	250	26	1:36.5
17	Ed Leslie	Webster Special-Climax	10	U2	59	2	-	50	10	1:30.1
18	Paul Scott	Lotus 23-Ferrari	63	U2	58	1	-	50	-	-
19	John Hall	Porsche 718 RSK	82	U2	55	-	-	50	24	1:35.4
20	Bud Morley	Elva Mk 7S-BMW	-	U2	48	-	-	50	19	1:32.6
21	Richard Macon	McLaren M1A-Oldsmobile	6	O2	45	-	-	50	12	1:30.2
22	Dick Guldstrand	Chevrolet Corvette	14	GTO	23	-	4	250	14	1:30.8
DNF	Paul Reinhart	Genie Mk 8-Chevrolet	-	O2	49	-	-	-	8	1:29.3
DNF	Stan Burnett	Burnett Mk 2-Chevrolet	13	O2	41	-	-	-	13	1:30.4
DNF	Bob Johnson	Cobra	33	GTO	37	-	-	-	16	1:31.9
DNF	Jerry Grant	Lotus 19-Chevrolet	8	O2	19	-	-	-	2	1:22.3
DNF	Monte Shelton	Cobra	57	GTO	11	-	-	-	-	-
DNF	Jerry Matthews	Cooper Monaco-Climax	72	U2	0	-	-	-	29	1:38.6
DNF	Pete Harrison	Genie Mk10-Ford	87	O2	-	-	-	-	25	1:35.4
DNF	Robert Erickson	Costin Lister	73	O2	-	-	-	-	28	1:38.1
DNF	Wayne Schmad	Plymouth Valiant	78	O2	-	-	-	-	30	2:09.7

Fastest Qualifier:	Jim Hall	Chaparral 2A-Chevrolet	1:22.0	98.78 mph
Race Distance:	153 miles	68 laps of 2.25 mile course		
Race Time:	1hr 42min 30.84sec			
Winner's Speed:	89.459 mph			
Victory Margin:	10 seconds			
Fastest Lap:	Jim Hall & Hap Sharp	Chaparral 2A-Chevrolet	1:23.8	96.66 mph

Lew Florence #20 with Rick Muther #11 in the Pacesetter Lola about to shoot by. Photo by Tom Lebo, courtesy Bill Lebo.

UNITED STATES
ROAD RACING
CHAMPIONSHIP

AUGUST 14TH, & 15TH, 1965

COLORADO REGION

OFFICIAL PROGRAM

25¢

SPONSORED BY CIRA INC.

CONTINENTAL DIVIDE RACEWAYS

CASTLE ROCK, COLORADO

SANCTIONED BY S.C.C.A. INC. NO. N20 INSURANCE NO. SF3 ACCUS-FIA LISTING NO. N20   PRIZE $11,400

Continental Divide race program cover. Scan courtesy Don Markle.

Jerry Grant leading Hap Sharp during the early laps. Photo by Ron Shaw.

Jerry Grant in the Pacesetter Homes Lola T70. Photo by Ron Shaw.

Continental Divide

Thirty-three cars started the race at Continental Divide Raceway. Of the twelve over two-liter sports cars the strongest entries were the Chaparrals of Jim Hall and Hap Sharp, Jerry Grant in a Lola and Lothar Motschenbacher in a Cooper. Other notable entries were Augie Pabst and Bud Gates in McLarens, Mike Hall in the LMD McKee, Don Skogmo and Pete Harrison in Genies, Charlie Cox and Roy Kumnick in Coopers and Skip Scott in a 427 Cobra. George Follmer, Jerry Titus and Gerry Bruihl were the top contenders of the under two-liter class. Ed Leslie in the Webster Special and Elva drivers, Bud Morley, Mak Kronn, Odie Fellows, Bill Bowman and Gary Stephenson were potential threats. There were three Cobras versus two Corvettes in the Manufacturers over two-liter class. Bob Johnson, Tom Payne and Dan Gerber were in the Cobras while Chuck Frederick and Jock Barker piloted the Corvettes. The Porsche 904's of Scooter Patrick and Dave Jordan were challenged by the Lotus Elans of Ray Steinhaltz and Ron Hunter, and Stan Schooley in an Alfa Romeo.

Recent flood and tornado damage forced Friday's practice to be cancelled for track repair. Practice was rescheduled to Saturday morning and qualifying to Saturday afternoon. After the morning practice session, the Chief Steward announced that qualifying would run an extra fifteen minutes, until 4:00pm.

The Chaparrals went out early and posted times three seconds quicker than Jerry Grant and six seconds faster than anyone else. Grant, however, was waiting for the final minutes of qualifying to show his real speed. At 3:45pm, Jerry stormed onto the track only to find the checkered flag waving to end the session, yet the starter waved Jerry onto the track. He stood on the gas and set a time .9 seconds faster than Sharp, at 1:55.8. Someone complained about Jerry getting a time after the finishing flag had been waved. The officials then disallowed Grant's time. Jerry filed a protest based on the announcement that qualifying would run until 4:00pm. Jerry's protest was not allowed, but an additional half-hour of qualifying was scheduled for Sunday morning.

There was still open practice time on Saturday after qualifying and the Chaparrals went out after changing gear ratios. They beat Grant's disallowed time by .4 seconds. Grant could not practice because an inspection of his car revealed a cracked rear brake disc. Phone calls were made across the country to find a disc and one was located at Dan Gurney's shop. The trouble was the shop mechanic could not release the part without Gurney's approval. Dan was out celebrating Joe Leonard's Indycar win at Milwaukee and not reachable. Someone thought to get Carroll Shelby (Gurney's AAR partner) to approve the release of the disc. Shelby gave his approval. The next problem was getting the part from Costa Mesa, California, to Castle Rock, Colorado. The LA Watts riots were in full swing and the roads between the AAR shop and the airport were all closed. In the meantime, Grant's crew reworked a front brake disc and hoped it would work.

The Chaparrals went out and set the pace right away during Sunday qualifying. Hap Sharp was the quickest with a time of 1:55.3 and Jim Hall had a 1:57.2. Grant roared onto the track with five minutes left in the session and, immediately, Sharp was on his tail. Jerry slowed down so much that Sharp was forced to pass him. Jerry let Hap get out of sight and then he stood on the gas. It worked, as Jerry turned in a 1:55.1 to get the pole position. During all this excitement Jim Hall was sitting in his car, in the pits, and fuel was added to his car. This was a definite

On the pace lap, Jerry Titus (Elva-Porsche #88), Mike Hall (McKee-Ford #4), George Follmer (Lotus 23-Porsche #16), and John Everly (Lotus 30-Ford #26). Photo by Ron Shaw.

Jim Hall drove his Chaparral to fourth place after three pitstops put him three laps down. Photo by Ron Shaw.

breach of the rules, yet no one protested.

The race began with Grant taking the lead from Sharp, Hall, Pabst, Titus and Follmer. Also near the front were Mike Hall, Lothar Motschenbacher and Skip Scott. Jim Hall looked like he had an afterburner in his Chaparral. He zoomed past Sharp and Grant on the eighth lap to take the lead and just disappeared into the distance. Grant's modified brake disc began to give him problems on the next lap and Sharp was able to get by him to take second place. About this time, Augie Pabst started a series of pitstops to cure overheating problems.

George Follmer and Jerry Titus were passing and repassing each other multiple times, lap after lap. Mak Kronn ran a steady pace to maintain third place in the under two-liter class, with Bud Morley fourth in class. Bob Johnson's Cobra controlled the Manufacturers over two-liter class, ahead of Dan Gerber

and Tom Payne. Scooter Patrick led the Manufacturers under two-liter class ahead of Dave Jordan.

Mike Hall retired his LMD McKee after twenty-one laps when the engine expired. Jim Hall came into the pits with a blown fuel pump fuse on lap twenty-seven. Hall pitted again for another fuse after a few laps, and his hopes of a win pretty much disappeared at this point. Sharp, Grant, Follmer and Titus had all gone by and Jim stopped twice more for fuses. Hall did tear up the old lap record trying to regain places.

Sharp cruised to the win by two laps over Grant. George Follmer finished third and got the under two-liter class win. Jim Hall was fourth overall, getting four points for third in class. Lothar Motschenbacher brought his Cooper home in fifth place, ahead of Skip Scott's 427 Cobra. Bob Johnson won the Manufacturers over two-liter

class by three laps over Tom Payne (twelfth) and Dan Gerber (thirteenth). Scooter Patrick finished a lap ahead of Dave Jordan to win the under two-liter Manufacturers class.

With his class win, the balance of the championship swung in Follmer's favor. He now had 57 points to Jim Hall's 50 points, with two races left. They both had scored in all the races and had five wins each. Follmer also had two second place finishes, while Hall had a third and a sixth. If either driver won their class, they would have to start dropping their lowest finish. Hap Sharp now had 33 points and took third place in the championship from Gerry Bruihl, who had 31 points. Skip Scott moved into a tie for fifth place with Don Wester, as both had 14 points. Mike Hall was seventh with 13 points, Chuck Dietrich and Mak Kronn both had 12, while Jerry Titus was tenth with 11 points.

1965 Continental Divide • Combined Race • USRRC

August 15, 1965, Continental Divide Raceway, Castle Rock, Colorado

Place	Driver	Car/Engine	Car #	Class	Laps	Driver Points	Mfg Points	Prize
1	Hap Sharp	Chaparral 2A-Chevrolet	65	O2	70	9	-	$2,000
2	Jerry Grant	Lola T70-Chevrolet	11	O2	68	6	-	1,250
3	George Follmer	Lotus 23-Porsche	16	U2	68	9	-	1,700
4	Jim Hall	Chaparral 2A-Chevrolet	66	O2	67	4	-	850
5	Lothar Motschenbacher	Cooper T61M-Ford	1	O2	66	3	-	700
6	Skip Scott	Cobra-Ford 427	91	O2	65	2	-	500
7	Bob Johnson	Cobra	33	GTO	65	-	9	900
8	Mak Kronn	Elva Mk 7S-BMW	71	U2	64	6	-	800
9	Scooter Patrick	Porsche 904GTS	38	GTU	64	-	9	500
10	Gerry Bruihl	Lotus 23-Climax	41	U2	64	4	-	400
11	Dave Jordan	Porsche 904GTS	34	GTU	63	-	-	300
12	Tom Payne	Cobra	13	GTO	62	-	-	100
13	Dan Gerber	Cobra	19	GTO	62	-	-	100
14	Roy Kumnick	Cooper T61-Ford	61	O2	62	1	-	100
15	Jerry Nelson	Porsche	18	U2	61	3	-	250
16	Roy Stenhaltz	Lotus Elan	48	GTU	60	-	4	100
17	Chuck Fredericks	Chevrolet Corvette	0	GTO	58	-	3	100
18	Jerry Titus	Elva Mk 7S-Porsche	88	U2	57	2	-	150
19	Stan Schooley	Alfa Romeo SZ	37	GTU	56	-	3	100
20	Jock Barker	Chevrolet Corvette	81	GTO	56	-	-	100
21	Odie Fellows	Elva Mk 4	12	U2	54	1	-	100
22	Del Taylor	Lotus 23-Alfa	44	U2	51	-	-	-
23	Bill Bowman	Elva Mk 7S-Porsche	77	U2	45	-	-	-
24	Gary Stephenson	Elva Mk 7S-Porsche	46	U2	40	-	-	-
DNF	Augie Pabst	McLaren M1A-Chevrolet	7	O2	54	-	-	-
DNF	Pete Harrison	Genie-Mk 10-Ford	87	O2	45	-	-	-
DNF	Bud Morley	Elva Mk 7S-BMW	67	U2	41	-	-	-
DNF	Charlie Cox	Cooper T61M-Ford	39	O2	29	-	-	-
DNF	Ron Hunter	Lotus Elan	21	GTU	22	-	-	-
DNF	Mike Hall	LMD McKee Mk 4-Ford	4	O2	21	-	-	-
DNF	Bud Gates	McLaren M1A-Chevrolet	28	O2	18	-	-	-
DNF	Don Skogmo	Genie Mk 10-Ford	31	O2	14	-	-	-
DNF	Ed Leslie	Webster Special-Climax	76	U2	6	-	-	-

Fastest Qualifier:	Jerry Grant	Lola T70-Chevrolet	1:55.1	87.58 mph
Race Distance:	196 miles	70 laps of 2.8 mile course		
Race Time:	2hr 19min 59.88sec			
Winner's Speed:	84.001 mph			
Victory Margin:	2 laps, 30 seconds			
Fastest Race Lap:	Unknown			

Lothar Motschenbacher took his Cooper-Ford (#1) to fifth place, while Charlie Cox retired his Cooper-Ford after twenty-nine laps. Photo by Ron Shaw.

Skip Scott took sixth place in his Cobra 427. Photo by Ron Shaw.

Don Skogmo (#31 Genie-Ford) leading Bob Johnson (#33 Cobra), Mak Kronn (#71 Elva-BMW), and the Cobras of Tom Payne and Dan Gerber. Photo by Ron Shaw.

Dan Gerber (#19 Cobra) leading Gerry Bruihl (#41 Lotus 23-Climax) and Scooter Patrick (#38 Porsche 904). Gerber finished thirteenth overall and third in the Manufacturers over two-liter class. Bruihl finished tenth overall and third in the Drivers under two-liter class. Patrick won the Manufacturers under two-liter class, finishing ninth overall. Photo by Ron Shaw.

George Follmer (Lotus 23-Porsche #16) on his way to finishing third overall and first in the Drivers under two-liter class. Photo by Ron Shaw.

Jerry Grant leading Hap Sharp and Jim Hall. Grant led the first eight laps, before Hall flew by. Hall's lead lasted until lap twenty-seven when his pitted with a blown fuel pump fuse. Sharp then took the lead and held it until the end of the race. Photo by Ron Shaw.

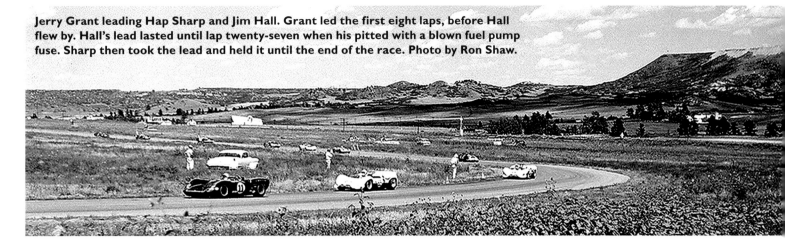

Jim Hall leading Grant and Sharp. Photo by Ron Shaw.

Mak Kronn (#71 Elva-BMW) leading John Everly (#26 Lotus 30-Ford), Tom Payne (#13 Cobra), Dan Gerber (#19 Cobra), and Pete Harrison (#87 Genie). Photo by Ron Shaw.

Augie Pabst debuted his McLaren M1A at Continental Divide. Augie ran in the top six for the first ten laps. Then overheating problems set in and he made multiple pitstops before retiring after fifty-four laps. Photo by Ron Shaw.

UNITED STATES
ROAD RACING
CHAMPIONSHIP
•
AUG. 28-29, 1965

OFFICIAL PROGRAM
FIFTY CENTS
•
ACCUS - FIA - SCCA
SANCTION NO. N-22

MID·OHIO SPORTS CAR COURSE
LEXINGTON, O.

1965 Mid Ohio program cover. Scan courtesy Don Markle.

The grid right before the start of the race. The front row from right to left; Jim Hall #66 is on the pole, Hap Sharp #65 is in the middle, Augie Pabst #7 is on the outside. Photo by Dave Arnold

Early laps with Hall leading Sharp, Sherman Decker, and Augie Pabst. Photo by Dave Arnold

Mid-Ohio

This race brought together a field of fifty-one entries vying for thirty-five starting positions. The Chaparrals of Jim Hall and Hap Sharp were again favored to win. The four McLarens of Charlie Hayes, Ludwig Heimrath, Richard Macon and Ralph Salyer were the main challengers. Skip Scott got a lot of attention with the Ford GT he entered. Augie Pabst ran a McLaren-Chevrolet, Lothar Motschenbacher had a Cooper, Sherman Decker was in a Lola T70 and Mike Hall ran a 427 Cobra. George Follmer and Gerry Bruihl were the strength of the under two-liter entries. Challenging them were the Lotus 23's of George Alderman and Doug Revson and four Elvas piloted by Joe Buzzetta, Chuck Dietrich, Gary Stephenson and Ralph Treischmann. The Manufacturers classes had a skimpy field, with five over two-liter entries and three in under two-liters. Three Cobras were entered for Bob Johnson, Tom Payne and Dan Gerber. Dave Heinz had a Corvette and Don Sesslar entered a Sunbeam Tiger. The under two-liter entries were Ray Cuomo in a Simca-Abarth, Max Nerriere in a Lotus Elan and Horst Kwech in an Alfa Romeo TI.

Practice and qualifying reduced the starting field to thirty-three cars. Jim Hall started on the pole position with a time of 1:37.2, while teammate, Hap Sharp, turned in a 1:37.6 for the second quickest time. Augie Pabst started from third place with a time of 1:41.6. Before the race, Pabst told the drivers behind him that he would be starting very slow. Ralph Salyer started in fourth spot with a 1:42.0, while fifth was Charlie Hayes (1:42.2).

Charlie Hayes got the drop on everyone at the start and took the lead from Hall, Sharp, Decker and Heimrath. They were followed by Lyall, Salyer, Dietrich, Al Schall, Pabst, Macon, Bruihl, Revson and Treischmann. George Follmer was nowhere. He had tried to pass Pabst on the right, got on the grass, spun and then slid back on the track facing the cars coming towards him. Follmer got out of the way as quickly as possible, but was tapped by Revson and spun back onto the grass. After everyone was gone, Follmer finally got underway.

Hayes stopped at the pits on the second lap to have a loose exhaust pipe removed and Jim Hall assumed the lead. Al Schall passed Dietrich and Gerry Bruihl got ahead of Macon. Further back, Bob Johnson, Dan Gerber, Joe Buzzetta, Lothar Motschenbacher and Mike Hall were swapping places at almost every corner. Ralph Salyer's McLaren retired with a broken halfshaft on lap four. Follmer was back on the track and now picking off car after car. Charlie Hayes was doing the same after his pit stop.

Chuck Dietrich was hit from behind and had an oil line break. He pitted to have the line repaired, but the engine cover did not get snapped down and it flew off as Dietrich re-entered the race. This gave the under two-liter lead to Gerry Bruihl. Lothar Motschenbacher retired his Cooper after twenty-seven laps. Sherman Decker also retired on the next lap, driving his Lola through the pits and straight onto the trailer. Follmer's bid ended after thirty-six laps with a broken suspension.

Charlie Hayes was driving like a man possessed. He worked up to sixth place, ahead of Augie Pabst and was ready to pass Lyall and Heimrath. Lyall's engine then threw a fan belt and immediately slowed down. Hayes made it past Heimrath, just as Hall and Sharp were coming up to lap both of them. Hall was about to lap Hayes when the Chaparral's gearbox broke and Hall coasted to the pits. Sharp took up the charge and passed both Heimrath and Hayes to assume the lead. The engine in Sharp's Chapar-

Winner Hap Sharp #65 passing second place Charlie Hayes #97. Photo by Dave Arnold.

Jim Hall retired with gearbox problems after leading most of the race. Photo by Dave Arnold.

George Follmer had a difficult time at Mid Ohio, retiring after thirty-six laps. This was the only race Follmer did not finish this year. Photo by Dave Arnold.

Skip Scott drove his Ford GT to four place. Photo by Bill Stowe.

Charlie Hayes brought his McLaren home in second place. Photo by Bill Stowe.

ral started to cut out a few laps later. Hap pitted for additional fuel and still had a thirty-six second lead when he returned to the track. Gerry Bruihl's Climax engine blew a valve after sixty laps and he dropped back, giving the under two-liter lead to Doug Revson.

Sharp won the race over Hayes and Heimrath. Skip Scott was fourth, in the Ford GT. Doug Revson won the under two-liter class over Ralph Treischmann and Joe Buzzetta. Dan Gerber was eighth and first in the Manufacturers over two-liter class, ahead of Tom Payne. Bob Johnson should have won the over two-liter class. He was leading by almost a lap when he flipped the reserve fuel switch. With all the right-hand corners, the reserve fuel sloshed to the main tank and Johnson ran out of fuel one lap from finishing the race. Ray Cuomo won the Manufacturers under two-liter class ahead of Max Nerriere.

The point standings remained much the same after this race. Follmer led with 57 points to Jim Hall's 50 points. Hap Sharp was in third place with 42 points. Gerry Bruihl's 31 points put him in fourth place. Skip Scott took sole possession of fifth place with 17 points. Mike Hall, Chuck Dietrich and Don Wester were tied for sixth place with 14 points. Mak Kronn was ninth, with 12 points and Jerry Titus was tenth, with 11 points, going into the last race.

1965 Mid Ohio • Combined Race • USRRC

August 29, 1965, Mid-Ohio Sports Car Course, Lexington, Ohio

Place	Driver	Car/Engine	Car #	Class	Laps	Driver Points	Mfg Points	Prize	Qual Place	Qual Time
1	Hap Sharp	Chaparral 2A-Chevrolet	65	O2	85	9	-	$2,400	2	1:37.6
2	Charlie Hayes	McLaren M1A-Chevrolet	97	O2	84	6	-	1,400	5	1:42.2
3	Ludwig Heimrath	McLaren M1A-Ford	15	O2	84	4	-	900	14	1:45.0
4	Skip Scott	Ford GT40	92	O2	83	3	-	700	13	1:48.2
5	Doug Revson	Lotus 23-Climax	23	U2	83	9	-	1,000	-	-
6	Ralph Treischman	Elva Mk 7S-Porsche	56	U2	82	6	-	600	-	-
7	Joe Buzzetta	Elva Mk 7S-Porsche	3	U2	82	4	-	400	-	-
8	Dan Gerber	Cobra	19	GTO	81	-	9	600	-	1:48.8
9	Tom Payne	Cobra	13	GTO	81	-	-	350	-	1:49.6
10	George Alderman	Lotus 23-Climax	22	U2	78	3	-	150	-	1:49.2
11	Ray Cuomo	Abarth-Simca	18	GTU	77	-	9	250	-	1:53.8
12	Max Nerriere	Lotus Elan	42	GTU	77	-	6	150	-	1:56.0
13	Chuck Dietrich	Elva Mk 7S-BMW	57	U2	76	2	-	100	9	1:42.8
14	Bill Seeley/Thomas Wood	Merlyn	2	U2	75	np	-	100	-	-
15	Dave Heinz	Chevrolet Corvette	52	GTO	73	-	4	100	-	-
16	Horst Kwech	Alfa Romeo TI	28	GTU	67	-	4	100	-	1:58.8
17	Gerry Bruihl	Lotus 23-Climax	49	U2	61	-	-	50	10	1:43.6
18	Glen Lyall	SCD 3-Ford	47	O2	61	2	-	50	7	1:42.8
19	Gary Stephenson	Elva Mk 7S-Porsche		U2	54	-	-	50	-	-
DNF	Bob Johnson	Cobra	33	GTO	81	-	-	-	-	1:48.8
DNF	Don Sesslar	Sunbeam Tiger	74	GTO	52	-	-	-	-	-
DNF	Dick Macon	McLaren M1A-Oldsmobile	8	O2	47	-	-	-	-	1:50.2
DNF	Al Schall	Carliss-Schall Special	71	O2	46	-	-	-	-	-
DNF	Augie Pabst	McLaren M1A-Chevrolet	7	O2	38	-	-	-	3	1:41.6
DNF	George Follmer	Lotus 23-Porsche	16	U2	36	-	-	-	8	1:42.8
DNF	Jim Hall	Chaparral 2A-Chevrolet	66	O2	35	-	-	-	1	1:37.2
DNF	Sherman Decker	Lola T70-Ford	67	O2	28	-	-	-	6	1:42.8
DNF	Lothar Motschenbacher	Cooper T61M-Ford	1	O2	27	-	-	-	-	1:49.0
DNF	Ed Hugus	Lotus 23-Ferrari	88	O2	13	-	-	-	-	-
DNF	Mike Hall	Cobra-Ford 427	91	O2	10	-	-	-	-	-
DNF	Ralph Salyer	McLaren M1A-Oldsmobile	26	O2	1	-	-	-	4	1:42.0

Fastest Qualifier:	Jim Hall	Chaparral 2A-Chevrolet	1:37.2	88.89 mph
Race Distance:	204.0 miles	85 laps of 2.4 mile course		
Race Time:	2hr 28min 20.76sec			
Winner's Speed:	82.51 mph			
Victory Margin:	1 lap, 72 seconds			
Fastest Race Lap:	Hap Sharp	Chaparral 2A-Chevrolet	1:40.6	85.88 mph

Mike Hall in Skip Scott's Cobra 427 lasted all of ten laps. Photo by Dave Arnold.

Chuck Dietrich in an Elva-BMW finished in thirteenth place and fifth in the under two-liter class. Photo by Dave Arnold.

ROAD AMERICA 500

SEPTEMBER 4 - 5 / 1965   SEVENTY FIVE CENTS

1965 Road America 500 program cover. Scan courtesy Don Markle.

The field coming around on the pace lap. Walt Hansgen in the Mecom Lola T70 is on the pole with Jim Hall's Chaparral next to him. Photo by Tom Schultz.

Road America 500

The showdown for the championship came to Road America with George Follmer leading Jim Hall, 57 points to 50 points, both from seven results. Since only the best seven results counted, each would have to drop a previous result to add to their current total. Follmer's worst result was a second place. He would have to win his class to drop the second place and gain three points. Hall's worst result was a sixth place. He would add points by finishing fifth place, or higher. Follmer would ensure the championship, regardless of where Hall finished, if he won his class. Hall needed to win his class and have Follmer finish second in his class, or lower, to win the championship.

There were over sixty entries and fifty-seven cars started the race. Naturally the two Chaparrals were the favorites in the over two-liter class. Jim Hall and Hap Sharp would share one car with Ron Hissom and the other with Bruce Jennings. Walt Hans-

gen and Mark Donohue in John Mecom's Lola T70, Ralph Salyer/Bill Mitchell and Bud Gates in McLarens, Skip Scott/Augie Pabst in a Ford GT, Mike Hall in the LMD McKee and Don Skogmo in a Genie were the strongest of the over two-liter challengers. George Follmer shared his regular Lotus-Porsche with Earl Jones and he shared Joe Buzzetta's Elva-Porsche, just in case his Lotus broke. There were fourteen other Elvas and three Lotus 23's challenging Follmer.

Walt Hansgen locked up the pole position during qualifying with a lap of 2:27.8. The Hall/Sharp/Hissom Chaparral qualified second with a time of 2:29.4. The other Chaparral (Hall/Sharp/Jennings) suffered an oil problem and was relegated to the sixth row of the grid with a time of 2:40.0. The McLaren of Ralph Salyer and the McKee Mk 2 Chevette of Jerry Hansen were on the second row. The third row was occupied by Skip Scott's Ford GT and Charles Cox' Cooper. Gerry Bruihl's Lotus 23 was the fastest

under two-liter qualifier, in ninth place with a time of 2:39.6. Follmer qualified his car in sixteenth spot with a 2:42.0. The Cobra shared by Dan Gerber and Tom Yeager was the fastest over two-liter Manufacturer entry at 2:38.2, while the next fastest was Bob Johnson's Cobra at 2:42.8. There were three under two-liter Manufacturer entries and Chuck Stoddard's Alfa Romeo TZ was the fastest in thirty-ninth place.

Raceday weather was cold and clear. A rolling start was used and as the cars came down the straight to take the flag, Hansgen punched it and pulled ahead of Hall's Chaparral. Giving chase were Ralph Salyer, Skip Scott, Jerry Hansen, Mike Hall, Charlie Cox and Dick Thompson. The under two-liter brigade was right behind Thompson, with Gerry Bruihl leading Joe Buzzetta and George Follmer. Skip Scott and Charlie Cox passed Ralph Salyer at the end of the first lap. Dick Thompson and Hap Sharp were seventh and eighth. Hall got his Chaparral

Looking down on the winning Chaparral, driven by Jim Hall, Hap Sharp, and Ron Hissom. Photo by Ron Shaw.

George Follmer on his way to clinching the championship. Earl Jones co-drove with George and they placed fourth overall and won the under two-liter class. Photo by Ron Shaw.

The second place Chaparral was driven by Jim Hall, Hap Sharp, and Bruce Jennings. Photo by Ron Shaw.

Ferrari 250LM driven to fifth place by Bob Grossman and Dick Holquist. Photo by Ron Shaw.

past Hansgen and into the lead on the second lap.

Hap Sharp moved into fourth place on the next lap and into third place on the fourth lap. He then began an intense battle with Walt Hansgen for second place. Hansgen had more top speed while Sharp had better handling and braking. Hansgen pulled ahead on the straights and Sharp out-braked him in the corners. Everytime Sharp pulled up on the inside, Hansgen would close the door on him.

Jerry Hansen moved ahead of Skip Scott's Ford GT for fourth place after ten laps. Joe Buzzetta passed Gerry Bruihl for the under two-liter lead. On lap sixteen, Jack Ensley, in the Apache Special, cut across the front of Clint Lindberg's Elva-BMW. Both cars

spun and climbed the embankment at turn eleven. As they came back down, Lindberg's Elva flipped, hit the front of the Apache and burst into flames in the middle of the track. Budd Clusserath, in a Cheetah, was the next racer on the scene. He stopped his car and pulled Lindberg out of his burning wreck. Thanks to Clusserath's quick work, Lindberg suffered only minor burns and abrasions. Ensley came away with a broken arm and two broken ribs.

Cleaning up the track and getting the cars lined up for the restart took an hour and a half. The cars were started in line, in the same order as when the race stopped. Hall jumped into the lead at the re-start and quickly built a margin between himself and Hansgen. Hansgen had Hap Sharp all over

his rear-end, trying to get by. Hap took second place on the next lap, at turn five. The running order now was Hall in first, then Sharp, Hansgen, Hansen, Scott, Mike Hall, Salyer, Thompson, Buzzetta and Follmer.

Hansgen dove into the pits with a jammed throttle after twenty-seven laps. Jerry Hansen was now third with Hansgen in fourth. Between lap thirty-six and thirty-eight, the Chaparrals pitted for driver changes. Bruce Jennings came out of the pitstop in fourth place, behind Jerry Hansen and Walt Hansgen, while Hap Sharp piloted the first place car. Hansgen pitted and turned the Lola over to Mark Donohue. Bruce Jenning's third place turned into second when Jerry Hansen's Chevette lost its engine after fifty-two laps. But Jennings spun the Chaparral,

Walt Hansgen piloting the Mecom Lola, lasted 83 laps before retiring. Photo by Ron Shaw.

Chuck Stoddard drove solo in his Alfa TZ to place fifteenth overall and first in the Manufacturers under two-liter class. Photo by Ron Shaw.

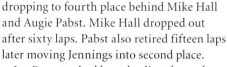

Ralph Salyer and Bill Mitchell drove Ralph's McLaren to a fifth place finish. Photo by Tom Schultz.

Joe Buzzetta shared his Elva-Porsche with George Follmer, but it didn't quite make it to the finish. Photo by Tom Schultz.

dropping to fourth place behind Mike Hall and Augie Pabst. Mike Hall dropped out after sixty laps. Pabst also retired fifteen laps later moving Jennings into second place.

Joe Buzzetta had been leading the under two-liter class. He pitted to hand his car over to George Follmer, giving Follmer's Lotus the lead, with Earl Jones driving. George put in the required amount of laps in Joe's car, right behind his own car and handed the Elva back to Buzzetta in a very long pitstop. Then George returned to his own car and the class lead.

The Chaparrals raced along in first and second, while Follmer, in third place overall, was leading the 427 Cobra of Dick Thomp-

son and Ed Lowther. Walt Hansgen retired the Mecom Lola with a broken transmission after eighty-three laps. After Joe Buzzetta returned to his Elva, he found it running progressively worse and retired after 104 laps.

The Jim Hall/Hap Sharp/Ron Hissom Chaparral crossed the finish line in first place with the Hall/Sharp/Jennings car one lap behind, in second place. The Dick Thompson/Ed Lowther 427 Cobra finished in third place. George Follmer and Earl Jones brought Follmer's Lotus-Porsche home in fourth place and first in under two-liters, clinching the championship. Ralph Salyer and Bill Mitchell's McLaren was

fifth with the Bob Grossman/Dick Holquist Ferrari 250LM in sixth. Tom Payne and Ray Cuomo were seventh and first in the Manufacturers over two-liter class. The under two-liter class was won by Chuck Stoddard's Alfa Romeo TZ, which finished fifteenth.

George Follmer, in his under two-liter Lotus 23-Porsche, won the championship with 60 points and Jim Hall finished second in the championship with 58 points. Hap Sharp was third with 51 points. Gerry Bruihl had 31 points, taking fourth in the championship. Skip Scott and Mike Hall tied for fifth place, both with 17 points. The Cobra team and Porsche shared the Manufacturers title with the maximum of 63 points each.

1965 Road America • Combined Race • Road America 500
September 5, 1965, Road America, Elkhart Lake, Wisconsin

Place	Driver	Car/Engine	Car #	Class	Laps	Driver Points	Mfg Points	Prize	Qual Place	Qual Time
1	Jim Hall/Hap Sharp/Ron Hissom	Chaparral 2A-Chev	66	O2	125	9	-	$3,000	2	2:29.4
2	Hap Sharp/Bruce Jennings/Jim Hall	Chaparral 2A-Chev	65	O2	124	6	-	2,000	12	2:40.0
3	Dick Thompson/Ed Lowther	Cobra 427	91	O2	118	4	-	1,200	10	2:39.6
4	George Follmer/Earl Jones	Lotus 23-Porsche	16	U2	118	9	-	1,200	16	2:42.0
5	Ralph Salyer/Bill Mitchell	McLaren M1A-Olds	26	O2	117	3	-	600	3	2:30.0
6	Bob Grossman/Dick Holquist	Ferrari 250LM	96	O2	116	2	-	500	27	2:48.8
7	Tom Payne/Ray Cuomo	Cobra	13	GTO	115	-	9	900	25	2:48.2
8	Bill Kimberly/Denise McCluggage	Elva Mk 7S-Porsche	51	U2	114	6	-	600	23	2:47.4
9	Lee (E.L.) Hall/Mike Hall	Elva Mk 7S-Porsche	69	U2	113	4	-	400	29	2:50.0
10	Peter Goetz/George Wintersteen	Elva Mk 8-BMW	9	U2	112	3	-	100	21	2:47.2
11	Gary Stephenson/Carl Haas	Elva Mk 7S-Porsche	6	U2	110	2	-	50	22	2:47.4
12	Budd Clusserath	Cheetah	64	O2	108	1	-	50	32	2:51.0
13	Bob Johnson/Don Sesslar	Cobra	33	GTO	108		--	350	19	2:42.8
14	John Martin/W. Marvin Shoenfeld	Corvette Grand Sport	27	O2	107	-	-	50	59	-
15	Chuck Stoddard	Alfa Romeo TZ	5	GTU	106	-	9	550	39	2:59.8
16	Ralph Scott/Alan Ross	Elva Mk 7-Climax	67	U2	105	1	-	50	41	3:00.2
17	Phil Seitz/George MacDonald	Elva Mk 6-Climax	72	U2	105	-	-	50	42	3:00.4
18	Jerry Nelson/Tom Countryman	Porsche 718 RS60	18	U2	103	-	-	50	34	2:51.8
19	George Dickinson/Wil-Hans Wiedmann	Porsche 718 RS60	36	U2	103	-	-	50	51	3:10.0
20	Doc (M.R.J.) Wyllie/Peg Wyllie	Lola Mk 1-Climax	2	U2	103	-	-	50	56	3:24.0
21	Bob Nagel/Peg Wyllie	Elva Mk 8-BMW	14	U2	102	-	-	50	38	2:57.4
22	William Cooper/Dick Irish	Ferrari 275P	22	O2	102	-	-	50	48	3:05.2
23	Chuck Dietrich/Alan Ross	Elva Mk 7S-BMW	57	U2	102	-	-	50	18	2:42.6
24	Dave Heinz/Paul Canary	Corvette Grand Sport	52	O2	102	-	-	50	62	-
25	Bob Bienerth/Andy Baumgartner	Chevrolet Corvette	10	GTO	101	-	4	250	55	3:18.8
26	Jerry Dunbar/Walter Gray	Chevrolet Corvette	32	GTO	101	-	-	50	45	3:01.6
27	Gene Parsons	Lotus Elan	45	GTU	100	-	6	350	46	3:03.8
28	Nick Hartman/Bill Bradley	Merlyn Mk 4	53	U2	93	-	-	50	53	3:14.8
29	Rich Dagiel/Guy Wooley	Dirty Pop Special	48	O2	92	-	-	50	54	3:17.8
30	Jack Brady/Bob Shufelt	Lotus 11	43	U2	79	-	-	50	64	-
31	Hugh Major/David Gulick	Elva Mk 7	41	U2	77	-	-	-	44	3:01.2
32	Dick Durant/John Martin	Durant Special-Chev	46	O2	74	-	-	-	14	2:41.8
33	Dan Gerber/Tom Yeager	Cobra	19	GTO	68	-	-	-	7	2:38.2
DNF	Joe Buzzetta/George Follmer	Elva Mk 7S-Porsche	3	U2	104	--	-	-	13	2:41.0
DNF	Bill Kirtley/Dale Lang	Elva Mk 6	15	U2	94	-	--	-	49	3:05.4
DNF	Walt Hansgen/Mark Donohue	Lola T70-Chevrolet	11	O2	83	-	--	-	1	2:27.8
DNF	James Marquardt	Chevrolet Corvette	97	GTO	77	-	--	-	52	3:12.4
DNF	Jack Baker/John Barlass	Black Jack Special	71	O2	77	-	--	-	40	3:00.2
DNF	Skip Scott/Augie Pabst	Ford GT40	92	O2	76	-	-	-	5	2:34.6

continued

Skip Scott and Augie Pabst had Skip's Ford GT inside the top ten, until they retired after 76 laps. Photo by Ron Shaw.

Jerry Hansen's McKee-Chevette also ran inside the top ten, until retiring. Photo by Ron Shaw.

DNF	Horst Kwech/Tom Terrell	Alfa Romeo TI	7	GTU	73	-	-	-	47	3:04.4
DNF	Doug Revson	Lotus 23B-Climax	24	U2	68	-	-	-	24	2:48.2
DNF	Bud Gates	McLaren M1A-Chev	73	O2	68	-	-	-	58	-
DNF	Mike Hall	LMD McKee Mk 4-Ford	4	O2	61	-	-	-	11	2:39.8
DNF	Jerry Hansen/Pat Manning	McKee Mk 2 Chevette	44	O2	52	-	-	-	4	2:32.0
DNF	Gerry Bruihl-Ed Leslie	Lotus 23-Climax	47	U2	47	-	-	-	9	2:39.6
DNF	Bob Shaw/Phillip Martin	Lotus 23B	1	U2	39	-	-	-	30	2:50.2
DNF	Mak Kronn/Jim Scott	Elva Mk 7-BMW	77	U2	32	-	-	-	17	2:42.4
DNF	Charlie Cox/Dan Fowler	Cooper T61M-Ford	39	O2	30	-	-	-	6	2:36.4
DNF	Dave Causey Allen Barker	Lotus 19-Ford	54	O2	23	-	-	-	8	2:39.4
DNF	Sam Eller/Lloyd Barton	Porsche 718 RSK	82	U2	21	-	-	-	36	2:55.4
DNF	Joe Scopelite	Bonanza-Chevrolet	63	O2	19	-	-	-	37	2:56.0
DNF	Dean Causey/Lyle York	Elva Mk 7S-BMW	81	U2	16	-	-	2	8	2:49.4
DNF	Clint Lindberg/Bob Kelce	Elva Mk 8-BMW	35	U2	13	-	-	-	20	2:44.2
DNF	Jack Ensley/Don Brady	Apache-Chevrolet	17	O2	13	-	-	-	35	2:53.2
DNF	Don Skogmo/Scott Beckett	Genie Mk 8-Ford	37	O2	10	-	-	-	15	-
DNF	Herb Swan	Elva Mk 7-BMW	99	U2	7	-	-	-	33	2:51.4
DNF	Byron Bossart	Laura Special	28	O2	2	-	-	6	3	-

Fastest Qualifier:	Walt Hansgen	Lola T70-Chevrolet	2:27.8	97.43 mph
Race Distance:	500 miles	125 laps of 4.0 mile course		
Race Time:	5hr 35min 5.88sec			
Winner's Speed:	89.526 mph			
Victory Margin:	1 lap, 1 second			
Fastest Race Lap:	Jim Hall	Chaparral 2A-Chevrolet	2:28.0	97.30 mph

Mike Hall drove his LMD McKee-Ford solo, before retiring after 61 laps. Photo by Ron Shaw.

Jim Hall at speed in the winning Chaparral. Photo by Tom Shultz.

1965 USRRC Drivers Championship Points

PEN Pensacola, RIV Riverside, LS Laguna Seca, BH Bridgehampton, WG Watkins Glen, PR Pacific Raceways, CD Continental Divide, MO Mid-Ohio, RA Road America

Place	Driver	PEN	RIV	LS	BR	WG	PR	CD	MO	RA	Best 7 Races	Total Points
1	George Follmer	9	9	6	9	9	6	9	-	9	60	66
2	Jim Hall	1	9	9	9	9	9	4	-	9	58	59
3	Hap Sharp	-	6	-	6	6	6	9	9	9	51	51
4	Gerry Bruihl	4	4	9	-	6	4	4	-	-	31	31
5	Skip Scott	6	-	-	2	4	-	2	3	-	17	17
6	Mike Hall	9	-	-	4	-	-	-	-	4	17	17
7	Don Wester	-	4	6	-	-	4	-	-	-	14	14
8	Chuck Dietrich	6	-	-	6	-	-	-	2	-	14	14
9	Mak Kronn	-	-	-	3	3	-	6	-	-	12	12
10	Jerry Titus	-	-	-	-	-	9	2	-	-	11	11
11	Ron Hissom	-	-	-	-	-	-	-	-	9	9	9
12	Earl Jones	-	-	-	-	-	-	-	-	9	9	9
13	Doug Revson	-	-	-	-	-	-	-	9	-	9	9
14	Augie Pabst	4	-	-	-	3	-	-	-	-	7	7
15	Charlie Hayes	-	-	1	-	-	-	-	6	-	7	7
16	Bruce Jennings	-	-	-	-	-	-	-	6	-	6	6
17	Bud Morley	-	6	-	-	-	-	-	-	-	6	6
18	Dave Ridenour	-	-	4	-	-	2	-	-	-	6	6
19	Jerry Grant	-	-	-	-	-	-	6	-	-	6	6
20	Ralph Treischman	-	-	-	-	-	-	-	6	-	6	6
21	George Wintersteen	-	-	-	3	-	-	-	-	3	6	6
22	Tony Settember	-	2	3	-	-	-	-	-	-	5	5
23	Paul Reinhart	-	2	3	-	-	-	-	-	-	5	5
24	Lothar Motschenbacher	-	-	-	2	-	-	-	3	-	5	5
25	Joe Buzzetta	-	-	-	-	1	-	-	4	-	5	5
26	Lee (E.L.) Hall	-	-	-	-	-	-	-	-	4	4	4
27	Ludwig Heimrath	-	-	-	-	-	-	-	4	-	4	4
28	Walter Mann	-	-	-	4	-	-	-	-	-	4	4
29	Ed Marshall	-	-	4	-	-	-	-	-	-	4	4
30	Dan Gerber	3	-	-	1	-	-	-	-	-	4	4
31	George Ralph	-	-	-	-	4	-	-	-	-	4	4
32	Dick Thompson	-	-	-	-	-	-	-	-	4	4	4
33	Ed Lowther	-	-	-	-	-	-	-	-	4	4	4
34	Ralph Salyer	-	-	-	-	-	-	-	-	3	3	3
35	Bill Mitchell	-	-	-	-	-	-	-	-	3	3	3
36	Peter Goetz	-	-	-	-	-	-	-	-	3	3	3
37	George Alderman	-	-	-	-	-	-	-	3	-	3	3
38	Rick Muther	-	-	-	-	-	3	-	-	-	3	3
39	Pierre Phillips	-	-	-	-	-	3	-	-	-	3	3
40	Miles Gupton	-	3	-	-	-	-	-	-	-	3	3
41	Bill Bowman	3	-	-	-	-	-	-	-	-	3	3
42	Bob Challman	-	3	-	-	-	-	-	-	-	3	3
43	Jerry Nelson	-	-	-	-	-	-	3	-	-	3	3
44	Bob Grossman	-	-	-	-	-	-	-	-	2	2	2
45	Dick Holquist	-	-	-	-	-	-	-	-	2	2	2
46	Bill Kimberly	-	-	-	-	-	-	-	-	6	2	2
47	Denise McCluggage	-	-	-	-	-	-	-	-	6	2	2
48	Gary Stephenson	-	-	-	-	-	-	-	-	2	2	2
49	Carl Haas	-	-	-	-	-	-	-	-	2	2	2
50	Glen Lyall	-	-	-	-	-	-	-	2	-	2	2
51	Ed Leslie	-	-	-	-	-	2	-	-	-	2	2
52	Mike Goth	-	-	-	2	2	-	-	-	-	2	2
53	Don Skogmo	-	-	-	-	2	-	-	-	-	2	2
54	Tom Tobin	-	-	2	-	-	-	-	-	-	2	2
55	Jerry Crawford	2	-	-	-	-	-	-	-	-	2	2
56	Roy Kumnick	-	-	-	-	-	-	1	-	-	1	1
57	Odie Fellows	-	-	-	-	-	-	1	-	-	1	1
58	Bob Montana	-	1	-	-	-	-	-	-	-	1	1
59	Nade Bourgeault	-	-	1	-	-	-	-	-	-	1	1
60	Jim Paul	-	1	-	-	-	-	-	-	-	1	1
61	Charlie Parsons	-	-	-	-	-	1	-	-	-	1	1

		PEN	RIV	LS	BR	WG	PR	CD	MO	RA	Total
62	Paul Scott	-	-	-	-	1	-	-	-	1	1
63	Budd Clusserath	-	-	-	-	-	-	-	1	1	1
64	Ralph Scott	-	-	-	-	-	-	-	1	1	1
65	Alan Ross	-	-	-	-	-	-	-	1	1	1
66	Al Schall	-	-	-	1	-	-	-	-	1	1

1965 Manufacturers' Championship Points

PEN Pensacola, RIV Riverside, LS Laguna Seca, BR Bridgehampton, WG Watkins Glen, PR Pacific Raceways, CD Continental Divide, MO Mid-Ohio, RA Road America

Place	Driver	PEN	RIV	LS	BR	WG	PR	CD	MO	RA	Best 7 Races	Total Points
1	Shelby-American (Cobra)	9	9	9	9	9	9	9	9	9	63	81
2	Porsche	9	9	9	9	9	9	9	-	-	63	63
3	Lotus	3	3	2	6	-	-	4	6	6	30	30
4	Chevrolet	-	4	4	3	-	-	3	4	4	26	26
5	Alfa-Romeo	1	-	1	-	-	4	3	4	9	18	18
6	Ford	4	3	2	-	-	-	-	-	-	9	9
7	Abarth-Simca	-	-	-	-	-	-	-	9	-	9	9
8	Jaguar	-	-	3	-	-	-	-	-	-	3	3
9	Volvo	-	-	-	3	-	-	-	-	-	3	3
10	BMC	-	1	-	-	-	-	-	-	-	1	1

1965 Season Summary

Everything clicked in 1965. Auto racing, in general, became popular enough to be featured in Time, Newsweek and other serious news magazines. ABC TV's Wide World of Sports regularly featured Grand Prix and Indycar races, plus Sebring, Le Mans and the Fall sports car races. Occasionally, even NASCAR got TV time.

The Chaparral team started the year off by winning the Sebring 12 hours. It was a nice David and Goliath story, "Private Chaparral Team Beats the Might of Ferrari and Ford". At Pensacola, the first USRRC race of the year, George Follmer pulled a win out of his helmet when the Chaparrals failed. Suddenly the Chaparral team goes from being the David, to being the Goliath and Jim Hall spent the year chasing George's points lead. Try as he might, Jim came up short. He and Follmer both scored six wins. The difference was that Hall was winning the races overall and Follmer was winning his class. Hall was a little perturbed that Follmer could finish in third place, or sixth place and score the same amount of points. The championship was scored on a best seven, out of nine, races. Follmer won the championship with a second place (in class) to Hall's next best

finish of third place (overall). The two-point margin was the closest in the USRRC's three-year history.

The SCCA was thrilled. Membership went from 15,545 at the end of 1964, to 16,757 by the end of 1965. Even the weather cooperated. Everywhere the USRRC went in 1965 the weather was hot and sunny. Spectators thronged to the races and paid admissions went from 144,000 for the ten races in 1964 to 156,000 for nine events in 1965.

The racing itself, unfortunately, was so-so. The early laps of most races were thrilling. Usually Walt Hansgen, Jerry Grant, or Charlie Hayes would lead at the start, with the Chaparrals close behind. After a handful of laps, the Chaparrals had the competition figured out, or worn out, and they would sail into the lead. There were a few occasions when Hall would take the lead at the start and fly away into the distance. Usually, there was more action in the under two-liter class as George Follmer would be fighting with the likes of Joe Buzzetta, Gerry Bruihl, Jerry Titus and Bud Morley. The dicing they provided usually lasted longer than the fight up front. Also, there was generally a nice amount of mid-field jockeying for position to hold the spectator's interest.

The Chaparrals scored five 1-2 finishes

with Hall leading Sharp by .2 seconds at Watkins Glen, ten seconds at Pacific Raceways, sixteen seconds at Riverside and over a minute at Bridgehampton. The closest third place finisher was Don Wester, at Riverside, fifty-one seconds behind the winner. Road America was the longest distance between first and third at seven laps, or twenty-eight miles. Follmer's run of wins in the under two-liter class was about the same. The only race in which George won his class by less than a lap was at Riverside. He won his class by four laps at the Continental Divide and Road America races.

The series had a total of 255 individual drivers starting races. Jim Hall and George Follmer were the only drivers to start all nine races. Hap Sharp and Gerry Bruihl both started eight races. Four drivers started in four, five and six races. Nine drivers started three races and twenty-six drivers started two races. 201 drivers made single race starts.

This was the last year of the Manufacturers championship. Total domination by the Cobra team and a lack of support from other Manufacturers were the major reasons for its demise. Although Porsche was "co-champions" with Cobra, they did not win their class at every race, like Cobra did.

1966

Stardust
Riverside
Laguna Seca
Bridgehampton
Watkins Glen
Pacific Raceways
Mid Ohio
Road America

1966 Introduction

The major change for the USRRC in 1966 was basing the championship solely on the overall race positions. Under two-liter finishers would no longer score the same points as the over two-liter finishers. This pretty much assured that an over two-liter car would win the championship. The under two-liter driver with the most overall points would only be the class champion.

For the Chaparral team, it was too little, too late. They won six of the seven 1965 Fall pro races, then decided to skip the USRRC in 1966. Instead, they ran cars in the World Championship of Makes and the Can-Am Series. For Chaparral fans, this was a bummer. In addition, John Mecom did not enter any cars in the 1966 USRRC. He decided to concentrate on the Can-Am series and Indycar racing.

There were quite a few new team and driver combinations. Dan Gurney's All-American Racers entered a new Lola T70 for Jerry Grant, powered by a Ford engine with Gurney-Weslake heads, reputed to put out 500 horsepower. Randy Hilton entered a Genie-Chevrolet for Charlie Parsons. Dan Blocker ("Hoss" from television's Bonanza series) also entered a Genie-Chevrolet for John Cannon. Pacesetter Homes entered a Lola T70 for Bill Krause. Skip Hudson and Buck Fulp also ran Lola T70's. Charlie Hayes, Mike Goth and Lothar Motschenbacher would run McLaren Mk 1's.

Even though the chance of winning the series championship was gone, the under two-liter class was still popular. Vasek Polak and Otto Zipper both entered the new Porsche Carrera 6 (also known as a 906) for a variety of drivers. The bulk of the under two-liter ranks were made up of local drivers racing other Porsche 906's and 904's, Lotus 23 variants, Elvas and Bobsys.

Also in 1966, there would be no Manufacturers Championship. This was due, in part, to a lack of participation from the Manu-facturers. During the past two years, the only real Manufacturer effort was the Shelby American Cobra team and the under two-liter Lotus Cortinas. The Porsche effort consisted of a few dealers and lots of customer cars, but not a real factory effort. That the Cobras won every Manufacturers race since the start of the USRRC, except Pensacola in 1963, with very little close competition, did not do the series any good. A dwindling amount of entries was also a contributing factor. In 1965, there were 115 starters in the Manufacturers classes, down from 148 in 1964. What probably sealed the fate of the Manufacturers Championship were the four races with single digit starters: three at Watkins Glen, eight at Pacific Raceways and Mid-Ohio, and nine at Road America.

1966 was a year the SCCA would build on the success of the USRRC with two new professional racing series. The Trans-American Sedan Championship, for cars like the Ford Mustang and Chevrolet Camaro, and the Canadian-American Challenge Cup, for USRRC-type cars. The Trans-Am series started in June, midway through the USRRC calendar. The Can-Am series started on September 11, one week after the Road America USRRC. The only date clash was the Pacific Raceway USRRC and the Virginia Trans-Am race, on July 31. There was some initial thought that the USRRC might suffer because entrants would save their cars for the more lucrative Can-Am series. This thought was soon dispelled by a large entry at the first race.

There would be eight USRRC races in 1966. Stardust Raceways, in Las Vegas, was new to the series and hosted the first round. Other West Coast events were held at Riverside, Laguna Seca and Pacific Raceways. The East Coast events were held at Bridgehampton, Watkins Glen, Mid-Ohio and Road America. Gone were the races at Pensacola and Continental Divide.

United States Road Racing Championship

April 22, 23 and 24, 1966

and Stardust Formula SCCA

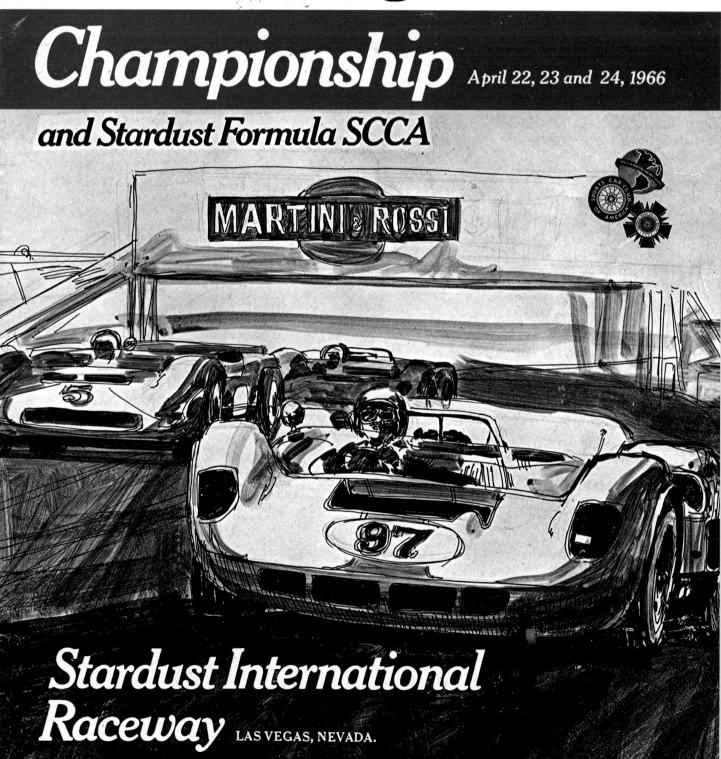

MARTINI & ROSSI

Stardust International Raceway
LAS VEGAS, NEVADA.

1966 Stardust program cover. Scan courtesy Don Markle.

Jerry Grant #8 jumps into the lead, ahead of Charlie Hayes #97, Charlie Parsons #10, and the rest of the field. Winner, John Cannon #62 is visible, on the far right, about four cars back. Photo from the collections of the Henry Ford.

Stardust

This would be the second professional sports car race at Stardust Raceway. The previous November, Hap Sharp won the inaugural Stardust Grand Prix in a Chaparral. During the winter, wind had blown sand across the track surface, erasing the layer of rubber that had been laid down by the previous race. There was a fine layer of dust and sand covering the track and there were a lot of rocks and pebbles on the ground by the side of the course. Stardust was a very desolate looking track. There was no grass or landscaping anywhere. The spectator's bleachers were simply set on the hard-scrabble dirt.

There was some pre-race worry of a thin race field due to drivers possibly saving their cars for the new Fall Can-Am series. Their worry was for naught. Fifty cars were entered for this race with thirty-four making the start.

Five of the starters were Lola T70's. Jerry Grant was in the All-American Racers car. Skip Hudson had the Lancer-sponsored car with a modified rear deck and nice looking air scoops. Ron Bucknum was in the Russkit-sponsored, Haskell Engineering car. Bill Krause was making a return to racing in the Pacesetter Lola and Buck Fulp

entered his own Lola. Also, five McLarens were on the starting grid. Charlie Hayes was in a Nickey sponsored car. Lothar Motschenbacher, Joe Starkey, Ralph Salyer and Jim Roe were in the other McLarens. Four Genies started the race. Dan Blocker entered a Genie, called a Vinegaroon Special. This was a two-year old Mark 10 that had been lightened and fitted with a strong Traco Chevrolet engine. It was sponsored by Nickey Chevrolet, for John Cannon to drive. Randy Hilton entered another Genie Mark 10 for Charlie Parsons. Bill Eve and Don Skogmo also entered their Genies.

Ed Hamill was entered in his self-built Hamill SR3. Bob Montana had a McKee Mk 5 stuffed with a 427 Plymouth engine in the rear. Budd Clusserath and Mak Kronn raced their Mk 6 McKees, with Oldsmobile and Chevrolet engines, respectively. Dick Guldstrand, Neben Evol and Paul Reinhart all raced Corvettes. Jerry Hansen and Steve Diulo were entered in Lotus 19's. Bob Drake was in an Ol' Yaller, entered as a Balchowsky Special and painted blue. Al Whatley ran his Ford GT. Dave Ridenour raced a Ford Mustang and Jim Chaffee raced his Pink Elephant Special.

The under-two liter contingent was

represented by George Follmer and John Morton in Lotus 23-Porsches, Ken Miles in Otto Zipper's new Porsche 906, Scooter Patrick and Norman Smith in Porsche 904's, Miles Gupton in his Platypus-Porsche and Harry Banta in the Ferharry Special.

Qualifying for 1966 races was a three-day affair. The first fifteen positions went to the fifteen fastest on Friday. The next ten spots were determined on Saturday and a race day morning session set the final ten spots. Right off the bat on Friday, Jerry Grant established his dominance with a time of 1:39.7. Charlie Hayes got second spot with a time of 1:40.3. Next up were Charlie Parsons (1:42.5), John Cannon (1:44.3) and Mak Kronn (1:44.6). George Follmer was initially credited with sixth fastest and the top under two-liter qualifier at 1:44.8. His time was later determined to be a mistake and he was moved back. Skip Hudson, Buck Fulp, Lothar Motschenbacher and Ralph Salyer, and Ron Bucknum completed the top ten. Bill Krause, Ed Hamill, Earl Jones and Ken Miles took the remaining Friday places. Jerry Hansen had the fastest time (1:45.3) on Saturday. This was the 6th fastest overall qualifying time, but Jerry

John Cannon #62 waving at a photographer and leading Mak Kronn #77. Cannon qualified fourth, dropped back early in the race, and worked his way up to the lead on lap thirty-four, when Grant dropped out. Kronn finished in fourth place. Photo from the collections of the Henry Ford.

Charlie Parsons #10 and Skip Hudson #9 finished second and third, respectively, after an early race duel. Photo from the collections of the Henry Ford.

had to start from 16th position. The other Saturday qualifiers were Budd Clusserath (1:48.5), Steve Diulo (1:48.6), Jim Dittemore (1:50.5), George Follmer (1:51.2), Mason O'Kieff (1:51.8), Joe Starkey, Dick Guldstrand, Don Skogmo and Miles Gupton.

Raceday was warm and sunny with 10,400 spectators on hand to witness the first race of the season. Charlie Hayes took the lead from Jerry Grant at the start. Grant muscled his way past Hayes going into the first turn. Following this pair were Charlie Parsons, Skip Hudson and Bill Krause. Before the first lap was over, Hudson and Krause had passed Parsons. Krause took third place from Hudson on the second lap. John Cannon recovered from a poor start and passed Krause for third place after a few more laps. Charlie Parsons took fifth place back from Hudson.

Hayes started closing the gap to Grant on the fourth lap. Grant went wide on a corner and his car slipped to the edge of the road. Two wheels went off the road and showered Hayes' car with pebbles and dust. The pebbles penetrated the radiator of Hayes' McLaren and he was out of the race. Hayes later made a point of telling reporters he

thought Grant went off course with the sole purpose of showering his car with stones.

Lothar Motschenbacher started late, after having his brakes adjusted on the grid. He tore through the field to join Parson and Hudson in the fight for fourth place. Jerry Hansen also recovered from a poor start to join the fight for fourth place. He retired with a smoking engine after eighteen laps.

An unidentified car dumped oil on the line through turn two on the sixteenth lap. Krause and Lothar got to the corner before the flag crew and both spun wildly. Krause kept his engine running and got back under way without losing a place. Lothar stalled his engine, got a push-start from an enthusiastic spectator and was black-flagged for it.

After twenty-five laps, Grant was thirty seconds ahead of Cannon, who had a similar lead over Krause. There were big gaps between Krause, Parsons and Hudson. Krause retired with a fried clutch after thirty laps and, four laps later, Grant was out with a broken transaxle. Grant was beset with reporters telling him what Hayes had said about him going off course on purpose. Jerry vehemently denied the accusation.

Cannon was now leading, with a one-minute gap over Parsons. Skip Hudson and Mak

Kronn were thirty seconds back in third and fourth places. Buck Fulp drove smoothly from the start of the race and worked his way up to fifth place on lap fifty, but retired when he got hit on the goggles by a flying stone. He was able to get back to the pits and went to the medical center for attention to his eye. With five laps to go, Cannon's Genie developed battery problems and his lead dwindled to thirty-three seconds by the end of the race. Chuck Parsons finished in second place, even though his Genie had developed fuel-feed pickup problems. Skip Hudson took third place, a minute behind Parsons and eighteen seconds ahead of Kronn. Ed Hamill was fifth. Ken Miles, in a Porsche 906, was sixth and the first under two-liter car. George Follmer was seventh, two laps behind Miles, in last year's championship winning car.

John Cannon led the championship with nine points. Charlie Parsons was second with six points and Skip Hudson was third with four points. Mak Kronn had three points and Ed Hamill got two points for fifth place. Since the under two-liter cars now scored points only for their overall finish positions, Ken Miles was in sixth place with only one point.

LEFT–Ed Hamill #6 finished the race in fifth place. Photo from the collections of the Henry Ford.

BELOW–Ken Miles #34, in Otto Zipper's Porsche 906 was the first under two-liter finisher, in sixth place. Under the new scoring rules Miles got one point for sixth place. Photo from the collections of the Henry Ford.

Buck Fulp #26, qualified in eighth place and in the race worked his way up to fifth place. With one lap to go, Fulp got hit in the eye by a flying stone and had to retire to seek medical attention. Photo from the collections of the Henry Ford.

1966 STARDUST • USRRC
April 24, 1966, Stardust Raceway, Las Vegas, Nevada

Place	Driver	Car/Engine	Car #	Class	Laps	Points	Prize	Qualifying Place	Qualifying Time
1	John Cannon	Genie Mk 10-Chevrolet	62	O2	60	9	$3,000	4	1:44.3
2	Charlie Parsons	Genie Mk 10-Chevrolet	10	O2	60	6	1,750	3	1:42.5
3	Skip Hudson	Lola T70-Chevrolet	9	O2	60	4	1,250	6	1:45.6
4	Mak Kronn	McKee Mk 6-Chevrolet	77	O2	60	3	900	5	1:44.6
5	Ed Hamill	Hamill SR3-Oldsmobile	6	O2	58	2	700	12	1:48.2
6	Ken Miles	Porsche 906	34	U2	58	1	1,500	14	1:49.7
7	George Follmer	Lotus 23-Porsche	16	U2	56	-	1,000	20	1:51.2
8	Budd Clusserath	McKee Mk 6-Oldsmobile	64	O2	55	-	300	17	1:48.5
9	Scooter Patrick	Porsche 904GTS	33	U2	55	-	650	-	-
10	John Morton	Lotus 23-Porsche	46	U2	54	-	500	-	-
11	Paul Reinhart	Chevrolet Corvette	11	O2	53	-	175	-	-
12	Steve Diulo	Lotus 19-Ford	29	O2	52	-	150	18	1:48.6
13	Jim Chaffee	Pink Elephant-Chevrolet	25	O2	50	-	150	-	-
14	Harry Banta	Ferharry-Climax	7	U2	50	-	350	-	-
15	Bob Drake	Balchowsky Spl-Ford	99	O2	49	-	150	-	-
16	Norm Smith	Porsche 904GTS	0	U2	48	-	225	-	-
17	Don Skogmo	Genie-Mk10-Ford	37	O2	44	-	125	24	1:52.8
DNF	Buck Fulp	Lola T70-Chevrolet	26	O2	59	-	125	7	1:46.0
DNF	Jerry Grant	Lola T70-Ford	8	O2	34	-	125	1	1:39.7
DNF	Bill Eve	Genie Mk 10-Ford	52	O2	30	-	125	13	1:49.0
DNF	Bill Krause	Lola T70-Ford	88	O2	30	-	100	11	1:47.0
DNF	Lothar Motschenbacher	McLaren M1B-Olds	27	O2	22	-	100	8	1:46.6
DNF	Jerry Hansen	Lotus 19-Chevrolet	44	O2	18	-	100	16	1:45.3
DNF	Joe Starkey	McLaren M1A-Chevrolet	21	O2	15	-	100	22	1:52.1
DNF	Jim Roe	McLaren M1A-Chevrolet	-	O2	13	-	100	-	-
DNF	Bob Montana	McKee Mk 5-Plymouth	15	O2	13	-	100	-	1:54.3
DNF	Miles Gupton	Platypus-Porsche	75	U2	12	-	100	25	1:53.1
DNF	Neben Evol	Chevrolet Corvette	-	O2	12	-	100	-	-
DNF	Dick Guldstrand	Chevrolet Corvette	18	O2	12	-	100	23	1:52.6
DNF	Al Whatley	Ford GT40	43	O2	7	-	100	-	-
DNF	Ralph Salyer	McLaren M1A-Oldsmobile	28	O2	7	-	-	9	1:46.8
DNF	Charlie Hayes	McLaren M1B-Chevrolet	97	O2	6	-	-	2	1:40.3
DNF	Ronnie Bucknum	Lola T70-Chevrolet	31	O2	5	-	-	10	1:46.9
DSQ	Dave Ridenour	Ford Mustang	71	O2	4	-	-	-	-
DNS	Jerry Titus	Elva Mk 7S-Porsche	58	U2	-	-	-	15	1:50.6
DNS	Jim Dittemore	Cobra	4	O2	-	-	-	19	1:50.5
DNS	Mason O'Keiff	McLaren M1B-Chevrolet	98	O2	-	-	-	21	1:51.8

Fastest Qualifier:	Jerry Grant	Lola T70-Ford		1:39.7	108.33 mph
Race Distance:	180 miles	60 laps of 3.0 mile course			
Race Time:	1hr 48min 44.7sec				
Winner's Speed:	99.31 mph				
Victory Margin:	33 seconds				
Fastest Race Lap:	Unknown				

Bill Krause #88 in the Pacesetter Homes Lola T70. Check the scoops and wing on the rear deck. Krause ran in third place until retiring with a burnt clutch. Photo from the collections of the Henry Ford.

UNITED STATES
ROAD RACING CHAMPIONSHIP
AND Mission Bell Trophy Race

RIVERSIDE INTERNATIONAL RACEWAY
April 30---May 1, 1966

CONDUCTED BY—California Sports Car Club Region of SCCA

1966 Riverside USRRC race program. Scan courtesy Don Markle.

ABOVE–Namaste! Jerry Grant and Charlie Hayes make up after accusations that Grant purposely sprayed Hayes' car with stones at Stardust. Photo from the collections of The Henry Ford.

LEFT–Grant qualified on the pole, but Hayes got the drop on him at the start and led. Photo from the collections of The Henry Ford.

1966 Riverside

There were forty-eight pre-race entries for the Riverside USRRC and thirty-one of them started the race. Earl Jones was in the Genie that Bill Eve raced at Stardust. They would swap drives in the car throughout the season. Dave Jordan joined the under two-liter ranks, in the Porsche 906 that Ken Miles raced at Stardust. Doug Revson entered a Lotus 23. Norm Smith, Jerry Titus, Nick Dioguardi, Charlie Kulman, Norm Sweetser and Joe Ward were all starting their only USRRC race for the year.

Jerry Grant won the pole position with a qualifying time of 1:26.4 (108.333 mph) and broke Bruce McLaren's 1:26.6 lap record. Charlie Hayes equaled Grant's time in the last five minutes of qualifying to take second on the grid. Next were Buck Fulp (1:29.2) and Skip Hudson (1:29.7). John Cannon was fifth (1:30.2) and Charlie Parsons started sixth (1:30.5).

Raceday was hot with the temperature in the nineties. Charlie Hayes shot off the grid at the start. Grant, Fulp, Charlie Parsons, Hudson and Bill Krause pursued in second through sixth places. Grant selected first gear instead of fourth and got sideways in turn two, on the second lap and Fulp whizzed by into second place. Grant pulled off the course at turn seven, after four laps, with an over-revved engine.

Hayes continued to lead, with a comfortable distance between himself and Buck Fulp. Ron Bucknum closed up on Fulp and they had a great battle for eight laps. Bucknum made a "did-you-see-that" pass on Fulp and began closing on Hayes. Before he got close to Hayes, Bucknum pulled into the pits with heat exhaustion and retired from the race

Lothar Motschenbacher worked his way from sixteenth on the grid, up to fourth place and joined Buck Fulp and Krause in the dice for second place. Four laps later, Lothar got by both for second place. Krause then took third place from Fulp. Hayes was way out in front looking invincible, when the ring and pinion gears broke on lap twenty-six and he coasted to a halt. Also on lap twenty-six, Ralph Salyer's McLaren got out of shape at turn two and flipped over. Salyer was unhurt, but his McLaren was very bent.

Lothar was now in the lead and followed by Krause, Fulp, Hansen, Parsons and Hudson. Lothar began putting distance between himself and Krause. Then Fulp started to reel in Krause. Suddenly, Krause got the bit between his teeth and for the next ten laps he pulled out five seconds on Fulp. Krause couldn't maintain the pace and Fulp eventually took second place from him.

Hansen held down fourth place until lap forty-four when Parsons got by. Hudson got inspired and passed Hansen two laps later. A front spindle broke on Hansen's Lotus and he retired after forty-seven laps. Hudson passed Parsons on lap fifty to take fourth place. After four more laps, Hudson took third place from Krause. Lothar spun at turn six on lap fifty. He got going again, in time to keep Fulp twenty seconds behind. Lothar's engine blew up eight laps later and Fulp inherited the lead.

Hudson was now in second place and really motoring. He was visibly faster than Fulp and closing at a rate of a second a lap. On the final lap, Hudson closed right up on Fulp's tail, going into the last turn. They came out of the turn side by side and it was a drag race to the finish, with Fulp winning by barely a second. Charlie Parsons was third and Krause was fourth. Scooter Patrick was fifth and the first under two-liter finisher in a Porsche 906. Ed Hamill scored the final point for sixth place.

With two races down Charlie Parsons and Skip Hudson led the series with 10 points each. Next up were John Cannon and Buck Fulp, each with 9 points. Fifth place was shared with Mak Kronn, Bill Krause and Ed Hamill having 3 points each. Scooter Patrick was in eighth place with 2 points and Ken Miles had 1 point.

Charlie Parsons #10 and Lothar Motschenbacher #27 dicing for third place. Photo from the collections of The Henry Ford.

Early in the race, the battle for fourth place was fought between Skip Hudson #9, John Cannon #62, Ron Bucknum #31, Bill Krause #88, Earl Jones #52, and Bud Morley #6. By the end of the race Hudson was second, Krause was fourth, and Morley was seventh. Photo from the collections of The Henry Ford.

Buck Fulp #26 and Bill Krause #88 fought over third place early in the race. Fulp won after Lothar's engine blew up and Krause finished in fourth place. Photo from the collections of The Henry Ford.

Scooter Patrick #33 was the top under two-liter finisher in fifth place. George Follmer #16 was eighth and Dave Jordan #34 retired after sixth two laps. Photo from the collections of The Henry Ford.

1966 RIVERSIDE • USRRC
May 1, 1966 Riverside International Raceway   Riverside, California

Place	Driver	Car/Engine	Car #	Laps	Points	Prize	Qualifying Place	Qualifying Time
1	Buck Fulp	Lola T70-Chevrolet	26	O2	70	9	$ 2,600	3 1:29.2
2	Skip Hudson	Lola T70-Chevrolet	9	O2	70	6	1,200	4 1:29.7
3	Charlie Parsons	Genie Mk 10-Chevrolet	10	O2	70	4	900	6 1:30.5
4	Bill Krause	Lola T70-Chevrolet	88	O2	70	3	700	12 1:32.7
5	Scooter Patrick	Porsche 906	33	U2	68	2	1,500	14 1:34.2
6	Ed Hamill	Hamill SR3-Oldsmobile	6	O2	67	1	300	20 1:36.3
7	Bud Morley	McLaren M1B-Oldsmobile	66	O2	67	-	250	8 1:30.9
8	George Follmer	Lotus 23-Porsche	16	U2	67	-	700	16 1:35.0
9	John Morton	Lotus 23-Porsche	46	U2	67	-	400	21 1:36.5
10	Don Skogmo	Genie Mk 10-Oldsmobile	37	O2	63	-	100	17 1:35.2
11	Budd Clusserath	McKee Mk 6-Oldsmobile	64	O2	63	-	100	--
12	Norm Smith	Porsche 904GTS	0	U2	61	-	300	--
13	Bill Young	Lotus Elan	99	U2	61	-	150	--
14	Jerry Titus	Porsche 911	81	U2	61	-	100	--
15	Charlie Kulman	Lotus 23B	-	U2	55	-	100	--
16	Norman Sweetser	Merlyn	-	U2	51	-	100	--
DNF	Lothar Motschenbacher	McLaren M1B-Oldsmobile	27	O2	62	-	50	9 1:31.2
DNF	Dave Jordan	Porsche 906	34	U2	62	-	50	15 1:34.5
DNF	Miles Gupton	Playtpus-Porsche	75	U2	59	-	50	18 1:35.8
DNF	Jerry Hansen	Lotus 19-Chevrolet	44	O2	47	-	50	10 1:32.0
DNF	Mason O'Keiff	McLaren M1B-Chevrolet	98	O2	35	-	50	22 1:37.1
DNF	Charlie Hayes	McLaren M1B-Chevrolet	97	O2	26	-	50	2 1:26.4
DNF	Ralph Salyer	McLaren M1A-Oldsmobile	28	O2	23	-	50	11 1:32.1
DNF	Joe Ward	Bobsy SR3	14	U2	22	-	50	--
DNF	Ron Bucknum	Lola T70-Chevrolet	31	O2	21	-	50	7 1:30.6
DNF	Al Whatley	Ford GT40	43	O2	17	-	50	23 1:39.2
DNF	Doug Revson	Lotus 23-Climax	23	U2	16	-	50	19 1:36.1
DNF	John Cannon	Genie Mk 10-Chevrolet	62	O2	12	-	50	5 1:30.2
DNF	Jerry Grant	Lola T70-Ford	8	O2	4	-	50	1 1:26.4
DNF	Earl Jones	Genie Mk 10-Ford	52	O2	4	-	50	13 1:33.4
DNF	Nick Dioguardi	Lotus 23	-	U2	4	-	50	--

Fastest Qualifier:	Jerry Grant	Lola T70-Ford	1:26.4	108.333 mph
Race Distance:	182.0 miles	70 laps of 2.6 mile course		
Race Time:	1hr 49min 26.0sec			
Winner's Speed:	99.786 mph			
Victory Margin:	1 second			
Fastest Race Lap:	Skip Hudson	Lola T70-Chevrolet	1:29.0	105.169 mph

Buck Fulp takes the checkered flag and his first USRRC win. Photo from the collections of The Henry Ford.

USRRC MAY 6·7·8 1966
LAGUNA SECA

1966 Laguna Seca USRRC program cover. Scan courtesy Don Markle.

Laguna Seca

When the teams arrived at Laguna Seca, there were twelve drivers who had competed at both Stardust and Riverside. The major players were John Cannon, George Follmer, Jerry Grant, Miles Gupton, Ed Hamill, Jerry Hansen, Charlie Hayes, Skip Hudson, Lothar Motschenbacher, Scooter Patrick, Charlie Parsons and Don Skogmo. This would be Follmer's last USRRC race of the year due to a lack of funds. It would also be Ken Miles last USRRC race ever. He lost his life testing the Ford GT J-car at Riverside in August. Drivers who had started at either Stardust or Riverside were Dave Jordan, now in Haskell Wexler's Russkit Lola, Dick Guldstrand, Bill Eve, Jim Roe, Steve Diulo, Norm Smith, Bud Morley, Harry Banta and Dave Ridenour who was now in a Lotus 23. Making their first USRRC start of the year were: Ludwig Heimrath, Bob Challman, Stan Burnett, Jerry Entin, Gerry Bruihl, Doug Walker, Bill Amick, R.J. Schmidt and Don Cummins. In all, there were twenty-two over two-liter starters and ten under two-liter starters.

Qualifying was a two-day affair for this race, due to a full schedule of regional races on Saturday. Friday would determine the first twenty-four grid positions, with the balance qualifying on Sunday morning

before the race. When qualifying began on Friday, Charlie Hayes turned in a few moderate laps before he cranked out a pole winning 1:08.98. Lothar Motschenbacher was next on the grid as he got his McLaren around in 1:09.16. John Cannon tied Lothar's time for the third grid spot. In fourth spot was Bud Morley (1:09.82) with Charlie Parsons next to him (1:10.33). Jerry Grant was at Indianapolis on Friday. His crew arrived at Laguna Seca with the Lola and a stock-looking Ford engine. Jerry flew in on Saturday morning and found out there would not be a qualifying session that day. He did not even set a qualifying time during the Sunday session and started the race from the back of the grid.

It was overcast, wet and windy on raceday. The start was wild. This race was the first time the cars would start on a false grid and then move up to the real grid to take the flag. Charlie Hayes missed the driver's meeting in which this was explained and as the cars rolled up to the startline Hayes put his car in neutral, expecting the usual wait. They were flagged away immediately and Hayes was sitting there looking for a gear with cars roaring by him on both sides.

John Cannon grabbed the lead from Lo-

thar going into the first turn. Bud Morley and Jerry Hansen were third and fourth. During the start, Harry Banta stalled his engine right in front of Jerry Grant. Somehow, Grant was able to slice around him on the right and got off the track. Grant was giving it everything he had when he got back on the track and passed six or seven cars before the end of the first lap. Hayes got his car into gear and worked up to sixth place by the end of the first lap. He was behind Dave Jordan but ahead of Scooter Patrick, Stan Burnett, Ken Miles, Charlie Parsons and Skip Hudson.

There was a lot of place shifting during the first four laps as Hayes worked his way into the lead. Cannon was a few seconds behind, in second place. Lothar had Grant trying to take third place away from him and Bud Morley was the first retirement of the race.

The under two-liter cars had their own excitement. John Morton snapped a halfshaft at the start. Scooter Patrick took the early lead and had Ken Miles on his tail. Miles got a little too close, missed a braking point and shoved Patrick into the hay bales. Scooter tried to find reverse but couldn't. He put it in first and plowed his way through the haybales to get back into

Skip Hudson followed Charlie Parsons for the whole race and finished in third place. Photo from the collections of The Henry Ford.

Dave Jordan ran in sixth place for most of the race and finished in fourth place, following the demise of Lothar and Cannon. Photo from the collections of The Henry Ford.

the race. As Scooter got back on the course, Miles Cobra spun right in front of him. George Follmer had to pit to have his gas filler cap secured.

Up front, Hayes was building up a lead. Grant was in fourth place when his engine starting steaming. Lothar passed John Cannon for second place on lap twenty-four and Grant pitted to have his engine looked at. The head gasket on Grant's Ford engine was beginning to self-destruct. The AAR crew did not have enough time to rebuild the Gurney-Weslake engine that got over-revved at last week's Riverside event. As a result, Grant's Lola was fitted with a basi-cally stock 289 Cobra engine. Grant had to park the Lola as the head gasket blew with

finality after thirty-five laps. Scooter Patrick retired his Porsche with a broken piston one lap later.

The race settled down with Hayes leading Lothar Motschenbacher, Cannon, Parsons, Hudson, Jordan and Miles. Around lap forty, Lothar picked up his pace and started closing in on Hayes. Ed Hamill had his transmission stick in low gear and he retired after fifty-nine laps. John Cannon's engine lost oil pressure, so he pulled off the course, turned off the engine and restarted it. He was able to get going again and still keep third place ahead of Parsons. However, it was to no avail as he retired after sixty-seven laps. After seventy laps, Lothar had moved his McLaren to within four seconds behind

Hayes. However, two laps later a halfshaft snapped and Lothar was out of the race.

The race ran out with Charlie Hayes winning by two laps over Charlie Parsons. Skip Hudson finished in third place and Dave Jordan brought the Wexler Lola home in fourth. Ken Miles was fifth and George Follmer grabbed the final point for sixth.

Charlie Parson's second place gave him a total of 16 points and sole possession of first place in the championship. Skip Hudson was in second with 14 points, while Cannon, Hayes and the absent Buck Fulp shared third place with 9 points each. Sixth place was a five-way tie between Mak Kronn, Ed Hamill, Bill Krause, Dave Jordan and Ken Miles with 3 points each.

Ken Miles got fifth place, in Otto Zipper's Porsche, and was the first under two-liter finisher. Photo from the collections of The Henry Ford.

George Follmer brought his Lotus-Porsche home in sixth place. This would be the last USRRC race in '66 for Follmer. The new points structure was not kind to under two-liter cars. Photo from the collections of The Henry Ford.

Jerry Grant missed qualifying and started the race from the back of the grid. He worked his way up to fourth place and held it for twenty laps before he pitted with engine problems. Photo by Gil Munz.

1966 LAGUNA SECA • USRRC

May 8, 1966, Laguna Seca Raceway, Monterey, California

Place	Driver	Car/Engine	Car #	Class	Laps	Points	Prize	Qualifying Place	Qualifying Time
1	Charlie Hayes	McLaren M1B-Chevrolet	97	O2	80	9	$ 2,750	1	1:09.98
2	Charlie Parsons	Genie Mk 10-Chevrolet	10	O2	78	6	1,700	5	1:10.33
3	Skip Hudson	Lola T70-Chevrolet	9	O2	78	4	1,200	-	-
4	Dave Jordan	Lola T70-Ford	51	O2	77	3	900	6	1:11.95
5	Ken Miles	Porsche 906	34	U2	76	2	1,350	10	1:12.89
6	George Follmer	Lotus 23-Porsche	16	U2	75	1	1,050	-	-
7	Don Skogmo	Genie Mk 10-Chevrolet	31	O2	73	-	500	-	-
8	Miles Gupton	Platypus-Porsche	75	U2	73	-	700	-	-
9	Doug Revson	Lotus 23-Climax	23	U2	72	-	500	-	-
10	Dave Ridenour	Lotus 23	14	U2	72	-	300	-	-
11	Bob Challman	Lotus 30-Ford	-	O2	70	-	150	-	-
12	Richard Schmidt	Lotus 23	41	U2	70	-	150	-	-
13	Dick Guldstrand	Chevrolet Corvette	18	O2	69	-	150	-	-
14	Ludwig Heimrath	McLaren M1A-Ford	95	O2	68	-	100	-	-
15	Stan Burnett	Burnett Mk 2-Chevrolet	61	O2	67	-	100	8	1:12.69
16	Jim Roe	McLaren M1A-Chevrolet	-	O2	55	-	100	-	-
17	Bill Eve	Genie Mk 10-Ford	52	O2	42	-	100	-	-
DNF	Lothar Motschenbacher	McLaren M1B-Ford	27	O2	72	-	100	2	1:09.16
DNF	John Cannon	Genie Mk 10-Chevrolet	62	O2	67	-	100	3	1:09.16
DNF	Ed Hamill	Hamill SR3-Oldsmobile	65	O2	59	-	100	9	1:12.89
DNF	Scooter Patrick	Porsche 906	32	U2	36	-	50	-	-
DNF	Pierre Phillips	Lotus 23-Porsche	33	U2	35	-	50	-	-
DNF	Jerry Grant	Lola T70-Ford	8	O2	35	-	50	33	-
DNF	Jerry Hansen	Lotus 19-Chevrolet	44	O2	31	-	50	7	1:12.09
DNF	Steve Diulo	Lotus 19-Chevrolet	29	O2	24	-	50	-	-
DNF	Jerry Entin	McLaren M1B-Oldsmobile	2	O2	23	-	50	-	-
DNF	Harry Banta	Ferharry-Ford	17	O2	22	-	50	-	-
DNF	Gerry Bruihl	Cooper-Chevrolet	-	O2	12	-	50	-	-
DNF	Doug Walker	Chaparral 1-Chevrolet	1	O2	11	-	50	-	-
DNF	Norm Smith	Porsche 904GTS	-	U2	10	-	50	-	-
DNF	Don Cummins	Genie Mk 4-Climax	64	-	9	-	50	-	-
DNF	Bill Amick	McLaren M1B-Chevrolet	19	O2	7	-	50	-	-
DNF	Bud Morley	McLaren M1B-Oldsmobile	6	O2	4	-	50	4	1:09.82
DNF	John Morton	Lotus 23-Porsche	4	U2	0	-	-	-	-
DNS	Bob Johnson	McKee Mk 4-Ford	33	O2	-	-	-	20	1:13.2

Fastest Qualifier:	Charlie Hayes	McLaren M1B-Chevrolet	1:09.98	97.742 mph
Race Distance:	152.0 miles	80 laps of 1.9 mile course		
Race Time:	1hr 35min 27.3sec			
Winner's Speed:	95.5 mp			
Victory Margin:	2 laps, 25 seconds			
Fastest Race Lap:	Charlie Hayes	McLaren M1B-Chevrolet	1:09.161	98.9 mph

Richard Schmidt #41 is about to be passed by Dave Ridenour #14. Photo by Gil Munz.

1966 Bridgehampton Vanderbilt Cup USRRC program cover. Scan courtesy Don Markle.

Race winner, Jerry Grant (#8) following Sherman Decker (#67) during practice. Decker ran in the top three for the first three laps, then retired due to a patch on the gas tank that did not hold. Photo by Dave Nicholas.

Bridgehampton

Bridgehampton had a strong entry with the series regulars: Charlie Parsons, Jerry Grant, Ed Hamill, Jerry Hansen, Lothar Motschenbacher, Bud Morley, Don Skogmo and Doug Revson. West Coast entrants were Bob Montana, John Morton, Earl Jones and Scooter Patrick. There were twenty East Coast entrants making their first start this year; Mike Goth, Dick Thompson, Bill Wonder, George Wintersteen, Oscar Kovelski, Bob Grossman, Peter Gregg and Skip Barber. Missing from this race were Charlie Hayes, Buck Fulp, George Follmer and Skip Hudson. Hayes' crew had two road accidents towing the McLaren. The second accident damaged the car enough that Charlie had to sit this one out. Fulp was still bothered by the Stardust eye injury. Follmer had sold his car and did not have a replacement. Hudson just decided to skip this race.

Long Island experienced unusually heavy rainfall during the week preceding the Bridgehampton race. Friday practice was cancelled to clean off the track. Saturday morning, there was light rain, followed by clearing skies and rising temperatures. It was eighty degrees and humid when qualifying started. Jerry Grant was one of the first

drivers on the track and he was quick immediately. At the end of the session, Sherman Decker tried following Grant around the course and ended up sharing the front row with him. Grant's time was 1:39.2 and Decker's was 1:39.4. Mike Goth was third on the grid with a 1:40.6.

Grant was first off the line when the race started, but was soon passed by Goth. As the cars came around at the end of the first lap, Goth was still leading Grant, who was followed by Decker, Lothar Motschenbacher, Bud Morley and Charlie Parsons. Decker retired after three laps because a patch on his gas tank did not hold. Grant retook the lead from Goth and started pulling away from the field at a rate of two seconds a lap. Lothar started closing in on Goth and passed him on the tenth lap.

John Cannon had started near the back of the grid and worked his way up to sixth place, behind Morley and Parsons. Cannon got fifth place when Charlie Parsons retired after thirty-two laps. This was Parsons' first retirement of the season. Cannon was able to get by both Morley and Goth to take third place after a few more laps.

Scooter Patrick led the under two-liter cars, with Peter Gregg following. Herb

Wetanson and Joe Buzzetta put on a show passing each other, until Buzzetta's engine broke a valve spring on lap thirty-one and he retired.

Cannon's car had fuel problems with less than twenty laps to go and he pitted for fuel. In haste to improve his position, Cannon spun his car into the sand. He did get it going again, but finished out of the points.

Morley was running in third place behind Grant and Lothar, when his engine started misfiring. Morley stumbled his way down the field to eleventh place by the end of the race. Grant won by forty-two seconds and his average speed of 97.46 mph was a new race record. Lothar finished in second, with Goth in third place, a lap back. Scooter Patrick was the first under two-liter finisher in fourth place. Herb Wetanson and Peter Gregg finished in fifth and sixth places.

Parsons and Hudson remained first and second in the championship with sixteen and fourteen points, respectively. Third was now a four-way tie as Cannon, Fulp, Hayes and Grant each had nine points. Lothar Motschenbacher was seventh with six points and Scooter Patrick was eighth with five points.

Oscar Kovelski, in his #64 Cooper-Chevrolet, was the last of twenty-three finishers. Photo by Dave Nicholas.

Jerry Hansen in the ex-Jerry Grant Lotus 19-Chevrolet DNF'd after three laps. Photo by Dave Nicholas.

George Wintersteen and Oscar Kovelski discussing things. Photo by Dave Nicholas.

Sherman Decker in the pits during practice. Photo by Dave Nicholas.

Skip Barber's Brabham BT8-Climax. Skip finished seventh overall and was fourth in the under two-liter class. Photo by Robert Raymond.

Jerry Grant's AAR Lola in the pits. After three and a half years of running at the front of races, only to DNF, Grant finally won a USRRC race. Photo by Robert Raymond.

1966 BRIDGEHAMPTON • USRRC

May 22, 1966, Bridgehampton Race Circuit, Long Island, New York

Place	Driver	Car/Engine	Car #	Class	Laps	Points	Prize
1	Jerry Grant	Lola T70-Ford	8	O2	70	9	$2,600
2	Lothar Motschenbacher	McLaren M1B-Olds	27	O2	70	6	1,300
3	Mike Goth	McLaren M1A-Chevrolet	96	O2	69	4	900
4	Scooter Patrick	Porsche 906	33	U2	68	3	1,700
5	Herb Wetanson	Porsche 906	15	U2	68	2	1,100
6	Peter Gregg	Porsche 906	1	U2	68	1	600
7	Skip Barber	Brabham BT8-Climax	18	U2	67	-	450
8	John Morton	Lotus 23-Porsche	46	U2	67	-	200
9	Don Skogmo	Genie Mk 10-Oldsmobile	31	O2	66	-	150
10	Bob Nagel	Elva Mk 8-BMW	4	U2	66	-	100
11	Bud Morley	McLaren M1B-Ford	66	O2	66	-	100
12	Ralph Treischmann	Porsche 906	56	U2	65	-	100
13	Dick Thompson	Ford GT-40	22	O2	64	-	100
14	Mike Hall	Porsche 906	69	U2	64	-	100
15	Bill Wonder	Ford GT-40	11	O2	64	-	100
16	John Cannon	Genie Mk 10-Chevrolet	62	O2	63	-	100
17	George Wintersteen	Corvette Grand Sport	12	O2	62	-	50
18	Doug Revson	Lotus 23-Climax	23	U2	62	-	50
19	Fred Ashplant	Elva Mk 8-BMW	73	U2	59	-	50
20	Bob Colombosian	Lotus-Elan	60	U2	58	-	50
21	Sam Posey	Porsche 904GTS	20	U2	56	-	50
22	Earl Jones	Genie Mk 10-Ford	52	O2	45	-	50
23	Oscar Koveleski	Cooper-Chevrolet	64	O2	38	-	50
DNF	Bob Grossman	Ferrari 330P	6	O2	53	-	-
DNF	George Ralph	Elva Mk 8-BMW	2	U2	51	-	-
DNF	Charlie Parsons	Genie Mk 10-Chevrolet	10	O2	32	-	-
DNF	Joe Buzzetta	Porsche 906	7	U2	31	-	-
DNF	Ed Hamill	Hamill SR3-Oldsmobile	65	O2	31	-	-
DNF	Bob Montana	McKee Mk 5-Plymouth	45	O2	14	-	-
DNF	Jerry Crawford	Lola T70-Chevrolet	70	O2	10	-	-
DNF	Alan Friedland	McKee Mk 3-Ford	19	O2	9	-	-
DNF	Jerry Hansen	Lotus 19-Chevrolet	44	O2	3	-	-
DNF	Sherman Decker	Lola T70-Ford	67	O2	3	-	-
DSQ	Sy Kabach	Elva Mk 7S-BMW	72	U2	-	-	-

Fastest Qualifier:	Jerry Grant	Lola T70-Ford	1:39.2	103.79 mph
Race Distance:	199.5 miles	70 laps of 2.85 mile course		
Race Time:	2hr 2min 4.8sec			
Winner's Speed:	97.46 mph			
Victory Margin:	42 seconds			
Fastest Race Lap:	Jerry Grant	Lola T70-Ford	1:40.4	102.6 mph

Earl Jones Genie Mk 10-Ford in the pits. Photo by Robert Raymond.

Bob Montana brought his McKee Mk5-Plymouth, with big hemi engine, but DNF'd after fifteen laps. Photo by Robert Raymond.

George Wintersteen's Corvette Grand Sport was dated compared to the Lolas and McLarens. Photo by Robert Raymond.

John Morton was eighth overall and the fifth under two-liter finisher in his Lotus 23-Porsche. Photo by Robert Raymond.

Charlie Parsons ran in the top ten for the first thirty laps before retiring. Photo by Dave Nicholas.

19th ANNUAL WATKINS GLEN

SPORTS CAR GRAND PRIX

JUNE 24, 25, 26, 1966   50 cents

1966 Watkins Glen Sports Car Grand Prix race program cover. Scan courtesy Don Markle.

Watkins Glen

The East Coast was in the middle of a heat wave when the series rolled into Watkins Glen. Temperatures were in the nineties and some of the cars were feeling the effects. One of Otto Zipper's Porsches blew an engine. When Otto could not get a replacement engine from the Porsche distributor, he withdrew both cars and immediately put them up for sale.

Once again, Jerry Grant took the pole position with a time of 1:15.0. This was in a new Lola T70 with a 500 horsepower Gurney-Weslake engine. Buck Fulp was second on the grid, 1.2 seconds behind Grant. On row two of the grid, were Mark Donohue and Mike Goth, both at 1:16.4.

Grant leaped into the lead when the race started, but was passed by Donohue before the end of the first lap. Charlie Parsons was third with Fulp, Kronn and Goth behind. Grant stopped in the pits after two laps, with a sticky throttle. He was told that nothing

could be done about it and was sent back out, a lap down.

Mike Goth retired after seven laps with a bum transmission. Lothar followed suit after eleven laps with a broken fan belt.

On lap nineteen, John Cannon came up to lap Joe Buzzetta's Porsche. They exchanged blows just over the hill, beyond turn two. Buzzetta spun off course, while Cannon spun and stalled, sideways, in the middle of the track. Donohue came flying around the corner and plowed into the left front of Cannon's Genie. Donohue's Lola burst into flames and he was lucky to get out with just minor burns. Although the fire crew responded quickly, part of the track melted from the heat of the fire. Donohue's car was a total write-off and Cannon's Genie needed a lot of work. The race was red-flagged and stopped for an hour, so the course could be cleaned up.

Charlie Parsons led off the line when the race was re-started, with Mak Kronn and

Buck Fulp close behind. Skip Barber was seventh and leading the under two-liter class in his Brabham BT8. Kronn spun on lap thirty-two, giving second place to Fulp. Parsons' car started slowing with transmission problems and Fulp passed him for the lead on lap thirty-four.

Barber's car developed suspension problems after sixty laps and he drifted down through the field. The race ran the final twenty laps with Fulp leading Mak Kronn, Bill Eve, Skip Hudson and Jerry Grant. Ralph Treischmann was the first under two-liter car in sixth place, ahead of Herb Wetanson and George Wintersteen.

Buck Fulp became the first driver to score two wins this season. His average speed for the race, 101.46 mph, was two miles an hour faster than Jim Hall's record from the previous year. Also, Fulp and Grant shared the fastest race lap at 1:17.2, two seconds faster than the previous record.

Skip Hudson #9 qualified seventeenth and finished in fourth place. Here Skip is taking his place on the grid, behind the Comstock Ford GT of Eppie Weitzes with Oscar Kovelski moving up on the left to take his place next to Skip. Photo by Gil Munz.

Behind Grant, Buck Fulp #26 led Mark Donohue #6, Mike Goth #96, Charlie Parsons #0, and Mak Kronn #77 across the line on the first lap. Photo by Gil Munz.

Going to the grid are Mak Kronn #77, Charlie Parson #0, and Ed Hamill #65. Kronn qualified sixth and finished second. Parsons qualified fifth and retired with transmission problems. Hamill qualified seventh, ran in third place for a while, then retired with an oil leak after fifteen laps. Photo by Gil Munz.

1966 WATKINS GLEN • USRRC Sports Car Grand Prix
June 26, 1966, Watkins Glen, Watkins Glen, New York

Place	Driver	Car/Engine	Car #	Class	Laps	Points	Prize	Qualifying Place	Qualifying Time
1	Buck Fulp	Lola T70-Chevrolet	26	O2	87	9	$3,250	2	1:16.2
2	Mak Kronn	McKee Mk 6-Chevrolet	77	O2	87	6	1,500	6	1:18.7
3	Bill Eve	Genie Mk 10-Ford	52	O2	85	4	1,200	11	1:20.3
4	Skip Hudson	Lola T70-Chevrolet	9	O2	85	3	1,000	17	1:22.6
5	Jerry Grant	Lola T70-Ford	8	O2	85	2	1,150	1	1:15.0
6	Ralph Treischmann	Porsche 906	56	U2	82	1	1,300	19	1:23.6
7	Herb Wetanson	Porsche 906	15	U2	81	-	900	23	1:24.3
8	George Wintersteen	Corvette Grand Sport	12	O2	81	-	300	26	1:26.1
9	Peter Gregg	Porsche 906	4	U2	81	-	575	21	1:23.9
10	John Dennis	Denmacher II	41	U2	74	-	400	29	1:28.4
11	Oscar Koveleski	Cooper-Chevrolet	64	O2	66	-	100	16	1:21.3
12	Skip Barber	Brabham BT8-Climax	48	U2	65	-	300	22	1:24.1
13	Chuck Dietrich	Elva Mk 7S-BMW	57	U2	63	-	225	20	1:23.6
14	Eppie Weitzes	Ford GT-40	95	O2	62	-	100	15	1:21.3
DNF	Bob Montana	McKee Mk 5-Plymouth	75	O2	62	-	100	18	1:23.3
DNF	John Morton	Lotus 23-Porsche	46	U2	48	-	100	25	1:25.6
DNF	Don Skogmo	Genie Mk 10-Chevrolet	31	O2	38	-	100	13	1:21.6
DNF	Charlie Parsons	Genie Mk 10-Chevrolet	0	O2	37	-	100	5	1:17.1
DNF	Bob Bucher	Lola T70-Ford	29	O2	34	-	100	8	1:19.8
DNF	Ludwig Heimrath	McLaren M1A-Ford	3	O2	25	-	100	9	1:19.9
DNF	John Cannon	Genie Mk 10-Chevrolet	62	O2	18	-	100	10	1:20.0
DNF	Mark Donohue	Lola T70-Chevrolet	6	O2	18	-	100	3	1:16.4
DNF	Joe Buzzetta	Porsche 906	7	U2	17	-	100	14	1:22.4
DNF	Ed Hamill	Hamill SR3-Oldsmobile	65	O2	15	-	100	7	1:17.1
DNF	Doug Revson	Lotus 23-Climax	23	U2	13	-	100	23	1:24.3
DNF	Lothar Motschenbacher	McLaren M1B-Olds	17	O2	11	-	100	12	1:20.3
DNF	Mike Goth	McLaren M1A-Chevrolet	96	O2	7	-	100	4	1:16.4
DNF	Hal Keck	Cobra	88	O2	6	-	100	24	1:25.2
DNF	Charlie Kolb	Porsche 906	1	U2	2	-	100	30	1:30.0
DNQ	Candido DaMota	Lotus-Climax	42	U2	-	-	-	31	1:30.4
DNQ	Ed Hessert	Elva Mk 7-Ford	19	U2	-	-	-	32	1:33.6
DNQ	Alvin Forsyth	Chevrolet Corvette	81	O2	-	-	-	33	1:34.0

Fastest Qualifier:	Jerry Grant	Lola T70-Ford		1:15.0	110.4 mph
Race Distance:	200.1 miles	87 laps of 2.3 mile course			
Race Time:	1hr 58min 20.3sec				
Winner's Speed:	101.46 mph				
Victory Margin:	48 seconds				
Fastest Race Lap:	Jerry Grant & Buck Fulp	Lola T70-Ford & Chev		1:17.2	107.25 mph

Eppie Weitzes at speed in the #95 Comstock Ford GT. Weitzes qualified fifteenth and ran in mid-field until he began a series of pitstops to cure a cooling problem. Photo by William Green.

On lap nineteen John Cannon, in Dan Blocker's Vinegaroon Genie, came up to lap Joe Buzzetta, in a Porsche 906, at turn two and they made heavy contact. Then Mark Donohue came along and spun into the driver's side of Cannon's Genie. Here is Cannon climbing out of the Genie after hitting Buzzetta and being hit by Donohue. Buzzetta's car is under the dustcloud. Photo by William Green.

The aftermath of the crashes. Cannon's car is still in the road. Buzzetta's car is to the right of Cannon's Genie. The nose of Cannon's car is on the ground, to the right of Buzzetta's Porsche. Peter Gregg's Porsche #4 is threading his way through the crash scene while Mark Donohue's Sunoco Lola is burning against the guardrail, under the Kendall sign. Photo by William Green.

Cannon's Genie being towed back to the paddock with massive leftside damage. Photo by William Green.

The right side of Cannon's Genie appears relatively undamaged. This car would race again, the following year at the Stardust Can-Am event. Photo by Gil Munz.

UNITED STATES ROAD
RACING CHAMPIONSHIP
JULY 30/31-1966
PACIFIC
RACEWAYS
KENT, WASHINGTON

VOORHIES-66

PROGRAM - FIFTY-CENTS

1966 Pacific Raceways USRRC program cover. Scan courtesy Don Markle.

1966 Pacific Raceways

There was a field of thirty cars at Pacific Raceways, including series regulars, John Cannon, Buck Fulp, Lothar Motschenbacher, Ed Hamill, Doug Revson, and local favorite Jerry Grant. Randy Hilton had taken delivery of a new McLaren M1B and Charlie Parsons spent the previous week here, shaking it down and setting it up. Skip Hudson and Charlie Hayes returned to the series after missing the Bridgehampton race. Mike Goth and Mark Donohue made the trek west for this race. Roger Penske had a new Lola for Donohue, to replace the one destroyed at Watkins Glen. Notable West Coast and local drivers racing were Ron Bucknum, Steve Diulo, Bill Eve, Bud Morley, Stan Burnett, Bill Amick, Lew Florence, Don Wester, Wade Carter, Gary Gove, Rick Stark and Pierre Phillips.

It was a hot and sunny Pacific Northwest weekend. After the East Coast heatwave, some competitors took extra cooling measures. The most obvious of these being Mike Goth's McLaren. It had a clear plexiglass spoiler with dryer hose duct-taped to it, to suck hot air out of the engine compartment.

For the third race in a row, Jerry Grant was the fastest qualifier with a time of 1:19.5. Charlie Hayes and Lothar Motschenbacher filled out the front row with times of 1:20.5 and 1:20.6. Mike Goth (1:21.1) and Mark Donohue (1:21.4) were on row two. Charlie Parsons (1:22.4), John Cannon (1:22.4) and Bill Amick (1:23.1) were on the third

row. Bud Morley (1:23.5) and Stan Burnett (1:23.5) started on row four.

On raceday, Charlie Hayes' crew discovered a water leak in the engine and swapped it out for an untested engine. They finished just minutes before the green flag fell to start the race. Jerry Grant grabbed the lead, as expected, with Lothar right behind him. A few seconds back were Goth, Donohue, Amick, Parsons, Cannon, Burnett, Eve, Hamill, Florence, Hudson and Fulp.

Ron Bucknum was the first to retire. He spun on the fifth lap and could not get going again. Bill Amick retired with no oil pressure on the tenth lap. About this time, the duct tape and flexible hosing on Goth's McLaren started unraveling and flying around behind the car. Goth pitted to have the shreds torn off and was a lap behind when he got underway again. This put Donohue in third place, about ten seconds behind Lothar.

It was fast becoming a race of attrition. The next to retire was local driver, Stan Burnett, who had been running in eighth place. Bud Morley retired after five more laps. Then Skip Hudson pitted with a blown head gasket and Ed Hamill retired after twenty-two laps.

Grant was running strong, with Lothar still right behind. The heat and the fast pace of the race took its toll. Lothar retired with a blown head gasket after twenty-seven laps. Donohue was now ten seconds behind in second place. Grant maintained his lead,

while more drivers back in the field were retiring. As Grant was going into turn two on lap forty-three, the left front brake on his Lola broke and sent him spinning. By the time Jerry recovered, Donohue had closed the gap to four seconds. Donohue was able to get by Grant after two more laps. After that, Grant couldn't even stay close. He dropped further back over the next ten laps and then retired.

Charlie Parsons and John Cannon were having a real tussle for second place. They passed and re-passed each other, until lap sixty, when Parsons' engine started sputtering. Parsons slowed dramatically and nursed his car to the finish. Charlie Hayes was closing quickly on Parsons, when a halfshaft broke and he retired with two laps to go in the race.

Mark Donohue easily had his first USRRC race win, eighty-five seconds ahead of Cannon. Parsons was third, a lap behind. Bill Eve was fourth, ahead of Lew Florence and Don Wester. With his third place, Charlie Parsons retook the championship lead with 20 points. Second was Buck Fulp with 18 points and Skip Hudson was third with 17 points. John Cannon moved up to fourth place with 15 points while Jerry Grant's 11 points put him in fifth place. Sixth was a three-way tie between Charlie Hayes, Mak Kronn and Mark Donohue with nine points each. With two races left, the championship was still wide open.

Race winner, Mark Donohue (#16) leading Mike Goth (#96) and Charlie Parsons #10). Photo by Tom Lebo, courtesy Bill Lebo.

Pacesetter Lola driven by Skip Hudson. Hudson took the rear deck with large airscoops off his Lola and put it on the Pacesetter car. Photo by Tom Lebo, courtesy Bill Lebo.

Dan Blocker (John Cannon's entrant) having a chat with Charlie Parsons. Photo by Gil Munz.

Charlie Parsons, in flight. This was the first race for the new McLaren and Charlie drove it to third place. Photo by Gil Munz.

Jerry Nelson's #18 Porsche 904 about to be lapped by Mike Goth #96, who has some flexible dryer ducting unraveling off the back of his McLaren. The ducting was to provide extra cooling to the brakes during the hot race. In the background is Jerry Grant. Photo by Tom Lebo, courtesy Bill Lebo.

Jerry Grant trying to win his "home" race. Photo by Gil Munz.

1966 PACIFIC RACEWAYS • USRRC

July 31, 1966, Pacific Raceways, Kent, Washington

Place	Driver	Car/Engine	Car #	Class	Laps	Points	Prize	Qualifying Place	Qualifying Time
1	Mark Donohue	Lola T70-Chevrolet	16	O2	68	9	$2,400	6	1:22.4
2	John Cannon	McLaren M1B-Chevrolet	62	O2	68	6	1,300	7	1:22.4
3	Charlie Parsons	McLaren M1B-Chevrolet	10	O2	67	4	900	5	1:21.4
4	Bill Eve	Genie Mk 10-Ford	52	O2	66	3	700	13	1:24.8
5	Lew Florence	Lotus 19-Chevrolet	4	O2	65	2	500	11	1:24.6
6	Don Wester	Porsche 906	60	U2	65	1	1,300	16	1:26.8
7	Doug Revson	Porsche 906	23	U2	65	-	750	19	1:28.8
8	Mike Fisher	Porsche 906	2	U2	64	-	500	17	1:28.6
9	Steve Diulo	Lotus 19-Ford	14	O2	61	-	150	20	1:28.8
10	Ken Legg	Lotus 23-Ford	73	U2	60	-	300	23	1:33.9
11	Wade Carter	Porsche 904GTS	22	U2	60	-	100	24	1:34.0
12	Gary Gove	Chevrolet Corvette 396	77	O2	57	-	100	26	1:34.6
13	Jerry Nelson	Porsche 904GTS	18	U2	55	-	100	-	-
14	Rick Stark	Chevrolet Corvette 396	11	O2	51	-	100	27	1:36.8
15	Pierre Philips	Lotus 23-Porsche	3	U2	49	-	100	22	1:30.4
16	Skip Hudson	Lola T70-Chevrolet	9	O2	39	-	100	15	1:25.1
DNF	Charlie Hayes	McLaren M1B-Chevrolet	97	O2	64	-	50	2	1:20.5
DNF	Buck Fulp	Lola T70-Chevrolet	26	O2	55	-	50	14	1:25.0
DNF	Jerry Grant	Lola T70-Ford	8	O2	52	-	250	1	1:19.5
DNF	Mike Goth	McLaren M1A-Chevrolet	96	O2	47	-	50	4	1:21.1
DNF	Terry Kniss	Cooper-Ford	47	O2	37	-	50	21	1:30.2
DNF	Erik Anderson	Lotus 23-Climax	69	U2	31	-	50	29	1:38.1
DNF	Paul Scott	Lotus 23-Ferrari	12	U2	29	-	50	25	1:34.6
DNF	Lothar Motschenbacher	McLaren M1B-Olds	1	O2	27	-	50	3	1:20.6
DNF	Ed Hamill	Hamill SR3-Oldsmobile	65	O2	22	-	50	12	1:24.6
DNF	Bud Morley	McLaren M1B-Ford	6	O2	20	-	50	9	1:23.5
DNF	Stan Burnett	Burnett Mk 2-Chevrolet	64	O2	15	-	50	10	1:23.5
DNF	John McCornack	McCornack Spl-Ford	13	U2	13	-	50	28	1:37.7
DNF	Bill Amick	McLaren M1B-Mercury	19	O2	9	-	50	8	1:23.1
DNF	Ron Bucknum	Lola T70-Chevrolet	31	O2	4	-	50	8	1:28.6

Fastest Qualifier:	Jerry Grant	Lola T70-Ford	1:19.5	101.9 mph
Race Distance:	153.0 miles	68 laps of 2.25 mile course		
Race Time:	1hr 35min 21.4sec			
Winner's Speed:	96.27 mph			
Victory Margin:	1 minute, 25 seconds			
Fastest Race Lap:	Unknown			

Grant ended his race parked on the back stretch next to Terry Kniss. Photo by Tom Lebo, courtesy Bill Lebo.

UNITED STATES
ROAD RACING
CHAMPIONSHIP
·
AUG. 27-28, 1966

OFFICIAL PROGRAM
FIFTY CENTS

MID·OHIO
SPORTS
CAR
COURSE
LEXINGTON, O.

ACCUS · FIA · SCCA
SANCTION N22-66

1966 Mid Ohio USRRC program cover. Scan courtesy Don Markle.

The field is on the grid and ready to go. Photo by Tom Schultz.

Mid-Ohio

Mark Donohue took pole position with a qualifying time of 1:37.8. John Cannon was second on the grid with the same time as Donohue and Lothar Motschenbacher had the final front row spot with a 1:38.4. On the second row were Charlie Hayes (1:38.6) and Ralph Salyer (1:39.4). Next up were Charlie Parsons (1:40.0), Jerry Hansen (1:40.4) and Ludwig Heimrath (140.6). Charlie Kolb's Dino Ferrari was the fastest under two-liter car with a time of 1:43.8, good enough for the sixth row of the grid. Jerry Grant and his car did not arrive until there was less than an hour left in the qualifying session. They got the Lola off the truck, checked the tire pressures and Grant smoked onto the track. The only trouble was that the Gurney-Weslake engine in Grant's Lola was also smoking. The best time Jerry could manage was a 1:43.2. Grant withdrew his entry, to save the car and engine for the upcoming Can-Am series.

Cannon launched his car ahead of Donohue and Lothar and into the lead when the race started. Heimrath, Parsons, Hayes and Hudson were following. Donohue passed Cannon on the fifth lap to assume the lead. Lothar then moved in closer to Cannon. Heimrath was now fourth, with Charlie Parsons a close fifth. Parsons had Charlie Hayes beside him and Skip Hudson following close behind. Hayes and Hudson both passed Parsons and Heimrath. Parsons got by Heimrath five laps later.

Donohue, Cannon and Lothar were battling it out for the lead. Donohue had the upper hand, but could not let his guard down. Skip Hudson looked like he was flying along in fifth place, but Parsons caught up and passed him after twelve laps and then set out after Hayes.

The leaders started lapping backmarkers. They lapped eighth place Jerry Hansen by the nineteenth lap. On lap twenty-five, Lothar passed Cannon, who was getting nauseated from exhaust fumes in the cockpit. Cannon's car had its transaxle break after nine more laps and he retired. Charlie Hayes started a succession of pitstops to have fuel pump and electrical problems fixed. Unfortunately, they couldn't be fixed and Hayes retired.

Lothar started reeling in Donohue. By lap forty-one, Lothar was just three seconds behind Donohue. The next fifteen laps were a great battle between them. Time and again, Lothar pulled up to Donohue going into a corner, only to have the door shut and Donohue then pulled away exiting the corner. Lothar started falling back on lap fifty-six. He was getting nauseated from Donohue's exhaust fumes. Lothar lost thirty seconds to Donohue during the next seven laps. Charlie Parsons, Buck Fulp and Dick Brown were running a lap behind Mark and Lothar. Joe Buzzetta and Charlie Kolb were the under two-liter leaders, a lap behind Brown. Skip Hudson was running in the top ten, until lap forty-eight. He

stopped at the pits to have oil added to the transaxle case. Hudson then retired with a broken suspension after fifty-seven laps.

The race wound down with no more changes in the top ten until lap seventy-six. Donohue suddenly started slowing down with a deflating rear tire. Lothar's crew hung out sign saying "Donohue coming in" and Lothar picked up his pace. Donohue pitted on lap seventy-eight. His crew added air to the deflated tire and sent him back out. Donohue was stopped for thirty seconds, which was enough time for Lothar to take the lead and pull out twenty seconds. Donohue's car lasted another lap and a half before the engine blew and he retired. Lothar took a very popular first USRRC victory. Charlie Parsons was second with Buck Fulp and Dick Brown two laps back in third and fourth places. Joe Buzzetta beat Charlie Kolb to fifth place and first in the under two-liter class.

The championship was shaping up into a three-horse race. Charlie Parsons still led with 26 points to Fulp's 22 points. Skip Hudson had a very outside chance with 17 points. If Hudson won the final race with Parsons and Fulp not scoring, he would tie Parsons and claim the championship with his wins. Tied for fourth were Lothar and Cannon with fifteen points. Grant still had eleven points and was sixth. Seventh remained a three-way tie between Charlie Hayes, Mak Kronn and Mark Donohue with nine points each.

John Cannon #62 launching into the lead, ahead of Lothar #96 on the left and Mark Donohue #6 on the right. Ludwig Heimrath #39 is behind, on the left and moving up ahead of Ralph Salyer, blue #25 to the right, and Charlie Hayes, white #97 to the right. Charlie Parsons is in the red #10 McLaren on the right and about to pass Hayes #97. Photo by Gil Munz.

Another view of the start with Cannon #62 just edging Lothar #96. Behind, Ludwig Heimrath #39 is a solid third ahead of Mark Donohue #6, with Charlie Parsons #10 in fifth place. Charlie Hayes #97 is sixth and has Jerry Hansen, #88 Wolverine, behind to the left, Mak Kronn, #77 McKee, directly behind, Earl Jones, #52 Genie, is behind to the right, and Skip Hudson #9 on the far right is just about to fly by all of them. Photo by Dave Arnold.

1966 MID-OHIO • USRRC
August 28, 1966, Mid-Ohio Sports Car Course, Lexington, Ohio

Place	Driver	Car/Engine	Car #	Class	Laps	Points	Prize	Qualifying Place	Qualifying Time
1	Lothar Motschenbacher	McLaren M1B-Olds	96	O2	85	9	$2,500	3	1:38.4
2	Charlie Parsons	McLaren M1B-Chevrolet	10	O2	85	6	1,500	6	1:40.0
3	Buck Fulp	Lola T70-Chevrolet	26	O2	83	4	1,100	13	1:42.8
4	Dick Brown	McLaren M1B-Ford	38	O2	83	3	900	10	1:41.8
5	Joe Buzzetta	Porsche 906	7	U2	82	2	1,500	16	1:43.8
6	Charlie Kolb	Ferrari Dino 206S	1	U2	82	1	1,100	15	1:43.2
7	Chuck Dietrich	Elva Mk 7S-BMW	57	U2	81	-	800	21	1:44.8
8	Peter Gregg	Porsche 906	4	U2	79	-	600	28	1:49.2
9	Brooke Doran	McLaren M1B-Chevrolet	3	O2	77	-	300	22	1:45.2
10	Bill Bowman	Porsche 906	87	U2	75	-	350	32	1:51.0
11	Don Skogmo	Lola T70-Chevrolet	31	O2	75	-	75	27	1:48.6
12	John Dennis	Denmacher 2-Porsche	44	U2	75	-	175	30	1:50.6
13	Ralph Treischmann	Porsche 906	56	U2	71	-	75	24	1:46.2
14	Art Seyler	Cooper-Ford	93	O2	68	-	75	19	1:44.4
15	Owen Russell	Russell Spl	83	O2	62	-	75	36	1:58.2
16	Mike Pung	Cheetah	85	O2	60	-	75	23	1:46.0
17	Bob Nagel	Elva Mk 8-BMW	14	U2	53	-	75	29	1:49.8
DNF	Mark Donohue	Lola T70-Chevrolet	6	O2	79	-	75	1	1:37.8
DNF	Skip Hudson	Lola T70-Chevrolet	9	O2	57	-	75	11	1:42.8
DNF	Earl Jones	Genie Mk 10-Ford	52	O2	41	-	75	9	1:41.6
DNF	Phil Seitz	Lotus 23-Climax	72	U2	41	-	50	34	1:55.1
DNF	Tom Jones	Ferrari 290	28	O2	40	-	50	-	-
DNF	John Cannon	McLaren M1B-Chevrolet	62	O2	36	-	50	2	1:37.8
DNF	Charlie Hayes	McLaren M1B-Chevrolet	97	O2	36	-	50	4	1:38.6
DNF	Dave Causey	Lotus 19-Ford	54	O2	35	-	50	25	1:46.4
DNF	Ludwig Heimrath	McLaren M1A-Ford	39	O2	28	-	50	8	1:40.6
DNF	Jerry Hansen	Wolverine-Chevrolet	88	O2	27	-	50	7	1:40.4
DNF	Tom Payne	Cobra 427	-	O2	25	-	50	20	1:44.6
DNF	Mike Hall	Porsche 906	69	U2	24	-	50	26	1:47.8
DNF	Mak Kronn	McKee Mk 6-Chevrolet	77	O2	20	-	50	12	1:42.8
DNF	Bob Harris	Genie Mk 10-Oldsmobile	95	O2	11	-	-	18	1:44.2
DNF	Ralph Salyer	McKee Mk 6-Oldsmobile	25	O2	9	-	-	5	1:39.4
DNF	Doug Revson	Porsche 906	23	U2	7	-	-	-	-
DNF	Scott Beckett	Genie Mk 8-Chevrolet	11	O2	6	-	-	31	1:51.0
DNF	Bud Gates	McLaren M1A-Chevrolet	73	O2	2	-	-	17	1:44.2

Fastest Qualifier:	Mark Donohue	Lola T70-Chevrolet	1:37.8	88.34 mph	
Race Distance:	204.0 miles	85 laps of 2.4 mile course			
Race Time:	1hr 35min 21.4sec				
Winner's Speed:	84.13 mph				
Victory Margin:	1 minute, 26.2 seconds				
Fastest Race Lap:	Mark Donohue & Lothar Motschenbacher		1:38.6	87.63 mph	

Lothar Motschenbacher speeding his way to victory.
Photo by Tom Schultz.

Lothar and wife, Marilyn, after taking a victory lap.
Photo by Dave Arnold.

Charlie Parsons' second race in Randy Hilton's McLaren netted him second place and kept him in the championship lead. Photo by Tom Schultz.

Buck Fulp qualified in mid-field and worked his way up the order as faster cars dropped out. He finished in third place and kept his championship hopes alive. He was four points behind Parsons after this race, with just Road America to go. Photo by Dave Arnold.

Dick Brown followed Fulp's strategy and took fourth place in his green McLaren. Photo by Tom Schultz.

Don Skogmo looks happy the first time out in his new Lola. Photo by Gil Munz.

Mark Donohue pitting with a deflated left rear tire. The mechanic on the right is about to add air to the deflated tire, while Roger Penske leans in to have a word with Donohue, as Al Holbert (behind Penske) is paying attention. Photo by Dave Arnold.

1966 Road America 500 program cover. Scan courtesy Don Markle.

Road America

The entry for the Road America race was pretty strong. Charlie Parsons planned to do the race solo in Randy Hilton's McLaren. Charlie Hayes and Earl Jones, Lothar Motschenbacher driving solo, Brooke Doran and Carl Haas, Bud Gates and Jack Ensley were the other McLaren drivers. Buck Fulp and Skip Hudson were the only Lola drivers. Mak Kronn and Ralph Salyer entered their McKee's. There were 6 Porsches piloted by Doug and Peter Revson, Joe Buzzetta and Gunter Klass (a German hillclimb and prototype racer), Ralph Treischmann and Chuck Dietrich, Mike Fisher and Pete Lovely, as well as Lee and Mike Hall. Dick Thompson and Ed Lowther shared a Ford GT.

Of the current top ten drivers, only John Cannon, Jerry Grant and Mark Donohue chose not to come. They decided to save their cars for the Can-Am series which started the following week.

Friday practice came to an early end. Don Skogmo was driving his new Lola T-70 when he lost control on the wet surface, hit a new guardrail that had just been installed at the pit entrance and died. No one wanted to go out after that. Don was very well known and liked by all. He helped found the Land

of Lakes region in 1950, served 13 years as a Regional Director and two terms as Regional Executive. Don won numerous races driving a Cad-Allard, a D-type Jaguar and a Birdcage Maserati.

Charlie Hayes took pole position in Saturday qualifying, with a time of 2:26.2. Hayes' time was 1.7 seconds faster than last year's pole time and 5.4 seconds quicker than Buck Fulp's second place time. Charlie Parsons and Mak Kronn were on the second row and Ralph Salyer and Bud Gates occupied the third row. The fastest under two-liter qualifier was Charlie Kolb in his Ferrari Dino with a time of 2:38.8.

A rolling start was used and Hayes jumped into the lead as they crossed the start line and was three seconds ahead of Parsons, Kronn and Hudson by the end of the first lap. Next in line were Fulp, Salyer, Gates, Lothar, Dick Thompson and Brooke Doran. Joe Buzzetta passed Charlie Kolb for the under two-liter lead. Lothar picked up his pace and began charging after a couple of laps. He passed Parsons on lap seventeen to claim second place, fourteen seconds behind the flying Hayes.

When Hayes was signaled that Lothar was fourteen seconds behind and closing,

he quickly put another six seconds between himself and Lothar. Skip Hudson was starting to fall back with transmission problems. Fulp and Kronn passed Hudson to take fourth and fifth places. Lothar stopped in the pits after thirty-three laps to have his shift linkage fixed. The fix took six laps and put him out of contention for the win. On lap thirty-three a slower car hit Mak Kronn's McKee, sending Kronn off course and into Ralph Salyer's parked McKee. The front bodywork of Kronn's McKee was torn off, but the strong tube frame held together preventing serious injury to Kronn's legs.

Buck Fulp had the bit between his teeth and was visibly the fastest car on the course. Fulp passed Parsons on lap thirty-nine. Then Fulp took the lead when Hayes stopped at the pits for fuel and a co-driver. Unfortunately for Fulp, his race ended with a broken shift linkage four laps later. This put Parsons in the lead. One of Parsons' mechanics ran across the pitroad to spread the news. He yelled out, "Charlie's leading". Team owner, Randy Hilton, was watching the action in Fulp's pits. He turned and asked, "Charlie who?" That broke the tension of the moment and had the team laughing.

Up close with Parsons and Hayes, just waiting. Photo by Gil Munz.

OWNER: R. HILTON
DRIVER: C. PARSONS
MECH.: BOB SMITH

Soon after Parsons took the lead, his spoiler came loose and was hanging off the rear of the car. The spoiler fell off just before he was about to be blackflagged. That was a good thing, as Parsons had planned to make only one pitstop for fuel at the halfway point. A stop then would have been too early. Parsons continued to lead Hudson by almost two minutes, with the Hayes/Jones McLaren even further back but on the same lap.

Hudson pitted first and was stopped for a long time. He was two laps down when he finally got back in the race. Parsons made his stop for fuel on lap sixty-six and it took three minutes. Parsons was second, to the Jones/Hayes McLaren, when he got back on the course. Jones stopped around lap eighty to hand the car back to Hayes. Parsons was still a minute behind when Hayes returned to the track.

The gap between Hayes and Parsons stayed at one-minute over the next fifteen laps. Then the engine in Hayes' McLaren blew a plug on lap ninety-five and started losing oil. Hayes pitted to add oil after a few more laps. Although it was a short stop, it allowed Parsons back into the lead. Hayes roared out of the pits after Parsons, set a new lap record in the process and caught him after three more laps. Hayes continued to rip around and built up a lead of ten seconds, while Parsons steadily motored along. Hayes' engine was seriously smoking and he slowed down with ten laps to go. Parsons picked up

The front of Don Skogmo's Lola, after hitting the new guardrail during practice. Don did not plan to pit. His car aquaplaned, got light, turned sideways and T-boned the guardrail. Don died instantly and was the only fatality of the USRRC series. Photo by Mike Odell.

his pace on the last three laps, chased down Hayes and took the lead on the last lap. Hayes took the lead right back from him, with his car still smoking heavily. Parsons ripped through the smoke cloud on the last corner, floored it and crossed the line three feet in front of Hayes, to win the race. Skip Hudson was three laps back in third place, followed by Lothar, the Buzzetta/ Klass Porsche and the Treischmann/Dietrich Porsche.

Parsons' win gave him the championship with a total of 35 points. Buck Fulp was second with 22 points. Skip Hudson

hung onto third place with 21 points. Lothar took sole possession of fourth place in the championship with 18 points. The six points Charlie Hayes got from this race moved him into a tie for fifth place with John Cannon at 15 points each. Jerry Grant dropped to seventh place with 11 points. Mark Donohue and Mak Kronn tied for eighth place with 9 points each. Bill Eve had 7 points and was tenth in the championship. Parsons, Fulp, Hudson and Lothar were the only drivers to score points in three or more races. Scooter Patrick was the under two-liter champion with 5 points in twelfth place overall.

Skip Hudson's Lola had a slick rear deck with big airscoops. Hudson placed third in this race and in the championship. Photo by Tom Schultz.

Lothar Motschenbacher drove solo to fourth place in his Nickey McLaren. Photo by Tom Schultz.

Joe Buzzetta's Porsche 906 which won the under two-liter class. Buzzetta shared the drive with European distance racer Gunter Klass. Photo by Tom Schultz.

The Kumnick/Spooner Hamill SR3 in the paddock. It lasted eleven laps in the race before retiring. Photo by Mike Odell.

Charlie Parsons on a victory lap with mechanic, Gil Munz. Photo by Ike Smith, courtesy Gil Munz.

ABOVE—Parsons after the race, with his arm around wife, Sherry, and on his left, ace mechanic, Gil Munz. Photo courtesy Gil Munz.

LEFT—Charlie Hayes leading the first lap. Photo by Tom Schultz.

The eighth place Porsche of Mike and Lee Hall. Photo by Mike Odell.

1966 ROAD AMERICA • USRRC Road America 500

September 4, 1966, Road America, Elkhart Lake, Wisconsin

Place	Driver	Car/Engine	Car #	Class	Laps	Points	Prize	Qualifying Place	Qualifying Time
1	Charlie Parsons	McLaren M1B-Chevrolet	10	O2	125	9	$3,500	3	2:31.8
2	Charlie Hayes - Earl Jones	McLaren M1B-Chevrolet	98	O2	125	6	2,700	1	2:26.2
3	Skip Hudson	Lola T70-Chevrolet	9	O2	122	4	1,500	7	2:36.4
4	Lothar Motschenbacher	McLaren M1B-Olds	96	O2	120	3	1,100	8	2:37.4
5	Joe Buzzetta - Gunter Klass	Porsche 906	7	U2	118	2	1,900	15	2:39.
6	Ralph Treischmann - Chuck Dietrich	Porsche 906	56	U2	118	1	1,200	14	2:40.2
7	Mike Fisher - Pete Lovely	Porsche 906	12	U2	117	-	850	21	2:42.2
8	Lee (E.L.) Hall - Mike Hall	Porsche 906	69	U2	115	-	600	23	2:48.6
9	William Cooper - Charlie Kolb	Ferrari 275P	21	O2	109	-	300	-	3:32.6
10	Peter Goetz - George Wintersteen	Elva Mk 7	19	U2	107	-	200	-	3:38.2
11	Bill Shoenfeld - John Martin	Corvette Grand Sport	27	O2	106	-	100	20	2:48.2
12	Bob Grossman - Denise McCluggage	Ferrari 275 GTB	36	O2	103	-	50	30	2:57.8
13	Ralph Scott - Alan Ross	Elva Mk 7-Climax	67	U2	102	-	50	32	3:06.6
14	Mike Rahal - Ted Rand	Elva Mk 7-Porsche	74	U2	100	-	50	34	3:10.4
DNF	Bob Nagel - Doc (M.R.J.) Wyllie	Elva Mk 8-BMW	14	U2	110	-	50	22	2:49.8
DNF	Brooke Doran - Carl Haas	McLaren M1B-Ford	3	O2	101	-	50	11	2:39.0
DNF	Dick Thompson - Ed Lowther	Ford GT-40	22	O2	100	-	50	16	2:41.0
DNF	Bud Gates - Jack Ensley	McLaren M1A-Chev	73	O2	98	-	50	6	2:36
DNF	Jerry Nelson - Tom Countryman	Porsche 904GTS	18	U2	97	-	50	24	2:52.4
DNF	Bruce Munroe - Baxter Rogers	Elva-Climax	66	U2	80	-	50	-	3:49
DNF	Jerry Rosbach - Jack Baker	Genie Mk 8-Chevrolet	81	O2	70	-	50	26	2:56.0
DNF	Robert Shaw - Rich Dagiel	Lotus 30-Ford	1	O2	61	-	50	25	2:51.0
DNF	Tom Tufts - Cliff Apel	Bobcat	-	-	-	-	-	-	-
DNF	Buck Fulp	Lola T70-Chevrolet	26	O2	48	-	50	2	2:31.6
DNF	Bob Harris - John Morton	Genie Mk 10-Olds	95	O2	43	-	50	12	2:39.2
DNF	Fred Pipin - Bill Morrison	Cooper T49-Ford	63	O2	41	-	50	29	2:57.0
DNF	Doc (M.R.J.) Wyllie - Bob Nagel	Bobsy SR3-Climax	2	U2	40	-	50	38	3:16.6
DNF	Dick Durant - John Martin	Durant-Chevrolet	47	O2	40	-	50	17	2:40.6
DNF	Mak Kronn	McKee Mk 6-Chevrolet	10	O2	32	-	50	4	2:31.8
DNF	Charlie Kolb	Ferrari 206 Dino	11	U2	32	-	150	10	2:38.8
DNF	Russ Tyndall - George Furman	Lotus 11	71	U2	28	-	-	37	3:12.4
DNF	Ralph Salyer - Bill Mitchell	McKee Mk 4-Olds	25	O2	22	-	-	5	2:32.4
DNF	Peter Dock - Jim Whelan	Chevrolet Corvette	5	O2	19	-	-	36	3:14.0
DNF	George Dickinson - Don Devine	Elva Mk 6	31	U2	19	-	-	31	2:57.4
DNF	Roy Kumnick - Bob Spooner	Hamill SR-3-Chevrolet	65	O2	11	-	-	19	2:41.8
DNF	Dave Causey - Allen Barker	Lotus 19-Ford	54	O2	9	-	-	9	2:38.0
DNF	Dale Lang - Frank Phillips	Elva	84	U2	0	-	-	-	no time
DSQ	Doug Revson - Peter Revson	Porsche 906	23	U2	61	-	-	18	2:42.0

Fastest Qualifier:	Charlie Hayes	McLaren M1B-Chevrolet	2:26.2	98.495 mph	
Race Distance:	500 miles	125 laps of 4.0 mile course			
Race Time:	5 hr 23 min 0.2 sec				
Winner's Speed:	92.879 mph				
Victory Margin:	0 .4 second				
Fastest Race Lap:	Charlie Hayes	McLaren M1B-Chevrolet	2:28.1 mph	97.232 mph	

Buck Fulp at speed in his Lola. Fulp retired after forty-eight laps with a broken shift linkage. Photo by Gil Munz.

1966 USRRC Drivers Championship Points

SD Stardust, RIV Riverside, LS Laguna Seca, BH Bridgehampton, WG Watkins Glen, PR Pacific Raceways, MO Mid-Ohio, RA Road America

Place	Driver	SD	RIV	LS	BH	WG	PR	MO	RA	Total Points
1	Charlie Parsons	6	4	6	-	-	4	6	9	35
2	Buck Fulp	-	9	-	-	9	-	4	-	22
3	Skip Hudson	4	6	4	-	3	-	-	4	21
4	Lothar Motschenbacher	-	-	-	6	-	-	9	3	18
5	John Cannon	9	-	-	-	-	6	-	-	15
6	Charlie Hayes	-	-	9	-	-	-	-	6	15
7	Jerry Grant	-	-	-	9	2	-	-	-	11
8	Mark Donohue	-	-	-	-	-	9	-	-	9
9	Mak Kronn	3	-	-	-	6	-	-	-	9
10	Bill Eve	-	-	-	-	4	3	-	-	7
11	Earl Jones	-	-	-	-	-	-	-	6	6
12	Scooter Patrick	-	2	-	3	-	-	-	-	5
13	Mike Goth	-	-	-	4	-	-	-	-	4
14	Joe Buzzetta	-	-	-	-	-	-	2	2	4
15	Ed Hamill	2	1	-	-	-	-	-	-	3
16	Bill Krause	-	3	-	-	-	-	-	-	3
17	Ken Miles	1	-	2	-	-	-	-	-	3
18	Dave Jordan	-	-	3	-	-	-	-	-	3
19	Dick Brown	-	-	-	-	-	-	3	-	3
20	Herb Wetanson	-	-	-	2	-	-	-	-	2
21	Lew Florence	-	-	-	-	-	2	-	-	2
22	Ralph Treischman	-	-	-	-	1	-	-	1	2
23	Gunther Klass	-	-	-	-	-	-	-	2	2
24	George Follmer	-	-	1	-	-	-	-	-	1
25	Peter Gregg	-	-	-	1	-	-	-	-	1
26	Don Wester	-	-	-	-	-	1	-	-	1
27	Charlie Kolb	-	-	-	-	-	-	1	-	1
28	Chuck Dietrich	-	-	-	-	-	-	-	1	1

1966 Season Summary

The racing in 1966 was about as close as in 1965. Two races were won by one second, or less. The closest finish was at Road America where Charlie Parsons won by four-tenths of a second. Three more races had a victory margin of less than one minute. The remaining three were won by more than a minute. The greatest victory margin was when Charlie Hayes won by two laps and twenty-five seconds, at Laguna Seca.

The championship lead changed hands four times during the series. John Cannon naturally had the lead after the first race. Charlie Parsons and Skip Hudson shared the lead after the second race. Then Parsons took sole possession after the third race. Buck Fulp led after the fifth race at Watkins Glen. Charlie Parsons retook the series lead after the sixth race and held it to the end. Seven other drivers were still in the championship hunt with two races left. However, Parsons, Fulp and Hudson were the only drivers who could win the championship going into the last race. Fulp retired from the lead, Hudson nursed a sick car and Parsons took the championship with a thrilling drive.

During 1966, the spectators and press reporters missed the Chaparral team. They were used to the sleek, white cars showing up and running away with races. More than once, it was mentioned in the press that "no one wants to win this series". However, with seven different winners (five of them scoring their first USRRC win), it was obvious they all wanted to win. Mechanical failure kept all but Parsons and Hudson from scoring in more than three races. Buck Fulp and Lothar did finish three races. Fulp was the only repeat winner. He won at Riverside and Watkins Glen, while Lothar scored his first USRRC win at Mid-Ohio. Five other drivers in the top ten finished in two races. Mark Donohue's win in a Roger Penske Lola, at Pacific Raceways, was his only finish out of three starts. Jerry Grant was a pre-season favorite in Dan Gurney's All-American Racers Lola T70. It had a small block Ford engine with Gurney-Weslake heads and 500 horsepower. However, Grant's season was fraught with bad mechanical luck. He suffered a broken gearbox at Stardust, an over-revved engine at Riverside and a blown head gasket in a stock Ford engine at Laguna Seca before getting his first USRRC win at Bridgehampton. He followed that up with a fifth place at Watkins Glen and then skipped the rest of the series so the car could be prepared for the coming Can-Am series. Charlie Hayes' season was similar to Grants. He suffered a holed radiator at Stardust, courtesy of Grant and a gearbox failure at Riverside before winning the Laguna Seca race. A road accident by his crew caused enough damage to the McLaren to put it out of the Bridgehampton and Watkins Glen races. He suffered a broken halfshaft at Pacific Raceways and a faulty fuel pump and electrical problems at Mid-Ohio. He then closed the season with a second place at Road America.

On a sad note, Don Skogmo's death during practice at Road America was a prime example of how outside influences could have a very negative effect on racing. Road America's insurance company insisted that a guardrail be installed between the pits and the track. Don was going full tilt, got sideways and hit the end of the guardrail. Although unfortunate, thankfully, Don's death would be the only fatality of the whole USRRC series.

Scooter Patrick was the under two-liter class champion. He finished fourth at Bridgehampton and fifth at Riverside, gaining five points and finished twelfth overall in the series. Joe Buzzetta was second in the under two-liter class with four points, from two fifth place finishes. If the old points scoring system had been kept Patrick would have finished tied for second place in the championship with 22 points.

The SCCA continued to grow in 1966. Membership increased from 16,757 at the end of 1965, to 17,670 by the end of 1966. The new Trans-Am and Can-Am series did not have much of an effect on the USRRC. The last two races may have suffered a few less entries from those who chose to prepare their cars for the Can-Am series, but it was not evident from the size of the grids.

The series had a total of 264 individual drivers starting races. Charlie Parsons and Lothar Motschenbacher were the only drivers to start all eight races. John Cannon, Skip Hudson and Doug Revson started seven races. Five drivers started six races and one started five races. There were nine drivers starting four races, fifteen starting three races and twenty-five drivers started two races. That left 204 drivers starting only one race in the series. Since the under two-liter class did not get separate points this year, only twenty-eight drivers scored championship points. Seventeen were Over Two-Liter drivers and eleven were Under Two-Liter drivers.

1967

Stardust
Riverside
Laguna Seca
Bridgehampton
Watkins Glen
Pacific Raceways
Road America
Mid Ohio

1967 Introduction

For 1967, the series schedule was basically the same as 1966. The only change was the Mid-Ohio race would close the season instead of Road America. As a result, the series would then end two weeks earlier, to give the Can-Am series an earlier start. The SCCA also introduced a new professional series for formula cars.

The new 1966 Can-Am series replaced the old, loosely organized, Fall Pro sports car races and USRRC drivers acquitted themselves quite well. Mark Donohue displayed his native talent by taking second place in the series. He won one race and placed third, fourth (twice) and fifth in the other races. 1964 USRRC Champion, Jim Hall, took his winged Chaparral to a couple of second place finishes. 1966 USRRC Champion, Charlie Parsons, finished third once and sixth twice. Other USRRC drivers to score points were John Cannon, George Follmer, Peter Revson, Earl Jones, Lothar Motschenbacher and Jerry Titus.

For the 1967 USRRC series, everyone knew the Penske team with Donohue

driving would be the combination to beat. Peyton Cramer's Dana Chevrolet team looked to be a strong threat with a couple of new McLarens for Peter Revson and Bob Bondurant. Carl Haas entered a McLaren for 1965 Le Mans co-winner, Masten Gregory. Running strong, private entries in McLarens and Lolas were George Follmer, Charlie Parsons, Lothar Motschenbacher, Bud Morley and Skip Scott. Almost unnoticed was Sam Posey, who first came to attention by qualifying fourth, in the wet, for the 1966 Mosport Can-Am race. When the qualifying times were posted, Jerry Grant was overheard saying, "Who the hell is Sam Posey?"

There were so many strong over two-liter entries that the under two-liter class got very little pre-season attention. Fred Baker would run his Porsche 906 in five races on both coasts. Otto Zipper entered a 906 for Scooter Patrick in the West Coast races. Joe Buzzetta, Mike Hall and Mak Kronn ran their 906's in the East Coast races. Other than that, the under two-liter entries varied from race to race.

UNITED STATES ROAD RACING CHAMPIONSHIP

STARDUST INTERNATIONAL RACEWAY
APRIL 21,22,23
1967
LAS VEGAS, NEVADA

The Penske Sunoco Lola T70 getting fettled for the race. Photo by Gil Munz.

Stardust

There were thirty-one pre-race entries for the first round of the 1967 series. Twenty-five of these entries were over two-liter cars, while six were under two-liter cars. Of the twenty-four cars that started the race, twelve were McLarens. The Dana Chevrolet team had Peter Revson and Bob Bondurant driving. Masten Gregory was back from Europe to pilot a car for Carl Haas. Lothar Motschenbacher, Charlie Parsons, Skip Scott, Bud Morley, Jerry Entin, Sam Posey, Mason O'Kieff, Jay Hills, Jim Adams and Ted Peterson all entered McLarens. There were five Lolas. The most prominent were Roger Penske's Sunoco sponsored T70 for Mark Donohue and George Follmer's self-entered car. Bill Eve, Mexican champ Moises Solana and Pierre Phillips also raced T70's. Ralph Salyer had the lone McKee and Bill Leonheart raced his ASR special. The under two-liter class shrank to five entries with two Porsche 906's, two Lotus 23's and an Elva-Porsche.

Qualifying at Stardust brought a new name to the fore, Sam Posey. He told the press he would get the pole position. Then he went out and did it, with a time of 1:36.1. George Follmer was .7 seconds slower and lined up on the front row with Posey. Skip Scott (1:37.0) and Mark Donohue (1:37.8) were on the second row. They were followed by Peter Revson (1:38.1), Charlie

Parsons (1:38.1), Jim Adams (1:39.0), who elected to start from the back of the grid and Bud Morley (1:39.5). Bill Eve and Ralph Salyer (both at 1:40.0) completed the top ten qualifiers. Bob Bondurant posted a qualifying time, but his engine blew up during Sunday's warm-up session. Mike Goth, Jerry Titus and Frank Matich were also qualifiers who did not start the race for various mechanical reasons.

Posey blew the start when he over-revved his engine. A newly installed tachometer, with a rev-limiter and automatic shut-off, killed the engine. Follmer took the lead with Donohue right behind. After some earlier regional races, there was some oil on the last corner that did not get cleaned up. As the field came around on the first lap, Follmer hit the oil and spun off course. The rocks lying on the ground tore a hole in the Lola's radiator and George retired. Donohue led the first lap with Skip Scott in second place, six seconds behind. Peter Revson blew his clutch on the first lap and coasted into the pits to retire. Ted Peterson spectacularly went off at turn two and smashed into the spectator fencing on the third lap. Fortunately, no one was hurt. Peterson's McLaren, on the other hand, was a mass of broken fiberglass and twisted metal.

Lothar Motschenbacher started from the seventh row of the grid and immediately set

about moving up through the field. Lothar was in fifth place after four laps. Seven laps later, Lothar passed Charlie Parsons for third place. Masten Gregory had started the race on the sixth row, with no clutch, and moved up a few places before retiring after twelve laps.

Sam Posey, recovered from his botched start and subsequent spin, was now motoring hard. He caught up to Lothar, who was in third spot behind Donohue and Scott.

Skip Scott flew into the pits on lap twenty-three with a leaking oil cooler and narrowly missed another competitor's crewman. This moved Lothar into second place and Posey into third place. Twenty laps later Scott returned to the pits. He was still too fast for the previously missed crewman and got a bucket full of water thrown at him. The force of the water broke the McLaren's windscreen, causing him to retire on the spot. Scott was naturally a bit angry and filed a protest.

Lothar came into the pits about the same time Scott retired. He had a sputtering engine which couldn't be immediately fixed and was sent back out to finish the race. Donohue ran the race out, winning by almost a lap over Posey. Bill Eve brought his Lola home in third place. Lothar was fourth, Moises Solana was fifth and Charlie Kolb, in a Porsche Carrera 6, finished in sixth place.

At the start, George Follmer #16 takes the lead from Mark Donohue, Skip Scott, Charlie Parsons #10, and Peter Revson #52.

Scooter Patrick #33 led the under two-liter class until he retired after forty-nine laps. Behind the following McLaren is Charlie Kolb's Porsche which did win the under two-liter class. Photo from the collections of The Henry Ford.

Sam Posey #2 qualified on the pole, had a rev limiter shut his engine off at the start, but worked his way back up to second place. Photo from the collections of The Henry Ford.

Bill Eve #1 in Woody Young's Lola T70 took third place. Bill ran in the top ten from the start and steadily worked his way up the order as faster cars dropped out. Photo from the collections of The Henry Ford.

Skip Scott #91 and Lothar Motschenbacher #11. They ran the early laps in second and third spots, respectively. Scott retired after having his windscreen broken by a member of another team. Lothar took over second place, until his engine lost power and finished in fourth place. Photo from the collections of The Henry Ford.

1967 STARDUST • USRRC
April 23, 1967, Stardust Raceway, Las Vegas, Nevada

Place	Driver	Car/Engine	Car #	Class	Laps	Points	Prize	Qualifying Place	Qualifying Time
1	Mark Donohue	Lola T70-Chevrolet	6	O2	61	9	$3,100	4	1:37.8
2	Sam Posey	McLaren M1B-Chevrolet	2	O2	61	6	2,500	1	1:36.1
3	Bill Eve	Lola T70-Chevrolet	1	O2	60	4	1,500	10	1:40.8
4	Lothar Motschenbacher	McLaren M1B-Chevrolet	11	O2	59	3	1,000	15	1:42.5
5	Moises Solana	Lola T70-Chevrolet	99	O2	58	2	800	13	1:42.0
6	Charlie Kolb	Porsche 906	22	U2	56	1	1,400	20	1:51.0
7	Pierre Phillips	Lola T70-Chevrolet	3	O2	56	-	450	14	1:42.0
8	Jerry Entin	McLaren M1B-Chevrolet	7	O2	55	-	350	24	-
9	Ed Bowman	Elva Mk 7S-Porsche	-	U2	51	-	750	22	1:56.9
10	Bud Morley	McLaren M1B-Chevrolet	71	O2	48	-	200	9	1:39.5
11	Charles Kulmann	Lotus 23B-Cosworth	68	U2	47	-	475	23	2:03.9
DNF	Scooter Patrick	Porsche 906	33	U2	49	-	400	18	1:47.0
DNF	Skip Scott	McLaren M1B-Ford	91	O2	47	-	150	3	1:37.0
DNF	Mason O'Keiff	McLaren M1B-Chevrolet	98	O2	42	-	150	17	1:45.3
DNF	Jay Hills	McLaren M1B-Chevrolet	81	O2	23	-	150	8	1:39.5
DNF	Bill Leonheart	ASR-Chevrolet	-	O2	19	-	125	21	1:54.5
DNF	Ralph Salyer	McKee Mk 7-Oldsmobile	25	O2	17	-	125	11	1:41.0
DNF	Jim Adams	McLaren M1A-Chevrolet	39	O2	15	-	125	7*	1:39.0
DNF	Charlie Parsons	McLaren M1B-Chevrolet	10	O2	14	-	125	6	1:38.1
DNF	Masten Gregory	McLaren M1B-Chevrolet	26	O2	12	-	125	12	1:41.0
DNF	Ted Peterson	McLaren M1B-Chevrolet	77	O2	2	-	100	16	1:43.4
DNF	John Morton	Lotus 23-Porsche	46	U2	2	-	100	19	1:49.9
DNF	George Follmer	Lola T70-Chevrolet	16	O2	1	-	100	2	1:36.8
DNF	Peter Revson	McLaren M1B-Chevrolet	52	O2	1	-	100	5	1:38.1

Fastest Qualifier:	Sam Posey	McLaren M1B-Chevrolet	1:36.1	112.28 mph
Race Distance:	183 miles	61 laps of 3.0 mile course		
Race Time:	1hr 42min 41.8sec			
Winner's Speed:	106.91 mph			
Margin of Victory:	1 minute 42 seconds			
Fastest Race Lap:	Mark Donohue	Lola T70-Chevrolet	1:38.1	109.09 mph

* = elected to start from the back of the grid

Moises Solana brought his Lola T70 up from Mexico and ran a steady race to finish in fifth place. Photo from the collections of The Henry Ford.

Charlie Kolb #22, drifting the under two-liter class winning Porsche 906. Photo from the collections of The Henry Ford.

UNITED STATES ROAD RACING CHAMPIONSHIP

50¢
TAX INC.

RIVERSIDE INTERNATIONAL RACEWAY
APRIL 29, 30, 1967

1967 Riverside USRRC program cover. Scan courtesy Don Markle.

At the start George Follmer #16 leads Mark Donohue #6, Bob Bondurant #51, Peter Revson (hidden behind Bondurant), Skip Scott #91, and Lothar Motschenbacher (behind Revson). Photo from the collections of The Henry Ford.

Riverside

Twenty drivers from the Stardust race were entered at Riverside. Additions to the field were Jerry Grant, Mike Goth and Skip Barber in Lolas, Jerry Titus in a Piper-Buick, Frank Matich in a Matich-Oldsmobile, Miles Gupton in a modified Merlyn, Andre Gessner in the Capello Special and a few under two-liter cars.

George Follmer wanted to see his son's ballgame on Saturday, so he set a time of 1:24.3 in the Friday qualifying session and didn't even show up on Saturday. Mark Donohue was beside Follmer on the front row with a time of 1:25.1. Lothar Motschenbacher (1:25.5) and Peter Revson (1:25.6) were on the second row of the grid. Behind them were Bob Bondurant, Bud Morley, Jerry Grant, Skip Scott, Charlie Parsons, Mike Goth, Sam Posey and Masten Gregory. The first under two-liter qualifier was Scooter Patrick on the outside of row twelve with a time of 1:32.8. Lothar's engine blew up in the final minutes of Saturday qualifying and he spent most of the night putting a new engine in his car.

The cars were on the grid and Masten Gregory was nowhere to be found. Follmer took the lead at the start and Donohue was right on his tail. Revson and Bondurant were close behind in third and fourth spots. Grant, Posey, Goth and Parsons were all dicing for position a few seconds back. Revson had trouble on the first lap when a bird got

sucked into his engine bay and stuck in the throttle linkage. The engine would not drop the revs below 3,800 rpm and Revson spun off course. He fell to the back of the field, got used to the stuck throttle and set about working his way back to the front of the running order. Lothar also had trouble at the start and fell from third on the grid to twelfth place.

Masten Gregory finally arrived at the track as the field was coming around on the first lap. He claimed he forgot about daylight savings time and hadn't adjusted his watch. Gregory wanted to get in the car and race, but Carl Haas was in no mood for it.

Donohue squeezed by Follmer and took the lead at the last corner of the third lap. Follmer didn't give Donohue any grief. He just sat right behind him, biding his time. Bondurant had third place all to himself. Grant and Posey had a real battle for fourth place, until Posey retired with an overheating engine on the nineteenth lap. Charlie Parsons caught up to Grant and tried hard to get by him. Grant's car was having suspension problems loud enough to be heard. This allowed Parsons to pass him on lap thirty-one. Grant retired on the next lap when the Lola's suspension collapsed.

Donohue and Follmer continued to lead Bondurant by twenty seconds. Lothar and Peter Revson climbed through the field and put on a great show as they passed back-

markers. Charlie Kolb and Moises Solana dueled for tenth place until lap forty-four, when Kolb's car expired.

Follmer's engine lost oil pressure on lap forty-eight and he retired. Donohue was left with a huge lead over Bondurant, who was caught up by Charlie Parsons. Parsons was actually gaining a second a lap on Donohue. It all came to an end for Parsons on lap fifty-three when he ran over a piece of tailpipe lying on the track. This put a hole in the oilpan of Parsons' McLaren and he retired on the next lap. Mike Goth was now in third place.

Goth's engine started running rough in the final laps and Lothar flew by him to take third place. Lothar's concentration lapsed with two laps remaining and he spun at turn seven. The hard-charging Revson passed Lothar right after he got turned around and going again. Donohue took the win by fifty-five seconds over Bondurant, who was twenty-six seconds ahead of Revson. Lothar finished in fourth place followed by Mike Goth and Bud Morley. Scooter Patrick was the first under two-liter finisher in tenth place, five laps behind Donohue.

Donohue received his trophy from British model, Twiggy. He also took command of the championship with 18 points. Lothar, Posey and Bondurant were tied for second with 6 points each. Peter Revson and Bill Eve were next up with 4 points apiece.

Donohue took the lead on the third lap and Follmer sat on his tail until his engine lost oil pressure on lap forty-eight. Photo from the collections of The Henry Ford.

Bob Bondurant, in one of the Dana Chevrolet McLarens, drove a lonely race, in third place, until Follmer retired. Bob then kept second place to the end. Photo from the collections of The Henry Ford.

Peter Revson, in the other Dana McLaren, had a race long duel with Lothar Motschenbacher. Revson finished in third place after Lothar spun with two laps to go. Photo from the collections of The Henry Ford.

Lothar Motschenbacher finished in fourth place, behind Revson, but in front of Goth. Photo from the collections of The Henry Ford.

Mike Goth placed fifth. He was in third place with a few laps left when his engine started running rough, allowing Revson and Lothar to pass him. Photo from the collections of The Henry Ford.

Scooter Patrick, in tenth place, was the top under two-liter finisher. Photo from the collections of The Henry Ford.

Jerry Grant #78 and Sam Posey #2 spent the early laps battling for fourth place. Posey retired after eighteen laps with an overheated engine. Grant's Lola lasted thirty-two laps before the Lola's suspension collapsed. Photo from the collections of The Henry Ford.

1967 RIVERSIDE • USRRC
April 30, 1967, Riverside International Raceway, Riverside, California

Place	Driver	Car/Engine	Car #	Class	Laps	Points	Prize	Qualifying Place	Qualifying Time
1	Mark Donohue	Lola T70-Chevrolet	6	O2	70	9	$ 3,100	2	1:25.1
2	Bob Bondurant	McLaren M1C-Chevrolet	51	O2	70	6	1,700	5	1:25.7
3	Peter Revson	McLaren M1C-Chevrolet	52	O2	70	4	1,300	4	1:25.6
4	Lothar Motschenbacher	McLaren M1B-Chevrolet	11	O2	69	3	950	3	1:25.5
5	Mike Goth	Lola T70-Chevrolet	4	O2	69	2	650	10	1:27.2
6	Bud Morley	McLaren M1B-Chevrolet	71	O2	68	1	500	6	1:26.6
7	Bill Eve	Lola T70-Chevrolet	1	O2	68	-	400	14	1:29.0
8	Moises Solana	Lola T70-Chevrolet	99	O2	68	-	300	19	1:30.1
9	Skip Barber	McLaren M1B-Chevrolet	14	O2	65	-	200	15	1:29.7
10	Scooter Patrick	Porsche 906	33	U2	65	-	675	23	1:32.
11	Mason O'Keiff	McLaren M1B-Chevrolet	98	O2	64	-	175	22	1:31.9
12	Fred Baker	Porsche 906	22	U2	64	-	475	24	1:33.9
13	Miles Gupton	Platypus-Oldsmobile	75	O2	62	-	150	29	1:41.5
14	Jerry Entin	McLaren M1B-Chevrolet	7	O2	61	-	150	17	1:29.7
15	Ed Bowman	Elva Mk 7S-Porsche	-	U2	61	-	350	27	1:39.
16	Charles Gates	Triumph GT-6	4	U2	57	-	150	30	1:42.8
DNF	Andre Gessner	Capello-Chevrolet	-	O2	56	-	125	25	1:36.3
DNF	John Morton	Lotus 23-Porsche	46	U2	55	-	125	26	1:37.2
DNF	Charlie Parsons	McLaren M1B-Chevrolet	10	O2	54	-	100	9	1:27.0
DNF	Jerry Titus	Piper-Buick	5	O2	51	-	100	21	1:31.4
DNF	George Follmer	Lola T70-Chevrolet	16	O2	48	-	275	1	1:24.3
DNF	Charlie Kolb	Lola T70-Chevrolet	12	O2	44	-	75	12	1:27.7
DNF	Jerry Grant	Lola T70-Chevrolet	78	O2	32	-	75	7	1:26.7
DNF	Frank Matich	Matich SR3-Oldsmobile	76	O2	19	-	75	13	1:28.9
DNF	Sam Posey	McLaren M1C-Chevrolet	2	O2	18	-	50	11	1:27.3
DNF	Ted Peterson	McLaren M1C-Chevrolet	77	O2	16	-	50	20	1:30.7
DNF	Pierre Phillips	Lola T70-Chevrolet	3	O2	16	-	50	18	1:30.0
DNF	Ralph Salyer	McKee Mk 7-Oldsmobile	25	O2	13	-	50	16	1:29.7
DNF	Skip Scott	McLaren M1C-Ford	91	O2	10	-	50	8	1:26.9
DNF	Richard Smith	Algeri Porsche	-	U2	10	-	450	28	1:39.8
DSQ	Warren Shamlian	Elva Mk 7S-Porsche	36	U2	31	-	-	31	1:42.8
DNS	Masten Gregory	McLaren M1B-Chevrolet	26	O2	-	-	-	-	-

Fastest Qualifier:	George Follmer	Lola T70-Chevrolet	1:24.3	111.03 mph
Race Distance:	182.0 miles	70 laps of 2.6 mile course		
Race Time:	1hr 43min 47.3sec			
Winners Speed:	105.21 mph			
Victory Margin:	55 seconds			
Fastest Race Lap:	Mark Donohue	Lola T70-Chevrolet	1:26.4	108.33 mph

Mark Donohue receives the trophy and winner's kiss from British model sensation, Twiggy. Photo from the collections of The Henry Ford.

USRRC

LAGUNA SECA 1967™

MAY 5 - 6 - 7
OFFICIAL PROGRAM $1.00

1967 Laguna Seca USRRC program cover. Scan courtesy Don Markle.

Laguna Seca

Laguna Seca had a strong entry with twenty-four drivers who had raced at either, or both, Stardust and Riverside. The major players being Mark Donohue, George Follmer, Sam Posey, Charlie Parsons, Bud Morley, Bill Eve, Lothar Motschenbacher, Peter Revson, Bob Bondurant and Skip Scott. Five drivers were appearing for the first time this year: John Cannon in a McLaren-Chevrolet; Stan Burnett, down from Seattle in his self-built Burnett Special; Ed Leslie driving a Lotus 23; Bob Jones in a Porsche RSK and Bill Amick in a McLaren-Chevrolet.

As if he could make up for missing the Riverside race, Masten Gregory was first in line for Friday qualifying at Laguna Seca. Unfortunately, Gregory got his McLaren out of shape at the corkscrew, had a tankslapper ride down the hill and came to a stop on top of a fire extinguisher. The extinguisher ruptured the fuel tank and the handling was not the same afterward and Gregory qualified twelfth.

George Follmer got the pole position for the second race in a row. His time was 1:06.2. Reporters kept asking him if the accusations at Riverside were true, that he used special qualifying tires. To quell the rumors, Follmer made a point of showing the reporters he used regular Firestone race tires to set his qualifying time. Lothar was second fastest with a 1:07.0. Mark Donohue's Penske Lola had a new rear spoiler and he was third on the grid with a time of 1:07.2. Peter Revson shared the second row, also with a time of 1:07.2. He was lucky to be on the grid at all. While qualifying, Revson looped it at the corkscrew, spun off course and then back onto the course, but facing backwards. Now he was staring straight at teammate, Bob Bondurant, bearing down on him. Somehow they synchronized their moves and missed each other. Skip Scott had a 400 cubic inch Ford engine installed in the Drummond McLaren and snatched fifth place on the grid from Sam Posey. Seventh and eighth on the grid were Mike Goth and Bob Bondurant. Next were Jerry Entin and Frank Matich, then John Cannon and Masten Gregory. The writing on the wall was becoming clearer for the under two-liter cars. Scooter Patrick was the lead car, with the twenty-third fastest practice time at 1:12.6.

Donohue shot between Follmer and Lothar to take the lead when the starter dropped the flag. Lothar was second. Follmer missed a shift getting off the line and was in third place. A few laps into the race, Follmer had a fuel line break right behind his head, squirting gasoline on the back of his driving suit. Follmer pitted on lap eight, found Don Wester who was a

At the start of the race Donohue #6 is leading Lothar Motschenbacher #11, George Follmer #16, Skip Scott #91, Mike Goth #4, and Sam Posey #2. Photo from the collections of The Henry Ford.\

similar size and whose suit had a Firestone patch on it. They both did a strip down to shorts in the pits. Follmer changed into Wester's dry suit, while Wester went looking for some street clothes to wear. Follmer got back in the race, but was hopelessly behind. Jerry Entin was running in fourth place, on the fifth lap, when Sam Posey made an optimistic move at turn nine. Posey hit the right front corner of Entin's car and bent the steering arm. Both were able to continue.

Donohue led Lothar after ten laps. Masten Gregory was in third place, Mike Goth in fourth and Frank Matich fifth. Gregory's engine overheated and lost power, so he parked it. Charlie Kolb was in sixth place and ahead of Peter Revson and Bob Bondurant. The oil cooler in Kolb's Lola blew after twenty-three laps and he retired. Revson was out after twenty-seven laps with a broken clutch. Ralph Salyer had a wild ride into retirement on lap twenty-nine, when his car lost a wheel

Mike Goth #4 finished the race in second place. Here he leads Frank Matich, who finished in eighth place. Photo from the collections of The Henry Ford.

With a rearranged nose, John Cannon #62 leads Skip Scott #91. Photo from the collections of The Henry Ford.

Fred Baker #22 was the first under two-liter finisher, in eleventh place. Photo from the collections of The Henry Ford.

at turn seven. Bob Bondurant retired after thirty-six laps with a broken gearshift linkage.

Up front, Donohue was pulling away from Lothar. Both were pulling away from Mike Goth, who had Frank Matich right on his tail. Following Matich were Sam Posey, John Cannon, Skip Barber, Bill Eve and Stan Burnett. Fred Baker was leading the under two-liter class. Sam Posey retired with no brakes after forty laps and a couple of spins. Frank Matich passed Mike Goth's Lola for third place on lap forty-two. A failed ring and pinion sent Jerry Entin into retirement after forty-eight laps.

The race had settled down into what looked like the finishing order and everyone was reeling off the laps. Donohue's car

started sputtering like it was out of gas. He was forty seconds ahead of Lothar on lap sixty-seven, when he dove into the pits to have fuel added. After the race his crew found out it was not transferring fuel from the left tank to the right tank, where the fuel pump was.

Lothar took the lead and Donohue returned to the race in second place. Matich and Goth were third and fourth. John Cannon was fifth and Jay Hills sixth, with Barber and Eve following in seventh and eighth places. When Donohue stopped for fuel, his crew had put it in the left tank so he had to stop again to have some more fuel put in the right tank. This dropped him to fourth place behind Lothar, Matich and Goth. Matich pitted with ignition problems after a few

more laps and dropped back to ninth place. The race ran out with Lothar taking a popular win. Mike Goth finished in second place. Donohue got third place and John Cannon had worked his way up to take fourth place. Skip Barber was fifth, in his second race in an over two-liter car. Bill Eve took the final point in sixth place. Fred Baker was the under two-liter class winner in twelfth place, six laps behind Lothar.

Donohue still got four points for his third place finish and left Laguna Seca still in the championship lead with 22 points. Lothar was second with fifteen points. Mike Goth had eight points for third place. Sam Posey and Bob Bondurant were tied for fourth place with six points and Bill Eve was sixth with five points.

Stan Burnett #64 going a bit wide and Sam Posey #2 looking to squeeze through. Both ran in the top ten. Burnett took his homebuilt car to seventh place. Posey retired after forty laps and a couple of spins. Photo from the collections of The Henry Ford.

For once, Penske preparation was not up to their usual standards. Lothar spent most of the race in second place, until Donohue had fuel feed problems. Here Lothar takes the checkered flag and the win. Photo from the collections of The Henry Ford.

1967 LAGUNA SECA • USRRC

May 7, 1967, Laguna Seca, Monterey, California

Place	Driver	Car/Engine	Car #	Class	Laps	Points	Prize	Qualifying Place	Qualifying Time
1	Lothar Motschenbacher	McLaren M1B-Chevrolet	11	O2	84	9	$ 3,850	2	1:07.0
2	Mike Goth	Lola T70-Chevrolet	4	O2	83	6	2,000	7	1:08.0
3	Mark Donohue	Lola T70-Chevrolet	6	O2	83	4	1,600	3	1:07.21
4	John Cannon	McLaren M1B-Chevrolet	62	O2	83	3	1,000	11	-
5	Skip Barber	McLaren M1B-Chevrolet	44	O2	81	2	800	19	-
6	Bill Eve	Lola T70-Chevrolet	14	O2	80	1	600	24	-
7	Stan Burnett	Burnett Mk 2-Chevrolet	64	O2	80	-	450	22	
8	Frank Matich	Matich SR3-Oldsmobile	76	O2	79	-	350	10	-
9	Bud Morley	McLaren M1B-Chevrolet	12	O2	79	-	250	16	1:09.9
10	Pierre Phillips	Lola T70-Chevrolet	3	O2	79	-	200	18	-
11	Charlie Parsons	McLaren M1B-Chevrolet	10	O2	78	-	175	14	1:09.4
12	Fred Baker	Porsche 906	22	U2	78	-	850	26	1:14.5
13	John Morton	Lotus 23-Porsche	46	U2	77	-	600	29	-
14	Ed Bowman	Elva Mk 7S-Porsche	15	U2	76	-	400	28	1:16.9
15	Ed Leslie	Lotus 23-Ford	98	U2	76	-	300	25	1:13.8
16	Skip Scott	McLaren M1C-Ford	91	O2	72	-	125	5	1:07.9
17	George Follmer	Lola T70-Chevrolet	16	O2	70	-	625	1	1:06.86
DNF	Jay Hills	McLaren M1B-Chevrolet	81	O2	79	-	125	15	-
DNF	Paul Reinhart	Genie Mk 8-Chevrolet	61	O2	49	-	125	27	1:16.7
DNF	Jerry Entin	McLaren M1B-Chevrolet	1	O2	48	-	125	9	-
DNF	Sam Posey	McLaren M1C-Chevrolet	2	O2	40	-	100	6	1:08.0
DNF	Bob Bondurant	McLaren M1B-Chevrolet	51	O2	36	-	100	8	1:08.1
DNF	Bob Jones	Porsche 718 RSK	7	U2	31	-	100	30	1:23.7
DNF	Ralph Salyer	McKee Mk 7-Oldsmobile	25	O2	28	-	100	20	1:12.0
DNF	Peter Revson	McLaren M1C-Chevrolet	52	O2	27	-	50	4	1:07.21
DNF	Charlie Kolb	Lola T70-Chevrolet	21	O2	23	-	50	13	1:09.0
DNF	Masten Gregory	McLaren M1C-Chevrolet	36	O2	13	-	50	12	1:08.3
DNF	Jerry Titus	Piper-Buick	5	O2	10	-	50	21	1:12.3
DNF	Scooter Patrick	Porsche 906	33	U2	8	-	250	23	1:12.6
DNF	Bill Amick	McLaren M1B-Chevrolet	19	O2	0	-	50	17	1:10.2
DNS	Don Wester	McLaren M1B-Ford	-	O2	-	-	-	-	-

Fastest Qualifier:	George Follmer	Lola T70-Chevrolet	1:06.2	103.32 mph
Race Distance:	159.6 miles	84 laps of 1.9 mile course		
Race Time:	1hr 44min 31.0sec			
Winner's Speed:	91.6 mph			
Victory Margin:	1 lap, 13.3 seconds			
Fastest Lap:	Lothar Motschenbacher	McLaren M1B-Chevrolet	1:03.5	107.69 mph

Lothar and wife, Marilyn, about to enjoy the spoils of victory. Photo from the collections of The Henry Ford.

USRRC

BRIDGEHAMPTON

MAY 20 & 21, 1967

Price 75¢

1967 Bridgehampton USRRC program cover. Scan courtesy Don Markle.

George Follmer #16 jumps into the lead at the start. He is followed by Lothar Motschenbacher #11, Mark Donohue #6, Bob Bondurant #51, Peter Revson #52, Mike Goth (right behind Revson), and Sam Posey #2. Photo from the collections of The Henry Ford.

Bridgehampton

As the USRRC hit the East Coast, there were fifteen drivers racing who competed in at least two of the previous three rounds. They included Mark Donohue, Lothar Motschenbacher, Sam Posey, Bill Eve, Charlie Kolb, Bud Morley, Skip Scott, Peter Revson, Bob Bondurant, George Follmer, Mike Goth, Skip Barber and Fred Baker. East Coast drivers competing in their first USRRC race of 1967 were Brett Lunger, Bruce Jennings, Candido DaMota, Jerry Crawford, Bob Nagel, George Ralph, John Poland, Peter Gregg, Gene Hobbs, Charles Sarle and Don Morin.

Once again, George Follmer was on the pole position. He beat the Can-Am qualify-

ing record (1:32.9) with a time of 1:32.6. This was the first time a Can-Am record was broken during a USRRC race. Follmer had to work for it though. He had posted a quicker time of 1:31.2, but it was protested and disallowed. Instead of sitting out the Saturday qualifying, Follmer sat in the pits until the last ten minutes of the session. Then he went out and set the pole winning time. Lothar Motchenbacher shared the front row with a time of 1:33.8. Mark Donohue (1:34.2) and Bob Bondurant (1:34.5) were on the second row. Next were Peter Revson (1:35.0), Sam Posey (1:35.2), Mike Goth (1:35.8) and Masten Gregory (1:36.4).

When the race started, Follmer blasted

into the lead. He had a six-second lead over Lothar, Donohue, Revson, Posey, Bondurant, Goth and Gregory at the end of the first lap. Skip Scott retired on the first lap with a blown head gasket on his Ford "development" engine. Donohue passed Lothar for second place on the next lap and moved within two car lengths of Follmer. Lothar started to slow down with a broken shock mounting that was just about to collapse. Charlie Kolb was another early retirement when the new two-speed automatic transaxle on his Lola blew a seal.

Peter Gregg took the under two-liter lead at the start, in his Porsche 906. The rear bodywork came off Gregg's Porsche after

Charlie Parson #10 and Masten Gregory #26 are heading the second group at the start. Following are: Skip Barber #44, Bud Morley #72, Charlie Kolb #21, Bill Eve, #1, Skip Scott #91, and the rest of the field. Photo from the collections of The Henry Ford.

At the end of the second lap, Donohue was a few car lengths behind Follmer and this much ahead of Lothar. Photo from the collections of The Henry Ford.

seven laps and he got blackflagged. Gregg retrieved the piece, pitted to reattach it and did five more laps before he figured he had lost too many laps. Bruce Jennings assumed the under two-liter lead in Herb Wetanson's topless 906.

Donohue passed Follmer to take the lead on lap thirteen. Revson passed Lothar for third place. Lothar, retired after fifteen laps with a hole in the engine sump. Sam Posey had a shift rod break on his McLaren when he went into the Echo Valley corner on lap fifteen. Rather than take anyone else out, Posey went straight at the corner, hit a bank and his car flipped over. Posey was unhurt and able to crawl out. Fortunately, damage to his McLaren was light. An ambulance was dispatched and while it was on course, Donohue slowed down and Follmer went by into the lead. After a few seconds, though, Follmer motioned Donohue to re-take the lead before they started racing again.

Follmer spun off the course around lap thirty and it was quite a few laps before he got going again. This moved Peter Revson up to second place. However, it was not long before Revson tangled with Jennings' Porsche and came off the worse for it, retiring with a broken suspension. Jennings was able to keep going and retained the under two-liter lead. Bob Bondurant followed Revson into retirement four laps later with engine problems.

With Revson out, Charlie Parsons took over second place. Parsons retired on lap thirty-nine when his gearbox gave up the ghost. Bud Morley assumed second place and had a huge margin over Mike Goth. Masten Gregory spun his McLaren and was stuck in the sand for two laps. By lap forty, Gregory was motoring though the field. Gregory got by Goth on lap fifty and engaged in a battle with Morley for second place. While all this was happening, Dono-

hue increased his lead to three laps ahead of Morley. Follmer was ten laps behind, going like a freight train and trying to make up laps and lost time.

Just when everyone thought the battle for second place would go down to the finish, Morley pitted for more fuel. He came out close behind Mike Goth, but another pitstop ensured Morley would remain in fourth place. Donohue won by four laps over Gregory. Goth took third place ahead of Morley and Brett Lunger was fifth. Bruce Jennings was sixth and first in the under two-liter class, six laps behind Donohue.

Donohue increased his championship lead to sixteen points over Lothar (31 points to 15 points). Mike Goth was third with twelve points. Sam Posey, Bob Bondurant and Masten Gregory were tied for fourth place with six points each. Bill Eve had five points, while Peter Revson and Bud Morley each had four points.

1967 BRIDGEHAMPTON • USRRC VANDERBILT TROPHY

May 21, 1967, Bridgehampton, Long Island, New York

Place	Driver	Car/Engine	Car #	Class	Laps	Points	Prize	Qualifying Place	Qualifying Time
1	Mark Donohue	Lola T70-Chevrolet	6	O2	70	9	$2,800	3	1:34.2
2	Masten Gregory	McLaren M1C-Chevrolet	26	O2	66	6	1,700	8	1:36.4
3	Mike Goth	Lola T70-Chevrolet	14	O2	65	4	1,300	7	1:35.8
4	Bud Morley	McLaren M1B-Chevrolet	72	O2	65	3	900	12	1:39.6
5	Brett Lunger	McLaren M1C-Chevrolet	25	O2	65	2	700	16	1:44.1
6	Bruce Jennings	Porsche Carrera 6	15	U2	64	1	1,300	22	1:49.7
7	Candido DaMota	McLaren M1B-Chevrolet	42	O2	63	-	500	17	1:44.4
8	Fred Baker	Porsche 906	22	U2	62	-	900	20	1:46.4
9	George Follmer	Lola T70-Chevrolet	16	O2	60	-	600	1	1:32.
10	Jerry Crawford	Lola T70-Chevrolet	0	O2	60	-	200	21	1:48.2
11	Charlie Parsons	McLaren M1C-Chevrolet	10	O2	40	-	100	9	1:37.8
DNF	George Ralph	Elva Mk 8-BMW	12	U2	43	-	400	24	1:52.2
DNF	Bob Bondurant	McLaren M1C-Chevrolet	51	O2	38	-	100	4	1:34.5
DNF	Peter Revson	McLaren M1C-Chevrolet	52	O2	34	-	100	5	1:35.0
DNF	Skip Barber	McLaren M1B-Chevrolet	44	O2	31	-	100	10	1:38.2
DNF	Bill Eve	Lola T70-Chevrolet	1	O2	30	-	100	13	1:39.8
DNF	Bob Nagel	McKee Mk 7-Chevrolet	24	O2	25	-	50	15	1:42.1
DNF	Lothar Motschenbacher	McLaren M1B-Chev	11	O2	15	-	50	2	1:33.8
DNF	Sam Posey	McLaren M1C-Chevrolet	2	O2	14	-	50	6	1:35.2
DNF	John Poland	Lola T70-Chevrolet	5	O2	14	-	50	19	1:46.2
DNF	Peter Gregg	Porsche 906	4	U2	12	-	150	18	1:45.0
DNF	Charlie Kolb	Lola T70-Chevrolet	21	O2	8	-	50	11	1:38.4
DNF	Gene Hobbs	Elva Mk 7S-BMW	56	U2	5	-	50	23	1:52.1
DNF	Skip Scott	McLaren M1C-Ford	91	O2	1	-	50	14	1:40.4
DNS	Dave Fenton	Elva Mk 7S-Porsche	-	U2	-	-	-	-	-

Fastest Qualifier:	George Follmer	Lola T70-Chevrolet	1:32.6	110.8 mph
Race Distance:	199.5 miles	70 laps of 2.85 mile course		
Race Time:	1hr 56min 7.4sec			
Winner's Speed:	103.6 mph			
Victory Margin:	4 laps			
Fastest Lap:	Mark Donohue	Lola T70-Chevrolet	1:34.0	109.15 mph

Masten Gregory #25 about to be lapped again by Mark Donohue #6. Even second place would not salvage Gregory's USRRC season and this would be his last race for Carl Haas. Photo courtesy of the Collier Collection.

Mike Goth's #14 Lola survived a munched fender to take him to third place. Photo courtesy of the Collier Collection.

Bud Morley was running in second, then third, place late in the race. A pit for fuel dropped him back to fourth. Photo courtesy of the Collier Collection.

Brett Lunger drove this McLaren to a fifth place finish. Photo by Robert Raymond.

Bruce Jennings #15 won the under two-liter class with a sixth place finish, in an open top Porsche 906. Photo from the collections of The Henry Ford.

Fred Baker's Porsche 906 getting ready for battle. Baker finished in eighth place and second in the under two-liter class. Photo by Robert Raymond.

Jennings enjoying his class victory. Photo from the collections of The Henry Ford.

20th Annual Sports Car Grand Prix

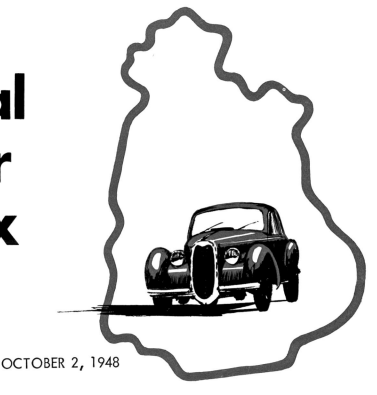

OCTOBER 2, 1948

at Watkins Glen
June 23-25, 1967

50¢

1967 Watkins Glen Sport Car Grand Prix race program cover. Scan courtesy Don Markle.

Mark Donohue pretty much dominated at Watkins Glen. He qualified on the pole and led every lap, but one. Photo by Jim Hayes.

Watkins Glen

All of the championship front runners were at Watkins Glen, except George Follmer and Masten Gregory. Charlie Parsons' sponsor, Randy Hilton, lost interest in racing. Carl Haas' sponsor lost faith in Masten Gregory. After two DNF's, not showing up on time for the Riverside race and one lackluster second place, Haas fired Gregory and hired Parsons. John Cannon, Brett Lunger, Candido DaMota, Bob Nagel and Charles Sarle were starting their second USRRC race of the year. For Joe Buzzetta, Skip Hudson, Brooke Doran, Ron Courtenay, Bill Brack, Dave Wolin, Ludwig Heimrath, John Cordts, Fred Pipin and Peter Lerch, this would be their first USRRC race of the year.

Mark Donohue won the pole position (1:13.7) from Sam Posey (1:13.9) in the last few minutes of qualifying. Lothar Motschenbacher (1:14.2) was third, with Charlie Parsons (1:14.2) beside him on row two. Peter Revson (1:14.6) and John Cannon (1:14.8) were on the third row. Bob Bondurant (1:15.8), Skip Hudson (1:16.2), Mike Goth (1:16.3) and Don Morin (1:16.7) were next on the grid. The first ten cars were all below Jerry Grant's 1:17.2 qualifying record from last year's race. Joe Buzzetta was the fastest under two-liter qualifier, in twenty-second place, with a time of 1:21.9.

Donohue took the lead at the start and was shadowed by Posey. John Cannon was in third place as the first lap ended. Following Cannon were Parsons, Morin, Goth, Lothar, Revson, Hudson and Ludwig

Heimrath. Goth retired with an oil leak after seven laps. After ten laps, Donohue continued to lead Posey, Cannon and Parsons. Lothar was fifth and bothered by a broken mount that caused his seat to move around in the cockpit. Revson, Morin, Hudson, Skip Barber and Bondurant were all behind Lothar.

Revson made his move from sixth place up to third place on lap fourteen. Unfortunately, on lap fourteen, Bondurant's car made a sideways move at 140 mph on the main straight. It then did a series of end over end somersaults and rolled up into a ball of metal and plastic. Although he broke a shoulder, both legs, got a concussion and many cuts and abrasions, Bondurant was lucky to be alive. The yellow flag came out and the field bunched up. Posey was right on Donohue's tail. The green flag was waved after Bondurant was pulled out of the wreckage and the mess was cleaned up. Posey got the jump on Donohue and took the lead. Posey led for one lap before Mark took the lead again and began to draw away.

Revson was holding down third place followed by Cannon, Parsons, Morin, Lothar, Barber, Heimrath and Hudson. Charlie Parsons retired with gearbox trouble after twenty-two laps. Don Morin went off the road on lap twenty-six. The front spoiler of Morin's car did a nice job of clipping the grass and collecting it in front of the radiator. Morin made a quick pitstop to have the grass removed and went back out in eleventh place. Candido DaMota flipped his

McLaren on lap twenty-eight and escaped with minor injuries. A young spectator, who was in a prohibited area close to the track, was also injured when he got hit with debris from DaMota's crash.

Peter Revson retired on lap thirty-four, giving third place to Charlie Parsons. Bud Morley and John Cordts also retired on lap thirty-four. Parsons retired with gearbox trouble after thirty-seven laps. Skip Barber was now in third place, followed by Lothar, Heimrath, Morin, Hudson, Nagel and Buzzetta. Meanwhile, Donohue was stretching his lead over Posey by a second a lap. Posey was doing the same to third place Skip Barber.

Joe Buzzetta made his Porsche fly, but it was no match for the leaders. Buzzetta managed to pass Bob Nagel for eighth place. Heimrath retired with a broken gearbox on lap forty-six. The last two passes of the race were Don Morin taking fourth place from Lothar and Bob Nagel re-taking seventh place from Buzzetta. Donohue finished seventy-three seconds ahead of Posey and over a lap ahead of Skip Barber. Don Morin took fourth place in his USRRC debut. Lothar was fifth and Skip Hudson took the last point for sixth place.

Donohue continued to lead the championship after this race, with forty points to Lothar's seventeen. Sam Posey and Mike Goth were tied for third place, with twelve points each. Skip Barber, Bob Bondurant and Masten Gregory were tied for fifth place, each with six points each.

Sam Posey had a good race with the second fastest qualifying time, running second to Donohue and leading the lap after the restart. Photo by Jim Hayes.

Skip Hudson drove a new Mk 7 McKee entered by Bob McKee and Gene Crowe. Hudson had to pit to have some fabric ducting removed, but carried on and finished in sixth place. Photo by Jim Hayes.

Donohue and Posey, running nose to tail during the first fifteen laps. Photo by Jim Hayes.

Skip Barber brought his McLaren home in third place. Photo by Jim Hayes.

Fred Baker was second in the under two-liter class in his Porsche 906. Photo by Jim Hayes.

1967 WATKINS GLEN • USRRC Sports Car Grand Prix

June 25, 1967, Watkins Glen Grand Prix Course, Watkins Glen, New York

Place	Driver	Car/Engine	Car #	Class	Laps	Points	Prize	Qualifying Place	Qualifying Time
1	Mark Donohue	Lola T70-Chevrolet	6	O2	87	9	$2,500	1	1:13.7
2	Sam Posey	McLaren M1C-Chevrolet	2	O2	87	6	1,500	2	1:13.9
3	Skip Barber	McLaren M1B-Chevrolet	44	O2	86	4	1,200	11	1:17.5
4	Don Morin	McLaren M1B-Chevrolet	36	O2	86	3	1,000	10	1:16.7
5	Lothar Motschenbacher	McLaren M1B-Chevrolet	11	O2	85	2	700	3	1:14.2
6	Skip Hudson	McKee Mk 7-Oldsmobile	9	O2	84	1	500	8	1:16.2
7	Bob Nagel	McKee Mk 7-Chevrolet	24	O2	81	-	400	18	1:20.1
8	Joe Buzzetta	Porsche 906	7	U2	80	-	1,000	22	1:21.9
9	Brett Lunger	McLaren M1C-Chevrolet	25	O2	79	-	220	15	1:19.5
10	Fred Baker	Porsche 906	22	U2	77	-	470	24	1:26.2
11	Brook Doran	McLaren M1B-Chevrolet	3	O2	76	-	150	19	1:21.1
12	Ron Courtney	McLaren M1B-Chevrolet	4	O2	73	-	150	21	1:21.7
13	Bill Brack	Lotus 47	85	U2	73	-	350	26	1:32.3
14	David Wolin	Porsche 718 RS	88	U2	64	-	150	27	1:35.1
DNF	Ludwig Heimrath	McLaren M1B-Chevrolet	39	O2	45	-	150	12	1:17.8
DNF	Charles Sarle	Piranha	74	O2	44	-	150	25	1:28.7
DNF	John Cannon	McLaren M1B-Chevrolet	62	O2	37	-	150	6	1:14.8
DNF	Peter Revson	McLaren M1C-Chevrolet	52	O2	34	-	150	5	1:14.6
DNF	John Cordts	McLaren M1B-Chevrolet	57	O2	34	-	150	16	1:19.6
DNF	Bud Morley	McLaren M1B-Chevrolet	13	O2	34	-	150	13	1:18.2
DNF	Candido DaMota	McLaren M1B-Chevrolet	42	O2	28	-	100	20	1:21.5
DNF	Fred Pipin	Cooper-Chevrolet	61	O2	23	-	100	23	1:23.6
DNF	Charlie Parsons	McLaren M1C-Chevrolet	26	O2	22	-	100	4	1:14.2
DNF	Bill Eve	Lola T70-Chevrolet	1	O2	18	-	100	17	1:20.0
DNF	Bob Bondurant	McLaren M1C-Chevrolet	51	O2	13	-	100	7	1:15.8
DNF	Mike Goth	Lola T70-Chevrolet	14	O2	7	-	100	9	1:16.3
DNF	Peter Lerch	McLaren M1B-Chevrolet	32	O2	7	-	100	28	1:38.9
DNF	Charlie Kolb	Lola T70-Chevrolet	21	O2	1	-	100	14	1:18.6

Fastest Qualifier:	Mark Donohue	Lola T70-Chevrolet	1:13.7	112.35 mph	
Race Distance:	200.1 miles	87 laps of 2.3 mile course			
Race Time:	1hr 53min 24.4sec				
Winner's Speed:	105.87 mph				
Victory Margin:	1 minute, 13 seconds				
Fastest Lap:	Peter Revson	McLaren M1C-Chevrolet	1:13.45	112.73 mph	

Lothar Motschenbacher #11 and Peter Revson #52 ran seventh and eighth in the early laps. Revson held third place for about twenty laps before retiring with no oil pressure. Photo by Jim Hayes.

UNITED STATES Road Racing

CHAMPIONSHIPS

July 16 1967

PACIFIC RACEWAYS

KENT, WASHINGTON   PROGRAM 50¢

1967 Pacific Raceways USRRC program cover. Scan courtesy Don Markle.

Pacific Raceways

The USRRC series went back to the West Coast for a race at Pacific Raceways in Kent, Washington. The weather was warm and there were thirty-two cars starting the race. Included were series regulars: Fred Baker, Mark Donohue, Bill Eve, Mike Goth, Bud Morley, Lothar Motschenbacher, Charlie Parsons, Sam Posey and Peter Revson. John Cannon, George Follmer, Scooter Patrick and Skip Scott all rejoined the series. West Coast and local racers bolstering the grid were: Bill Amick, Eric Anderson, Ed Bowman, Merle Brennan, Gerry Bruihl, Stan Burnett, Mike Eyerly, Lew Florence, Jerry Grant, Charlie Hayes, Jay Hills, Sid Horman, Don Jensen, Ken Legg, John McCornack, Ted Peterson, Monte Shelton and Paul Scott.

Mark Donohue methodically worked his time down during qualifying. Donohue put in four laps at the end of the session that were under the lap record of 1:19.5. His best time was 1:18.7. After Donohue returned to the pits, Jerry Grant took to the track in Tom Friedkin's Lola-Chevrolet. He had enough time for a warm-up and three flying laps. The official timers had Grant doing his fastest flyer in 1:18.3 and gave him the pole position for the race. Pit-side timers had Grant's best lap in the 1:20's. When asked about his time, Grant's response was, "No comment". George Follmer turned in a 1:19.4 to share the front row with Grant and Donohue. Skip Scott and Lothar Motschenbacher were on

the second row of the grid, both with a time of 1:19.7. Mike Goth (1:19.9), Peter Revson (1:20.1) and Sam Posey (1:20.2) occupied the third row. Charlie Parsons (1:20.3) and Jim Adams (1:20.5) completed the top ten qualifiers.

When the race started, George Follmer screeched off the grid and into the lead with Grant and Donohue were close behind. Donohue passed Grant for second place on the next lap. Charlie Hayes spun his McKee twice on the second lap. He got back to the pits and his crew found a screwdriver sticking out of the bottom of the gas tank. Many laps went by before it was repaired and Hayes got back into the race. Follmer's scavenging pump broke and dumped oil through the S-turns on the third lap. Donohue, Grant, Lothar and Skip Scott got through the oil without spinning. Bill Amick wasn't so lucky. He hit the oil and did a couple of 360's. Amick then re-entered the track without noticing Jay Hills aiming for the same piece of road. Contact was made and both were out of the race.

Mark Donohue continued to lead and was pulling away from Jerry Grant. Grant was also putting distance between himself and Lothar. Skip Scott, Peter Revson and Charlie Parsons were right behind Lothar. Bill Eve, Bud Morley and Sam Posey were a little further back and trying to keep the group ahead in sight. Posey stopped at the pits for new goggles, on the eighth lap, and fell out of the

group. Revson got a little too close to Skip Scott's McLaren and gave him a push. The push damaged Scott's shift linkage, causing his retirement after nineteen laps. Grant was starting to slow down with a leaking tire after twenty-one laps. Lothar passed him to take second place on the next lap. Grant fell out of contention when he pitted for a new tire.

Donohue's lead over Lothar was fifty seconds at the halfway point. Parsons was third with Revson fourth, Morley fifth, Eve sixth and Posey seventh. This order remained the same until lap fifty-five when Charlie Parsons pitted to have a flat tire replaced. On lap sixty, Donohue passed second place Lothar to put him a lap down. Lothar started to slowly fall back after that and got passed by Revson. Bud Morley pitted with tire problems.

Donohue was now a lap ahead of Revson with Lothar in third place. Posey passed Bill Eve to take fourth place and Stan Peterson was sixth. The race finished in this order.

With this win and only two races left, Donohue clinched the championship with 49 points. Lothar was second with 21 points and Sam Posey took sole possession of third place with 15 points. Mike Goth was fourth with 12 points and Peter Revson's 10 points were good enough for fifth place. Bill Eve was sixth with 7 points. Seventh place was a three-way tie between Bob Bondurant, Masten Gregory and Skip Barber, each with 6 points.

Around turn two on the pace lap, Jerry Grant #78 is on the pole, next to him is Mark Donohue #6, with George Follmer #16 on the far right. The second row has Skip Scott #91 and Lothar Motschenbacher #11. Mike Goth #14 and Peter Revson #52 are on the third row. Photo by Ron Miller.

On the first lap, at turn two, George Follmer has taken the lead. Unfortunately, it lasted only two laps before the oil pump gave out, sending George into retirement. Behind George is Lothar, Dono-hue, and Grant. Photo by Ron Miller.

Peter Revson #52 leading Charlie Parsons. Revson finished in second place a lap behind Donohue. Photo by Ron Miller.

Jerry Grant was always fast at Pacific Raceways. He ran in second place for the first twenty laps, before suffering a deflating tire. Photo by Ron Miller.

ABOVE and **RIGHT**–Mark Donohue running away with his fifth win in six races. Note the spoiler between the headlights has been given the Penske treatment of tape in the same color as the bodywork and the number roundel placed just so. Photos by Ron Miller.

PACIFIC RACEWAYS • USRRC

July 18, 1967, Pacific Raceways, Kent, Washington

Place	Driver	Car/Engine	Car #	Class	Laps	Points	Prize	Qualifying Place	Qualifying Time
1	Mark Donohue	Lola T70-Chevrolet	6	O2	70	9	$2,700	2	1:18.
2	Peter Revson	McLaren M1B-Chevrolet	52	O2	69	6	1,500	7	1:20.1
3	Lothar Motschenbacher	McLaren M1B-Chevrolet	11	O2	68	4	1,000	5	1:19.7
4	Sam Posey	McLaren M1B-Chevrolet	2	O2	68	3	750	8	1:20.2
5	Bill Eve	Lola T70-Chevrolet	1	O2	66	2	575	14	1:21.5
6	Ted Peterson	McLaren M1B-Chevrolet	77	O2	65	1	400	18	1:24.6
7	Charlie Parsons	McLaren M1B-Chevrolet	26	O2	64	-	300	9	1:20.3
8	Scooter Patrick	Porsche 906	33	U2	64	-	900	19	1:26.0
9	Merle Brennan	Genie Mk 10-Chevrolet	17	O2	64	-	175	22	1:27.8
10	Bud Morley	McLaren M1B-Chevrolet	13	O2	64	-	150	17	1:22.1
11	Monte Shelton	Lola T70-Chevrolet	-	O2	64	-	125	21	1:27.5
12	Fred Baker	Porsche 906	22	U2	64	-	400	23	1:28.9
13	Don Jensen	Burnett Mk 2-Chevrolet	0	O2	63	-	100	12	1:21.3
14	Mike Goth	Lola T70-Chevrolet	14	O2	62	-	100	6	1:19.9
15	Ken Legg	Lotus 23-Cosworth	73	U2	62	-	250	26	1:33.0
16	Paul Scott	Lotus 23-Ferrari	12	U2	61	-	75	28	1:33.1
17	Ed Bowman	Elva Mk 7S-Porsche	15	U2	60	-	75	27	1:33.0
18	Mike Eyerly	Bourgeault	54	U2	59	-	75	24	1:30.5
19	Jerry Grant	Lola T70-Chevrolet	78	O2	58	-	75	1	1:18.3
20	John McCormack	Lotus 23-Porsche	43	U2	58	-	50	30	1:36.1
21	Sid Horman	Elva Mk 8-BMW	-	U2	52	-	50	29	1:34.5
22	Charlie Hayes	McKee Mk 7-Chevrolet	97	O2	42	-	50	15	1:21.6
23	Gerry Bruihl	Lotus 23-Climax	41	U2	35	-	50	20	1:26.9
DNF	Lew Florence	Genie Mk 10-Chevrolet	4	O2	33	-	50	16	1:22.1
DNF	Skip Scott	McLaren M1B-Ford	91	O2	19	-	50	4	1:19.7
DNF	Eric Anderson	Lotus 23B-Cosworth	69	U2	16	-	50	25	1:32.9
DNF	John Cannon	McLaren M1B-Chevrolet	62	O2	6	-	50	31	-
DNF	Jay Hills	McLaren M1B-Chevrolet	81	O2	2	-	50	13	1:21.4
DNF	Stan Burnett	Burnett Mk 2-Chevrolet	64	O2	2	-	50	32	-
DNF	George Follmer	Lola T70-Chevrolet	16	O2	2	-	50	3	1:19.4
DNF	Jim Adams	McLaren M1A-Chevrolet	3	O2	1	-	50	10	1:20.5
DNF	Bill Amick	McLaren M1B-Chevrolet	19	O2	0	-	50	11	1:21.1

Fastest Qualifier:	Jerry Grant	Lola T70-Chevrolet	1:18.3	103.45 mph
Race Distance:	157.5 miles	70 laps of 2.25 mile course		
Race Time:	1hr 37min 7.1sec			
Winner's Speed:	97.27 mph			
Victory Margin:	1 lap, 40 seconds			
Fastest Race Lap:	Mark Donohue	Lola T70-Chevrolet	1:20.2	101.00 mph

Lew Florence #4 leading Ted Peterson #77 early in the race. Florence retired after thirty-three laps. Peterson was eighteenth on the grid and through attrition, moved up to sixth place by the end of the race. Photo by Ron Miller.

BADGER 200
ROAD
AMERICA
500
JULY 29/30

75¢

ELKHART LAKE, WISCONSIN

1967 Road America 500 race program cover. Scan courtesy Don Markle.

The winning car of Charlie Parsons and Skip Scott in the paddock. Photo by Gil Munz.

Road America 500

The Road America 500 had one of the smallest fields in recent years, with only twenty-one cars starting the race. Charlie Parsons had two opportunities to win as he shared both of Carl Haas' McLarens; one with Skip Scott and the other with Jerry Hansen. Peter Revson and Lothar Motschenbacher were entered in the Sunray DX McLaren. Ralph Salyer shared his McKee with Bill Mitchell. Sam Posey and Bud Morley both co-drove with Jerry Entin. Bob Nagel had Ed Lowther co-driving his McKee. Skip Barber shared the driving in Don Morin's McLaren. The Penske team decided to give the Road America race a miss to get their new Lola ready for the Mid-Ohio race and the Can-Am series. In the under two-liter class, Joe Buzzetta and Scooter Patrick shared Joe's Porsche 906 and Mak Kronn had Chuck Dietrich co-driving in his Porsche 906.

Charlie Parsons had a lock on the front row. The McLaren he was sharing with Skip Scott won the pole position with a time of 2:22.8. Jerry Hansen turned in the second fastest time (2:23.2) in the McLaren he shared with Parsons . Ralph Salyer (2:25.8) and Peter Revson (2:27.0) were on the second row. Brooke Doran was fifth with a time of 2:27.6 in his McLaren. Jerry Entin (2:29.4) was next to Doran on the third row.

Don Morin (2:29.7) and Bob Nagel (2:31.0) started from seventh and eighth spots. Joe Buzzetta (2:33.1) and Mak Kronn (2:39.7) completed the top ten starters.

Jerry Hansen jumped into the lead at the start, followed by Charlie Parsons, Peter Revson and Jerry Entin. Hansen led for the first four laps before Revson passed him. Revson's lead lasted for three laps. Hansen retook the lead with Parsons in second and Revson back to third place. Brian O'Neill retired his Lola after eight laps with brake trouble.

Bill Mitchell sent Ralph Salyer's McKee spinning and retired after twenty-seven laps. Revson had the right front wheel lock up on lap thirty. That sent his car into a spin and blew out the left rear wheel. Revson was able to get back to the pits for repairs, but was two laps down when he returned to the course. To make up for lost time, Revson set a new course record of 2:23.2. It was the first race lap over 100 mph (100.559 mph, to be exact) at Road America. Parsons pitted to turn his car over to Skip Scott on lap forty.

Revson pitted on lap forty-two to replace another flat tire. The starter burned out when he tried to restart his car and he retired from the race. Hansen brought his McLaren into the pits for gas and to hand

it over to Charlie Parsons. Parsons kept the lead until lap fifty-five. Then he pitted for oil and that gave the lead to his other car, with Skip Scott driving. The running order was now Parsons/Scott, Parsons/Hansen, Don Morin/Skip Barber, Sam Posey/Jerry Entin/Bud Morley, Mak Kronn/Chuck Dietrich and Joe Buzzetta/Scooter Patrick.

In the last half of the race, the Parsons/Scott and Parsons/Hansen McLarens rolled on to finish first and second. Don Morin and Skip Barber brought their car home in third place. Joe Buzzetta and Scooter Patrick were able to pass the Mak Kronn/Chuck Dietrich car for fourth place and won the under two-liter class. The McLaren of Jerry Entin/Sam Posey/Bud Morley fell back to sixth place for the final championship point.

The first four places in the championship standings remained the same. Mark Donohue had clinched the Championship in the last round and had 49 points. Lothar was second with 21. Sam Posey had 16 points for third place with Mike Goth fourth with 12 points. Skip Barber now tied Peter Revson for fifth place, each with 10 points. Charlie Parsons and Skip Scott were tied for seventh with 9 points each. With his third place, Don Morin now tied Bill Eve for ninth place with 7 points. Mid-Ohio would be the decider for second place on down.

Parsons' and Scott's second place car in action.
Photo by Tom Schultz.

The third place McLaren of Don Morin and Skip Barber. Photo by Tom Schultz.

The under two-liter class winning Porsche 906 #7 shared by Joe Buzzetta and Scooter Patrick ahead of Brooke Doran's McLaren. Buzzetta won the under two-liter class at Watkins Glen and Patrick won it at Riverside and Pacific Raceways, but they were not in the top six to score points. In sharing this class win they shared the championship. Photo by Tom Schultz.

1967 ROAD AMERICA • USRRC

Road America 500
July 31, 1967, Road America, Elkhart Lake, Wisconsin

Place	Driver	Car/Engine	Car #	Class	Laps	Points	Prize	Qualifying Place	Qualifying Time
1	Charlie Parsons/Skip Scott	McLaren M1C-Chevrolet	26	O2	125	9	$3,700	1	2:22.8
2	Jerry Hansen/Charlie Parsons	McLaren M1C-Chevrolet	44	O2	124	6	2,500	2	2:23.2
3	Don Morin/Skip Barber	McLaren M1C-Chevrolet	36	O2	119	4	1,500	7	2:29.7
4	Joe Buzzetta/Scooter Patrick	Porsche 906	7	U2	119	3	2,200	9	2:33.1
5	Mak Kronn/Chuck Dietrich	Porsche 906	77	U2	118	2	1,400	10	2:39.7
6	Jerry Entin/Sam Posey/Bud Morley	McLaren M1B-Chevrolet	1	O2	118	1	700	6	2:29.4
7	Lee (E.L.) Hall/Mike Hall	Porsche 906	69	U2	117	-	850	11	2:41.4
8	Mike Rahal/Ralph Trieschmann	Elva Mk 7S-Porsche	68	U2	114	-	600	14	2:46.4
9	Werner Frank/Horst Kwech	Porsche 904	99	U2	113	-	300	18	2:48.2
10	William Cooper/Dick Drexler	Ferrari 275P	21	O2	102	-	200	17	2:47.9
11	Bill Shoenfeld/Dick Durant	Corvette Gran Sport	27	O2	95	-	100	19	2:28.9
12	Bill Tuttle/Gloria Tuttle	Elva Mk 7S-Porsche 9	1	U2	94	-	50	20	3:14.1
13	Rich Dagiel/Guy Wooley	Lister-Chevrolet	49	O2	87	-	50	16	2:47.1
14	Jim Place/George Dickinson	Lotus 23-Porsche	13	U2	75	-	50	21	3:35.6
DNF	Brooke Doran	McLaren M1B-Chevrolet	31	O2	61	-	50	5	2:27.6
DNF	Lothar Motschenbacher/Peter Revson	McLaren M1B-Chevrolet	52	O2	42	-	50	4	2:27.0
DNF	Peter Helferich	Pariah-Oldsmobile	57	O2	40	-	50	12	2:42.0
DNF	Robert Nagel/Ed Lowther	McKee Mk 7-Chevrolet	24	O2	38	-	50	8	2:31.0
DNF	Ralph Salyer/Bill Mitchell	McKee Mk 6-Oldsmobile	25	O2	27	-	50	3	2:25.8
DNF	Brian O'Neill	Lola T70-Ford	14	O2	8	-	50	13	2:45.5
DNF	George Alderman/Bob Gardner	McLaren M1B-Chevrolet	23	O2	5	-	50	15	2:46.8

Fastest Qualifier:	Chuck Parsons	McLaren M1C-Chevrolet	2:22.8	100.83 mph
Race Distance:	500 miles	125 laps of 4.0 mile course		
Race Time:	5hrs 23min 42.8sec			
Winner's Speed:	92.67mph			
Victory Margin:	1 lap, 55 seconds			
Fastest Race Lap:	Peter Revson	McLaren M1B-Chevrolet	2:23.2	100.559 mph

Jerry Entin's McLaren, shared with Sam Posey and Bud Morley. They took sixth place. Photo by Tom Schultz.

Jerry Hansen leading Charlie Parsons and Peter Revson. Photo by Tom Schultz.

The Dana Chevrolet McLaren driven by Peter Revson fought for the early lead only to spin, then stop to change a deflated tire, but could not get the starter to engage. Lothar Motschenbacher never got into the car. Photo by Mike Odell.

The Ralph Salyer/Bill Mitchell McKee lasted twenty-seven laps. Photo by Mike Odell.

UNITED STATES ROAD RACING CHAMPIONSHIP

•

AUGUST 19-20, 1967

OFFICIAL PROGRAM • SCCA - ACCUS SANCTION N - 25 - 67
Restricted Event Sanction 67 - RS - 52 • **FIFTY CENTS**

1967 Mid Ohio USRRC race program cover. Scan courtesy Don Markle.

Close racing back in the pack. Mak Kronn #77 Porsche 906 leads Ludwig Heimrath #39 McLaren, Mike Hall #69 Porsche 906, Gary Wilson #19 McLaren, and Dave Heinz #97 McKee. Photo by Gerry Melton.

The first two rows of the grid on the pace lap. Mark Donohue #16 is on the pole. Charlie Parsons #26 is on the left of Donohue. Charlie Hayes #25 qualified third in a new McKee Mk 7. Next to Hayes is Jerry Hansen #47, who finished second. Photo by Gerry Melton.

Mid-Ohio

With the championship already decided, Mid-Ohio still had a good turnout with twenty-five cars taking the starter's flag. Bud Morley, Lothar Motschenbacher, Charlie Parsons and Sam Posey were the only drivers to start all eight races. Mark Donohue and Mike Goth were back for the Mid-Ohio round after missing the Road America race. Other semi-regular competitors present were Skip Barber, Joe Buzzetta, John Cannon, Don Morin and Bob Nagel. George Alderman, Ron Courtenay, Brooke Doran, Mike Hall, Jerry Hansen, Charlie Hayes, Ludwig Heimrath, Gene Hobbs, Mak Kronn, Brian O'Neill, Jim Place, Art Seyler and Phil Seitz made up the rest of the grid.

Lothar's Dana Chevrolet team had a rough time getting to the race. The mechanics trailering the McLaren to the race were in Indiana when they swerved to avoid a car stopped in the road and got hit head-on by a truck coming from the opposite direction. Both mechanics ended up in the hospital and the McLaren suffered front-end damage. Lothar phoned his wife, Marilyn, to have her fly to Chicago, rent a truck, pick up parts from Carl Haas' shop and drive them to the track. Lothar spent Saturday rebuilding the front-end of the McLaren with Peyton Cramer's help, so he could qualify Sunday morning.

Qualifying was two sessions on Saturday

and one session Sunday morning. Charlie Parsons had the fastest time at 1:35.0 at the end of Saturday. His teammate, Jerry Hansen, was second fastest with a 1:35.4. These times ended up being good enough for only the second row of the grid. Sam Posey used Saturday to try his new Caldwell D7, with a driver-actuated rear airfoil. But a 1:44.2 was the best he could manage. Sam then took over the McLaren he entered for Brett Lunger on Sunday and put in a 1:35.6. That was good enough for fifth on the grid. The Penske team arrived late Saturday with a 427 Chevrolet engine fitted in the Lola. In transit to the race course, the windscreen flew off the Lola and broke. Donohue was allowed to practice without the windscreen, but was told he could not race without one. Penske had a new windscreen flown in and installed Sunday morning. Mark went out and took the pole position with a 1:33.4. Charlie Hayes urged Ralph Salyer's McKee around the course in 1:35.0 for second on the grid. Bud Morley was sixth on the grid at 1:36.8. Mike Goth (1:37.2) was on the fourth row of the grid with Lothar Motschenbacher (1:37.4).

Donohue took the lead right at the start. Charlie Parsons, Charlie Hayes, Sam Posey and Jerry Hansen were all close behind. Ludwig Heimrath was disqualified after six laps for getting a push-start at turn eleven. Parsons took fifteen laps before he decided

to let Charlie Hayes go by. Parsons was close to Donohue, but still losing ground. Parsons thought Hayes might catch Donohue and they might race each other to the point of breaking their cars. It didn't quite work that way. Parsons' car broke on lap twenty. The distributor rotor tip got dislodged and Parsons was able to borrow a screwdriver from a spectator to fix it. He did lose five laps with the repair.

Hayes caught up with Donohue after twenty-four laps. Donohue responded to Hayes' challenge with a new course record to put a little distance between them. Donohue lost second gear after twenty laps, but it wasn't noticeable by his smooth driving. The running order, after thirty laps, was Donohue, Hayes, Hansen, Lothar, Mike Goth, Bud Morley, Skip Barber and Sam Posey. Gary Wilson, Brian O'Neil, Dave Heinz and Art Seyler had all retired.

On lap forty-three, Lothar's McLaren broke a halfshaft, got airborne and sailed off course towards some spectators. The car flipped over and hit a post broadside. The impact ruptured the fuel cell and a girl sitting nearby got doused with gasoline, but was not injured. Lothar tore some rib ligaments, but otherwise escaped serious injury. This moved Mike Goth up to fourth place. Bud Morley, Skip Barber, Don Morin and Sam Posey all followed Goth. Joe Buzzetta was the first under two-liter contender and

Mark Donohue is looking very intent as he speeds to victory. He was so intent he won by three laps. Photo by Dave Arnold.

Jerry Hansen enters the track in his McLaren. Hansen ran in the top five for all of the race, moved up as others dropped out, and finished in second place. Photo by Gerry Melton.

Bud Morley drove a smooth race inside the top ten and finished in third place. Photo by Gerry Melton.

Skip Barber finished in fourth place. Photo by Gerry Melton.

Don Morin qualified tenth and finished in fifth place. Photo by Gerry Melton.

This was the first race appearance of Sam Posey's Caldwell D7. Sam drove it in practice but it was about ten seconds off the pace and he reverted to his McLaren for the race. Photo by Gerry Melton.

he was running in eleventh place. The race ran its course until Mike Goth ran out of gas on lap seventy-five and handed fourth place to Bud Morley.

The cars were very spread-out at this point. Donohue was leading Charlie Hayes by a few seconds. Jerry Hansen, in third place, was over three laps behind. Bud Morley was fourth, about a minute behind Hansen and five seconds in front of Skip Barber. Don Morin was a lap behind Barber and Sam Posey was a lap behind Morin. This order remained until the last lap when

Charlie Hayes' McKee ran out of gas and sputtered to a stop with a little more than a mile to the finish line. His pit crew was prepared for him to stop because they knew the gas tank was about ten gallons less than a McLaren or Lola. However, Charlie never stopped because the gas gauge did not flicker at all.

Donohue took the win and nine points. He finished three laps and five seconds ahead of Jerry Hansen. Bud Morley was third, with Skip Barber fourth, Don Morin fifth and Sam Posey taking the final point

for sixth place. Mark Donohue had won the championship earlier in the season and now finished with a total of 54 points, from his best six results. His grand total was 58 points. Lothar Motschenbacher was second with 21 points. Third was Sam Posey with 17 points while Skip Barber was fourth with 13 points. Mike Goth and Jerry Hansen tied for fifth place with 12 points each. Peter Revson was seventh with 10 points. Rounding out the top ten were Don Morin, Charlie Parsons and Skip Scott all tied for eighth place, each with 9 points.

1967 MID-OHIO • USRRC wwww1967 BUCKEYE CUP

August 20, 1967, Mid-Ohio Sports Car Course, Lexington, Ohio

Place	Driver	Car/Engine	Car #	Class	Laps	Points	Prize	Qualifying Place	Qualifying Time
1	Mark Donohue	Lola T70-Chevrolet	16	O2	85	9	$3,800	1	1:33.4
2	Jerry Hansen	McLaren M1B-Chevrolet	47	O2	82	6	2,300	4	1:35.4
3	Bud Morley	McLaren M1B-Chevrolet	13	O2	82	4	1,500	6	1:36.8
4	Skip Barber	McLaren M1B-Chevrolet	44	O2	82	3	1,200	11	1:39.0
5	Don Morin	McLaren M1B-Chevrolet	36	O2	81	2	1,000	10	1:38.8
6	Sam Posey	McLaren M1C-Chevrolet	4	O2	80	1	800	5	1:35.6
7	Charlie Parsons	McLaren M1B-Chevrolet	26	O2	79	-	900	3	1:35.0
8	George Alderman	McLaren M1B-Chevrolet	27	O2	78	-	500	12	1:39.6
9	Joe Buzzetta	Porsche 906	7	U2	76	-	600	14	1:42.4
10	Ron Courtney	McLaren M1B-Chevrolet	41	O2	76	-	300	16	1:42.6
11	Mike Hall	Porsche 906	69	U2	76	-	250	21	1:45.6
12	Bob Nagel	McKee Mk 7-Chevrolet	24	O2	75	-	225	13	1:41.0
13	Mak Kronn	Porsche 906	77	U2	73	-	200	20	1:45.0
14	Jim Place	Lotus 23-Porsche	43	U2	69	-	175	25	1:56.4
15	John Cannon	McLaren M1B-Chevrolet	6	O2	52	-	175	9	1:38.2
DNF	Charlie Hayes	McKee Mk 7-Oldsmobile	25	O2	84	-	175	2	1:35.0
DNF	Mike Goth	Lola T70-Chevrolet	14	O2	75	-	150	7	1:37.2
DNF	Gene Hobbs	McLaren M1B-Chevrolet	56	O2	60	-	150	15	1:42.4
DNF	Lothar Motschenbacher	McLaren M1B-Chev	11	O2	42	-	150	8	1:37.4
DNF	Art Seyler	Cooper-Chevrolet	93	O2	31	-	150	18	1:43.
DNF	Dave Heinz	McKee-Chevrolet	97	O2	26	-	100	19	1:44.6
DNF	Brian O'Neill	Lola T70-Ford	5	O2	19	-	100	24	1:49.2
DNF	Phil Seitz	Lotus 23	72	U2	13	-	100	23	1:48.8
DNF	Gary Wilson	McLaren M1B-Chevrolet	19	O2	10	-	100	22	1:48.0
DSQ	Ludwig Heimrath	McLaren M1B-Chevrolet	39	O2	-	-	-	17	1:42.8

Fastest Qualifier:	Mark Donohue	Lola T70-Chevrolet	1:33.4	92.51 mph
Race Distance:	204.0 miles	85 laps of 2.4 mile course		
Race Time:	2hr 17min 6.6sec			
Winners Speed:	87.11 mph			
Victory Margin:	3 laps, 5 seconds			
Fastest Race Lap:	Mark Donohue	Lola T70-Chevrolet	1:34.6	91.33 mph

Charlie Parsons #26 is leading Charlie Hayes early in the race. Hayes drove an inspired race and was robbed of second place when he ran out of gas on the last lap. Photo by Gerry Melton.

George Alderman qualified twelfth and finished in eighth place. Photo by Gerry Melton.

Joe Buzzetta with his Porsche 906 in the paddock. Joe finished in ninth place and was the under two-liter winner.

1967 USRRC Drivers Championship Points

SD Stardust, RIV Riverside, LS Laguna Seca, BH Bridgehampton, WG Watkins Glen, PR Pacific Raceways, MO Mid-Ohio, RA Road America

Place	Driver	SD	RIV	LS	BH	WG	PR	MO	RA	Total Points	Best 6 Points
1	Mark Donohue	9	9	4	9	9	9	-	9	58	54
2	Lothar Motschenbacher	3	3	9	-	2	4	-	-	21	21
3	Sam Posey	6	-	-	-	6	3	1	1	17	17
4	Skip Barber	-	-	2	-	4	-	4	3	13	13
5	Mike Goth	-	2	6	4	-	-	-	-	12	12
6	Jerry Hansen	-	-	-	-	-	-	6	6	12	12
7	Peter Revson	-	4	-	-	-	6	-	-	10	10
8	Don Morin	-	-	-	-	3	-	4	2	9	9
9	Charlie Parsons	-	-	-	-	-	-	9	-	9	9
10	Skip Scott	-	-	-	-	-	-	9	-	9	9
11	Bud Morley	-	1	-	3	-	-	-	4	8	8
12	Bill Eve	4	-	1	-	-	2	-	-	7	7
13	Bob Bondurant	-	6	-	-	-	-	-	-	6	6
14	Masten Gregory	-	-	-	6	-	-	-	-	6	6
15	John Cannon	-	-	3	-	-	-	-	-	3	3
16	Joe Buzzetta	-	-	-	-	-	-	3	-	3*	3*
17	Scooter Patrick	-	-	-	-	-	-	3	-	3*	3*
18	Moises Solana	2	-	-	-	-	-	-	-	2	2
19	Brett Lunger	-	-	-	2	-	-	-	-	2	2
20	Mak Kronn	-	-	-	-	-	-	2	-	2	2
21	Chuck Dietrich	-	-	-	-	-	-	2	-	2	2
22	Charlie Kolb	1	-	-	-	-	-	-	-	1	1
23	Bruce Jennings	-	-	-	1	-	-	-	-	1	1
24	Skip Hudson	-	-	-	-	1	-	-	-	1	1
25	Ted Peterson	-	-	-	-	-	1	-	-	1	1

* Under Two-Liter Co-champions

1967 Season Summary

Nineteen Sixty-Seven was the "Summer of Love" in cities and parks around America. Racing enthusiasts showed their love by attending USRRC races in record numbers. There were 171,125 paid admissions for the eight events. That was 35,000 more than the previous year and averaged out to over 21,000 spectators per race. The race promoters, in turn, showed their love to the racers by paying out $109,750 in prize money. That was another record. The tire companies, Goodyear and Firestone, plus Union Oil, Pure Oil, Champion Spark Plug and Bell Helmets provided $43,800 in contingency money for winning drivers who used their products.

On the racetrack it was the "Summer of Mark Donohue". From the first race at Stardust Raceway Donohue stamped his authority on the series. Starting in seven races, he won six of them and placed third in the other. Donohue clinched the championship at Pacific Raceways, with two races left in the series. He skipped the Road America race and won the final event at Mid-Ohio. Donohue scored fifty-eight total points and his best of six score was fifty-four points. Lothar Motschenbacher was a distant second with twenty-one points. There was an eight-way battle for third place going into the final event. Sam Posey was third (seventeen points), while Skip Barber was fourth (thirteen). Mike Goth and Jerry Hansen tied for fifth with twelve points and Peter Revson was seventh (ten points). Don Morin, Charlie Parsons and Skip Scott all tied for eighth place with nine points each.

In the early races, George Follmer usually grabbed the lead at the start. Donohue would take up to fifteen laps waiting for Follmer's car to break, or to find a way by him. At Laguna Seca, Watkins Glen and Mid-Ohio Donohue took the lead right at the start. The only time he got passed was at Watkins Glen, when Sam Posey got the jump on him as the race was restarted after Bondurant's accident.

There were no close finishes this year. In fact, the victory margins were measured in time at only three races. It was measured in laps, or miles at the rest of the races. The shortest victory margin was fifty-five seconds at Riverside. The greatest divide between first and second place was at Bridgehampton where Donohue beat Masten Gregory by four laps, or 11.4 miles.

Once again, the under two-liter class was based on overall points. Scooter Patrick and Joe Buzzetta co-drove a Porsche 906 to fourth place at Road America and scored three points each to share the title. Mak Kronn and Chuck Dietrich also co-drove at Road America and got two points. Charlie Kolb and Bruce Jennings each got a sixth place, the only other under two-liter drivers to score points. Joe Buzzetta and Scooter Patrick each won their class individually, two other times, but finished below sixth place and did not score points. Fred Baker was the only other class winner to not score points. As with the bigger cars, the class-winning margin was measured in laps. Pacific Raceways and Mid-Ohio were the only races where first and second in class finished on the same lap.

There were 225 individual drivers who started races. Charlie Parsons, Lothar Motschenbacher and Sam Posey started all eight races. Mark Donohue, Peter Revson and Bud Morley each started seven races. Four drivers started six races and another four drivers started five races. Six drivers started four races while seven started in three. Twenty-one drivers started twice and 177 started a single race. Twenty-five drivers scored points.

176 of the 225 starters were over two-liter cars. 150 of these were Lolas, McLarens, or McKees. The other over two-liter cars were specials like the Burnett, Capello, Piper, Piranha and Pariah. There were also some older Genies, Coopers and Ferraris. That left forty-nine starts for under two-liter cars which was an average of 6 per race. Things did not bode well for the under two-liter class in 1968.

1968

Mexico City
Riverside
Laguna Seca
Bridgehampton
St. Jovite
Pacific Raceways
Watkins Glen
Road America
Mid Ohio

1968 Introduction

The end of the USRRC was not apparent at the beginning of the season. 1967 was another record-setting year and the SCCA was taking the series to a new level in 1968. The USRRC became an international, or at least North American, series with the addition of races in Mexico City and St Jovite, Canada. The seven other races were held at Riverside, Laguna Seca and Pacific Raceways on the West Coast and at Bridgehampton, Watkins Glen, Road America and Mid-Ohio on the East Coast.

Pre-season interest by teams and drivers ran high, as the SCCA announced a big increase in prize money, plus a $15,000 points fund for the top ten finishers in the championship.

Fan and spectator interest was high as well. All of the past series champions, except Bob Holbert, were expected to take part. This included Jim Hall and his Chaparral, who skipped the last two years after losing the 1965 title.

A lot of this interest in the USRRC was an offshoot of the more lucrative Can-Am series, which featured international entries and driving talent. The USRRC was a great "development" series in which to get cars, drivers and teams ready for the Can-Am series, which followed the end of USRRC season by a couple of weeks. This made the USRRC a "must watch" series for both serious and casual race fans.

USRRC drivers acquitted themselves very well in the 1967 Can-Am series, although Bruce McLaren and Denny Hulme won all but one race and took first and second places in the championship. Mark Donohue scored two second place and one third place finish, to tie John Surtees for third in the series. Jim Hall was fifth with two second places and a fourth place. George Follmer tied Mike Spence for sixth place. Bud Morley and Peter Revson were eighth and ninth. Also scoring points were Charlie Hayes, Lothar Motschenbacher, Skip Scott, Jerry Hansen, Charlie Parsons and Bill Eve.

After the 1967 Can-Am series, Roger Penske bought Bruce McLaren's championship winning car for Mark Donohue to run in the '68 USRRC and Can-Am series. It was a McLaren M6A, with a 427 inch Chevrolet engine. Jim Hall was expected to race a development of the Chaparral 2G he used in the '67 Can-Am. Carl Haas had two Lola-Chevrolets and Simoniz sponsorship for Charlie Parsons and Skip Scott. Carroll Shelby entered a Lola-Ford for Peter Revson. Strong private entries were fielded by Sam Posey, Lothar Motschenbacher, Bud Morley, John Cannon, John Cordts and Canadian, George Eaton.

Under two-liter cars were still allowed to enter USRRC races. However, there was not a separate class for them and they had to race for overall results. Consequently, no under two-liter teams were prepared to enter the whole series.

Let the end begin.

CARRERA INTERNACIONAL CIUDAD DE MEXICO

Domingo 31 marzo de 1968 a las 11 a. m. Autódromo de México.

Programa oficial $2.00

1968 Mexico City USRRC program cover. Scan courtesy Don Markle.

Race winner, Moises Solana, passes the almost empty grandstand during practice. Solana ran the first thirty laps in second place to Skip Scott and took the lead when Scott's Lola developed transmission problems. Solana's new McLaren started smoking with ten laps to go, but he was able to stay ahead of Scott. Photo by Gil Munz.

Mexico City

International flavor was added to the USRRC in 1968, with a race in Mexico City to start the series. Unfortunately, part of the flavor included multiple-day waits at the border and bribes paid to get equipment into Mexico. Once at the race course however, the US and Canadian teams enjoyed delightful local hospitality.

Twenty drivers started the race. Three were Canadian, five were Mexican and twelve were American. Lola and McLaren were equally represented with eight entries each. The top teams and drivers included Mark Donohue in Roger Penske's Sunoco McLaren M6A-Chevrolet, the car Bruce McLaren used to win the 1967 Can-Am series. Carl Haas had Charlie Parsons and Skip Scott driving Lola T70 Mark 3's sponsored by Simoniz. Carroll Shelby entered Peter Revson in a Lola T70-Ford. Sam Posey

entered his Caldwell D7B. Lothar Motschenbacher had a new McLaren M6B running a 377-cubic-inch Ford engine with Gurney-Weslake heads. Local hero, Moises Solana, had a McLaren M6B, which he took delivery of Tuesday before the race. His team finished installing the engine after they arrived at the racetrack. Other Lola racers were Jerry Entin, Bud Morley, Jack Milliken, George Hollinger and Hernan Solana (Moises' brother). En-

1968 MEXICO CITY • USRRC Carrera Internacional Ciudad de Mexico

March 31, 1968, Magdalena Circuit, Mexico City, Mexico

Place	Driver	Car/Engine	Car #	Laps	Points	Prize	Qualifying Place	Qualifying Time
1	Moises Solana	McLaren M6B-Chevrolet	99	50	9	$ 4,000	7	1:53.28
2	Skip Scott	Lola T70-Chevrolet	26	50	6	2,400	3	1:49.40
3	Peter Revson	Lola T70-Ford	52	50	4	2,000	1	1:48.41
4	Sam Posey	Caldwell D7-Chevrolet	1	50	3	1,700	4	1:49.84
5	Bud Morley	Lola T70-Chevrolet	14	50	2	1,400	5	1:51.65
6	Lothar Motschenbacher	McLaren M6B-Chev	11	50	1	1,200	2	1:48.99
7	Jerry Entin	Lola T70-Chevrolet	12	49	-	1,100	14	2:02.32
8	Charlie Parsons	Lola T70-Chevrolet	10	49	-	900	6	1:52.46
9	George Eaton	McLaren M1C-Ford	98	48	-	700	10	1:57.40
10	Jack Milliken	Lola T70-Chevrolet	77	47	-	600	12	1:58.20
11	Jerry Crawford	McLaren M1B-Chevrolet	7	45	-	500	13	1:59.51
12	Werner Frank	Porsche 906	88	44	-	500	17	2:06.74
13	Rubin Navoa	Porsche 906	5	44	-	500	16	2:06.61
14	Paco Pineiro	Lotus 40-Chevrolet	21	42	-	500	15	2:05.14
15	Ludwig Heimrath	McLaren M1B-Chevrolet	39	41	-	500	9	1:56.94
16	Ron Courtney	McLaren-Chevrolet	8	28	-	500	11	1:58.19
DNF	Fred Van Beuren	McLaren M1B-Chevrolet	33	30	-	500	19	2:17.61
DNF	Hernan Solana	Lola T70-Chevrolet	2	27	-	500	8	1:55.49
DNF	George Hollinger	Lola T70-Chevrolet	37	23	-	500	18	2:10.92
DNF	Max Beimler	Chinook Mk 2-Chevrolet	34	18	-	500	20	2:33.10

Fastest Qualifier:	Peter Revson	Lola T70-Ford	1:48.41	102.441 mph
Race Distance:	155.0 miles	50 laps of 3.1 mile course		
Race Time:	1hr 33min 36sec			
Winner's Speed:	99.58 mph			
Victory Margin:	13 seconds			
Fastest Race Lap:	Peter Revson	Lola T70-Ford	1:48.91	102.47 mph

tered in other McLarens were Ron Courtney, Jerry Crawford, Fred Van Buren and Canadians Ludwig Heimrath and George Eaton. Werner Frank and Rubin Navoa had the Porsches. Paco Pineiro had a Lotus 40 and Max Beimler raced a Chinook-Chevrolet.

Mark Donohue got down to business and recorded a lap of 1:50.0 in the first qualifying session. An oil pump in Donohue's car failed in the last few minutes of the morning session. It damaged the crankshaft and a couple of rods and the Penske crew did not have a spare engine. They ordered parts to be flown in from Traco and spent Saturday evening rebuilding the engine. Skip Scott had the fastest time (1:51.8) when the Saturday afternoon session opened. During the last half-hour of the session, things got serious. Lothar thought he had the pole sewn up with a time of 1:48.99. Peter Revson went out in the last few minutes and threw down a 1:48.41 to take the pole position. Revson's time compared well with Jim Clark's lap record of 1:48.0, in a Formula One Lotus. Skip Scott and Sam Posey were on the second row with times of 1:49.4 and 1:49.84, respectively. Donohue's time was good enough for fifth spot on the grid with Bud Morley next quickest (1:51.65).

Rounding out the top ten qualifiers were Charlie Parsons (1:52.45), Moises Solana and his brother Hernan (1:53.28 and 1:55.49), as well as Canadians Ludwig Heimrath and George Eaton (1:56.94 and 1:57.4).

The oil pump in Donohue's rebuilt engine failed again during morning warm-up on raceday and he was out of the race. Peter Revson took the lead from Sam Posey when the race started. Skip Scott was third and followed by Moises Solana, Lothar, Morley and Charlie Parsons. Revson pitted on the next lap to have a broken battery strap fixed. Posey took the lead and Skip Scott moved in to challenge him. Posey's Caldwell started leaking fuel into the cockpit after another lap. Sam got soaked with fuel and then started feeling groggy. He backed off the pace and sat up into the airstream to get fresh air. Moises Solana was then able to get by Posey and he started challenging Scott for the lead. Sam and Lothar were scrapping for third place, while Revson was charging through the field to make up for his pitstop.

On lap fifteen, Scott still led over Moises Solana, Lothar, Posey, Morley, Jerry Entin and Charlie Parsons. Hernan Solana came off the last turn on lap twenty-seven and the left rear suspension of his Lola collapsed. The car spun, bounced off a guardrail and

continued to spin several times before stopping. Hernan stepped out of the car, walked back to the pits and waved at his brother the next time he came around. Skip Scott began to have transmission problems on lap thirty and Moises challenged him at every corner. Moises took the lead on the next lap and the crowd roared their approval.

Fred Van Buren had a wheel come off his car at the last corner on lap thirty. He parked the car on the inside of the corner while his wheel wandered down the track. It was chased down by a corner worker. Revson moved into sixth place a few laps later. A bolt holding the rear subframe to the transmission of Lothar's car loosened itself, causing the subframe to drag on the track. Bud Morley, who was right behind Lothar, was showered with the resulting sparks. Lothar tried to keep Morley behind him, but decided to slow up, in hopes of reaching the finish. While Lothar and Morley were having it out, Revson passed both of them to take third place.

With ten laps to go, Solana's car started smoking and Scott harbored thoughts of winning. He had to settle for second place, thirteen seconds behind Solana. Peter Revson finished in third place with Posey fourth, Morley fifth and Lothar in sixth.

RIVERSIDE RACEWAY APRIL 27, 28 1968   program 1.00

1968 Riverside program cover. Scan courtesy Don Markle.

The first three rows coming around on the pace lap. Mark Donohue #6 is on the pole with Lothar Motschenbacher #11 beside. Peter Revson is on the second row, behind Donohue, with Skip Scott #26 on the left. Sam Posey #1 and Moises Solana #99 are on row three. Photo by Ron Miller.

Riverside

The big news at Riverside was the return of Jim Hall in a Chaparral 2G. There were also ten McLarens, nine Lolas, three Porsches and Sam Posey's Caldwell D7. Mark Donohue, Lothar Motschenbacher, Moises Solana, John Cannon, George Eaton, Leonard Janke, Ron Herrera, Doug Hooper, Jay Hills and Jim Paul were all in various McLarens. The Lolas were piloted by Charlie Parsons, Skip Scott, Peter Revson, Bud Morley, Swede Savage, Jerry Entin, Tony Settember, Jack Milliken and Bill Young. Don Wester, Scooter Patrick and Milt Minter handled the Porsches.

Shortly after qualifying started, Jim Hall and Mark Donohue started trading fastest laps. The current lap record was 1:19.4, set by Dan Gurney in his Eagle Indy car. Hall broke Gurney's record as he took the Chaparral around the course in 1:19.0. Mark Donohue settled for second place on the grid with a time of 1:19.4. Lothar was third (1:20.7) and Peter Revson turned in a 1:21.0 for fourth spot. Following them were Skip Scott (1:21.9), Sam Posey (1:21.9), Moises Solana

(1:22.2), Chuck Parsons (1:22.5), John Cannon (1:22.5) and Jerry Entin (1:22.6).

Unfortunately, the transmission of the Chaparral broke in the morning warm-up and Hall did not start the race. When the race started, Donohue took the lead with Lothar in hot pursuit. Following them were Peter Revson, Skip Scott and Sam Posey. Donohue stretched his lead by two seconds a lap on Lothar. In turn, Lothar was a second a lap faster than Revson. This order stayed the same until Revson retired with a lack of oil pressure on lap twenty-two.

After Revson retired, Posey tried to out-brake Scott as they approached turn nine, but didn't quite make it. Posey followed Scott through the corner and they had a drag race toward turn one, an uphill left-hand bend. Scott had the correct line and entered the turn barely ahead of Posey. Posey took to the outside and in a move that defied gravity, he passed Scott at the apex of the corner, doing over 100 mph. Scott's car lasted about ten more laps before he retired with an over-heated engine.

Back at the front, Donohue had a seventy-second lead over Lothar. In turn, Lothar was thirty seconds ahead of Posey. Charlie Parsons was fourth and catching up with Posey. Moises Solana and Swede Savage were battling for fifth place.

Parsons closed up on Posey as the race wound down and they dueled for third place. Donohue had an ignition resistor break halfway through the last lap. He coasted through turns seven and eight and down the short straight. Donohue got through turn nine and up to the finish by flipping switches. Lothar had closed the gap to forty-nine seconds in the final lap. Posey finished in third place, a lap behind. Parsons was fourth, one second behind Posey. Solana was fifth and Savage got sixth place, two laps behind Donohue.

After two races, Solana had the championship lead with eleven points. Donohue was second with nine points and Lothar was tied with Posey for third place, with seven points each. Skip Scott had six points for fifth place. Parsons was next with three points to Morley's two points and Savage's one point.

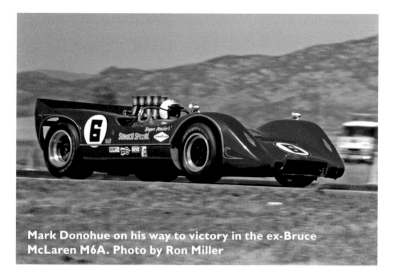

Mark Donohue on his way to victory in the ex-Bruce McLaren M6A. Photo by Ron Miller

Lothar Motschenbacher took second place in a McLaren M6B. This was the customer version of the McLaren M6A. Photo by Ron Miller.

Moises Solana followed up his win at Mexico City with a fifth place at Riverside. Photo by Ron Miller.

Jim Hall returned to the USRRC series at Riverside and won the pole position. Unfortunately the Chaparral 2G broke in the Sunday morning warm-up and did not start the race. Photo by Ron Miller.

1968 RIVERSIDE • USRRC
April 28, 1968, Riverside International Raceway, Riverside, California

Place	Driver	Car/Engine	Car #	Laps	Points	Prize	Qualifying Place	Qualifying Time
1	Mark Donohue	McLaren M6A-Chevrolet	6	60	9	$3,500	1	1:19.4
2	Lothar Motschenbacher	McLaren M6B-Ford	11	60	6	2,100	2	1:20.7
3	Sam Posey	Caldwell D7-Chevrolet	1	59	4	1,600	5	1:21.9
4	Charlie Parsons	Lola T70-Chevrolet	10	59	3	1,200	7	1:22.5
5	Moises Solana	McLaren M6B-Chevrolet	9	58	2	1,000	6	1:22.2
6	Swede Savage	Lola T70-Ford	36	58	1	900	11	1:23.8
7	Jerry Entin	Lola T70-Chevrolet	12	58	-	800	9	1:22.6
8	Don Wester	Porsche 910	60	55	-	700	17	1:29.3
9	Leonard Janke	McLaren M1C-Chevrolet	7	54	-	600	21	1:31.1
10	Tony Settember	Lola T70-Chevrolet	76	53	-	500	12	1:24.2
11	Scooter Patrick	Porsche 906	33	52	-	400	19	1:29.7
12	Ron Herrera	McLaren M1B-Chevrolet	38	44	-	300	16	1:27.8
13	John Cannon	McLaren M1B-Chevrolet	62	32	-	200	8	1:22.5
DNF	George Eaton	McLaren M1C-Ford	98	39	-	100	15	1:26.3
DNF	Skip Scott	Lola T70-Chevrolet	26	34	-	100	4	1:21.9
DNF	Bud Morley	Lola T70-Chevrolet	14	29	-	100	10	1:23.7
DNF	Doug Hooper	McLaren M1A-Chevrolet	91	28	-	100	23	1:32.7
DNF	Peter Revson	Lola T70-Ford	52	21	-	100	3	1:21.0
DNF	Jack Milliken	Lola T70-Chevrolet	77	13	-	100	18	1:29.6
DNF	Bill Young	Lola T70-Chevrolet	99	11	-	100	13	1:24.2
DNF	Jay Hills	McLaren M1B-Chevrolet	81	8	-	50	14	1:25.7
DNF	Milt Minter	Porsche 906	61	7	-	50	20	1:30.7
DNF	Jim Paul	McLaren M1B-Chevrolet	21	6	-	50	22	1:32.2
DNS	Jim Hall	Chaparral 2G-Chevrolet	66	0	-	-	1*	1:19.0

* did not start race

Fastest Qualifier:	Jim Hall	Chaparral 2G-Chevrolet	1:19.0	118.481 mph
Race Distance:	156.0 miles	60 laps of 2.6 mile course		
Race Time:	1hr 23min 1.3sec			
Winner's Speed:	112.742 mph			
Victory Margin:	49 seconds			
Fastest Race Lap:	Mark Donohue	McLaren M6A-Chevrolet	1:20.0	117.0 mph

Don Wester #60 leading Skip Scott. Wester is driving a topless Porsche 910 and was the top under two-liter finisher in eighth place. Scott ran in the top ten for thirty laps before retiring with a blown engine. Photo by Ron Miller.

The Carl Haas-owned and Skip Scott-driven Lola sitting outside the Riverside garage. Photo by Gil Munz.

1968 Laguna Seca USRRC race program cover. Scan courtesy Don Markle.

Jim Hall rips into the lead at the start. Right behind are Lothar Motschenbacher #11, Mark Donohue #6, Bud Morley #14, Skip Scott #26, John Cannon #62, Moises Solana #99 gold McLaren, Jerry Entin #12, and Scooter Patrick, in the topless Porsche 906. There is a big gap back to Charlie Parsons #10 McLaren, who stalled on the grid. Next to Parsons is Sam Posey and Stan Burnett. Photo by Ron Miller.

Laguna Seca

The entry for the Laguna Seca race was much the same as at Riverside. Absent were Peter Revson (waiting for a 427 engine to be installed in the Shelby Lola), George Eaton, Swede Savage, Doug Hooper and Don Wester. Wester chose not to race Otto Zipper's Porsche 910 after Zipper said he did not want Wester's mechanic working on his car. Joining the action for this race were Merle Brennan in a Super Genie-Chevrolet, Bill Leonheart in his ASR-Chevrolet and Stan Burnett from Seattle in his Burnett Mk 3-Chevrolet.

Qualifying was held on Friday and Saturday. Both Donohue and Hall did not run on Friday. They both received permission to run their cars during Saturday morning practice for the regional races. Their cars were warmed up and ready to go when qualifying began. Hall was quick from the outset and got down to 1:02.89. Lothar Motschenbacher turned in a time of 1:03.41 and Mark Donohue was in the 1:03's. When the qualifying times were posted, Donohue was credited with a 1:02.05. Hall and Lothar did not believe Donohue's time. When they questioned the officials, they were told the posted times were provisional. After the officials reviewed the watches that timed Donohue, he was credited with a 1:03.87, for third place on the grid. Fourth was Bud Morley with a 1:04.07, fifth was Chuck Parsons (1:04.85), while Skip Scott was sixth (1:05.40), John Cannon was seventh (1:06.10) and Moises Solana was eighth (1:06.96).

Hall grabbed the lead as the race started, with Donohue and Lothar right behind. At the end of the first lap, Hall ran wide and Donohue took the lead. Skip Scott was fourth, followed by Parsons, Morley, Cannon, Solana, Entin and Settember. During the next five laps, Donohue pulled out a six second lead over Hall. Lothar was within striking distance and hoping their engines would break. They started lapping backmarkers on the seventh lap and Hall gained back five seconds. Bill Leonheart was the first DNF with engine problems. John Cannon retired on lap seven with a broken driveshaft.

Hall's goggles steamed up on lap twenty-five and he ripped them off. Lothar took second place during the two laps it took Hall to get his spare goggles on and adjusted. Then Lothar started closing in on Donohue. The gearbox in Tony Settember's Lola broke on lap twenty-eight and he was out of the race. Skip Scott pulled into the pits a couple laps later to have his throttle linkage repaired. It took twenty-one laps for Scott's crew to repair the linkage and get him back in the race.

Lothar kept the pressure on Donohue, but his 377 Ford was no match for Donohue's 427 Chevy. There was never more than three seconds between them, but Lothar's engine did not have the low-end power that Donohue's had. Donohue and Lothar led Hall's Chaparral by ten seconds. Moises Solana was lapping Stan Burnett when they collided on lap thirty-four. Solana retired with steering problems and Burnett lasted seven more laps before he also retired. Lothar tried to pass Donohue on lap forty-eight and almost hit the haybales. He was able to avoid them and stay with Donohue. The Chaparral's handling deteriorated and Hall started dropping further back. On lap seventy Donohue and

Donohue leads Hall out of the last corner. Photo by Ron Miller.

Donohue exits the corner right next to the hay bales and his front wheel is turned to catch the drift. Photo by Ron Miller.

Jim Hall exits the same corner, a little further away from the bales and front wheel straight. Photo by Ron Miller.

Lothar, still racing nose to tail, lapped Hall.

On lap seventy-eight, Donohue lapped Jerry Entin and then put some distance between himself and Lothar. With a lighter engine, Lothar's McLaren was more nimble than Donohue's. Lothar clawed back the time finishing just half a second behind Donohue. Jim Hall claimed third place, a lap down. Chuck Parsons was fourth, two laps back. Fifth was Bud Morley and Jerry Entin got the last point for sixth place.

After three races, Donohue led the championship with eighteen points to Lothar's thirteen. Moises Solana still had eleven points, but this would be his last USRRC race. His engine was down on power, compared to the 427's and he was having trouble sorting his new McLaren. Sam Posey was fourth with seven points and tied for fifth were Charlie Parsons and Skip Scott with six points each. Peter Revson, Jim Hall and Bud Morley were tied for seventh with four points. Swede Savage and Jerry Entin each had one point.

Lothar Motschenbacher was within striking distance of Donohue for the whole race and finished just half a second behind in second place. Photo by Ron Miller.

Carl Haas' Simoniz Lolas in the paddock, driven by Skip Scott #26 and Charlie Parsons #10. Photo by Gil Munz.

Early in the race Bud Morley #14 leads John Cannon #62 and Moises Solana #99. Morley finished in fifth place while Cannon and Solana both retired. Photo by Ron Miller.

After two points finishes, Sam Posey finished in seventh place at Laguna Seca. Photo by Jim Hayes.

1968 LAGUNA SECA • USRRC

May 5, 1968, Laguna Seca Raceway, Monterey. California

Place	Driver	Car/Engine	Car #	Laps	Points	Prize	Qualifying Place	Qualifying Time
1	Mark Donohue	McLaren M6A-Chevrolet	6	80	9	$4,100	3	1:03.87
2	Lothar Motschenbacher	McLaren M6B-Ford	11	80	6	3,250	2	1:03.41
3	Jim Hall	Chaparral 2G-Chevrolet	66	79	4	2,700	1	1:02.80
4	Charlie Parsons	Lola T70-Chevrolet	10	78	3	1,700	5	1:04.85
5	Bud Morley	Lola T70-Chevrolet	14	77	2	1,500	4	1:04.07
6	Jerry Entin	Lola T70-Chevrolet	12	76	1	1,300	10	1:07.82
7	Sam Posey	Caldwell D7-Chevrolet	1	74	-	1,100	11	1:08.00
8	Scooter Patrick	Porsche 906	33	74	-	900	12	1:08.18
9	Bill Young	Lola T70-Chevrolet	9	73	-	750	16	1:09.90
10	Jay Hills	McLaren M1B-Chevrolet	81	72	-	600	13	1:08.20
11	Jack Milliken	Lola T70-Chevrolet	7	72	-	450	17	1:10.39
12	Milt Minter	Porsche 906	61	72	-	300	18	1:10.49
13	Leonard Janke	McLaren M1C-Chevrolet	77	70	-	200	22	1:16.01
14	Jim Paul	McLaren M1B-Chevrolet	21	68	-	100	19	1:12.21
15	Ron Herrera	McLaren M1B-Chevrolet	38	67	-	100	20	1:12.41
16	Skip Scott	Lola T70-Chevrolet	26	58	-	100	6	1:05.40
DNF	Merle Brennan	Genie Mk 8-Chevrolet	17	44	-	100	15	1:09.60
DNF	Stan Burnett	Burnett Mk 3-Chevrolet	64	41	-	50	14	1:08.40
DNF	Moises Solana	McLaren M6B-Chevrolet	99	34	-	50	8	1:06.96
DNF	Tony Settember	Lola T70-Chevrolet	76	26	-	50	9	1:07.72
DNF	John Cannon	McLaren M1B-Chevrolet	10	22	-	50	7	1:06.10
DNF	Bill Leonheart	ASR Special-Chevrolet	16	4	-	50	21	1:13.49

Fastest Qualifier:	Jim Hall	Chaparral 2G-Chevrolet	1:02.89	108.761 mph
Race Distance:	152.0 miles	80 laps of 1.9 mile course		
Race Time:	1hr 26min 17.99sec			
Winner's Speed:	105.68 mph			
Victory Margin:	0.77 second			
Fastest Race Lap:	Mark Donohue	McLaren M6A-Chevrolet	1:03.2	108.22 mph

Charlie Parsons #10 leads teammate, Skip Scott #26, out of the last turn. Photo by Jim Hayes

Lothar Motschenbacher #11 puts a lap on Bill Young #9. Photo by Jim Hayes.

1968

BRIDGE HAMPTON

AMERICA'S ROAD RACING CAPITAL

100 MILES FROM TIMES SQUARE

VANDERBILT CUP RACE

SOUVENIR PROGRAM: $1.00

MAY 17-19   UNITED STATES ROAD RACING CHAMPIONSHIP

1968 Bridgehampton USRRC race program cover. Scan courtesy Don Markle.

Charlie Parsons' car #10 in the pits. His engine did not have the oomph that Scott's had and Charlie took second place. Photo by Gil Munz.

The #26 Carl Haas Simoniz Lola of race-winner Skip Scott having the gasoline topped up. Scott took a fine win after Mark Donohue and Lothar Motschenbacher dropped out. Photo by Gil Munz.

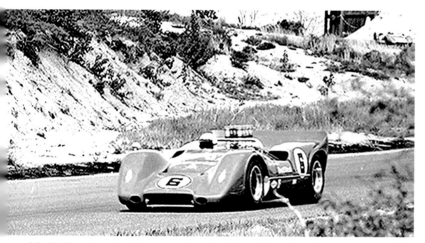

Mark Donohue led the race for the first thirty-five laps before suffering a broken halfshaft. Photo courtesy of the Collier Collection.

Early in the race, Lothar Motschenbacher held second place ahead of Scott and Parsons. A broken transmission put Lothar out of the race after eighteen laps. Photo courtesy of the Collier Collection.

Bridgehampton

Nineteen cars started the Bridgehampton race. Seven of them were front-running series regulars; Mark Donohue, Lothar Motschenbacher, Sam Posey, Charlie Parsons, Skip Scott, George Eaton and John Cannon. Jerry Crawford, Leonard Janke and Werner Frank joined the series again. First time East Coast entrants included John Cordts, Bob Nagel, George Ralph, Dick Jacobs, Brian O'Neill, Candido DaMota, Bill Howell, Horst Kwech and Bob Lande. Horst Kwech was running an Alfa Romeo T33 he had purchased. The Alfa was built as an under two-liter, long-distance sports prototype racer. It was light and nimble, but not very powerful.

Lothar was on pole position with a qualifying time of 1:30.6 and Mark Donohue was second on the grid with a 1:30.7. Charlie Parsons (1:32.9) and Skip Scott (1:33.3) occupied the second row. John Cannon (1:34.0) and Sam Posey (1:34.6) were on row three. Filling out the top ten were John Cordts (1:35.7), George Ralph (1:38.6), Bob Nagel (1:39.0) and Brian O'Neill (1:39.1). The last six qualifiers were seventeen to twenty-three seconds per lap slower than Lothar's pole time.

Mark Donohue grabbed the lead at the start. He had four seconds in hand over Lothar by the end of the first lap. Skip Scott, Charlie Parsons and Sam Posey were running behind Lothar. Donohue started to lap backmarkers at the end of the fifth lap. Sam Posey retired after nine laps. Sam Posey's Caldwell was not handling very well and he sent the corner workers at turn one running when he came over the hill with his car sliding back and forth. He retired after nine laps. Six cars dropped out with various mechanical maladies during the first ten laps. They included Horst Kwech, George Ralph, Candido DaMota, Jerry Crawford and Bob Lande.

Mark's lead was eighteen seconds over Lothar by the fifteenth lap. George Eaton retired with a bum engine after eighteen laps. Lothar's transmission broke on the next lap and he retired. With twenty laps run, Donohue had a forty-two second lead over Skip Scott. John Cannon and Brian O'Neill had both retired after thirty laps and Donohue now had a one-minute lead over Scott. Charlie Parsons and John Cordts

were running in third and fourth places.

After thirty-four laps, Donohue had a lead of seventy-five seconds over Scott. Two laps later, a halfshaft suddenly broke on Donohue's McLaren resulting in a very wild slide and retirement. Skip Scott inherited the lead and had ten seconds in hand over teammate, Charlie Parsons. Team owner, Carl Haas, hung out a pitboard telling his drivers to dead heat at the finish. Scott was obviously not paying attention and he took the win from Parsons and Cordts. Leonard Janke was fourth with Werner Frank fifth and Dick Jacobs sixth. With a high attrition rate, the last car running at the checker was Bill Howell in seventh place. Scott had the distinction of running out of gas on the backside of the course during his cooling down lap. Parsons stopped and gave him a ride back to the pits.

Donohue still clung to the championship lead with 18 points to Scott's 15. Lothar was third with 13 points and Charlie Parsons was fourth with 12 points. Fifth was Moises Solana (11 points) sixth was Sam Posey with 7 points and Jim Hall, Bud Morley and John Cordts were tied for seventh with 4 points each.

1968 BRIDGEHAMPTON • USRRC The Vanderbilt Cup Race

May 19, 1968, Bridgehampton, Long Island, New York

Place	Driver	Car/Engine	Car #	Laps	Points	Prize	Qualifying Place	Qualifying Time
1	Skip Scott	Lola T70-Chevrolet	26	60	9	$5,300	4	1:33.3
2	Charlie Parsons	Lola T70-Chevrolet	10	60	6	2,700	3	1:32.9
3	John Cordts	McLaren M1B-Chevrolet	57	59	4	2,000	7	1:35.7
4	Leonard Janke	McLaren M1C-Chevrolet	77	54	3	1,200	12	1:47.4
5	Werner Frank	Porsche 906	88	53	2	1,000	14	1:50.1
6	Dick Jacobs	Elva Mk 8-BMW	22	50	1	900	19	1:54.0
7	Bill Howell	McLaren-Chevrolet	7	48	-	800	13	1:49.7
DNF	Mark Donohue	McLaren M6A-Chevrolet	6	35	-	700	2	1:30.7
DNF	Bob Nagel	McKee Mk 7-Ford	24	35	-	600	9	1:39.0
DNF	John Cannon	McLaren M1B-Chevrolet	62	28	-	500	5	1:34.0
DNF	Brian O'Neill	Lola T70-Chevrolet	71	24	-	400	10	1:39.1
DNF	Lothar Motschenbacher	McLaren M6B-Ford	11	18	-	300	1	1:30.6
DNF	George Eaton	McLaren M1C-Ford	98	17	-	200	11	1:39.5
DNF	Sam Posey	Caldwell D7-Chevrolet	1	9	-	100	6	1:34.6
DNF	Horst Kwech	Alfa-Romeo T33	33	9	-	100	15	1:50.2
DNF	George Ralph	Lola T70-Chevrolet	3	8	-	100	8	1:38.6
DNF	Candido DaMota	McLaren M1B-Chevrolet	42	3	-	100	16	1:50.4
DNF	Jerry Crawford	Lotus 40-Ford	12	2	-	100	17	1:51.4
DNF	Bob Lande	Genie Mk 8-Ford	2	2	-	100	18	1:52.5

Fastest Qualifier:	Lothar Motschenbacher	McLaren M6B-Ford	1:30.6	113.242
Race Distance:	151.0 miles	60 laps of 2.85 mile course		
Race Time:	1hr 35min 29.78sec			
Winner's Speed:	107.868 mph			
Victory Margin:	3 seconds			
Fastest Race Lap:	Mark Donohue	McLaren M6A-Chevrolet	1:31.3	112.826 mph

Leonard Janke was fourth in the race. Here he has John Cannon on his tail. Photo courtesy of the Collier Collection.

Werner Frank #88 was the first under two-liter finisher, in fifth place. Photo courtesy of the Collier Collection.

Skip Scott takes the checkered flag ahead of teammate, Charlie Parsons. Photo by Gil Munz.

COMPETITION
VOL. I — NO. 1 — 0.75¢

JUNE 2 JUIN 1968

CHAMPIONNAT NORD - AMÉRICAIN
OFFICIAL PROGRAM(ME) OFFICIEL
NORTH AMERICAN CHAMPIONSHIP

NE MANQUEZ PAS NOTRE
PROCHAINE COURSE
"TRANS-AM"
JUILLET 21-1968

VISIT US FOR
THE "TRANS-
AM" RACE
JULY-21-68

7

USRRC

GROUPE

1968 St Jovite USRRC program cover. Scan courtesy Don Markle.

It was wet. Nat Adams spun his Chinook on the main straight, ended up off course and not able to get going again. Photo by Gil Munz.

St. Jovite

The series held its second international race at the St. Jovite circuit in Canada. This round had twenty-seven starters as opposed to Bridgehampton's nineteen. The usual series front-runners present were Donohue, Scott, Parsons, Motschenbacher, Posey, Morley, Cordts, Cannon, and Eaton. East Coast drivers participating included Bob Nagel, George Ralph, Brian O'Neill, Werner Frank, and Ron Courtney. Canadian and first time East Coast drivers filled the rest of the grid. They included Ludwig Heimrath, Max Beimler, Eppie Weitzes, Rich Galloway, Horst Kroll, Andre Samson, Jean-Pierre Ostiguy, Nick Adams, Anson Johnson, Dave Wolin, Phil Seitz, Andre Prefontaine, and Al Justason.

The weather was clear and sunny for Saturday qualifying. Mark Donohue got the pole position with a time of 1:35.0 and Lothar Motschenbacher (1:35.6) was second on the grid. The next four cars were over three seconds slower than Donohue's time, but within one second of each other. Skip Scott was third with a 1:38.1, Bud Morley (1:38.5) was fourth, Sam Posey (1:38.8) was fifth, and Charlie Parsons was sixth with a 1:38.9. Rounding out the top ten were John Cordts (1:39.2), John Cannon (1:40.6), Eppie Weitzes (1:42.5), and George Eaton (1:42.5).

The weather on race day was overcast. The heavens let loose half an hour before the start and rain poured down. Mark Donohue made the most of his pole position and took

the lead at the start. Lothar was in second place, trying to hold off John Cannon. Bud Morley was in fourth place, ahead of Charlie Parsons, Sam Posey, Eppie Weitzes, John Cordts, Ludwig Heimrath, and George Eaton. Skip Scott pitted after the first lap with misted goggles and dropped to twenty-first place.

Dave Wolin completed one lap before his Lotus 40 died from drowned electrics. Cannon passed Lothar to take second place and tried unsuccessfully to catch Donohue. Behind Lothar, Bud Morley was holding down fourth place, ahead of Charlie Parsons and Sam Posey. Next was a gap back to Wietzes, Cordts, Eaton and Heimrath.

On the eighth lap Posey got by Parsons for

1968 ST JOVITE • USRRC North American Championship Race

June 2, 1968, Le Circuit Mt Tremblant-St Jovite, St Jovite, Canada

Place	Driver	Car/Engine	Car #	Laps	Points	Prize	Qualifying Place	Qualifying Time
1	Mark Donohue	McLaren M6A-Chevrolet	6	60	9	$ 4,000	1	1:35.0
2	John Cannon	McLaren M1B-Chevrolet	62	60	6	2,500	8	1:40.6
3	Lothar Motschenbacher	McLaren M6B-Ford	11	59	4	2,000	2	1:35.6
4	Bud Morley	Lola T70-Chevrolet	14	58	3	1,600	4	1:38.5
5	John Cordts	McLaren M1B-Chevrolet	57	58	2	1,300	7	1:39.2
6	Charlie Parsons	Lola T70-Chevrolet	10	58	1	1,100	6	1:38.9
7	Eppie Weitzes	McLaren M1B-Chevrolet	15	58	-	950	9	1:42.5
8	Sam Posey	Caldwell D7-Chevrolet	1	57	-	800	5	1:38.8
9	George Eaton	McLaren M1C-Ford	98	57	-	650	10	1:42.5
10	Rich Galloway	Lola T70-Chevrolet	43	56	-	500	13	1:48.3
11	George Ralph	Lola T70-Chevrolet	3	56	-	400	17	1:51.3
12	Ludwig Heimrath	McLaren M1B-Chevrolet	39	56	-	300	11	1:42.6
13	Horst Kroll	Kelly-Porsche	37	54	-	250	16	1:49.6
14	Andre Samson	Cobra	170	54	-	200	23	1:58.1
15	Fred Werner	Porsche 906	88	52	-	150	19	1:53.4
16	Ron Courtney	McLaren M1B-Chevrolet	8	51	-	125	18	1:52.6
17	Jean Paul Ostiguy	Porsche GT	906	49	-	125	21	1:55.6
18	Skip Scott	Lola T70-Chevrolet	26	34	-	100	3	1:38.1
DNF	Nat Adams	Chinook-Chevrolet	36	22	-	100	15	1:48.6
DNF	Bob Nagel	McKee Mk 7-Ford	24	18	-	100	12	1:42.7
DNF	Brian O'Neill	Lola T70-Chevrolet	71	16	-	75	20	1:53.3
DNF	Anson Johnson	Lola T70-Chevrolet	17	2	-	75	22	1:57.0
DNF	David Wolin	Lotus 40-Chevrolet	41	-	-	75	27	2:08.4
DSQ	Craig Fisher	Chinook-Chevrolet	34	10	-	-	24	1:59.1
DSQ	Phil Seitz	Elva Mk 8-BMW	72	5	-	-	25	2:02.0
DSQ	Al Justason	Elva Mk 6-Climax	411	3	-	-	26	2:06.4
DSQ	Andre Prefontaine	Lotus 47	-	3	-	-	-	-

Fastest Qualifier: Mark Donohue   McLaren M6A-Chevrolet   1:35.0   106.11 mph
Race Distance: 162.0 miles   60 laps of 2.7 mile course
Race Time: 2 hr 5 min 17.6 sec
Winner's Speed: 80.44 mph
Victory Margin: 39.9 seconds
Fastest Race Lap: Mark Donohue   McLaren M6A-Chevrolet   1:58.5   85.07 mph

fourth place and Skip Scott had worked his way back up to fourteenth. Three laps later, Cordts and Eaton passed Weitzes for seventh and eighth places. Scott passed Samson for thirteenth. Four drivers were disqualified during the first ten laps for driving too slowly.

Morley spun on lap nineteen and fell to eighth place, behind Cordts, Eaton, and Weitzes. He spent the next ten laps dicing with this group, and then set out to catch up to Parsons and Posey again. Skip Scott spun out on lap twenty-one, pitted, and fell to last place.

Donohue led Cannon by twenty seconds after thirty laps. Lothar was third with Posey fourth, Morley fifth, and Parsons sixth. Weitzes, Cordts, and Eaton battled behind Parsons. It continued to rain and there was a small river running across the track right before turn one. Ludwig Heimrath hit the river and spun. He was able to keep racing, but had lost touch with Cordts, Eaton and Wietzes.

Donohue continued to lead Cannon by thirty seconds after forty-five laps and both had lapped Lothar. Morley, Posey, Parsons, Wietzes, Eaton, and Cordts were a lap behind Lothar. The race appeared to be running out with the order remaining the same. Posey dashed into the pits for more fuel with six laps left and fell back to eighth place. Then Cordts made his move and took fifth place from Parsons. Donohue splashed across the finish line to a wet win by forty seconds over Cannon.

Mark increased his lead in the championship with twenty-seven points, while Lothar moved up to second place with seventeen points. Skip Scott was third with fifteen points and Parsons had thirteen points for fourth place. Moises Solana was still in fifth place with the eleven points he earned in the first two races. Bud Morley was now tied with Sam Posey for sixth place with seven points. With their respective second and fifth place finishes, John Cannon and John Cordts were tied for eighth place with six points.

U.S. ROAD RACING CHAMPIONSHIP

FOR SPORTS CARS

PROGRAM 50 CENTS

PACIFIC RACEWAYS
JUNE 29 and 30, 1968

1968 Pacific Raceways USRRC program cover. Scan courtesy Don Markle.

Pacific Raceways

The entry for the race at Pacific Raceways was pretty strong. There were eight Lola's, six McLarens, two Burnett Specials, two Porsche 906's, a Genie, a Chinook and a Lotus 23. Peter Revson was back in Shelby's Lola, now with a 427 Ford stuffed in the rear end. The other Lolas were all Chevrolet powered and driven by Eric Anderson, Jerry Entin, Bud Morley, Charlie Parsons, Skip Scott, Tony Settember and Bill Young. Lothar Motschenbacher and George Eaton had Ford powered McLarens. John Cannon, John Cordts, Mark Donohue and Dick Hocking raced the McLarens with Chevy engines. Stan Burnett and Don Jensen were in the Burnett Specials while Lew Florence and Monte Shelton raced the Porsches. Max Beimler made the trip west to race his Chinook. Merle Brennan came up from the Bay Area with his Genie and Ken Legg raced his Lotus 23 with a BRM engine.

Mark Donohue lost the pole position to Peter Revson. In the second session, Mark worked his time down to 1:16.5 and thought that was fast enough. With fifteen minutes left in the session and being two seconds faster than the next fastest qualifier, the Penske crew rolled Donohue's McLaren into the paddock and onto the trailer. There were just a few minutes left in the session when it was announced that qualifying would be extended by twenty-five minutes. The Penske crew chose to sit-out the rest of qualifying and just watch. With ten minutes left in the extended session Peter Revson rolled onto the track and steadily whittled his time down. With a few minutes left, he put in two laps at 1:16.3 to take the pole. Skip Scott and teammate, Charlie Parsons were on the second row both with a time of 1:17.6. Bud Morley (1:20.0) and George Eaton (1:20.1) were on the third row. Filling out the top ten were Jerry Entin (1:20.3), John Cordts (1:20.5), John Cannon (1:20.6) and Tony Settember (1:20.9). Lothar Motschenbacher, usually a front-runner, was plagued with engine problems and had to start from seventeenth position with a time of 1:28.2.

From the start, Donohue took the lead with Revson right on his tail. Behind were Parsons, Scott, Morley, Eaton and Cannon. Revson's challenge lasted just one lap before the ring and pinion failed and he retired, giving second place to Parsons.

After twelve laps, Parsons' engine fouled a plug and started sputtering. Parsons let Skip Scott go by to try and chase down Donohue who was twenty seconds ahead. Cannon passed Eaton for fifth place, but then retired on lap sixteen with a broken gear selector.

On the first lap, going down the hill towards turn three, Peter Revson barely leads Mark Donohue. Photo by Tom Lebo, courtesy Bill Lebo.

Eventual winner, Skip Scott, leads teammate Charlie Parsons #10, Bud Morley #14, George Eaton # 98, Jerry Entin #12, John Cordts, #5, and John Cannon #62. Photo by Tom Lebo, courtesy Bill Lebo.

Mark Donohue makes it look so smooth and easy. Photo by Ron Miller.

Bill Young finished fourth in his Lola. Photo by Tom Lebo, courtesy Bill Lebo.

Local drivers Lew Florence #4 and Monte Shelton #57 traded places many times during the race, but finished in this order in fifth and sixth places. Photo by Ron Miller.

In the early laps John Cannon #62 led Bud Morley #14, and Jerry Entin #12. All three retired from the race. Photo by Ron Miller.

Lothar had moved up to seventh place then pitted for more oil on lap eighteen. It was all for naught as he retired after two more laps with a blown engine. George Eaton also retired on lap twenty with gearbox problems. Donohue now had a thirty-six second lead over Skip Scott. Charlie Parsons was still third, despite his engine problems. Jerry Entin was fourth, with Tony Settember fifth and John Cordts sixth.

Settember and Cordts had a nice battle for position, which ended when Settember retired after twenty-eight laps. The shocker of the race came when Mark Donohue rolled into the pits, after thirty-six laps, with a blown engine. Skip Scott was now leading the race by fifteen seconds over teammate, Charlie Parsons. Jerry Entin was now third with John Cordts fourth, Bill Young fifth and Lew Florence sixth. After fifty-five laps Entin retired with a blown engine. From this point, the race finished with no further position changes. Skip Scott won over Charlie Parsons, with John Cordts third, Bill Young fourth, Lew Florence fifth and Monte Shelton sixth. This was another race with a high attrition rate. The last two finishers were Ken Legg and Max Beimler in seventh and eighth places.

The championship point race was tightening up. Mark Donohue was still leading with 27 points and Skip Scott, with 24 points, moved ahead of Charlie Parsons (19 points) and Lothar Motschenbacher (17 points). Moises Solana was fifth with 11 points and John Cordts was sixth with 10 points.

1968 PACIFIC RACEWAYS • USRRC

June 30, 1968, Pacific Raceways, Kent, Washington

Place	Driver	Car/Engine	Car #	Laps	Points	Prize	Qualifying Place	Qualifying Time
1	Skip Scott	Lola T70-Chevrolet	26	70	9	$ 3,500	3	1:17.0
2	Charlie Parsons	Lola T70-Chevrolet	10	70	6	2,100	4	1:17.6
3	John Cordts	McLaren M1B-Chevrolet	5	69	4	1,600	8	1:20.5
4	Bill Young	Lola T70-Chevrolet	99	68	3	1,200	13	1:22.6
5	Lew Florence	Porsche 906	4	65	2	1,000	15	1:25.0
6	Monte Shelton	Porsche 906	57	65	1	900	16	1:27.3
7	Ken Legg	Lotus 23-BRM	73	62	-	800	20	1:32.0
8	Max Beimler	Chinook Mk 2-Chevrolet	34	57	-	700	21	1:32.2
DNF	Jerry Entin	Lola T70-Chevrolet	12	55	-	600	7	1:20.3
DNF	Mark Donohue	McLaren M6A-Chevrolet	6	35	-	500	2	1:16.5
DNF	Don Jensen	Burnett Mk 2-Chevrolet	0	31	-	400	12	1:22.0
DNF	Tony Settember	Lola T70-Chevrolet	76	28	-	300	10	1:20.9
DNF	George Eaton	McLaren M1C-Ford	98	20	-	200	6	1:20.1
DNF	Lothar Motschenbacher	McLaren M6B-Ford	11	20	-	100	17	1:28.2
DNF	John Cannon	McLaren M1C-Chevrolet	62	16	-	100	9	1:20.6
DNF	Eric Anderson	Lola T70-Chevrolet	69	12	-	100	19	1:29.6
DNF	Stan Burnett	Burnett Mk 3-Chevrolet	64	11	-	100	11	1:22.0
DNF	Bud Morley	Lola T70-Chevrolet	14	4	-	100	5	1:20.0
DNF	Richard Hocking	McLaren-Chevrolet	15	4	-	100	18	1:28.9
DNF	Merle Brennan	Genie Mk 10-Chevrolet	17	3	-	100	14	1:23.6
DNF	Peter Revson	Lola T70-Ford	52	1	-	50	1	1:16.3

Fastest Qualifier:	Peter Revson	Lola T70-Ford		1:16.3	106.159 mph
Race Distance:	155.5 miles	70 laps of 2.25 mile course			
Race Time:	1hr 36min 41.6sec				
Winner's Speed:	97.83 mph				
Victory Margin:	6.5 seconds				
Fastest Race Lap:	Mark Donohue	McLaren M6A-Chevrolet		1:18.3	103.45 mph

Stan Burnett in his Burnett Mk 3. Photo by Ron Miller.

6 HOUR WORLD
MANUFACTURERS' CHAMPIONSHIP
AND THE USRRC

21st Annual Watkins Glen
SPORTS CAR ROAD RACE

July 12-13-14, 1968 $1.00

1968 Watkins Glen USRRC program cover. Scan courtesy Don Markle.

Sam Posey qualified second fastest and held second place for the first twenty laps. The Caldwell was still not sorted. Photo by William Green.

Nat Adams in the Canadian Chinook-Chevrolet dropped out, early in the race. Photo by Gerry Melton.

Skip Scott qualified the Carl Haas Lola for sixth place on the grid. Scott ran as high as third, before dropping out. Photo by Gerry Melton.

George Ralph qualified his Lola in eleventh place and ran in mid-pack before retiring at half-distance. Photo by Gerry Melton.

Watkins Glen

When the teams went back east for the race at Watkins Glen, the entry was similar to the Bridgehampton and St Jovite races. Present were the Penske team, with Mark Donohue driving, and the Carl Haas Simoniz team of Skip Scott and Charlie Parsons. Lothar Motschenbacher, John Cannon, John Cordts and George Eaton were also there. Rejoining the series were Sam Posey, Werner Frank, Max Beimler, Ludwig Heimrath, Ron Courtney, Bob Nagel and George Ralph. This was the second USRRC race of the year for Bill Howell, Candido DaMota, Rich Galloway, Horst Kroll and Jean-Paul Ostiguy. Art Kijek, Nat Adams, George Fejer and Jim Place were having their first USRRC race of the season.

Qualifying lacked drama as Mark Donohue set his pole-winning time (1:06.85) in the first thirty minutes of the first session.

Sam Posey, thinking the past handling problems of the Caldwell were behind him, set the second fastest time of 1:07.71. Lothar Motschenbacher (1:07.73) and John Cannon (1:08.06) shared the second row of the grid. Charlie Parsons (1:08.5) and Skip Scott (1:09.16) were on the third row. George Eaton (1:09.31), John Cordts (1:09.6), Ludwig Heimrath (1:12.2) and Bob Nagel (1:13.0) filled out the top ten.

Donohue wasted no time pulling out two seconds a lap on Sam Posey when the starter dropped the flag. John Cannon was third and right on Posey's tail. Lothar, Charlie Parsons and Skip Scott were all within striking distance. Donohue had a ten-second lead after five laps and the first six were starting to lap the backmarkers. John Cannon was taking the fight to Posey for second place, until the tenth lap, when his oil pan gasket started leaking. As he lost

oil pressure, Cannon shut the engine down and coasted into the pits for a forty-minute repair job. Lothar inherited third place but retired three laps later, with an overheating engine.

Donohue now had a thirty-second lead over Posey, with Charlie Parsons third, Skip Scott fourth, George Eaton fifth and John Cordts sixth. Posey retired after twenty-one laps, with a myriad of problems and Scott retired seven laps later. The race ran out with Donohue taking the win, by over a lap ahead of Charlie Parsons. George Eaton was third, with John Cordts fourth, Werner Frank fifth and Jean-Paul Ostiguy sixth.

In the point standings, Mark Donohue led with 36 points and Charlie Parsons took over second place with 25 points. Skip Scott's 24 points put him in third place. Lothar was fourth with 17 points and John Cordts was fifth with 13 points.

1968 WATKINS GLEN • USRRC Watkins Glen Sports Car Road Race
July 13, 1968, Watkins Glen Grand Prix Course, Watkins Glen, New York

Place	Driver	Car/Engine	Car #	Laps	Points	Prize	Qualifying Place	Qualifying Time
1	Mark Donohue	McLaren M6A-Chevrolet	6	87	9	$ 4,300	1	1:06.85
2	Charlie Parsons	Lola T70-Chevrolet	10	86	6	2,500	5	1:08.50
3	George Eaton	McLaren M1C-Ford	98	83	4	2,000	7	1:09.31
4	John Cordts	McLaren M1B-Chevrolet	57	81	3	1,500	8	1:09.60
5	Werner Frank	Porsche 906	88	74	2	1,200	16	1:19.30
6	Jean-Paul Ostiguy	McLaren M1C-Chevrolet	96	73	1	1,000	17	1:20.90
7	Ludwig Heimrath	McLaren M1B-Chevrolet	39	70	-	900	9	1:12.20
8	Art Kijek	Ford Special	68	69	-	800	21	1:28.00
9	Horst Kroll	Kelly-Porsche	37	65	-	700	15	1:18.90
10	Dick Jacobs	Elva Mk 8-BMW	22	58	-	600	18	1:21.10
11	John Cannon	McLaren M1B-Chevrolet	62	52	-	500	4	1:08.06
DNF	George Ralph	Lola T70-Chevrolet	3	43	-	400	11	1:31.10
DNF	Bob Nagel	McKee Mk 7-Ford	24	36	-	300	10	1:13.00
DNF	Rich Galloway	Lola T70-Chevrolet	43	33	-	200	13	1:14.10
DNF	Skip Scott	Lola T70-Chevrolet	26	28	-	100	6	1:09.1
DNF	Sam Posey	Caldwell D7-Chevrolet	1	21	-	100	2	1:07.71
DNF	Nat Adams	Chinook-Chevrolet	36	17	-	100	19	1:21.80
DNF	Lothar Motschenbacher	McLaren M6B-Ford	11	13	-	100	3	1:07.73
DNF	Max Beimler	Chinook Mk 2-Chevrolet	34	13	-	100	20	1:25.10
DNF	Candido DaMota	McLarenM1B-Chevrolet	42	8	-	100	14	1:14.80
DNF	Ron Courtney	McLaren M1B-Chevrolet	8	7	-	100	12	1:13.80
DNF	George Fejer	Chinook-Chevrolet	15	2	-	100	23	1:31.90
DNF	Jim Place	Lotus 23-Porsche	18	2	-	100	22	1:30.20
DNS	Skipp Walther	Lola T70-Chevrolet	23	-	-	-	-	1:39.3

Fastest Qualifier:	Mark Donohue	McLaren M6A-Chevrolet	1:06.85	123.86 mph
Race Distance:	200.1 miles	87 laps of 2.3 mile course		
Race Time:	1hr 41min 46.33sec			
Winner's Speed:	117.969 mph			
Victory Margin:	1 lap, 72 seconds			
Fastest Race Lap:	Mark Donohue	McLaren M6A-Chevrolet	1:07.6	122.48 mph

Lothar Motschenbacher is on the grid and ready to go. Lothar ran in the top three until his engine expired after thirteen laps. Photo by Gerry Melton.

Mark Donohue ran away with the race. He qualified on the pole by .86 of a second and ran two seconds a lap faster than everyone else. Mark won by a lap, or 2.3 miles. Photo by Gerry Melton.

This is the view most drivers got of Donohue. Although he beat Charlie Parsons by a lap, he was four laps ahead of third place finisher, George Eaton. Photo by Gerry Melton.

BADGER 200
ROAD AMERICA
500
JULY 27-28
75¢

ELKHART LAKE, WISCONSIN

1968 Road America 500 program cover. Scan courtesy of Don Markle.

Road America 500

There were thirty-four starters for the Road America 500. The Penske team drafted Jerry Hansen to help Mark Donohue with the driving chores. Sam Posey was slated to share one of Carl Haas' Lolas with Charlie Parsons while Parsons shared the other Lola with Skip Scott. John Cannon teamed up with George Eaton. Charlie Hayes showed up to drive the brand new wedge-shaped McKee Mk 10, with a 427 Oldsmobile engine intending to share it with Charlie Gibson. Other notable pairings were Jerry Entin and Fred Pipin, Ludwig Heimrath and Rudy Bartling, plus Bob Nagel and Ed Lowther.

In qualifying, Mark Donohue got the pole position for the race with a time of 2:15.9. Charlie Parsons and Skip Scott were second and third on the grid, both at 2:19.9. Charlie Hayes had the McKee on the third row with Posey, both with a time of 2:21.5. The fourth row had George Eaton/John Cannon (2:24.6) and George Ralph/Bruce Jennings (2:27.1). The slowest qualifier's lap time was 3:05.1 and the Brian O'Neil/Geoffrey Stevenson Lola was allowed to start last on the grid with no qualifying time.

Charlie Hayes' McKee blew its oil filter off and dumped a load of oil on the track while on the grid waiting for the start. The start was delayed for fifteen minutes to get the oil cleaned up. Hayes' mechanic was able to remount the filter so Charlie could start the race. When the race started, Mark Donohue sped away into the lead with Hayes right on his tail. The rest of the field was spread out behind them. Hayes retired after ten laps and Skip Scott took over second place with teammate, Charlie Parsons, in third place. Scott's engine blew-up on the next lap and he retired the first of Haas' Lolas leaving Sam Posey out of a ride.

The McLaren of Ralph Salyer/Leonard Janke retired on lap eighteen with a blown head gasket. Jerry Entin's Lola blew its engine after twenty-seven laps and the George Ralph/Bruce Jennings Lola was finished after thirty laps. By lap forty-four, Donohue had built up a one-lap lead when he turned his car over to Jerry Hansen. Parsons persevered in second place. The Lola of Brian O'Neil and Geoffrey Stevenson started the race in last place and steadily worked their way through the field to run in fifth place.

The surprise of the race was the retirement of the lead car on lap fifty-seven. Hansen was driving the Penske McLaren along the backstretch when something let loose in the engine and he coasted to a stop. Skip Scott now in the second Haas Lola took the lead when Hansen retired. The McKee of Bob Nagel and Ed Lowther was now in second place, about a lap behind. The McLaren of Heimrath and Bartling was in third place and the O'Neil/Stevenson Lola was fourth.

With a big lead in hand, Skip Scott heeded Carl Haas' pleas to slow the pace down. Even with a slower pace Scott kept increasing his lead over the Nagel/Lowther McKee. Scott brought the Lola into the pits for fuel, oil and to hand it over to Charlie Parsons on lap ninety-three. Parsons brought the Lola back into the pits for more oil nine laps later. When Parsons left the pits, the car was visibly dropping gas onto the track. Concern was mounting that the car might not have enough fuel to finish the race. Parsons came in for a few gallons of fuel with a six lap lead and seven laps left to run. Then Parsons went back out, finished the race and took the win. Bob Nagel and Ed Lowther brought their McKee home in second place. Albeit nine laps behind the winner, Brian O'Neil and Geoffrey Stevenson took their car from last on the grid, to third place. Ludwig Heimrath and Rudy Bartling were fourth. F.P. Rafferty and Larry Brock brought their McLaren home in fifth place, eleven laps back. The final point winners were Gary Wilson and Vic Campbell.

This left Mark Donohue with the same thirty-six points he brought to the race and a two-point lead in the championship over Charlie Parsons. Skip Scott had 33 points for third place. Lothar was still in fourth place with 17 points and John Cordts had 13 points for fifth place. Now it was all down to the final race.

The front row getting ready for the start. Mark Donohue is on the left and Skip Scott is on the right. Photo by Gil Munz.

Bob Nagel and Ed Lowther shared Nagel's McKee and brought it home is third place. Photo by Tom Schultz.

Mark Donohue shared the Penske McLaren with Jerry Hansen. They led for the first half of the race, before retiring with a blown engine. Photo by Tom Schultz.

The Kelly Special, driven by Wayne Kelly and Horst Kroll, was the last car to finish. Photo by Tom Schultz.

1968 ROAD AMERICA • USRRC Road America 500
July 28, 1968, Road America, Elkhart Lake, Wisconsin

Place	Driver	Car/Engine	Car #	Laps	Points	Prize	Qualifying Place	Qualifying Time
1	Skip Scott/Charlie Parsons	Lola T70-Chevrolet	26	1259	9	$4,000	4	2:21.5
2	Bob Nagel/Ed Lowther	McKee Mk 7-Chevrolet	24	1196	6	2,800	9	2:27.8
3	Brian O'Neill/Jeff Stevens	Lola T70-Chevrolet	15	1164	4	2,200	34	no time
4	Lugwig Heimrath/Randy Bartling	McLaren M1B-Chevrolet	39	1163	3	2,700	5	2:22.7
5	F.P. Rafferty/Larry Bock	McLaren M1B-Chevrolet	33	1142	2	1,300	18	2:38.3
6	Gary Wilson/Vic Campbell	McLaren M1B-Chevrolet	19	1111	1	1,150	13	2:32.6
7	Cliff Phillips/Al Cervenka	Porsche 906	12	110	-	1,050	26	2:47.9
8	George Dickinson/Joe Jann	Elva Mk 7S-Porsche	30	108	-	950	25	2:46.1
9	Bud Morley/Bob Betts	Lola T70-Chevrolet	14	106	-	850	14	2:33.2
10	Art Kijek/Mike Cronin	KT Ford Special	68	104	-	750	24	2:44.1
11	Jean Paul Ostiguy /Jacques Couture	McLaren M1C-Chevrolet	96	102	-	650	11	2:31.0
12	Dick Jacobs/Dave Morrell	Elva Mk 8-BMW	22	99	-	550	20	2:39.5
13	George Eaton/John Cannon	McLaren M1C-Ford	98	96	-	450	7	2:24.6
14	Rich Dagiel/Guy Wooley	Lotus 30-Ford	49	93	-	350	29	2:55.7
15	James Place/Bill Blackmore	Lotus 23-Porsche	13	92	-	250	32	3:00.8
16	Max Beimler/David Wolin	Chinook Mk 2-Chevrolet	34	82	-	150	33	3:05.1
17	Bill Tuttle/Gloria Tuttle	Elva Mk 7S-Porsche	91	77	-	150	31	2:58.8
18	George Drolsom /Mak Kronn	Lola T70-Chevrolet	76	77	-	150	28	2:49.8
19	Horst Kroll/Wayne Kelly	Kelly-Porsche	37	76	-	450	16	2:36.8
DNF	Mike Robbins/Jack Cooper	Porsche 904	17	68	-	150	27	2:49.3
DNF	Mark Donohue/Jerry Hansen	McLaren M6A-Chevrolet	6	56	-	900	1	2:15.9
DNF	Phil Seitz/John Cordts	Elva Mk 8-BMW	72	40	-	100	22	2:41.3
DNF	Rich Galloway/Hank Candler	Lola T70-Chevrolet	43	32	-	100	12	2:31.9
DNF	George RalphBruce Jennings	Lola T70-Chevrolet	31	30	-	100	8	2:27.1
DNF	Fred Pipin/Jerry Entin	Lola T70-Chevrolet	61	27	-	100	6	2:24.4
DNF	Frank Opalka/Robert Lyon	Wolverine-Chevrolet	9	24	-	100	15	2:35.0
DNF	Leonard JankeRalph Salyer	McLaren M1C-Chevrolet	77	17	-	100	10	2:30.4
DNF	Charlie Parsons/Skip Scott	Lola T70-Chevrolet	10	11	-	100	2	2:19.9
DNF	Charlie Hayes/Charles Gibson	McKee Mk 7-Oldsmobile	25	10	-	100	3	2:21.5
DNF	Werner Frank/Ralph Treischmann	Porsche 906	88	10	-	100	17	2:37.9
DNF	Anson Johnson/Geoffrey Stevens	Lola T70-Chevrolet	28	6	-	75	21	2:41.3
DNF	Paul Canary/Tom Tufts	Cooper T61M-Chevrolet	14	3	-	75	30	2:57.9
DNF	Chuck Frederick/Keith Hardy	Lotus 19-Ford	3	2	-	75	23	2:43.1
DNF	Lee Hall/Mike Hall	Porsche 906	69	1	-	-	19	2:38.8

Fastest Qualifier:	Mark Donohue	McLaren M6A-Chevrolet	2:15.9	105.882 mph
Race Distance:	500 miles	125 laps of 4.0 mile course		
Race Time:	5hrs 16min 41.4sec			
Winner's Speed:	94.730 mph			
Victory Margin:	6 laps, .4 second			
Fastest Race Lap:	Mark Donohue	McLaren M6A-Chevrolet	2:18.1	104.272 mph

George Fejer in the Chinook Mk 2 drove a steady race from last on the grid to sixteenth at the finish. Photo by Tom Schultz.

1968 Mid-Ohio USRRC race program cover. Scan courtesy Don Markle.

LEFT–Mark Donohue in the Penske Sunoco Special on his way to winning the final USRRC race and the 1968 championship. Photo by Dave Arnold.

BELOW–Lothar Motschenbacher took second place at Mid Ohio, ensuring fourth place in the championship. Photo by Jim Hayes.

Mid-Ohio

Coming into the last race of the season, Mark Donohue had a two-point lead over Charlie Parsons and a three-point lead over Skip Scott. Mark just needed to finish ahead of them to win the championship. For Charlie Parsons to win the title, he needed to win, or finish fourth or higher, with Donohue out of the points and Skip Scott, fifth or lower. Skip Scott's task to win the championship was a little more difficult. He needed to win, or finish third or higher, with Donohue out of the points and Parsons fifth or lower.

Lothar Motschenbacher got the pole position with a time of 1:30.8. Mark Donohue was second on the grid at 1:31.2. Charlie Hayes (1:33.0) and Charlie Parsons (1:33.6) shared the second row. Behind were Fred Pipin (1:34.4) and Sam Posey (1:34.6). Skip Scott (1:35.0) and John Cordts (1:35.4) were on the fourth row. George Eaton (1:36.0) and Ludwig Heimrath (1:36.4) filled out the top ten.

When the flag dropped, Donohue beat Lothar into turn one and started putting distance between them. Charlie Hayes was third, followed by Charlie Parsons, Sam Posey and Skip Scott. Scott passed Posey on the third lap to take fifth place. Parsons took third place from Charlie Hayes on the next lap. Unfortunately, Parsons pitted for oil after seventeen laps. Skip Scott passed Posey for fifth place and on lap eighteen he took fourth place from Charlie Hayes. When Parsons retired after twenty-four laps, Scott inherited third place.

Donohue led Lothar by thirty seconds. Skip Scott was third, Charlie Hayes fourth, Sam Posey fifth and John Cordts sixth. Charlie Hayes' McKee retired with a wheel bearing failure after twenty-nine laps. This moved Posey up to fourth place, Cordts to fifth and Ludwig Heimrath to sixth place as the race ended. Donohue beat Lothar by one lap and four seconds. Skip Scott was third, three laps behind.

Mark Donohue became the only driver to win the series more than once. He finished with 45 points. Skip Scott was second with 37 points and Charlie Parsons was third with 34 points. Lothar Motschenbacher had 23 points for fourth place while John Cordts was fifth with 15 points. Moises Solana had 11 points, from the first two races, which was good enough for sixth place in the championship. Sam Posey had 10 points and Bud Morley's 7 points gave him eighth place. John Cannon, Bob Nagel and Ed Lowther tied for ninth with 6 points. In all, thirty-one drivers scored at least 1 point in this year's championship.

Sam Posey qualified sixth, in his Caldwell D7, and finished in fourth place. Photo by Jim Hayes.

Charlie Hayes in the McKee Mk 7 (#25) ahead of Sam Posey's Caldwell. Photo by Jim Hayes.

The pace car has entered pit road and the cars are coming up to take the green flag. Lothar #11 is on the pole with Donohue #6 beside him on the front row. Charlie Hayes #25 and Charlie Parsons #10 are on the second row. Photo by Jim Hayes.

Mark Donohue leading Nat Adams' Chinook. Photo by Jim Hayes.

During Sunday morning practice Skip Scott had a brake line burst. Here the team tunesmith plays the repair song while crew members inspect shoes and the scene. Photo by Jim Hayes.

1968 MID-OHIO • USRRC

August 18, 1968, Mid-Ohio Sports Car Course, Lexington, Ohio

Place	Driver	Car/Engine	Car #	Laps	Points	Prize	Qualifying Place	Qualifying Time
1	Mark Donohue	McLaren M6A-Chevrolet	6	75	9	$ 8,000	2	1:31.2
2	Lothar Motschenbacher	McLaren M6B-Ford	11	74	6	4,500	1	1:30.8
3	Skip Scott	Lola T70-Chevrolet	26	72	4	3,000	7	1:35.0
4	Sam Posey	Caldwell D7-Chevrolet	1	71	3	2,000	6	1:34.6
5	John Cordts	McLaren M1B-Chevrolet	57	70	2	1,500	8	1:35.4
6	Ludwig Heimrath	McLaren M1B-Chevrolet	39	69	1	1,000	10	1:36.4
7	Fred Pipin	Lola T70-Chevrolet	61	68	-	700	5	1:34.4
8	Rich Galloway	Lola T70-Chevrolet	43	68	-	400	15	1:42.0
9	Leonard Janke	McLaren M1C-Chevrolet	77	68	-	250	14	1:40.8
10	Mike Hall	Porsche 906	69	67	-	150	18	1:45.2
11	Dick Brown	McLaren-Chevrolet	28	66	-	100	11	1:38.2
12	Horst Kroll	Kelly-Porsche	37	65	-	100	19	1:45.2
13	Dick Jacobs	Elva Mk 8-BMW	22	63	-	100	20	1:46.
14	Art Kijek	Ford Special	67	59	-	100	27	1:50.
15	F.P. Rafferty	McLarenM1B-Chevrolet	30	55	-	100	24	1:48.4
16	Candido DaMota	McLarenM1B-Chevrolet	42	55	-	100	17	1:44.0
17	Ron Courtney	McLaren M1B-Chevrolet	8	53	-	100	13	1:30.4
18	Pete Ledwith	McLaren-Chevrolet	32	51	-	100	26	1:50.0
19	George Drolsom	Lola T70-Chevrolet	76	50	-	100	22	1:48.0
DNF	Phil Seitz	Elva Mk 8-BMW	12	47	-	100	30	1:52.6
DNF	Nat Adams	Chinook-Chevrolet	33	47	-	50	28	1:50.2
DNF	Pete Dawson	PMD-Chrysler Special	44	33	-	50	25	1:49.6
DNF	Jerry Crawford	McLarenM1B-Chevrolet	47	32	-	50	16	1:42.8
DNF	Tom Swindell	McLaren-Chevrolet	3	29	-	50	21	1:47.6
DNF	Charlie Hayes	McKee Mk 7-Oldsmobile	25	29	-	50	3	1:33.0
DNF	Bob Nagel	McKee Mk 7-Ford	24	28	-	50	12	1:39.6
DNF	Charlie Parsons	Lola T70-Chevrolet	10	24	-	50	4	1:33.6
DNF	Jim Place	Lotus 23-Porsche	23	22	-	50	23	1:48.0
DNF	Merv Rosen	Porsche 906	17	21	-	50	29	1:51.0
DNF	George Eaton	McLaren M1C-Ford	98	15	-	50	9	1:36.0

Fastest Qualifier:	Lothar Motschenbacher	McLaren M6B-Ford	1:30.8	95.15 mph
Race Distance:	180 miles	75 laps of 2.4 mile course		
Race Time:	1hr 58min 59.2 sec			
Winner's Speed:	90.77 mph			
Victory Margin:	1 lap, 72 seconds			
Fastest Race Lap:	Mark Donohue	McLaren M6B-Chevrolet	1:32.2	93.71mph

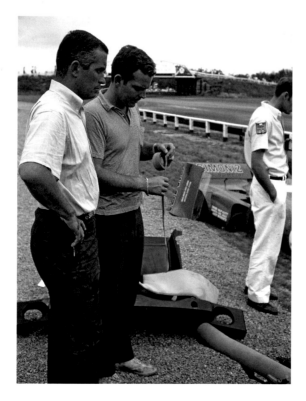

Roger Penske commiserates with Skip Scott. Photo by Jim Hayes.

1968 USRRC Drivers Championship Points

MC Mexico City, RIV Riverside, LS Laguna Seca, BH Bridgehampton, MT Mont Tremblant, PR Pacific Raceways, WG Watkins Glen, RA Road America, MO Mid-Ohio

Place	Driver	MC	RIV	LS	BH	MT	PR	WG	RA	MO	Total Points
1	Mark Donohue	-	9	9	-	9	-	9	-	9	45
2	Skip Scott	6	-	-	9	-	9	-	9	4	37
3	Charlie Parsons	-	3	3	6	1	6	6	9	-	34
4	Lothar Motschenbacher	1	6	6	-	4	-	-	-	6	23
5	John Cordts	-	-	-	4	2	4	3	-	2	15
6	Moises Solana	9	2	-	-	-	-	-	-	-	11
7	Sam Posey	3	4	-	-	-	-	-	-	3	10
8	Bud Morley	2	-	2	-	3	-	-	-	-	7
9	John Cannon	-	-	-	-	6	-	-	-	-	6
10	Bob Nagel	-	-	-	-	-	-	-	6	-	6
11	Ed Lowther	-	-	-	-	-	-	-	6	-	6
12	Peter Revson	4	-	-	-	-	-	-	-	-	4
13	Jim Hall	-	-	4	-	-	-	-	-	-	4
14	Werner Frank	-	-	-	2	-	-	2	-	-	4
15	Brian O'Neil	-	-	-	-	-	-	-	4	-	4
16	Jeff Stevens	-	-	-	-	-	-	-	4	-	4
17	Ludwig Heimrath	-	-	-	-	-	-	-	3	1	4
18	George Eaton	-	-	-	-	-	-	4	-	-	4
19	Leonard Janke	-	-	-	3	-	-	-	-	-	3
19	Randy Bartling	-	-	-	-	-	-	-	3	-	3
21	Bill Young	-	-	-	-	-	3	-	-	-	3
22	F.P. Rafferty	-	-	-	-	-	-	-	2	-	2
23	Larry Bock	-	-	-	-	-	-	-	2	-	2
24	Lew Florence	-	-	-	-	-	2	-	-	-	2
25	Swede Savage	-	1	-	-	-	-	-	-	-	1
26	Jerry Entin	-	-	1	-	-	-	-	-	-	1
27	Dick Jacobs	-	-	-	1	-	-	-	-	-	1
28	Gary Wilson	-	-	-	-	-	-	-	1	-	1
29	Vic Campbell	-	-	-	-	-	-	-	1	-	1
30	Jean-Paul Ostiguy	-	-	-	-	-	-	1	-	-	1
31	Monte Shelton	-	-	-	-	-	1	-	-	-	1

1968 Season Summary

Nineteen Sixty Eight was a lot more exciting and suspenseful than 1967. Although Mark Donohue led the championship from the third race and won the title with five wins, it was close. Four drivers won races during the season and there were three drivers who had a shot at the title going into the last race.

The season started in Mexico City at the Magdalena circuit with local driver, Moises Solana, taking the victory from Skip Scott and Peter Revson. The next race at Riverside saw the return of Jim Hall and his Chaparral. Hall set the fastest qualifying time, but had to scratch from the race with a broken transmission. So Mark Donohue took his first win of the season. At Laguna Seca, Jim Hall won the pole again, and this time was able to start the race. In his last USRRC appearance, Hall brought the ill-handling Chaparral home in third place. Donohue scored his second victory at Laguna Seca and followed it with wins at St Jovite, Watkins Glen and Mid-Ohio. Skip Scott won the high attrition races at Bridgehampton and Pacific Raceways. Plus he shared the win at Road America with his teammate, Charlie Parsons.

The Laguna Seca race provided the closest finish, with Lothar trailing Donohue by three-quarters of a second. Skip Scott's two victories were by three seconds and six and a half seconds. It looked close. Their shared win at Road America was the greatest victory margin of the year at six laps, or twenty-four miles.

The 1968 USRRC season set records for attendance and prize money paid out. Paid admissions grew from 171,725 in 1967 to 210,000 in 1968. Prize money went from $109,750 to $186,000. Contingency money provided by oil, tire and accessory suppliers topped $45,000. Plus there was a $15,000 championship point funds for the top ten finishers.

There were a total of 219 individual start-ers for the nine races. Skip Scott and Charlie Parsons were the only drivers to compete in all nine races. Mark Donohue, Lothar Motschenbacher and George Eaton made eight races. Sam Posey and John Cannon started seven races while Bud Morley and John Cordts took in six races. Four other drivers started five races and six drivers started four races. Twelve drivers started three races and fifteen drivers started in two races. That left 173 drivers starting just a single race. Of the 219 starters only 39 were under two-liters.

By the end of the series, it was known that this would be the last season for the USRRC series. The SCCA wanted to expand the Can-Am series and the only way to do that was to start earlier in the summer. Their professional formula car series was showing tremendous potential. Giving it the promotional attention it needed just didn't leave room for the USRRC. It died a quiet, sudden death.

USRRC Epilogue

Over the years there has been a lot of conjecture about why the SCCA gave up on the USRRC. There has been mention of dwindling spectator attendance, less race entries, more sponsorship and contingency money for amateur racers, the start of the SCCA Runoffs, the demise of the Manufacturers Championship and there being less opportunity for under two-liter cars. The answer was more simple than that. It became a victim of the SCCA's success with their multiple pro-racing series.

The USRRC faded away because the SCCA wanted to promote the Formula SCCA/Grand Prix Championship as the series that determined their "National Driving Champion" and they wanted to add more races for the Can-Am series.

1968 was the second year of the SCCA's Grand Prix Championship. It was also the first year that five-liter stock-block engines were allowed. The races were good and three of them were won by less than two seconds. Race fans were excited to see and hear formula cars with big V8 engines. The paid attendance was good and growing. The SCCA thought they had another hot property that would keep them at the forefront of sports

car racing in America and they planned a big promotional campaign for 1969.

Although the USRRC was an increasingly popular series with the race fans, the Can-Am races drew almost twice the number of paying spectators and there were race circuits clamoring to host a Can-Am race. The Can-Am series grew from six to ten races in 1969. This gave fans across the US and Canada more opportunities to see national drivers take on international drivers.

Between the Can-Am, Trans-Am and Formula series, the SCCA had a full calendar of race dates.

There were quite a few drivers participating in multiple series and keeping the USRRC would have created serious overlap of race dates between the different series. Consequently, the USRRC had to go.

The SCCA cautiously provided very little publicity about why they were getting rid of the USRRC. Instead, they put forth an optimistic spin on the opportunities the new Grand Prix Championship and the expansion of the Can-Am series would provide.

John Bishop has been acknowledged by many as being the main proponent for pro-racing in the SCCA during the early 1960's.

He left the SCCA management at the end of 1968 when the USRRC disappeared. Bishop and NASCAR's Bill France founded the International Motor Sports Association (IMSA) in 1969. Although IMSA took a few years to grow in strength and stature, by the mid-70's it began filling the hole in sports car racing left by the demise of the USRRC. Bishop and France eventually sold IMSA to Don Cone, twenty years later, in 1989, beginning a chain of ownership changes.

In 1998 a group of unhappy IMSA competitors, with cooperation from the SCCA, revived the USRRC name for an alternative series to IMSA, which had become the Professional Sports Car Racing series. This lasted two years before the USRRC then morphed into the Grand-Am sports car series, run by NASCAR.

In vintage racing, *Victory Lane* magazine started the USRRC Seniors Tour in 1993 to promote the cars that raced in the original USRRC series. This series is still alive and well. Race fans can still see the cars that paved the way for professional sports car racing in America, running on some of the original race tracks.

Appendix: Charts

Drivers Races • Overall Race Winners

Driver	Total	Races							
Mark Donohue	11	66 PR	67 SD	67 Riv	67 PR	67 WG	67 BR	67 MO	68 Riv
		68 LS	68 WG	68 SJ	68 MO				
Jim Hall	10	63 Day	64 Pen	64 LS	64 WG	64 MD	65 Riv	65 LS	65 PR
		65 WG	65 BR	65 RA (s)					
Charlie Parsons	4	63 LS	66 RA	67 RA (s)	68 RA (s)				
Hap Sharp	4	64 MO	65CD	65 MO	65 RA (s)				
Skip Scott	4	67 RA (s)	68 PR	68 BR	68 RA (s)				
Augie Pabst	3	63 CD	63 RA (s)	64 RA (s)					
Bob Holbert	2	63 Pen (s*)	63 WG						
Ken Miles	2	63 Pen (s*)	63 MO						
Dave MacDonald	2	64 Aug	64 PR						
Buck Fulp	2	66 Riv	66 WG						
L. Motschenbacher	2	66 MO	67 LS						
Moises Solana	1	68 Mex							
Pedro Rodriguez	1	63 PR							
Bill Wuesthoff	1	63 RA (s)							
Skip Hudson	1	64 Riv							
Ed Leslie	1	64 Grn							
Walt Hansgen	1	64 RA (s)							
George Follmer	1	65 Pen							
Ron Hissom	1	65 RA (s)							
John Cannon	1	66 SD							
Charlie Hayes	1	66 LS							
Jerry Grant	1	66 BR							
Moises Solana	1	68 Mex							

Key: (s) = shared win. "(s*) =shared win, but no points"

Aug-Augusta, **BR-**Bridgehampton, **CD-**Continental Divide, **Day-**Daytona, **Grn-**Greenwood, **LS-**Laguna Seca, **MD-**Meadowdale, **Mex-**Mexico City, **MO-**Mid Ohio, **Pen-**Pensacola, **PR-**Pacific Raceways, **RA-**Road America, **Riv-**Riverside, **SJ-**San Jovite, **WG-**Watkins Glen

Drivers Races • Class Winners

Driver	Total	Races						
Mark Donohue	12	66 PR (O2)	67 SD (O2)	67 Riv (O2)	67 PR (O2)	67 WG (O2)	67 BR (O2)	67 MO (O2)
		68 Riv	68 LS	68 WG	68 SJ	68 MO		
Jim Hall	11	63 Day (O2)	64 Pen (O2)	64 LS (O2)	64 WG (O2)	64 MD (O2)	65 Riv (O2)	65 LS (O2)
		65 PR (O2)	65 WG (O2)	65 BR (O2)	65 RA (s-O2)			
Joe Buzzetta	7	64 MD (U2)	64 RA (U2)	66 MO (U2)	66 RA (s-U2)	67 WG (U2)	67 MO (U2)	67 RA (s-U2)
Ken Miles	6	63 Pen (s-U2)	63 WG (O2)	63 RA (O2)	63 MO (O2)	66 SD (U2)	66 LS (U2)	
George Follmer	6	65 Pen (U2)	65 Riv (U2)	65 BR (U2)	65 WG (U2)	65 CD (U2)	65 RA (s-U2)	
Hap Sharp	5	63 MO (U2)	64 MO (O2)	65 CD (O2)	65 MO (O2)	65 RA (s-O2)		
Scooter Patrick	5	66 Riv (U2)	66 BR (U2)	67 Riv (U2)	67 PR (U2)	67 RA (s-U2)		
Bob Holbert	4	63 Day (U2)	63 Pen (s-U2)	63 WG (U2)	63 RA (O2)			
Charlie Parsons	4	63 LS (U2)	66 RA (O2)	67 RA (s-O2)	68 RA (s)			
Bill Wuesthoff	4	63 RA (s-U2)	64 Grn (U2)	64 RA (s-U2)	64 MO (U2)			
Charlie Hayes	4	64 Aug (U2)	64 LS (U2)	64 WG (U2)	66 LS (O2)			
Skip Scott	4	67 RA (s-O2)	68 PR	68 BR	68 RA (s)			
Augie Pabst	3	63 CD (O2)	63 RA (s-U2)	64 RA (s-U2)				
Don Wester	3	63 PR (U2)	63 RA (s-U2)	66 PR (U2)				
Skip Hudson	2	63 LS (S2)	64 Riv (O2)					
Dave MacDonald	2	64 Aug (O2)	64 PR (O2)					
Buck Fulp	2	66 Riv (O2)	66 WG (O2)					
L. Motschenbacher	2	66 MO (O2)	67 LS (O2					
Pedro Rodriguez	1	63 PR (O2)						
Tim Mayer	1	63 Pen (O2)						
Ed Leslie	1	64 Grn (O2)						
Walt Hansgen	1	64 RA (s-O2)						
Ed Hugus	1	64 Pen (U2)						
Bobby Unser	1	64 Riv (U2)						
Tony Settember	1	64 PR (U2)						
Mike Hall	1	65 Pen (O2)						
Ron Hissom	1	65 RA (s-O2)						
Gerry Bruihl	1	65 LS (U2)						
Jerry Titus	1	65 PR (U2)						
Doug Revson	1	65 MO (U2)						
Earl Jones	1	65 RA (s-U2)						
John Cannon	1	66 SD (O2)						
Jerry Grant	1	66 BR (O2)						
Ralph Treischmann	1	66 WG (U2)						
Gunter Klass	1	66 RA (s-U2)						
Charlie Kolb	1	67 SD (U2)						
Fred Baker	1	67 LS (U2)						
Bruce Jennings	1	67 BR (U2)						
Moises Solana	1	68 Mex City						

There was not an under two-liter class for 1968. The drivers listed below were the highest placed under two-liter finishers in the 1968 races.

Driver	Total	Races		
Werner Frank	3	68 Mex (U2)	68 BR (U2)	68 WG (U2)
Don Wester	1	68 Riv (U2)		
Scooter Patrick	1	68 LS (U2)		
Horst Kroll	1	68 SJ (U2)		
Lew Florence	1	68 PR (U2)		
Cliff Phillips	1	68 RA (s-U2)		
Al Cervenka	1	68 RA (s-U2)		
Mike Hall	1	68 MO (U2)		

Key to parentheses: (O2) = Over two-liters, (U2) = Under two-liters, (s) = shared win

Aug-Augusta, **BR-**Bridgehampton, **CD-**Continental Divide, **Day-**Daytona, **Grn-**Greenwood, **LS-**Laguna Seca, **MD-**Meadowdale, **Mex-**Mexico City, **MO-**Mid Ohio, **Pen-**Pensacola, **PR-**Pacific Raceways, **RA-**Road America, **Riv-**Riverside, **SJ-**San Jovite, **WG-**Watkins Glen

Manufacturers Races • Overall Race Winners

Driver	Total	Races							
Ken Miles	8	64 Aug	64 Pen	64 Riv	64 WG	64 PR	64 MD	65 Riv	65 LS
Bob Johnson	2	63 WG	64 MO						
Roger Penske	1	63 Pen							
Dave MacDonald	1	63 PR							
Bob Holbert	1	63 MO							
Ed Leslie	1	64 LS							

Manufacturers Races • Class Winners

Driver	Total	Races							
Ken Miles	10	64 Aug (O2)	64 Pen (O2)	64 Riv (O2)	64 PR (O2)	64 WG (O2)	64 Grn (O2)	64 MD (O2)	64 RA (s-O2)
		65 Riv (O2)	65 LS (O2)						
Bob Johnson	5	63 WG	64 MO (O2)	65 WG (O2)	65 BR (O2)	65 CD (O2)			
Chuck Stoddard	4	64 WG (U2)	64 MD (U2)	64 RA (U2)	65 RA (U2)				
Scooter Patrick	4	64 Riv (U2)	65 LS (U2)	65 PR (U2)	65 CD (U2)				
Tom Payne	3	65 Pen (O2)	65 PR (O2)	65 RA (s-O2)					
Bob Bondurant	2	63 CD	63 RA (s)						
Bob Holbert	2	63 LS	63 MO						
Dave MacDonald	2	63 PR	63 RA (s)						
John Whitmore	2	64 Pen (U2)	64 Grn (U2)						
Don Wester	2	64 LS (U2)	64 PR (U2)						
Ray Cuomo	2	65 MO (U2)	65 RA (s-U2)						
Roger Penske	1	63 Pen							
Bruce Jennings	1	64 Aug (U2)							
Ed Leslie	1	64 LS (O2)							
Bill Wuesthoff	1	64 MO (U2)							
John Morton	1	64 RA (s-O2)							
Skip Scott	1	64 RA (s-O2)							
Charlie Kolb	1	65 Pen (U2)							
Dave Jordan	1	65 Riv (U2)							
Herb Wetanson	1	65 WG (U2)							
George Drolsom	1	65 BR (U2)							
Dan Gerber	1	65 MO (O2)							

There was no Manufacturer race/class at Daytona 1963 and there was not an under two-liter class in 1963.
Also, the Manufacturers class was eliminated after the 1965 season.

Aug-Augusta, **BR-**Bridgehampton, **CD-**Continental Divide, **Day-**Daytona, **Grn-**Greenwood, **LS-**Laguna Seca, **MD-**Meadowdale, **Mex-**Mexico City, **MO-**Mid Ohio, **Pen-**Pensacola, **PR-**Pacific Raceways, **RA-**Road America, **Riv-**Riverside, **SJ-**San Jovite, **WG-**Watkins Glen

Drivers Races • Fastest Qualifiers

Driver	Total	Races										
Jim Hall	12	64 Aug	64 WG	64 PR	64 Grn	64 RA	64 MO	65 LS	65 PR	65 WG	65 MO	68 Riv	68 LS
Jerry Grant	10	63 LS	63 PR	63 CD	65 CD	66 SD	66 Riv	65 PR	66 WG	66 BR	67 PR	
Mark Donohue	6	66 MO	67 WG	67 MO	68 WG	68 SJ	68 RA					
George Follmer	3	67 Riv	67 LS	67 BR								
Roger Penske	2	63 Pen	64 Pen									
Bob Holbert	2	63 WG	64 LS									
Walt Hansgen	2	65 Pen	65 RA									
Hap Sharp	2	65 Riv	65 BR									
Charlie Hayes	2	66 LS	66 RA									
Peter Revson	2	68 Mex	68 PR									
L. Motschenbacher	2	68 BR	68 MO									
Harry Heuer	1	63 Day										
Ken Miles	1	63 RA										
Skip Hudson	1	63 MO										
Dave MacDonald	1	64 Riv										
Ed Leslie	1	64 MD										
Sam Posey	1	67 SD										
Charlie Parsons	1	67 RA										

Manufacturers Races • Fastest Qualifiers

Driver	Total	Races					
Ken Miles	9	64 Aug (O2)	64 Pen (O2)	64 Riv (O2)	64 PR (O2)	64 WG (O2)	64 Grn (O2)
		64 MD (O2)	64 RA (O2)	65 LS			
Bob Holbert	2	63 PR	63 MO				
Dave MacDonald	1	63 Pen					
Bob Johnson	1	63 WG					
unknown	1	65 Riv					

Drivers Races • Fastest Race Laps

Driver	Total	Races										
Mark Donohue	14	66 MO (s)	67 SD	67 Riv	67 PR	66 BR	67 MO	68 Riv	68 LS	68 PR	68 WG	68 BR	68 SJ	68 RA
		68 MO										
Jim Hall	8	64 WG	64 PR	64 RA	64 MO	65 Pen	65 LS	65 MO	65 RA			
Jerry Grant	4	63 PR	65 CD	66 WG	66 BR							
Peter Revson	3	67 WG	67 RA	68 Mex								
Harry Heuer	2	63 WG	63 CD									
Roger Penske	2	63 Pen	64 Pen									
Hap Sharp	2	65 Riv	65 BR									
Charlie Hayes	2	66 LS	66 RA									
L. Motschenbacher	2	66 MO (s)	67 LS									
Charlie Parsons	1	63 LS										
Ken Miles	1	63 RA										
Ed Hamill	1	63 MO										
Dave MacDonald	1	64 Riv										
Charlie Cox	1	64 Grn										
Ed Leslie	1	64 MD										
Skip Hudson	1	66 Riv										
unknown	6	63 Day	64 Aug	64 LS	65 Riv	65 CD	66 SD					

Manufacturers Races - Fastest Race Laps

Driver	Total	Races					
Ken Miles	6	63 MO	64 Pen	64 Riv	64 WG	64 MO (s)	65 LS
Bob Holbert	1	63 Pen					
Dave MacDonald	1	63 WG					
Ed Leslie	1	64 LS					
Bob Johnson	1	64 MO (s)					
Tom Payne	1	64 MO (s)					
unknown	5	63 PR	64 Aug	64 PR	64 MD	65 Riv	

Manufacturers Races • Fastest Qualifiers

Driver	Total	Races				
Ken Miles	9	64 Aug (O2)	64 Pen (O2)	64 Riv (O2)	64 PR (O2)	64 WG (O2)
		64 Grn (O2)	64 MD (O2)	64 RA (O2)	65 LS	
Bob Holbert	2	63 PR	63 MO			
Dave MacDonald	1	63 Pen				
Bob Johnson	1	63 WG				
unknown	1	65 Riv				

Manufacturers Races • Fastest Race Laps

Driver	Total	Races				
Ken Miles	6	63 MO	64 Pen	64 Riv	64 WG	64 MO (s)	65 LS
Bob Holbert	1	63 Pen				
Dave MacDonald	1	63 WG				
Ed Leslie	1	64 LS				
Bob Johnson	1	64 MO (s)				
Tom Payne	1	64 MO (s)				
unknown	5	63 PR	64 Aug	64 PR	64 MD	65 Riv

Drivers Race Victories by Car/Engine

Car	Engine	Total Overall Race Victories	Races									
Chaparral 2	Chevrolet	13	64 Pen	64 LS	64 WG	64 MD	64 MO	65 Riv	65 LS	65 PR	65 WG	65 BR
			65 CD	65 MO	65 RA							
Lola T70	Chevrolet	12	66 Riv	66 PR	66 WG	67 SD	67 Riv	67 PR	67 WG	67 BR	67 MO	68 PR
			68 BR	68 RA								
McLaren M6A	Chevrolet	5	68 Riv	68 LS	68 WG	68 SJ	68 MO					
Cooper T61M	Ford	3	64 Aug	64 PR	64 Grn							
McLaren M1B	Chevrolet	3	66 LS	66 RA	67 LS							
Porsche RS-61	Porsche	2	63 Pen	63 WG								
Cooper T57	Climax	1	63 Day									
Lotus 23	Ford (t/c)	1	63 LS									
Genie Mk 8	Chevrolet	1	63 PR									
Scarab	Chevrolet	1	63 CD									
Elva Mk 7S	Porsche	1	63 RA									
Cobra	Ford	1	63 MO									
Cooper T61	Chevrolet	1	64 Riv									
Ferrari 250LM	Ferrari	1	64 RA									
Lotus 23	Porsche	1	65 Pen									
Genie Mk 10	Chevrolet	1	66 SD									
Lola T70	Ford	1	66 BR									
McLaren M1B	Oldsmobile	1	66 MO									
McLaren M1C	Chevrolet	1	67 RA									
McLaren M6B	Chevrolet	1	68 Mex									

Manufacturers Race Victories by Car/Engine

Car	Engine	Total Overall Race Victories	Races								
Cobra	Ford	13	63 WG	63 PR	63 MO	64 Aug	64 Pen	64 Riv	64 LS	64 PR	64 WG	64 MD
			64 MO	65 Riv	64 LS							
Ferrari 250 GTO	Ferrari	1	63 Pen									

Aug-Augusta, **BR-**Bridgehampton, **CD-**Continental Divide, **Day-**Daytona, **Grn-**Greenwood, **LS-**Laguna Seca, **MD-**Meadowdale, **Mex-**Mexico City, **MO-**Mid Ohio, **Pen-**Pensacola, **PR-**Pacific Raceways, **RA-**Road America, **Riv-**Riverside, **SJ-**San Jovite, **WG-**Watkins Glen

Drivers Class Victories by Car/Engine

Car	Engine	Total Class Victories	Races
Porsche 906	Porsche	16	66 Grn(U2), 66 Riv (U2), 66 LS (U2), 66 BR (U2), 66 WG (U2), 66 PR (U2), 66 MO (U2), 66 RA (U2), 67 Grn(U2), 67 Riv (U2), 67 LS (U2), 67 BR (U2), 67 WG (U2), 67 PR (U2), 67 MO (U2), 67 RA (U2)
Chaparral 2	Chevrolet	13	64 Pen (O2), 64 LS (O2), 64 WG (O2), 64 MD (O2), 64 MO (O2), 65 Riv (O2), 65 LS (O2), 65 PR (O2), 65 WG (O2), 65 BR (O2), 65 CD (O2), 65 MO (O2), 65 RA (O2)
Lola T70	Chevrolet	12	66 Riv (O2), 66 PR (O2), 66 WG (O2), 67 Grn(O2), 67 Riv (O2), 67 PR (O2)
Elva Mk 7S	Porsche	9	63 RA (U2), 64 Aug (U2), 64 LS (U2), 64 WG (U2), 64 Grn (U2), 64 MD (U2)
Lotus 23	Porsche	6	65 Pen (U2), 65 Riv (U2), 65 BR (U2), 65 WG (U2), 65 CD (U2), 65 RA (U2)
Porsche RS-61	Porsche	5	63 Day (U2), 63 Pen (U2), 63 WG (U2), 63 PR (U2), 63 CD (U2)
McLaren M6A	Chevrolet	5	68 Riv (O2), 68 LS (O2), 68 WG (O2), 68 SJ (O2), 68 MO (O2)
Lotus 23	Climax	4	64 Riv (U2), 64 PR (U2), 65 LS (U2), 65 MO (U2)
Cobra	Ford	3	63 WG (O2), 63 RA (U2), 63 MO (O2)
Cooper T61M	Ford	3	64 Aug (O2), 64 PR (O2), 64 Grn (O2)
McLaren M1B	Chevrolet	3	66 LS (O2), 66 RA (O2)., 67 LS (O2)
Lotus 23	Ford (t/c)	2	63 LS (U2), 64 Pen (U2)
Cooper T57	Climax	1	63 Day (O2)
Genie Mk 8	Chevrolet	1	63 PR (O2)
Scarab	Chevrolet	1	63 CD (O2)
Cooper T61	Chevrolet	1	64 Riv (O2)
Ferrari 250LM	Ferrari	1	64 RA (O2)
Genie Mk 10	Chevrolet	1	66 Grn(O2)
Lola T70	Ford	1	66 BR (O2)
McLaren M1B	Oldsmobile	1	66 MO (O2)
McLaren M1C	Chevrolet	1	67 RA (O2)
McLaren M6B	Chevrolet	1	68 Mex (O2)
Chaparral 1	Chevrolet	1	63 LS (O2)
McKee Mk 4	Ford	1	65 Pen (O2)
Elva Mk 7	Ford (t/c)	1	63 MO (U2)
Cooper T57	Climax	1	63 Pen (O2)

Manufacturers Class Victories by Car/Engine

Car	Engine	Total Class Victories	Races
Cobra	Ford	25	63 LS, 63 WG, 63 PR, 63 CD, 63 RA, 63 MO, 64 Aug (O2), 64 Pen (O2), 64 Riv (O2), 64 LS (O2), 64 PR (O2), 64 WG (O2), 64 Grn (O2), 64 MD (O2), 64 MO (O2), 64 RA (O2), 65 Pen (O2), 65 Riv (O2), 65 LS (O2), 65 BR (O2), 65 WG (O2), 65 PR (O2), 65 CD (O2), 65 MO (O2), 65 RA (O2)
Porsche 904	Porsche	11	64 Riv (U2), 64 LS (U2), 64 PR, 64 MO (U2), 65 Pen (U2), 65 Riv (U2), 65 LS (U2), 65 BR (U2), 65 WG (U2), 65 PR (U2), 65 CD (U2)
Alfa Romeo TZ	Alfa Romeo	4	64 WG (U2), 64 MD (U2), 64 RA (U2), 65 RA (U2)
Lotus Cortina	Ford (t/c)	2	64 Pen (U2), 64 Grn (U2)
Porsche Carrera 356B	Porsche	1	64 Aug (U2)
Abarth-Simca	Simca	1	65 MO (U2)

Aug-Augusta, **BR-**Bridgehampton, **CD-**Continental Divide, **Day-**Daytona, **Grn-**Greenwood, **LS-**Laguna Seca, **MD-**Meadowdale, **Mex-**Mexico City, **MO-**Mid Ohio, **Pen-**Pensacola, **PR-**Pacific Raceways, **RA-**Road America, **Riv-**Riverside, **SJ-**San Jovite, **WG-**Watkins Glen

Appendix: Course Maps

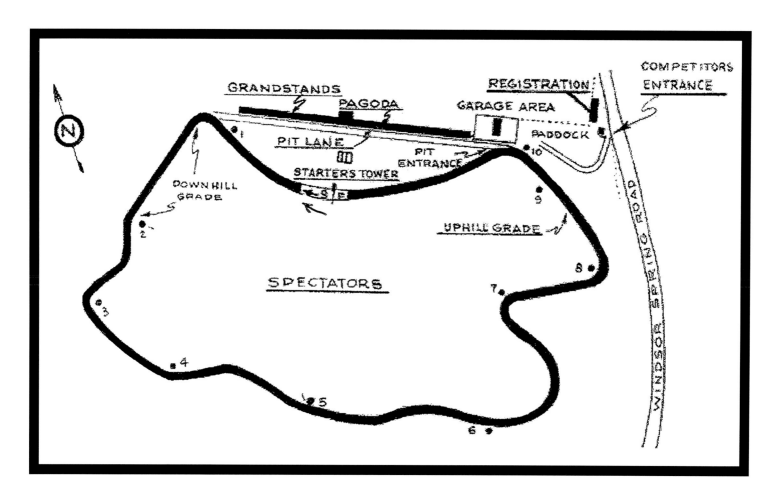

Augusta International Speedway
Augusta, Georgia

Augusta International Speedway sat on a 1,000 acre parcel of land. It was a combination 1/2 mile oval and three mile road course. The grandstands were on the far side of the 3,000 foot pit road which sat at the top of a bowl. The spectators had a nice view of the pits, the front "straight" and quite a bit of the track.

On the backside of the course, the lowest section is within 5 feet of the infield lake. NASCAR racer, Joe Weatherly, is credited with naming this Alligator Hole, after crashing here in practice for the NASCAR race in 1963. That NASCAR race was the only other major race to be held at Augusta. It was won by Fireball Roberts, driving a Ford and averaging 86.32 mph.

Fastest Qualifier – Drivers Race

1964	Jim Hall	Chaparral 2-Chevrolet	1:47.2	100.8 mph

Winners Speed – Drivers Race

1964	Dave MacDonald	Shelby Cooper T61M-Ford		97.65 mph

Fastest Qualifier – Manufacturers Race

1964	Ken Miles	Shelby Cobra	1:54.0	97.74 mph

Winners Speed – Manufacturers Race

1964	Ken Miles	Shelby Cobra		87.9 mph

Fastest Race Laps
unknown

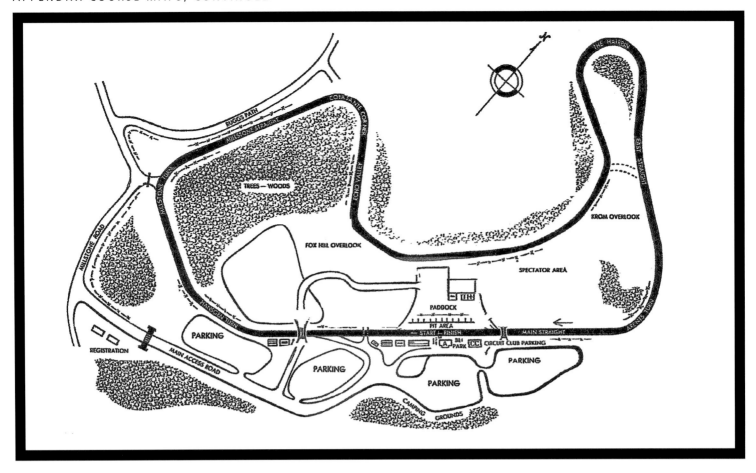

Bridgehampton Race Circuit
Bridgehampton, Long Island, New York

Bridgehampton's history with auto racing goes back to 1915 when auto races were held on the public roads and ran through 1921, then again from 1949 until 1952. The closed circuit road course opened in 1957. SCCA National Championship races were held from 1957, which Hansgen won every year through 1963. From 1962 through 1965 the Double 400 races were held and counted for the World Manufacturer's GT Championship. The feature race combined all-out sports racing cars with the top GT class. The USRRC races came along in 1965 and ran until the end in 1968. Along the way, Bridgehampton joined the Can-Am series when it started in 1966. This race was the scene of the only Can-Am win for a Ford engine, with Dan Gurney taking the honors. During 1967, Gus Hutchison scored a win in the only pro formula car race held at Bridgehampton. The last major race held at the Bridge was the Trans-Am race won by Mark Donohue in an AMC Javelin.

Fastest Qualifier
1965	Hap Sharp	Chaparral 2-Chevrolet	1:40.3	101.29 mph
1966	Jerry Grant	Lola T70-Gurney-Weslake Ford	1:39.2	103.8 mph
1967	George Follmer	Lola T70-Chevrolet	1:32.6	110.6 mph
1968	L. Motschenbacher	McLaren M6B-Ford	1:30.71	113.12 mph

Fastest Race Lap
1965	Jim Hall	Chaparral 2-Chevrolet	1:38.9	103.8 mph
1966	Jerry Grant	Lola T70-Gurney-Weslake Ford	1:40.4	102.6 mph
1967	Mark Donohue	Lola T70-Chevrolet	1:34.0	109.15 mph
1968	Mark Donohue	McLaren M6A-Chevrolet	1:31.33	112.826 mph

Winners Speed
1965	Jim Hall	Chaparral 2-Chevrolet	97.46 mph
1966	Jerry Grant	Lola T70-Gurney-Weslake Ford	98.39 mph
1967	Mark Donohue	Lola T70-Chevrolet	103.6 mph
1968	Skip Scott	Lola T70-Chevrolet	107.868 mph

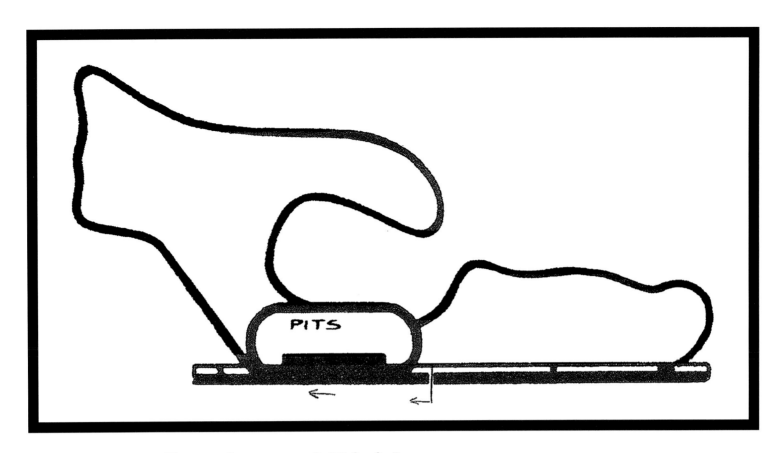

Continental Divide
Castle Rock, Colorado

Continental Divide Raceway was situated at 6,200 feet in the Rocky Mountains, outside of Castle Rock, Colorado, about thirty miles South of Denver. It was carved out of the desert floor with the main straight also serving as a drag strip and one of the straights of a half-mile oval. This 2.8 mile, ten turn course was built and opened in 1959.

The first pro race was a 1960 USAC road race won by Carroll Shelby driving a Scarab. Continental Divide hosted a pro formula car race in 1965, which was won by Hap Sharp in a 2.5 liter Cooper-Climax. The SCCA pro formula series race was run here in 1967 through 1969. Trans-Am races were staged in 1966 and 1967, won by Jerry Titus and Mark Donohue, respectively. An Indycar race was held in 1968 with A.J. Foyt being the victor. Further Indycar races were held in 1969 and 1970, with the latter being the final major pro race held at Continental Divide and it was won by Mario Andretti. Continental Divide continued operation with SCCA regional races until early 1979.

Fastest Qualifier

1963	Jerry Grant	Lotus 19-Chevrolet	2:04.2	81.16 mph
1965	Jerry Grant	Lola T70-Chevrolet	1:55.1	87.58 mph

Fastest Race Lap

1963	Harry Heuer	Chaparral I-Chevrolet	2:06.9	79.3 mph
1965	unknown			

Winners Speed

1963	Augie Pabst	Scarab-Chevrolet		77.19 mph
1965	Hap Sharp	Chaparral 2-Chevrolet		84.001 mph

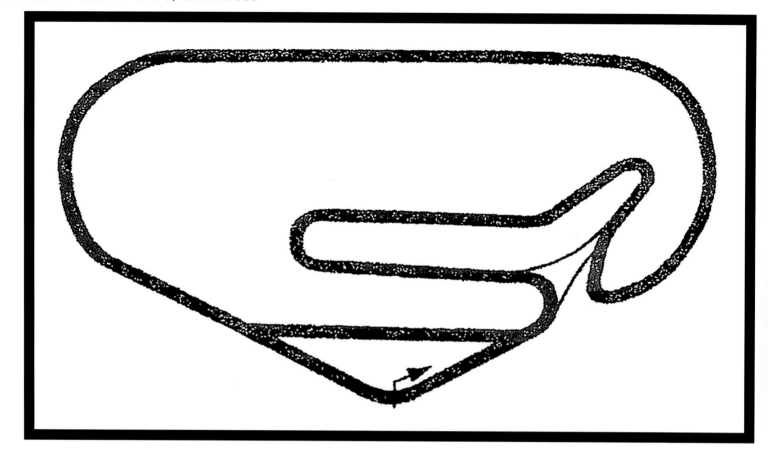

Daytona International Speedway
Daytona, Florida

SCCA amateur races had been held at Daytona since 1959 and the 1959 USAC road race was its first professional sports car race. Still, Daytona was an unusual choice for the SCCA's first USRRC race, since it was the home of NASCAR racing.

The road course comprised the banked corners, the backstretch, and an infield road course. It was fairly hard on the sports cars' brakes. The winter weather on the northern Florida coast was usually warmer than most other parts of the country. However, the day of the very first USRRC race was the exception. The wind blew, the rain poured down, and the spectators stayed home. The official attendance was 1,200. Journalists estimated the race day attendance to be closer to 300, and that included all of the officials, drivers, mechanics and the ducks in the infield lake. The race was not considered a success and the series did not return to Daytona.

Fastest Qualifier			
1963 Harry Heuer	Chaparral I-Chevrolet	2:05.01	108.852 mph
Fastest Race Lap			
1963 unknown			
Winners Speed			
1963 Jim Hall	Cooper T57-Climax		90.21 mph

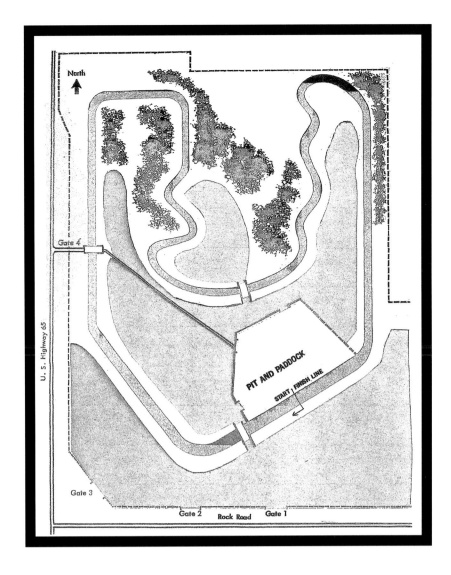

Greenwood Roadway

Indianola, Iowa

The founders of Greenwood Roadway optimistically thought the Midwest wanted another road racing circuit, and if they built it, the spectators would come and the profit could be put into finishing development of the racecourse. The track was bulldozed out of rolling farmland and forest, outside of Indianola, thirty miles south of Des Moines, Iowa.

An outline of the track looks like the jaws of a crab cracker. The start/finish line was at the end of a quarter mile long, uphill straight. The track then dropped downhill into a fast, banked right-hand corner followed by a short straight. It kept going slightly downhill around a softly banked right-hander and the beginning of a half-mile straight. The straight then went uphill to two banked right hand corners that led onto a short straight, followed by a couple of uphill S-turns. The S-turns exited into a long, fast and banked uphill left-hander that led into some downhill S-bends. These were followed by two tight, slightly uphill right-handers that exited onto a long straight. The start of the straight dipped downhill then rose uphill for half a mile to a banked right-hander that kept going uphill and back onto the main start/finish straight.

Greenwood held its first sports car race in June of 1963. The 1964 USRRC was the largest race it hosted. The following year USAC ran a stock car race won by Norm Nelson in a Plymouth, averaging 83.37 mph. After a few more years of running amateur events, Greenwood ceased operations.

Fastest Qualifier

1964	Jim Hall	Chaparral 2-Chevrolet	1:57.0	92.31 mph

Fastest Race Lap

1964	Charlie Cox	Cooper-Chevrolet	1:56.4	92.78 mph

Winners Speed

1964	Ed Leslie	Cooper-Ford	87.24 mph

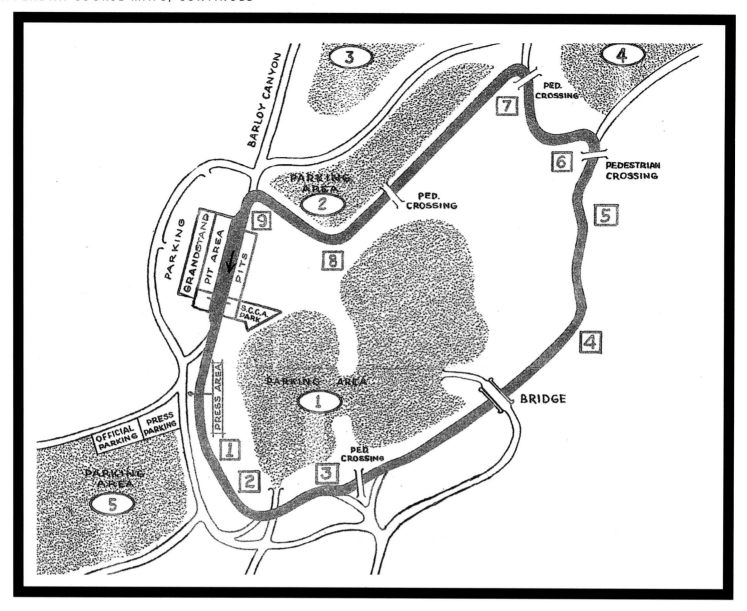

Laguna Seca
Salinas, California

The Monterey Peninsula, in California, is arguably the spritual home of West Coast sports car racing with the Pebble Beach road races dating back to 1950. Laguna Seca came into being after the last Pebble Beach race of 1956. The Monterey Peninsula business leaders realized how beneficial the annual road races were to the local economy. So they got together with the local racers and found a site for a permanent racetrack on the backside of a local Army base.

Since Pete Lovely won the first race in November of 1957, Laguna Seca has hosted races for most of the major sports car and formula racing series in America. It is one of the five tracks to host a USRRC race every year of the series. Can-Am, Trans-Am, Formula 5000, IMSA and Indycars all have significant history at Laguna Seca.

Fastest Qualifier – Drivers Race

Year	Driver	Car	Time	Speed
1963	Jerry Grant	Lotus 19-Chevrolet	1:16.6	89.3 mph
1964	Bob Holbert	Shelby Cooper T61M-Ford		timing equipment broken
1965	Jim Hall	Chaparral 2A-Chevrolet	1:09.81	97.98 mph
1966	Charlie Hayes	McLaren M1B-Chevrolet	1:09.98	97.74 mph
1967	George Follmer	Lola T70-Chevrolet	1:06.2	103.32 mph
1968	Jim Hall	Chaparral 2G-Chevrolet	1:02.89	108.761mph

Fastest Race Lap - Drivers Race

Year	Driver	Car	Time	Speed
1963	Charlie Parsons	Lotus 23-Climax	1:17.8	87.92 mph
1964	unknown			
1965	Jim Hall	Chaparral 2A-Chevrolet	1:10.05	97.65 mph
1966	Charlie Hayes	McLaren M1B-Chevrolet	1:09.161	98.9 mph
1967	L. Motschenbacher	McLaren M1C-Chev	1:03.5	107.69 mph
1968	Mark Donohue	McLaren M6A-Chevrolet	1:03.2	108.22 mph

Winners Speed - Drivers Race

Year	Driver	Car	Speed
1963	Charlie Parsons	Lotus 23-Climax	86.2 mph
1964	Jim Hall	Chaparral 2-Chevrolet	88.0 mph
1965	Jim Hall	Chaparral 2A-Chevrolet	94.62 mph
1966	Charlie Hayes	McLaren M1B-Chevrolet	95.5 mph
1967	L.Motschenbacher	McLaren M1C-Chevrolet	91.6 mph
1968	Mark Donohue	McLaren M6A-Chevrolet	105.68 mph

Fastest Qualifier – Manufacturers Race

Year	Driver	Car	Time	Speed
1964	Ken Miles	Shelby Cobra	time unknown	
1965	Ken Miles	Shelby Cobra	1:14.79	91.46 mph

Fastest Race Lap - Manufacturers Race

Year	Driver	Car	Time	Speed
1964	Ed Leslie	Shelby Cobra	1:17.58	88.17 mph
1965	Ken Miles	Shelby Cobra	1:16.24	89.72 mph

Winners Speed - Manufacturers Race

Year	Driver	Car	Speed
1964	Ed Leslie	Shelby Cobra	87.4 mph
1965	Ken Miles	Shelby Cobra	88.49 mph

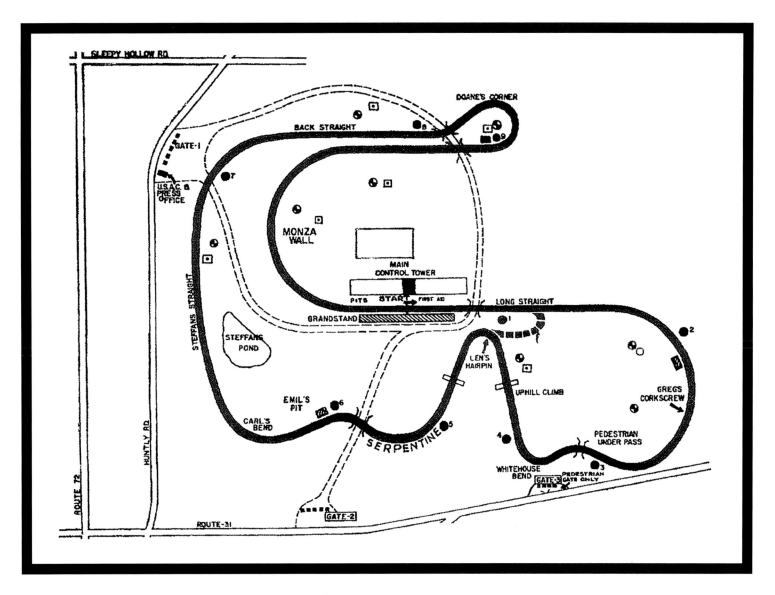

Meadowdale Raceway
Carpentersville, Illinois

Meadowdale was another race course born out of the mid-fifties ban of racing on public roads. It was located in the farmland near Carpentersville, Illinois, about 40 miles northwest of Chicago. Meadowdale's heyday was the USAC sports car races of the late 50's and early 60's. It was a very challenging track and featured a high-banked Monza Wall, plus a 3/4-mile straight.

The SCCA held regional and national races since the circuit opened. Professional sports car racing at Meadowdale began to decline after 1961. The only USRRC race held at Meadowdale was the 1964 race and the last major pro race was the 1968 Trans-Am won by Mark Donohue.

Drivers Fastest Qualifier
1964 Ed Leslie   Shelby Cooper T61M-Ford   1:58.4   99.43 mph
Drivers Fastest Race Lap
1964 Ed Leslie   Shelby Cooper T61M-Ford   1:59.4   98.59 mph
Drivers Winners Speed
1964 Ed Leslie   Shelby Cooper T61M-Ford   95.4 mph
Manufacturers Fastest Qualifier
1964 Ken Miles   Shelby Cobra   2:05.2   94.03 mph
Manufacturers Fastest Race Lap
1964 Ken Miles   Shelby Cobra   2:04.6   94.48 mph
Manufacturers Winners Speed
1964 Ken Miles   Shelby Cobra   91.49 mph

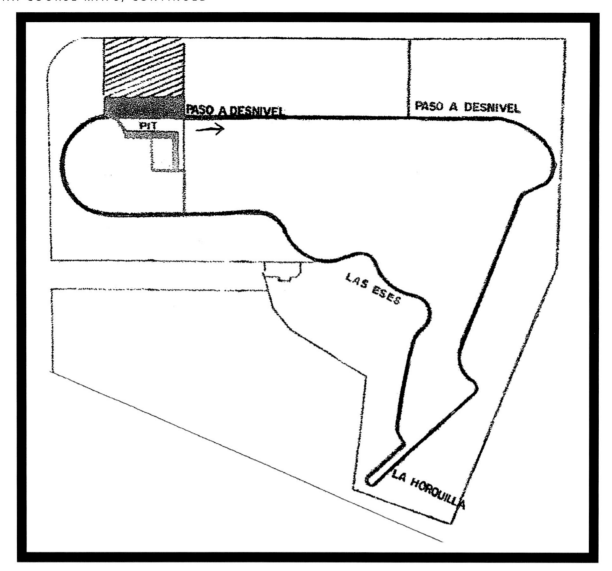

Autodromo de Mexico
Mexico City, Mexico

The popularity of the Ricardo and Pedro Rodriguez was the driving factor for the construction of the Autodromo de Mexico. It was built inside the pubic park, Magdalena Mixhuca, in Mexico City in 1962. This course was 3.1 miles, had 12 turns, and was flat, except for the mildly banked final parabolica, or peraltada, turn.

Unfortunately, Ricardo Rodriguez died in a practice accident during the first non-championship Mexican GP in 1962. This was usually the last Grand Prix of the season, from 1963 through 1970. The Grand Prix championship was decided here in 1964 and 1968.

The 1968 USRRC was the first major non-F1 race on this course, until the Trans-Am series came in1978 and 1979. The CART Indycars raced here in 1980 and `81. Both races were won by Rick Mears.

In more recent years CART came back for races from 2002 through the series end in 2007. The A1 GP series held two races here in 2006 and 2007, while NASCAR held Busch/Nationwide races from 2005 through 2008.

Fastest Qualifier

1968	Peter Revson	Lola T70-Ford	1:48.41	102.943 mph

Fastest Race Lap

1968	Peter Revson	Lola T70-Ford	1:48.91	102.470 mph

Winners Speed

1968	Moises Solana	McLaren M6B-Chevrolet		99.58 mph

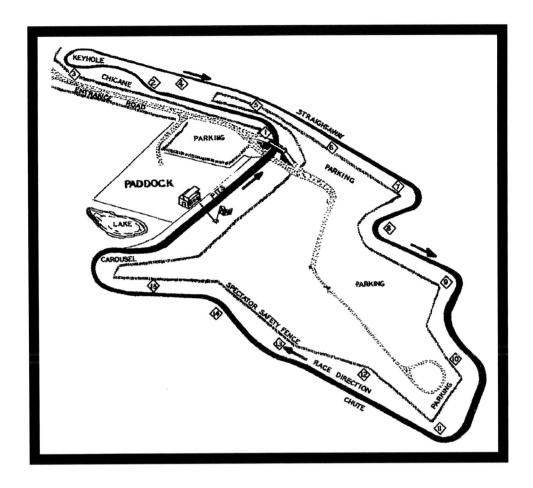

Mid Ohio Sports Car Course
Lexington, Ohio

Mid Ohio is another of the five courses that held USRRC races each year of the series. It is a challenging 2.4 mile course with fifteen turns and some moderate elevation changes.

Mid Ohio held its first SCCA races in the spring of 1962 and the USRRC races of 1963 were the first major pro races staged here. The 1963 Drivers race was notable because it was the only Drivers race won by a Manufacturers car, with Ken Miles winning in a Shelby Cobra.

Almost every major sports car series has had lengthy stays at Mid Ohio. There were: Can-Am races from 1969 through 1982; Trans-Am races from 1967 to 1972 and again from 1982 through 1992; Formula 5000 races from 1970 to 1976 (excluding 1972); IMSA races from 1972 to 1993; Indycars from 1990 to present, and ALMS from 2001 to present.

Fastest Qualifier - Drivers Race

1963	Skip Hudson	Cooper T61-Chevrolet	1:48.6	79.56 mph
1964	Jim Hall	Chaparral 2-Chevrolet	1:42.8	84.21 mph
1965	Jim Hall	Chaparral 2A-Chevrolet	1:37.2	88.89 mph
1966	Mark Donohue	Lola T70-Chevrolet	1:37.8	88.34 mph
1967	Mark Donohue	Lola T70-Chevrolet	1:33.4	92.51 mph
1968	Lothar Motschenbacher	McLaren M6B-Ford	1:30.8	95.15 mph

Fastest Race Lap - Drivers Race

1963	Ed Hamill	Cooper T61-Ford	1:44.24	82.89 mph
1964	Jim Hall	Chaparral 2-Chevrolet	1:44.0	83.01 mph
1965	Hap Sharp	Chaparral 2A-Chevrolet	1:40.6	85.88 mph
1966	Mark Donohue & Lothar Motschenbacher		1:38.6	87.63 mph
1967	Mark Donohue	Lola T70-Chevrolet	1:34.6	91.33 mph
1968	Mark Donohue	McLaren M6A-Chevrolet	1:32.2	93.71 mph

Winners Speed - Drivers Race

1963	Ken Miles	Shelby Cobra	77.41 mph
1964	Hap Sharp	Chaparral 2-Chevrolet	80.33 mph
1965	Hap Sharp	Chaparral 2A-Chevrolet	82.51 mph
1966	Lothar Motschenbacher	McLaren M1B-Oldsmobile	84.13 mph
1967	Mark Donohue	Lola T70-Chevrolet	87.11 mph
1968	Mark Donohue	McLaren M6A-Chevrolet	90.77 mph

Fastest Qualifier - Manufacturers Race

1963	Bob Holbert	Shelby Cobra	time unknown
1964	Ken Miles	Shelby Cobra	time unknown

Fastest Race Lap - Manufacturers Race

1963	Ken Miles	Shelby Cobra	1:48.4	79.71 mph
1964	Bob Johnson, Ken Miles & Tom Payne		1:51.0	85.55 mph

Winners Speed - Manufacturers Race

1963	Bob Holbert	Shelby Cobra	75.67 mph
1964	Bob Johnson	Shelby Cobra	76.43 mph

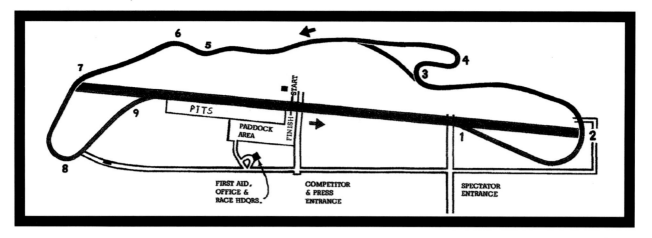

Pacific Raceways
Auburn/Kent, Washington

Pacific Raceways was often referred to as Kent. It is fairly close to Kent, but is a lot closer to the town of Auburn. The first race was held in August 1960 and organized by the Puget Sound Sports Car Club. The first pro race was the 1962 Northwest Grand Prix, won by Dan Gurney in a Lotus 19. A USRRC race was held every year of the series. The 1964 race being the last race Dave MacDonald won before perishing in that year's Indy 500 inferno.

Other series to make stops at Pacific Raceways were the Trans-Am from 1967 to 1970, Formula 5000 in 1969 to 1971, and USAC Indycars from 1969 to 1971. Other major races were held, on and off again.

At the time of the USRRC series, Pacific Raceways was very picturesque with tall evergreen trees surrounding the property. One popular viewing spot was at the top of the hill above the downhill stretch to the S-turn. From there one could watch the cars barrel down the straight, through turn one, around turn two, down the hill, through the S-turns, and onto the backstretch.

Fastest Qualifier - Drivers Race

Year	Driver	Car	Time	Speed
1963	Jerry Grant	Lotus 19-Chevrolet	1:30.4	89.6 mph
1964	Jim Hall	Chaparral 2-Chevrolet	1:38.7	82.07 mph
1965	Jim Hall	Chaparral 2A-Chevrolet	1:22.0	98.78 mph
1966	Jerry Grant	Lola T70-Ford	1:19.5	101.9 mph
1967	Jerry Grant	Lola T70-Chevrolet	1:18.3	103.45 mph
1968	Peter Revson	Lola T70-Ford	1:16.3	106.159 mph

Fastest Race Lap - Drivers Race

Year	Driver	Car	Time	Speed
1963	Jerry Grant	Lotus 19-Chevrolet	1:30.4	89.6 mph
1964	Jim Hall	Chaparral 2-Chevrolet	1:26.8	93.318 mph
1965	Jim Hall & Hap Sharp	Chaparral 2A-Chevrolet	1:23.8	96.66 mph
1966	unknown			
1967	Mark Donohue	Lola T70-Chevrolet	1:20.2	101.00 mph
1968	Mark Donohue	McLaren M6A-Chevrolet	1:18.3	103.45 mph

Winners Speed - Drivers Race

Year	Driver	Car	Speed
1963	Pedro Rodriguez	Genie Mk 10-Chevrolet	82.99 mph
1964	Dave MacDonald	Shelby Cooper T61M-Ford	91.5 mph
1965	Jim Hall	Chaparral 2A-Chevrolet	89.459 mph
1966	Mark Donohue	Lola T70-Chevrolet	96.27 mph
1967	Mark Donohue	Lola T70-Chevrolet	97.27 mph
1968	Skip Scott	Lola T70-Chevrolet	97.83 mph

Fastest Qualifier - Manufacturers Race

Year	Driver	Car	Time	Speed
1963	Bob Holbert	Shelby Cobra	1:34.1	86.08 mph
1964	Ken Miles	Shelby Cobra	time unknown	

Fastest Race Lap - Manufacturers Race

1963	unknown
1964	unknown

Winners Speed - Manufacturers Race

Year	Driver	Car	Speed
1963	Dave MacDonald	Shelby Cobra	83.49 mph
1964	Ken Miles	Shelby Cobra	85.9 mph

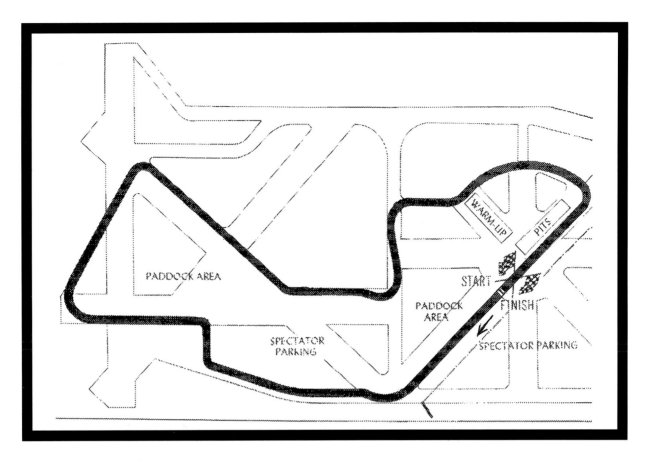

NAS Corry Field
Pensacola, Florida

The Pensacola USRRC races were held at Corry Field, a naval air station. The Gulf Coast SCCA region, the local Chamber of Commerce, and the US Navy combined forces to promote the annual Fiesta of Five Flags celebration with an annual road race on a little used portion of the naval base. These races started in 1959 and became part of the USRRC in 1963.

This was a challenging, if flat, 3.0 mile course, in a bow-tie configuration. The concrete road surface was bumpy and hard on the cars and the drivers in 1963 and 1964. For the 1965 races the course got a new asphalt surface and the speeds increased dramatically.

Fastest Qualifier - Drivers Race

1963	Roger Penske	Zerex Special-Climax	2:06.8	85.17 mph
1964	Roger Penske	Cooper T61-Chevrolet	2:00.8	89.4 mph
1965	Walt Hansgen	Lola T70-Chevrolet	1:45.2	102.66 mph

Fastest Race Lap - Drivers Race

1963	Roger Penske	Zerex Special-Climax	2:03.0	87.80 mph
1964	Roger Penske	Cooper T61-Chevrolet	2:03.8	87.24 mph
1965	Walt Hansgen	Lola T70-Chevrolet	1:45.0	102.85 mph

Winners Speed - Drivers Race

1963	Bob Holbert/Ken Miles	Porsche 718 RS61	70.77 mph
1964	Jim Hall	Chaparral 2-Chevrolet	84.22 mph
1965	George Follmer	Lotus 23-Porsche	92.07 mph

Fastest Qualifier - Manufacturers Race

1963	Dave MacDonald	Shelby Cobra	time unknown	
1964	Ken Miles	Shelby Cobra	2:12.6	81.45 mph

Fastest Race Lap - Manufacturers Race

1963	Bob Holbert	Shelby Cobra	2:14.0	80.70 mph
1964	Ken Miles	Shelby Cobra	2:12.6	81.45 mph

Winners Speed - Manufacturers Race

1963	Roger Penske	Ferrari 250 GTO	77.10 mph
1964	Ken Miles	Shelby Cobra	75.47 mph

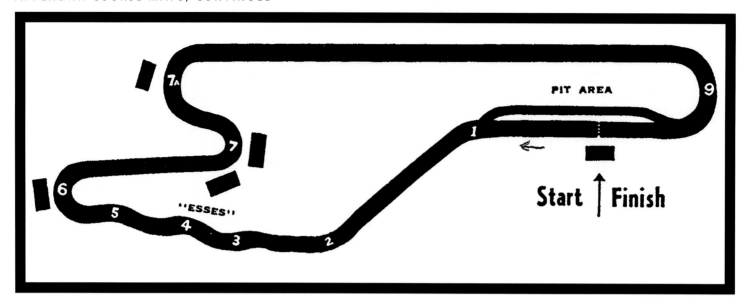

Riverside International Raceway
Riverside, California

Riverside was the most well known West Coast race course during its time. The first pro sports car race was won by Carroll Shelby in 1957. The Los Angeles Times sponsored the 1958 USAC road race in the Fall and it became famous as "The Times Grand Prix". This became part of the Can-Am series in 1966. These races always brought out the best international drivers and the racing was fierce. Riverside held its first USRRC race in 1964, with local driver, Skip Hudson, taking the win. During its time Riverside hosted races for Trans-Am, Indy cars, NASCAR, the Formula One US GP in 1960, Formula 5000, and IMSA. It ceased operations in 1989.

Fastest Qualifier - Drivers Race

1964	Dave MacDonald	Shelby Cooper T61M-Ford	1:32.6	101.08 mph
1965	Hap Sharp	Chaparral 2A-Chevrolet	1:28.0	106.363 mph
1966	Jerry Grant	Lola T70-Ford	1:26.4	108.333 mph
1967	George Follmer	Lola T70-Chevrolet	1:24.3	111.03 mph
1968	Jim Hall	Chaparral 2G-Chevrolet	1:19.0	118.481 mph

Fastest Race Lap - Drivers Race

1964	Dave MacDonald	Shelby Cooper T61M-Ford	1:34.0	99.58 mph
1965	unknown			
1966	Skip Hudson	Lola T70-Chevrolet	1:29.0	105.169 mph
1967	Mark Donohue	Lola T70-Chevrolet	1:26.4	108.33 mph
1968	Mark Donohue	McLaren M6A-Chevrolet	1:20.0	117.0 mph

Winners Speed - Drivers Race

1964	Skip Hudson	Cooper T61-Chevrolet	95.8 mph
1965	Jim Hall	Chaparral 2A-Chevrolet	100.38 mph
1966	Buck Fulp	Lola T70-Chevrolet	99.786 mph
1967	Mark Donohue	Lola T70-Chevrolet	105.21 mph
1968	Mark Donohue	McLaren M6A-Chevrolet	112.742 mph

Fastest Qualifier - Manufacturers Race

1964	Ken Miles	Shelby Cobra	1:38.4	95.12 mph
1965	Ed Leslie	Shelby Cobra	1:36.5	96.995 mph

Fastest Race Lap - Manufacturers Race

1964	Ken Miles	Shelby Cobra	1:40.0	93.6 mph
1965	unknown			

Winners Speed - Manufacturers Race

1964	Ken Miles	Shelby Cobra	92.55 mph
1965	Ken Miles	Shelby Cobra	93.60 mph

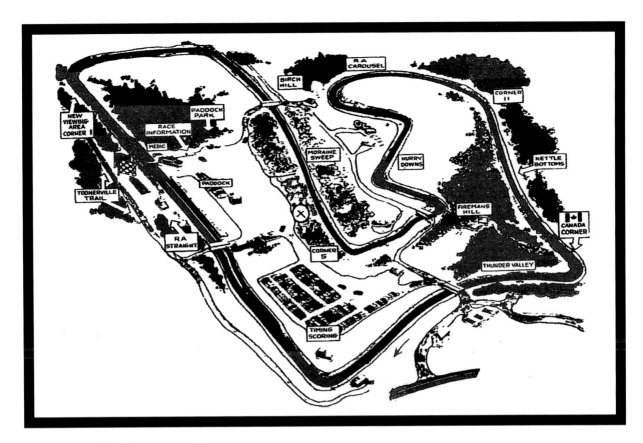

Road America
Elkhart Lake, Wisconsin

Known as Road America, Elkhart Lake, or just Elkhart, it's set in the middle of Wisconsin farmland, carved out of 523 hilly acres, and it's one of the most picturesque race courses in America. Racing started in 1950 on public roads around the village of Elkhart Lake. The next two years the course went through the village and around the lake. Racing on public roads in Wisconsin, and in most other states, ended after the 1952 races and it took Cliff Tufte two years to get his plan for Road America finalized and accepted by the SCCA. The hardscaping work of cutting and clearing trees and grading the road course began in April of 1955.

Phil Hill won the first feature race on September 11, 1955. Since then Road America has played a vital role in all forms of amateur and professional sports car racing. It was also one of the five courses to host USRRC races each year of the series and has been the scene of many fine Can-Am, Trans-Am, Formula 5000, CART, Formula Atlantic, and IMSA races.

Fastest Qualifier

Year	Driver	Car	Time	Speed
1963	Ken Miles	Shelby Cobra	2:40.8	89.55 mph
1964	Jim Hall	Chaparral 2-Chevrolet	2:32.0	94.7 mph
1965	Walt Hansgen	Lola T70-Chevrolet	2:27.8	97.43 mph
1966	Charlie Hayes	McLaren M1B-Chevrolet	2:26.2	98.495 mph
1967	Charlie Parsons	McLaren M1C-Chevrolet	2:22.8	100.83 mph
1968	Mark Donohue	McLaren M6A-Chevrolet	2:15.9	105.882 mph

Fastest Race Lap

Year	Driver	Car	Time	Speed
1963	Ken Miles	Shelby Cobra	2:41.6	89.109 mph
1964	Jim Hall	Chaparral 2-Chevrolet	2:32.2	94.55mph
1965	Jim Hall	Chaparral 2A-Chevrolet	2:28.0	97.30 mph
1966	Charlie Hayes	McLaren M1B-Chevrolet	2:28.1	97.232 mph
1967	Peter Revson	McLaren M1B-Chevrolet	2:23.2	100.559 mph
1968	Mark Donohue	McLaren M6A-Chevrolet	2:18.1	104.272 mph

Winners Speed

Year	Driver	Car	Speed
1963	Augie Pabst/Bill Wuesthoff	Elva Mk 7S-Porsche	84.507 mph
1964	Augie Pabst/Walt Hansgen	Ferrari 250LM	87.66 mph
1965	Jim Hall/Hap Sharp/Ron Hissom	Chaparral 2A-Chevrolet	89.526 mph
1966	Charlie Parsons	McLaren M1B-Chevrolet	92.879 mph
1967	Charlie Parsons/Skip Scott	McLaren M1C-Chevrolet	92.67 mph
1968	Skip Scott/Charlie Parsons	Lola T70-Chevrolet	94.73 mph

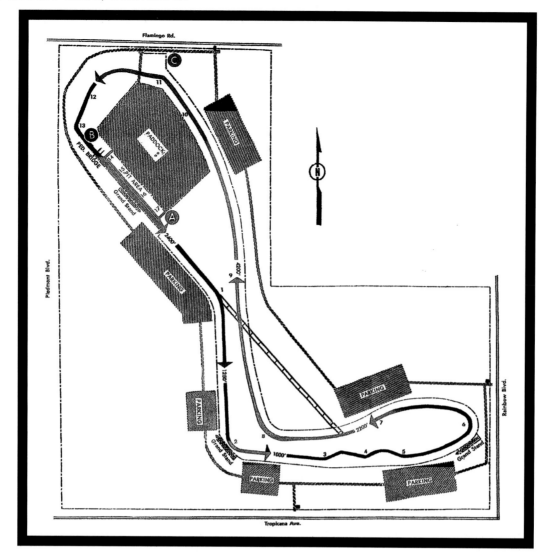

Stardust Raceways

Las Vegas, Nevada

Stardust Raceways was located about 2 miles west of the strip in Las Vegas, between Flamingo Road on the North, Tropicana Avenue on the South, Rainbow Road to the East, and Piedmont Boulevard to the West. In 1965 this was desert scrubland with lots of rocks and sagebrush. As with most attractions in Las Vegas, it was built to bring sports car racers and their fans to give them an activity to do in between gambling, eating and sleeping.

The first professional sports car race at Stardust was held in November 1965 and won by Hap Sharp in the Chaparral. The opening USRRC rounds of 1966 and 1967 were held here. Stardust hosted the final Can-Am races of the 1966, 1967, and 1968 seasons and they were rough and tumble affairs. Jim Hall basically had a career-ending crash here in 1968, suffering multiple broken bones and a very broken car. The Trans-Am series made one appearance in 1967 which was won by Mark Donohue. Bobby Unser won the only Indycar race in 1968. After the 1968 season the attraction of Stardust wore off and the track closed.

Fastest Qualifier

1966	Jerry Grant	Lola T70-Ford	1:39.7	108.33 mph
1967	Sam Posey	McLaren M1C-Chevrolet	1:36.1	112.28 mph

Fastest Race Lap

1966	unknown			
1967	Mark Donohue	Lola T70-Chevrolet	1:38.1	109.09 mph

Winners Speed

1966	John Cannon	Genie Mk10-Chevrolet		99.31 mph
1967	Mark Donohue	Lola T70-Chevrolet		106.91 mph

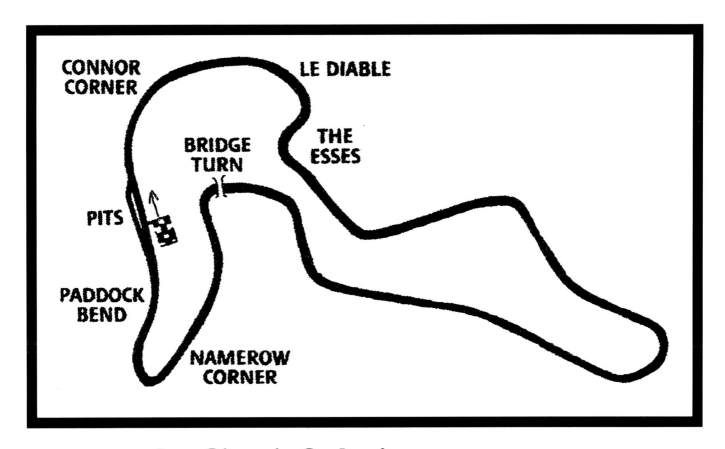

Le Circuit St Jovite
Mt Tremblant, Canada

Le Circuit St Jovite is located in the heart of the Laurentian hills, in Quebec, Canada. It was carved out of the forest and follows the natural up and down hill contours of the land. From above it looks like a melted plastic high-heel shoe. It is a very hilly, challenging course that opened in 1964.

Pedro Rodriguez won the first international race in September of 1964. Further Fall races continued with St Jovite hosting the first Can-Am race in 1966 won by series victor, John Surtees. Mario Andretti won both USAC Indycar races here, in 1967 and 1968. Trans-Am races were held here in 1968 through 1971 and all were won by Mark Donohue. St Jovite hosted the F1 Canadian Grand Prix in 1968 and 1970, both times won by Jackie Ickx. The USRRC visited St Jovite only once, in 1968, as part of an effort to be an international series.

Fastest Qualifier
1968 Mark Donohue McLaren M6A-Chevrolet 1:35.0 106.11 mph
Fastest Race Lap
1968 Mark Donohue McLaren M6A-Chevrolet 1:58.5 85.07 mph
Winners Speed
1968 Mark Donohue McLaren M6A-Chevrolet 80.44 mph

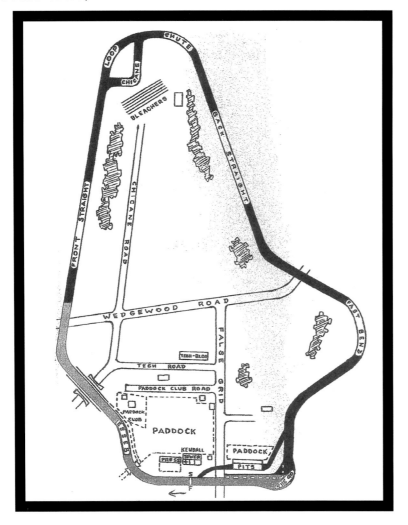

Watkins Glen Grand Prix Race Course

Watkins Glen, New York

Watkins Glen is widely acknowledged as the home of American sports car racing. The first race at "The Glen" was held in 1948 on the public roads. The closed-course road circuit opened in 1956. Watkins Glen hosted a Fall sports car race, starting in 1956, with George Constantine winning in a D-type Jaguar. The first professional road race was held in 1957 for NASCAR Grand National cars. Then the Fall sports car race became a pro race in 1958, as part of the USAC Road Racing Championship. Watkins Glen leaped onto the world stage by hosting the Formula One world championship, U.S. Grand Prix in 1961, with Innes Ireland taking the first victory for Team Lotus. Grand Prix races continued through 1980. The Glen was one of the courses which held USRRC races every year of the series.

Fastest Qualifier - Drivers Race

1963	Bob Holbert	Porsche 718 RS61	1:28.1	93.98 mph
1964	Jim Hall	Chaparral 2-Chevrolet	1:20.0	103.53 mph
1965	Jim Hall	Chaparral 2A-Chevrolet	1:16.5	108.09 mph
1966	Jerry Grant	Lola T70-Ford	1:15.0	110.4 mph
1967	Mark Donohue	Lola T70-Chevrolet	1:13.7	112.35 mph
1968	Mark Donohue	McLaren M6A-Chevrolet	1:06.85	123.86 mph

Fastest Race Lap - Drivers Race

1963	Harry Heuer	Chaparral I-Chevrolet	1:27.7	94.31 mph
1964	Jim Hall	Chaparral 2-Chevrolet	1:22.2	100.22 mph
1965	Hap Sharp	Chaparral 2A-Chevrolet	1:19.9	103.6 mph
1966	Jerry Grant & Buck Fulp	Lola T70-Ford & Chevrolet	1:17.2	107.25 mph
1967	Peter Revson	McLaren M1C-Chevrolet	1:13.45	112.73 mph
1968	Mark Donohue	McLaren M6A-Chevrolet	1:07.6	127.48 mph

Winners Speed - Drivers Race

1963	Bob Holbert	Porsche 718 RS61		90.63 mph
1964	Jim Hall	Chaparral 2-Chevrolet		96.81 mph
1965	Jim Hall	Chaparral 2A-Chevrolet		99.11 mph
1966	Buck Fulp	Lola T70-Chevrolet		101.46 mph
1967	Mark Donohue	Lola T70-Chevrolet		105.87 mph
1968	Mark Donohue	McLaren M6A-Chevrolet		117.969 mph

Fastest Qualifier - Manufacturers Race

1963	Bob Johnson	Cobra	1:29.3	92.72 mph
1964	Ken Miles	Shelby Cobra	1:24.3	98.23 mph

Fastest Race Lap - Manufacturers Race

1963	Dave MacDonald	Shelby Cobra	1:29.2	92.83 mph
1964	Ken Miles	Shelby Cobra	1:24.8	97.67 mph

Winners Speed - Manufacturers Race

1963	Bob Johnson	Cobra		92.33 mph
1964	Ken Miles	Shelby Cobra		93.48 mph

INDEX: Drivers and Race Courses

Drivers